SKYSCRAPER CINEMA

SKYSCRAPER
CINEMA

ARCHITECTURE AND GENDER
IN AMERICAN FILM

MERRILL SCHLEIER

University of Minnesota Press
Minneapolis • London

The University of Minnesota Press gratefully acknowledges the work of Edward Dimendberg, editorial consultant, on this project.

A portion of chapter 3 was previously published as "Ayn Rand and King Vidor's Film *The Fountainhead*: Architectural Modernism, the Gendered Body, and Political Ideology," *Journal of the Society of Architectural Historians* 61 (March 2002): 310–30; reprinted by permission of the Society of Architectural Historians. Another version of chapter 3 was published as "The Grid, the Spectacle, and the Labyrinth in *The Big Clock*'s Skyscraper: Queered Space and Cold War Discourse," *Film Studies* 11 (Winter 2007): 37–48.

"Portrait of a Cog," by Kenneth Fearing, is reprinted with the permission of Russell and Volkening as agents for the author. Copyright 1940 by Kenneth Fearing; renewed in 1968 by the estate of Kenneth Fearing.

Published by the University of Minnesota Press
111 Third Avenue South, Suite 290
Minneapolis, MN 55401-2520
http://www.upress.umn.edu

Library of Congress Cataloging-in-Publication Data

Schleier, Merrill.
    Skyscraper cinema : architecture and gender in American film / Merrill Schleier.
        p.   cm.
    Includes bibliographical references and index.
    ISBN 978-0-8166-4281-6 (hc : alk. paper) — ISBN 978-0-8166-4282-3 (pb : alk. paper)
        1. Skyscrapers in motion pictures.   2. Sex role in motion pictures.   3. Masculinity in motion pictures.
    4. Social classes in motion pictures.   5. Motion pictures—United States—History.   I. Title.
    PN1995.9.S5535S35 2009
    791.43'657—dc22

                                                                                        2008045191

Printed in the United States of America on acid-free paper

The University of Minnesota is an equal-opportunity educator and employer.

15 14 13 12 11 10 09   10 9 8 7 6 5 4 3 2 1

Contents

Constructing the American Skyscraper Film

In an act of defiance and resolve, Howard Roark (Gary Cooper), the hero of the film *The Fountainhead* (1949), bombs a housing project, intending to replace it with a towering skyscraper that is meant to redeem the government-subsidized property. This act of vandalism, which he accomplishes with the help of his wife-to-be Dominique Francon (Patricia Neal), is symptomatic of novelist and screenwriter Ayn Rand's intention to juxtapose these two building types as illustrating antithetical concepts. To the author, housing projects were the product of Roosevelt's New Deal, representative of federal handouts, community-based decisions, and collectivism, everything she found objectionable. Roark's gesture is thus meant to stamp out not only the dwellings but the ideas they represent. In contrast, Rand viewed skyscrapers as the epitome of capitalist achievement, upward aspiration, and democratic values, which symbolized the hope of the future. Tall buildings are also linked to all aspects of Roark's masculinity, from his refusal to adopt historical styles that Rand associated with decadent femininity, to his final triumph at the crest of the tower. The hero's gender identity is explored in relation to those of others, from craven bureaucrats to homosexually inflected dissemblers who are employed to buttress Roark's instrumentality. A virtual "cowboy of the sky," this lofty conqueror of space is poised to restore private ownership and individual initiative, which Rand believed had been severely compromised under the Roosevelt administration.

The Fountainhead underscores the manner in which skyscrapers in cinema are often invested with ideological significance, meant to reinstitute partisan values, economically based philosophies, and gender positions. Over fifty years later these ideas are still being debated in the public square. The events surrounding the destruction of Yamasaki's World Trade Center (1966–75) and the deliberations swirling around the efforts to rebuild at Ground Zero bear an uncanny resemblance to various issues explored in *The Fountainhead*. In accord with Rand, many of the commissioners entrusted with the site's reconstruction subscribe to the view that the skyscraper is a symbol of all that America holds dear—its entrepreneurial spirit, bold conquest of space, and importance as a national public monument. Many have also invested the skyscraper with democratic import in an effort to contrast it with the barbarism of those that destroyed it. In the context of global politics, these "American" values are frequently reversed and the skyscraper becomes a symbol of western imperialism, neocolonialism, and oppression. Dubbed the Freedom Tower by Governor George Pataki, Daniel Libeskind's original design (2003) for a 1,776-foot building, whose razor sharp skyward profile echoed the Statue of Liberty's welcoming gesture, underscores the manner in which skyscrapers still serve as potent sources of political ideologies.[1] The unfortunate events of September 11, 2001, have reinforced my commitment to a three-decade-long effort to define how tall buildings may both reflect and prescribe cultural meaning in a perpetual dialogue between diverse constituencies, including architects, politicians, and a viewing public, among others.[2]

Rand's creation of class-inflected and gendered characters in the service of her conservative political and economic convictions also prompted me to reflect on the meanings ascribed to tall buildings in cinema at various moments in film history, seen variously as symbols of class aspiration and upward mobility, seminal masculine genius, tombstones of capitalism, hotbeds of illicit eroticism, beacons of democracy, or well-oiled business machines assisted by computer technology. The explosion in scholarship in gender and space inspired me to consider the manner in which these buildings affect male and female, rich and poor, and various racial and sexual identities in different ways.[3] This led me to explore how "real" buildings, architectural discourses, and gender are inextricably linked, often employed by cinema's cultural producers (e.g., novelists, screenwriters, art directors, directors, and actors), either advertently or inadvertently, for ideological ends.[4]

This study builds upon the recent, burgeoning interest in cinema and architecture in general, and cinema and the city in particular. Donald Albrecht's pioneering *Designing Dreams* (1986) initiated an exploration of the relationship between set designs and extant buildings, concluding that cinematic architects were instrumental in "constructing" their own brand of modernism, often more influential than their actual counterparts.[5] Albrecht's study was followed by Dietrich Neumann's *Film Architecture* (1996), which augmented the former's research and valuable filmography with several scholarly essays on discreet aspects of cinematic architecture, a descriptive and visual analysis of selected films in which buildings were prominently featured, and useful information on previously unacknowledged set designers who helped fashion cinematic architecture.[6] Neumann's work was succeeded shortly thereafter by David Clarke's edited anthology *The Cinematic City* (1997) in which the author asserted that there was still "relatively little theoretical attention directed toward understanding the relationship between urban and cinematic space," a gap his book attempted to fill with the inclusion of essays exploring cinematic and architectural genres from *film noir* to the postmodern city by authors employing diverse methodological approaches and critical perspectives.[7] *Cinema and the City* (2001), an anthology edited by Mark Shiel and Tony Fitzmaurice, expanded the inquiry still further by considering the intersections between "spatialization" in cinema and the way power relations are inscribed into social life. Operating from a Marxist perspective, the authors explored how cinema and the city interface to include the ways power is invested in certain metropolises such as Los Angeles, paying close attention to how films are produced, distributed, and consumed globally.[8] The present full-length study seeks to build upon the explosion of scholarship of the last two decades by considering how skyscrapers as a particular building type and the discourses surrounding them, particularly those related to gender, were translated into cinema.[9]

Why separate cinematic depictions of skyscrapers from those of other architectural types, such as hotels, department stores, or banks? A skyscraper's height, suggestive phallic shape, grid-like shaft, and often particular components (e.g., elevators, penthouses, theatrical lobbies, boardrooms, dramatic pinnacles, etc.) generate their own iconographies and spatial practices in concert with prevailing cultural attitudes, which distinguish it from other buildings. These, in turn, create special cinematic conventions that are in a perpetual dialogue with their actual counterparts, hence the necessity to gauge a film's tall building in light of extant architecture and the issues swirling around it. For example, rapid, upward-moving skyscraper elevators crowded to capacity with male and female passengers in close proximity prompted scenes of flirtation or "elevator antics" in Depression-era cinema, which spoke to the continued discomfort that accompanied women's entrance into the labor force and the perception that skyscraper space was sexually charged. These images not only reflect subjectively material conditions and the social spaces of 1930s skyscrapers, but they often stipulate appropriate gender behavior in concert with the film's overriding prescriptive intent.

Before proceeding, it is necessary to clarify what is meant by a skyscraper, let alone a skyscraper film. Architectural historians are not in total agreement on what constitutes a skyscraper, although most concur on its structural components, including height, a steel skeleton frame, an elevator, and fire-cladding. Yet even an accord concerning purely material characteristics may be fraught with difficulties. As Sarah Landau and Carl Condit's *Rise of the New York Skyscraper* (1996) demonstrated, in order to determine whether early tall buildings were actual skyscrapers, constructed with a steel or iron frame, it would be necessary to perform architectural autopsies on extant structures, a nearly impossible task.[10] Moreover, skyscrapers also include seemingly diverse structures, including tall office buildings, high-rise apartments, and lofty hotels. They may be early twentieth-century ten-story monoliths, all-purpose Depression-era edifices, or automated, modernist buildings of the 1950s. Thus, one must not view skyscrapers in monolithic terms, but as a constantly evolving building type, the parts of which hold particular resonance at various times in history and in various locations (e.g., Los Angeles or New York). Skyscrapers also borrow or absorb parts of other buildings (e.g., gymnasiums, gardens, storefronts), creating a difficult task for the architectural and cultural historian who must disentangle the additional functional and symbolic intent of these appropriations. For example, a Depression-era cinematic skyscraper bathhouse comes freighted with meaning concerning class, leisure, patriarchal privilege, and homosocial and homoerotic bonding, among other meanings.

When I refer to skyscraper films, I am not seeking to invent another category, such as the western or musical, which is limiting to thinking about issues that are explored across cinematic genres.[11] I consider American skyscraper films those that include tall buildings as one of the main protagonists or necessary components of the narrative rather than mere backdrops or settings. This explains, in part, why this study commences in the 1910s during the silent era, when skyscrapers, like Hollywood stars, became an integral part of a film's story line. I have selected those films that I believe best characterize prevailing attitudes toward American skyscrapers during the eras in which they were produced rather than considering every film that includes a tall building.

The chronological parameters of this study also require further explanation because they adhere neither to the "classical" era of Hollywood, which lasts until the 1960s, nor to architectural histories of modernism, which often terminate in the late 1970s with the advent of postmodernism. Instead, I have chosen to end in the late 1950s during a period when modernization and renewed calls for gender realignment were being jointly touted by business as utopian hopes for the future, perhaps betraying my inclination to conclude on a positive note. These changes in material culture and gender ideology ushered in partly by William Henry Leffingwell's scientific office management in the 1910s, which was reintroduced in the 1950s, in turn affected the way skyscrapers were rendered in cinema. By 1960 and the film *The Apartment,* the depiction of cinematic skyscraper space shifted anew, being seen as dehumanizing and given over to quantification, bureaucratization, and mercenary behavior. In succeeding decades, the effects of multinational capitalism and globalization are explored in *Network* (1976) and *Wall Street* (1987), films in which bland and colorless skyscrapers with mutable cubical interiors and encroaching desktop computers threaten to overtake their human counterparts.

The subject of this book requires a serious grounding in architectural history and material culture in order to determine the subjective manner in which cinema's cultural producers appropriated or created skyscrapers in the formation of meaning. However, this is not simply a study of architectural adaptations in cinema, but includes a consideration of the way that prevailing discussions surrounding actual tall buildings circulate in and out of the films under discussion. Borrowing terminology from film historians and acknowledging the importance of intertextuality and intervisuality, this book seeks to explore how extra-architectural discourses, including publicity events, images of construction workers, and the often class-inflected and gendered rhetoric about buildings disseminated to the media, are inscribed in skyscraper cinema. To further accomplish this task, this book also relies on extracinematic materials to help explain how skyscraper imagery was produced and publicized to viewers by Hollywood studios. For example, one of the keys to understanding the film *Desk Set* (1957), which takes place in a large Rockefeller Center skyscraper, is in light of the prevailing debates surrounding the inclusion of computers in business buildings. Automation experts and apologists promised to liberate workers from mundane tasks by both measuring and mechanizing space, thereby inspiring leisure and creativity both within and without the buildings while strengthening profits, leading to a more benevolent capitalism.

Architectural discourses of a given period may also include pitched debates about the most appropriate style for skyscrapers, which are often heralded in times of strife as peculiarly American inventions that require a consonant formal idiom. One of the more pressing issues in the years during and immediately following World War II was whether historical or modernist styles imported from Europe could serve as suitable design solutions for office buildings that were increasingly thought of as beacons of democracy. Lewis Mumford reintroduced this view in his *New Yorker* "Skyline" column in 1947, which, in turn, prompted a debate among architectural professionals. In concert with Mumford and novelist Kenneth Fearing's intent, the art directors of the film *The Big Clock* (1948) pictured the tall office building in the International Style, which they associated with despotism, homosexual infiltrators, and evil feminized masculinity. By gauging cinematic skyscrapers in view of the current dialogue concerning style, one also learns about the role of art directors, many of whom were well versed in architectural research and practice, in staging meaning.

Equally significant is analyzing the cinematic mise-en-scène in order to more fully grasp architectural meaning and the simulation of social space. The rhetoric of the shot, which may be suggested by a director (e.g., Robert Wise in *Executive Suite* [1954]) or even a screenwriter (e.g., Ayn Rand), supplements the thematic and iconographic significance of skyscraper imagery offered by novelists, short story writers, or those adapting literary works to the screen. Perhaps the most common device associated with cinematic skyscrapers is the panning of buildings from floor to pinnacle to underscore their mammoth proportions and register awe. Another familiar method is the bird's-eye view taken from skyscraper crests, which reduces the rushing mob to infinitesimal proportions, meant to convey the often dehumanizing character of working in an urban environment. Often deep-focus cinematography combined with close-up shots alternate in films such as *The Big Clock* to vicariously re-create the crushing claustrophobia of a mechanical building while underscoring the confounding nature of a labyrinth.

Several important theoretical sources have assisted me in the rather daunting enterprise of interpreting both architectural and gendered imagery simultaneously, while interpreting films from the inside out (e.g., cultural producers) and the outside in (e.g., cultural context), and the various intersections between the two. Walter Benjamin's *Arcades Project* (1930s) serves as a model for analyzing architecture as a purveyor of desire and class values, one that is readily adaptable to film.[12] By implication, Benjamin shifted attention from a building's exterior to its interior, which is replete with implications for analyzing social space. In his magisterial work, he explored the cloistered, visually alluring spaces of the nineteenth-century Parisian arcade, glass-enclosed passageways that linked various commercial establishments, providing shoppers, strollers, and gawkers the opportunity for the pleasurable consumption of commodities. The author provides a strategy for grappling with a single architecture type, the arcade, while I explore the peculiarity of skyscrapers. Benjamin also deconstructed the myriad ways that architectural space is implicated in the production of ideology. Of particular significance for this study is his notion of architecture's "embedded" character; that is, buildings often serve as a palimpsest, preserving both a diachronic and a synchronic relationship to past and present buildings and their attendant associations in culture.

My discussion of skyscraper space is indebted to the writings of Henri Lefebvre, who offered a bridge for theorists exploring gender and spatiality.[13] Lefebvre provided the initial tools for thinking outside the constraints of traditional architectural discourse, envisioning architectural space as the production of its inhabitants rather than as an inert, inanimate materiality. In accord with Benjamin, he viewed representations of space (e.g., buildings) as organizing principles of both ideology and production, while defining representational spaces (e.g., film, painting, sculpture) as the coded results of human creation that also embody various economic and ideological intentions. According to Lefebvre, various categories of space continually intersect with and mediate one another, often preserving existing power relationships. He asserted that the imaginary spaces of film are not simply apprehended on the cerebral level, but provide conventions for how people inhabit and mediate space in their lives, which aids in the formulation of their subjectivities. One may use Lefebvre to understand actor Harold Lloyd's cinematic skyscraper-climbing gambits, which were based on the real efforts of working-class men who were trying to gain a leg up in a capitalist society given over to status seeking, the valorization of individual selfhood, and the pressure to differentiate oneself from the crowd. Yet Lloyd's antics, in turn, created a fad, laced with humor and thrills, conflating work and leisure, encouraging men to be risk-taking daredevils. The instructive message that reinforced capitalist modes of production is clear: one is responsible for one's own destiny through individual initiative and performative advertising, which took the onus off corporations for improving the lot of workers.

This study would have been impossible without the explosion in scholarship in the areas of gender studies, and gender and spatiality. Judith Butler is one of the most important scholars for any discussion of cinema and gender, and she anticipates many of the important discussions on gender and space. She discloses the manner in which gender is an impersonation or a "performative," or to use Lefebvre's terminology, a representational strategy, not predicated on the sex of the actor.[14] Butler argues that gender is produced as a "doing" rather than a material fact, requiring a set of negotiations with other gendered actors in a given context. Gender identity is thus a copy or a representation of past conventions that are perpetually negotiated and renegotiated. Extending Butler's analysis, cinematic depictions of gender identity may also be viewed as a series of representations by an array of gendered cultural producers (screenwriters, directors, art directors, actors, etc.) who are creating visual reproductions of already extant copies. As feminist sociologist Judith Lorber argues, these representations hold particular power as a way to both describe and prescribe dominant or hegemonic models of gender.[15]

Butler was one of the first to refute the binary model (masculinity versus femininity) employed to explain the formation of gender identity, which she attributes to the heterosexist underpinnings of much psychoanalytic and anthropological discourse. She posits the idea of a multiplicity of genders, a notion that has been amplified by scholars such as sociologist Robert Connell. In his book *Masculinities* (1995), Connell argues that all societies produce ideal or hegemonic models of masculinity.[16] Dominant forms of masculinity are not only forged in relation to femininity, but are in perpetual dialogue with other masculinities, including subordinate, marginal, and complicit, among others, which they require to buttress their theoretical and practical strength, hence power. Frequently, marginalized (homosexual men) and subordinate (men of color) masculinities (and femininities) overlap, strengthening Butler's assertion that any discussion of gender also implicates issues of race, class, and sexual identity. One might extend Butler's and Connell's assertions by envisioning an endless grid, or even a Deleuzean rhizomatic arrangement, in which a plethora of masculinities and femininities are in perpetual interplay in actual and representational space. In cinema, these varieties of gender are often superimposed or embedded in the depiction of professional identity. Thus in order to fully comprehend Harold Lloyd's enactment of hegemonic white masculinity in *Safety Last!* (1923), it is necessary to examine it in relation to the film's other men, who are employed to strengthen the masculinity of Harold's salesman: an acquisitive Jewish shop owner, a superstitious African American porter, a muscular construction worker, and a slothful drunkard. In accord with Connell, who begins with a structural method of analysis, this study recognizes that gender in cinema must be historicized in time and place.

I am also indebted to the legions of feminist film scholars for their interrogation of the cinematic text, including analyses of the representations of women, and the power dynamics often implicit in such depictions, the way both women and men gaze at the screen, including their often oppositional stances, and the debates concerning the construction of the female and other spectators. Rather than summarize the immense body of scholarship here, the reader will find the ideas of numerous feminist scholars interspersed liberally throughout this study. In addition to informing my analysis of constructions of femininity in film, these scholars have also influenced my discussions of masculinity, sexual identity, race, and class in a myriad of ways.

The work of feminist architectural historians concerned with the way gender is literally built into American corporate skyscraper space is equally necessary for a consideration of how film engages in a dialogue with actual settings, and their ideological underpinnings.[17] When women entered the workforce in the years after the Civil War, they were subject to spatial segregation. Up until 1920, men and women often worked in different locations in the same building, rode in separate elevators, and ate their meals in distinct areas. Women were relegated to lower-paying, clerical jobs, a fact exacerbated by the introduction of scientific office management, which increased the routinization and mechanical character of their tasks. Their male counterparts were appointed to managerial positions that required the supervision of their female subordinates, hence transferring paternalistic separate-sphere ideology into the workplace. Status was also equated with spatial allocation and the quality of decor, resulting in women's occupation of large, nondescript community work rooms, where they could be more readily surveyed. In contrast, managers and bosses were frequently afforded luxurious suites with breathtaking views, which echoed their class and patriarchal privilege.

An endemic power dynamic fraught with tension ensued; bosses were often wealthy older men, while clericals were young, single white women who had few legitimate opportunities for advancement. As both Kwolek-Folland and Wilson observed, the appearance of female employees in skyscraper offices led male commentators to regard it as a sexually charged sphere, which required monitoring.[18] Paternalistic companies such as Metropolitan Life sought to patrol the boundaries of female sexuality, regarding themselves as stewards of morality whose responsibility was to preserve purity in a woman's inevitable journey to the altar, rather than the boardroom.

Chapter 1 is devoted to Harold Lloyd, the premier skyscraper filmmaker of the silent era, who also starred as the main character in his tales of tall buildings. The comedic actor and frequent formulator of his own cinema stories and star persona, he appeared in five skyscraper films from 1919 to 1930, in which he found himself, either by serendipity or by resolve, hanging from an errant beam or climbing a towering pinnacle. Implicit in these productions is the idea that the quintessential monument to modernity, the skyscraper, part of a comprehensive urban nexus, which included crowds, billboards, and vehicular traffic, served initially as an emasculating force that the hero was poised to conquer in order to achieve the full realization of his gender identity. These films are all shot on location in the burgeoning Los Angeles metropolis, which is employed as a signifier of modernity on par with New York City. Constantly under siege, Harold succeeds by recourse to humorous exploits or performatives that temporarily thwart modernity's regimentation and undermine its bureaucratic practices while seeking reintegration in the business world. The character's masculinity is also formulated in relation to the prevailing advice literature pitched to an aspiring middle class, which encouraged the individual man to combine ingenuity with instrumental action, thereby ultimately supporting corporate values of success.

Lloyd's most sustained skyscraper film, *Safety Last!,* is evaluated in view of various paradigms of racial and ethnic masculinity to understand the way the actor exploited stereotypes to buttress his provisionally destabilized gender identity. Finally, class issues undergird many of Lloyd's films and his construction of ideal masculinity, which served to fuse brain and brawn in the often craven Harold, a character often haunted by the specter of feminization. His skyscraper-climbing escapades were formulated in a dialogue with real working-class human flies, men who climbed tall buildings for fun, fame, and profit after World War I, enacting the self-invention credo of advice peddlers while creating a new form of urban entertainment. Performing one's masculinity through strength or prowess emerged at the end of the nineteenth century, epitomized by the exploits of strongman Eugen Sandow, a product of the emergent mass-media society.[19]

The cinematic skyscraper as a symbol of debased urbanism during the Depression dominates chapter 2. An anonymous writer in the *New Republic* summed up these dominant sentiments, presaged by Lewis Mumford in the 1920s, referring to tall office buildings as "the material embodiment of the late bull market," which "soar boldly above a mesa of roofs, very much as the spire-graph of 1929 equity prices" but now serve as "ironic witnesses of collapsed hopes."[20] The emphasis shifts to studio-fabricated skyscraper interiors, which are employed to highlight their adverse effects on urban inhabitants, serving as a microcosm of various classes and gender positions, rife with sexual predation, corruption, suicide, and murder. Unlike Lloyd's location shots, New York's new megalopolitan, multipurpose skyscrapers' varied parts were appropriated by cinema's visual and textual producers to serve their thematic ends, reinforcing the necessity to gauge these images in relation to developments in material culture. Penthouse suites, spectacular lobbies, crowded elevators, and homosocial bathhouses were borrowed in general terms from actual buildings or simply fabricated to reinforce moralistic, class-conscious tales. In concert with a complex array of gendered character types, they sought to warn both men and women to remain within their own class boundaries and traditional gender positions. A popular Depression-era cinematic office trope was dubbed the office triangle, comprising the boss, wife, and secretary, or office wife. This novel ternary formulation with boss at the pinnacle invested films with the requisite erotic tension and entertainment value, ultimately resolved in favor of class and gender realignment.

This chapter also seeks to perform a textual exegesis of the often female-authored short stories and pulp-fiction novels that served as springboards for these cinematic tales, to ascertain the manner in which spatiality was prescriptively and ideologically constructed by the studios' textual and visual producers. A comparative analysis of Faith Baldwin's novel *Skyscraper* (1931) and short story "Wife versus Secretary" (1935) with their filmic adaptations reveals how protofeminist female voices were altered at the preproduction level. Baldwin sought to offer expanded options available for women, affording them the opportunity to enjoy a rewarding professional career and personal life, thereby inhabiting both public and private spheres.

In spite of their repression at the level of production, the studios' recommendations were not passively or uniformly received at the level of consumption. At least one group, namely secretaries and female clerical workers, resisted the ideological underpinnings of these films, referring to them as falsely salacious renderings of their labor, thus restoring Baldwin's message, in part, at the level of reception. This analysis corroborates the view of Italian Marxist Antonio Gramsci, who identified the heterogeneous nature of responses to cultural invention, which are dependent on audience members' class and gender positions.[21] Just as architectural space is a virtual palimpsest, drawing on past visual and textual regimes for sustenance, cinematic space is also saturated by a complex array of producers for their own ideological purposes, often the reinscription of normative views on gender, race, and class. One must disentangle these disparate threads to determine a film's overriding prescriptive pleas and alternative messages that are inserted spatially.

Pulp-fiction novels also serve as the springboard for the films considered in chapter 3, reinforcing the need for intertextuality in assessing cinema. The tall office building is no longer a microcosm of urban life; after World War II, it becomes a symbol of so-called American political and economic values. Both Ayn Rand's *The Fountainhead* (1943) and Kenneth Fearing's *The Big Clock* (1946) represent highly partisan novels in which skyscrapers are employed to promote their authors' respective ideologies. Their adaptations to the screen preserved their political intentions, although Fearing's left-wing sympathies are partially compromised in the translation from novel to script. In spite of their antithetical positions, both self-proclaimed propagandists designated the skyscraper as a site of collectivist-like intrigue in which conspiracies lurk and effeminate, homosexually inflected characters, depicted as foreign "others," threaten to dominate the skyscraper territory and deprive workers of their individuality and freedom. Repressive cold war ideology is also used to clarify the manner in which these films interface with larger political discourses concerning conformity, sexual identity, and persecution.

Architectural modernism is used in both to represent wholly different principles: for Rand, it is a harbinger of experimentation and freedom, while for Fearing and screenwriter Jonathan Latimer, it represents stultifying conformity. To support her contentions, Rand did extensive research on America's premier architectural nationalists, Louis Sullivan and Frank Lloyd Wright, which situates her work between popular fiction and highbrow architectural dogma. In this chapter, prevailing ideological debates concerning the skyscraper's legitimacy to embody putative American values are assessed, in order to define the ways it circulates through the films, employed by authors, screenwriters, and set designers to highlight thematic quests for independence. *The Big Clock*'s spatiality is not only re-created stylistically; the entire mise-en-scène is marshaled to establish vicariously feelings of entrapment and claustrophobia, which represent the ill effects of authoritarianism. The only hope of release is through the heroic efforts of lone men, with the assistance of female mates, to rout out the perverse foreign interlopers, thereby simultaneously reinstituting heterosexual normativity and putative democratic values, while rescuing capitalism, embodied in skyscrapers.

The last chapter explores how mid-century skyscraper films reengage with domestic business issues and the challenge to modernize occasioned by a new period of economic prosperity, accompanied by a call for capitalist revitalization in the new age. For the first time in American history, white-collar workers dominated the labor force while unions were marginalized, changing the nature of employment and the character of interior space. Chapter 4 explores the up-and-coming executive and his participatory wife, or Mrs. Executive, the new bulwarks of cinematic office space, who struggle to balance their public and private lives in relation to a more overarching corporation. *Executive Suite* (1954), *The Man in the Gray Flannel Suit* (1956), *Patterns* (1956), and *Women's World* (1957) examine the experiences of maladjusted white-collar workers who suffer from a variety of physical and mental ailments, straw men who are employed to make way for the reemergence of individualists who triumph over Organization Men. A healthy balance of work and private life, seen in the valorization of the nuclear family, is offered as the only way to avoid being swallowed up by the ever-increasing demands of business.

The subtexts of *Executive Suite* and *Desk Set* also concern the modernization of interior skyscraper space and business procedures, which are in danger of losing momentum, hence profitability. Significantly, Don Walling (William Holden) of *Executive Suite* was based on perhaps the most famous designer of the period, Charles Eames, who employed novel technologies, materials, and design strategies in the mass production of domestic and business furniture. Walling's ascension to the head of the corporation is employed in order to rejuvenate its business practices and its decayed, lugubrious environs. Likewise, the computer, which was introduced to skyscrapers in the 1950s, served as one of the main protagonists in *Desk Set* in order to prescribe the refashioning of spatial practice, or the way humans interact with machines, one of the earliest positive cinematic treatments of cyberspace. Its delineation was itself the product of a corporate partnership between Twentieth Century–Fox and IBM, designed to promote the "mechanical brain" as the only resolution to efficiency and gender harmony. Both films will be examined in light of the inclusion of new technologies, particularly automation in the office interior, and the concomitant discussions concerning their supposed space- and time-saving character, cost efficiency, and liberatory potential for workers. This, coupled with the emergence of new mid-century professionals, the spatial administrator and the automation expert, charged with the rehabilitation of actual skyscrapers, will illuminate the depiction of fictive cinematic skyscraper space and its characters.

The organization of this book is chronologically and thematically bound, with close readings of individual films while amplifying key concepts concerning skyscrapers and gender across several films during a given period. Since skyscrapers functioned as business buildings in these films, I have sought to historicize them in the context of discourses concerning gender and professionalism, changes in material culture, and debates concerning architectural styles. I have also tried to remain sensitive to the diverse depictions of skyscrapers throughout the book, identifying location shots, fictional interiors, skyline backdrops, and even fabricated studio miniatures whenever possible. As film historian Geoffrey Nowell-Smith claims, city films may be either studio-shot, in the service of a fictional, often dystopian city, or largely filmed on location in which specific cities (e.g., New York, Los Angeles) are part of the thematic. I have discovered that more often than not, cinematic skyscrapers are hybrids, comprising location and studio-fabricated imagery to create fictional metropolises in order to place buildings at the service of what Nowell-Smith refers to as "the dictates of the imagination."[22] I remain convinced that even what appear to be "real" skyscrapers are themselves, like the masculinities and femininities that mediate them, "constructions" in the service of particular ideologies.

ONE

From Stumbling Blocks to Stepping Stones: Harold Lloyd's Skyscraper Films

"Mystery Man in Death Defying Thrill: To Climb Wall of Towering Skyscraper" proclaimed the bold headline in a fictional tabloid newspaper in the film *Safety Last!* (1923). The sturdy physique of an anonymous daredevil appeared beneath the announcement with his face obliterated, to increase the suspense and the feat's promotional appeal.[1] This scene served multiple functions and summarizes the intent of many of Harold Lloyd's films; it demonstrated the inextricable link between dual tropes of modernity—tabloid sensationalism and skyscrapers— and their relationship to the realization of a temporarily destabilized masculinity. A bodily image without a face also enabled Lloyd to conflate seemingly antithetical types of manhood, that of his roommate "The Pal," also known as Limpy Bill (Bill Strothers), an instrumental construction worker, whose muscular build was featured in the picture, with that of a bookish-looking, upwardly mobile department store employee in the lady's fabric division. In the film, "The Boy" or Harold, replaces Bill and ultimately ascends a skyscraper shaft replete with difficulties.[2] In one of the most dramatic and humorous scenes in silent cinema, the bespectacled, slightly ruffled aspirant clutches desperately onto the bent hands of its clock and dangles precariously high above the hustle-bustle of metropolitan Los Angeles, a split figure whose suit and glasses prefigure Superman's mild-mannered disguise, but who is also ultimately able to "leap tall buildings," albeit not in a single bound. Although he begins as a browbeaten feminized salesman, through gumption he arrives at the skyscraper's summit as a man. By hatching the idea for the stunt in accord with the era's self-help credo and physically actualizing it, he has absorbed the construction worker's courage, in a perfect fusion of brain and brawn, which is necessary for his integrated, fully realized masculine identity.

Lloyd's films follow in the tradition of several films made during the silent era that featured men either high atop skyscraper scaffolds or bravely scaling tall building exteriors in search of their virility.[3] They emerged in part as a result

Newspaper headline in Safety Last!

of the new more lightweight mobile cameras, which literally permitted camera-men to scale skyscrapers along with actors. One of the earliest was *The Sky-scrapers of New York* (1906), which concerned all aspects of skyscraper building viewed from dizzying heights, including a "thrilling hand-to-hand encounter on one of the highest buildings ever erected in New York" between a working-class lout and his well-dressed foreman, which anticipated the appearance of a class disparity between Bill and Harold.[4]

The postwar popularity of this theme was also due to the building boom and the concomitant spectacle of male workers engaged in all aspects of skyscraper construction. In an article entitled "Titanic Forces Rear a New Skyline" (1925), a *New York Times* reporter observed the unprecedented building sweeping Manhattan, where 250 tall buildings were currently under construction, while noting the fusion between urban metamorphosis and masculine agency: "The remaking of New York is at full tilt. Upon every hand power-driven hammers split the air. . . . Bundles of steel beams ascend to startling heights, often with a steel worker standing amid ship, his hand upon the fall of the derrick."[5] A simi-lar display was evident in Los Angeles and most of the major cities in America during the Machine Age of the interwar years.

Harold hanging from the clock in Safety Last!

These inadvertent urban theatrics prompted a new type of performative: men began to climb skyscrapers in a quest for glory and profit. They were preceded by the strongman routines of Eugen Sandow or the death-defying antics of stuntman Harry Houdini in the 1890s, which in turn inspired common workmen to prove their prowess.[6] Known as human flies or human spiders, their temporary conquests of space became a fad after World War I, which, in turn, prompted Hollywood imitators. Drawing on these traditions, Harold Lloyd was the most popular and prolific practitioner of these particular "thrill" or "stunt" pictures, which introduced hapless innocents who found themselves high atop unstable beams or wildly swinging boatswains, echoing the risk-taking behavior of jazz-age youth and providing a forum for Lloyd to prove his manhood.

Lloyd's five skyscraper films concern the relationship between masculinity and modernity, of which the skyscraper serves as the overarching symbol; it is a metaphor for upward mobility and capitalist achievement. All shot on location in the burgeoning Los Angeles metropolis, the films collectively explore all facets of the city's modernity, on par with the large and small cinematic urban symphonies of the early twentieth century. The camera is often used to create vicariously the discomfort and fright experienced by a temporarily unrealized man in order that the viewer may identify with his eventual triumph. By conquering the tall building, Harold the climber attains success while simultaneously trying to thwart its bureaucratic character. Skyscraper scaling is also similar to mountain climbing or "the king of sports for the strenuous man," which gained popularity in America in the last quarter of the nineteenth century; early practitioners set out to conquer nature's most difficult and awe-inspiring monuments in a virtual duel with the ineffable.[7] Harold's climb up the enormous shaft of the Bolton Building in *Safety Last!,* coupled with the destabilizing character of the urban jungle that he sought to surmount, which included careening autos, buzzers gone awry, and errant I beams, was staged as a necessary rite of passage.

The character employed slapstick comedic devices and irony, among other ploys, to undermine modernity's seemingly all-pervasive confusion, its call to conformity, transforming its work-a-day character to an enormous theater in the round, attended by a mass audience who craved urban pleasure and release. Harold the hero and Lloyd the actor and publicist both subscribed to the individualist credo that exhorted men to create themselves, through ingenuity and instrumental action, one of the prevailing precepts of capitalist discourses on success, which in turn supported the same regime he meant to subvert. Sporting a three-piece suit and the latest rage in celluloid glasses, the fashionable hero was a paragon of advertising panache, an analogue to the adjacent billboards and towers. Hence, when evaluating Harold and Lloyd's masculinity, one must view it in dialectical terms, both in collusion with and in opposition to an all-pervasive modernity. Lloyd's self-fabrication is further highlighted in relation to racialized and ethnic "others," who are rendered as either timeless Old World stereotypes or essentialized, childish buffoons, incapable of progressive action.

EARLY SKYSCRAPER SHORTS

Lloyd's skyscraper films, which range from single-reel shorts to full-length features, linking him in the public mind with tall office buildings and daredevil antics, include *Look Out Below* (1919), *High and Dizzy* (1920), *Never Weaken* (1921), *Safety Last!* (1923), and *Feet First* (1930).[8] Seeking to capitalize on the actor's sustained exploration of this novel genre, in 1921 Pathé Exchange claimed that their young star suffered from "the blues if the sun set on a day" in which he did "not frolic about on a skyscraper iron framework as nonchalantly as a hungry goat on a tin can dump!" "Skyscrapers are the playthings of Harold Lloyd."[9] By 1923, reviewers also made the sought-after connection of Lloyd and skyscrapers, noting that *Safety Last!* was the kind of film "Harold goes in for."[10] A female fan watching him perform a daredevil stunt on location in Los Angeles concurred, exclaiming, "High and Dizzy again! Gee what a nerve!"[11]

Lloyd's skyscraper stunt films fall into two categories. Early efforts such as

Look Out Below and *High and Dizzy* present Harold as an insouciant youth who literally and figuratively goes out on a limb for the sake of love, or as a hapless innocent who is hoisted aloft and must hang on for dear life. *Never Weaken* is a transitional film, which continues with Harold as the accidental acrobat, but introduces the fusing of skyscrapers and individual initiative. Continuing in this vein, *Safety Last!* melds the tall office building with masculine striving and eventual triumph, seen in the hero's ascension to the skyscraper's pinnacle, where he is rewarded monetarily and romantically. The actor's last skyscraper film and his second sound feature, *Feet First,* resumes the subject of the upwardly mobile, smitten hero, who overcomes all odds in the pursuit of business and love. It repeats the formula that characterizes the initial silent films, of an unsuspecting Harold who is carried upward and clamors to return to firmer ground.[12]

The one-reel short *Look Out Below* introduces the theme of skyscrapers, heterosexual coupling, and virility, with two lovers who find themselves lifted from a bench to the highest beam of an emergent skyscraper's steel frame.[13] A reviewer in *Moving Picture World* commented, "They ascend a twenty-story building in the course of construction and do some breath-taking stunts in mid-air. . . . A novel

Harold and Bebe sitting on a beam in Look Out Below.

offering."[14] These seemingly death-defying antics coincided with the exuberant risk taking of the nation's youth, many of whom were smoking, drinking, necking, and fitfully trying to cast off the restraints of Victorian morality. It is Lloyd's only film in which he and a female protagonist, played by Bebe Daniels, perform equally hair-raising exploits on the skyscraper scaffold. Harold served the role of the contemporary Everyman, while Daniels's character was a New Woman, a variation of the flapper. The transformation of a skyscraper into an enormous plaything or jungle gym for high-wire stunts undercut its skeleton's functionality. By subverting the steel frame's purpose as the building's load-bearing member, and the skyscraper's intended business use, the actors render the nascent building a site of leisure rather than work. Their antics represent youth's ability to ward off responsibilities in the pursuit of unfettered pleasure. The undermining of conventionality, the flouting of authority, and the use of an unfinished office building for recreational purposes rather than labor, thereby critiquing its containment, were subjects consistently explored by Lloyd.

The daredevil stunts performed by the couple in midair served to signify their unfettered passions, which echoed their offscreen romance, and their willingness to experiment. These scenes were filmed on top of the Hill Street Tunnel in downtown Los Angeles, but many of the shots create the illusion of infinite height. As the couple ascends, they seem to achieve greater levels of enjoyment, thereby associating the tall building with erotic stimulation and orgasmic pleasure.[15] Lloyd was borrowing from an already established tradition of skyscraper iconography, albeit recasting it in a novel manner. Since the late nineteenth century, the erect vertical shape of the skyscraper spawned associations with male virility and conquest. Frank Norris's description of Chicago in his novel *The Pit* (1902) is typical: "Here, of all her cities, throbbed the true life—the true power and spirit of America; gigantic, crude with the crudity of youth . . . sane and healthy and vigorous . . . infinite in its desire."[16] When women entered the labor force, skyscraper interiors were regarded as sites of erotic liaisons between older bosses and their aspiring, lowly paid secretaries. Fictional portrayals of office labor pitched to women often encouraged them to advance their class positions by marrying the boss, rather than through professional means.[17]

Tall buildings and the ecstasies of heterosexual coupling are explored further in *High and Dizzy,* a two reeler released in July 1920, in which Harold plays the physician Dr. Harold Hall, who is redeemed by his twofold triumph over modernity and alcohol. The title is composed of double entendres: high refers to Harold's inebriated state and his precarious position on a skyscraper ledge, while dizzy suggests both vertiginous sensations and his overwhelming feelings for "The Girl," a female somnambulist (Mildred Davis). Dr. Hall promises to treat her but gets sidetracked by a bootlegging colleague in an adjacent office, who offers him some homebrew. The inebriated Harold proceeds to a skyscraper hotel, where he causes all kinds of mischief: the frustrated, amorous physician even tries several times to steal women away from their suitors.

From his hotel window, Harold spies his patient in her night dress and high heels walking on a skyscraper ledge outside his window. A long shot from above pictures her high over Los Angeles while capturing the depth of the street, which creates the vicarious feeling that the audience is in as much danger as the sleepwalker. She proceeds to his room and exits, prompting Dr. Hall to follow her in an act of drunken devotion. He soon realizes that his unsteady condition coupled with his precarious position on the outcrop could result in disaster. The camera is at a forty-five degree angle from the building's facade, which produces the impression that the audience is again hovering in space high above the metropolis with Harold. A close-up of his frightened face and upturned hair announces that he has finally sobered up. Realizing that he is literally out on a limb, Harold tries in vain to grasp onto something solid, but he trips, which results in his dangling from dangerous heights. The vagaries of modernity provide a challenge for the hero who must possess the requisite manly fortitude and sobriety to prevail.

Mildred on the hotel's skyscraper ledge in High *and* Dizzy.

Harold teeter-tottering on the skyscraper ledge in High and Dizzy.

Dr. Hall enters his room once again and finds his patient asleep in his bed, which lends a risqué element to the scene. In order to restore her honor, the resourceful suitor finds a minister a floor below who marries them from his window. Reminiscent of *Look Out Below,* the amorous encounter is forged on a skyscraper crest, which is associated with risk-taking behavior and overwhelming sensations. This modern Olympian sphere is free of the confines of convention, represented here by paternal authority, which has been soundly undermined. "He gets over a good one on an angry parent," the studio reported gleefully.[18]

The publicity for *High and Dizzy* illustrates that Pathé Exchange sought to associate Lloyd with daredevil escapades as early as 1920. An article in the press book sent to theaters and distributors reported that Lloyd had visited New York and made his way to the Brooklyn Bridge, to the very spot where an earlier stuntman, Steve Brodie, had jumped. In order to reinforce his youthful insouciance, the studio claimed that Lloyd also visited Atlantic City and Coney Island for more thrilling escapades.[19] "Make Exploitation Extra Whizzy *[sic]* When You're Showing 'High and Dizzy,'" the press book advised further. In order to accomplish these exploits, they suggested a tie-in with the "human fly" craze that was sweeping the nation, which was inspired by the adventurous activities of real construction workers and steeplejacks. One campaign called for the placement of a Lloyd dummy high atop a building, thereby associating the character Harold with youthful experimentation and intrepid masculinity. "Hoist him upon a flagpole" or "balance him on your marquee or electric sign" for maximum exposure, they urged.[20]

A threefold test of masculinity is introduced in the three-reel film *Never Weaken* and offered up anew two years later in Lloyd's tour de force, *Safety Last!* In addition to the skyscraper's association with manhood, romance, and unnerving sensations, *Never Weaken* asserts that an integrated masculine identity is the result of creative ingenuity in business matters and instrumental courage in the face of danger. The young man or Harold has initiative but lacks enough gumption in the area of romance. Only after swinging from the rafters of an enormous steel frame does he finally find the courage to propose to his sweetheart.

The press material for *Never Weaken* again linked the tall building with erotic encounters, referring to skyscrapers as "beehives of romance."[21] The opening intertitle for the film underscored this angle:

> In a certain city
> Each crowded skyscraper
> Holds a budding romance
> It's the one and only thing
> The janitor can't smash.

The following scene featured two fawning lovers, staring out at each other from the windows of their respective offices, as the reclining Harold dangles a ring on a fishing pole in the direction of "The Girl" or his beloved, played by Mildred. From his lowly vantage point seen in reverse, a tunnel-like long shot features an adjacent steel skeleton frame, auguring the hero's subsequent contest with modernity. Due to his "fishing" and flirting rather than working, the hero is intercepted by his boss, who demands more productive activity from his dallying employee.

Harold's masculinity is partially redeemed when he hears that his lover is about to be fired by Dr. Carter, an osteopath. He concocts a scheme to procure patients by teaming up with E. J. Reese (Mark Jones), in the office next door, who specializes in acrobatics. They take to the streets, where the entertainer feigns a tumbling injury, which the ersatz specialist, Harold, cures by recourse to showmanship. The amazed crowd, which includes the crippled and the infirm, are then given the doctor's business card, and they rush to his office to be healed.[22] This episode reflects a recurrent theme in Lloyd's films that self-promotion and performance, creativity, and wits are the only ways to succeed. As Mildred exclaims, "He can do anything he tries. Why he even learned the names of all the vice presidents."

Boss watching Harold in Never Weaken.

Harold is temporarily stopped short when he finds Mildred in the arms of a large man (Roy Brooks) who promises to marry her immediately. Instead of facing a man-to-man confrontation with the seemingly threatening interloper, Harold is intimidated by his girth and returns to his office despondently—his masculinity has suffered a setback. This juxtaposition of small and large male bodies is often employed by Lloyd and Charlie Chaplin (e.g., *Modern Times* [1936]) to convey either masculinity in provisional deficit or as a challenge to hegemonic models of manhood. Harold is both dejected and highly suggestible, but his cowardice prompts an adventure that will result in his achievement. When he reads of two suicides of spurned lovers in a tabloid newspaper, he decides to follow suit. After contemplating various self-destructive strategies, the coward opens the window, inadvertently allowing a swinging I beam to enter his office and transport him onto a steel skeleton frame high above the city. After peaking out from his protective blindfold, Harold realizes that the only way down is to tangle courageously with the building.

For the remaining third of the three-reel comedy, Harold is transformed into an acrobat fighting for his life, and he performs a variety of accidental and purposeful stunts on the steel frame.[23] His metamorphosis from a young man who lacks daring in romance to an intrepid actor prefigures the browbeaten Harold in *Safety Last!,* who also attains his newfound manhood in relation to the sky-scraper and Los Angeles's burgeoning modernity. He teeter-totters with knocking knees, bucks up and traverses an I beam as if it were a tightrope, and crawls back like an insect, prompting viewers to again vicariously identify with his imbalance and eventual triumph. In one shot, a mobile beam moves back and forth, prompting Harold to jump, while in another the camera's rapid tracking creates a feeling of vertigo. Construction workers are seen building the metropolis, hoisting ladders and tossing rivets confidently; their purposeful activities are juxtaposed with Harold's comedic antics. In several scenes, they seem to be the cause of his near brushes with death: one grabs the ladder that Harold thought was secure, while another throws a red-hot bolt, which he inadvertently sits on. The discombobulated suitor is eventually carried to the ground on an errant I beam, where he is reunited with Mildred and they are finally married. Harold's reluctant contest with the skyscraper signals his newly acquired masculine daring and paves the way for the consummation of his relationship. As the film's title suggests, to be a real man one must never weaken even in the face of danger.

While the ersatz acrobat carries out his entertaining, albeit perilous routine,

Harold holding on for dear life in Never Weaken.

Construction worker in Never Weaken.

Harold and Mildred on firmer ground in Never Weaken.

the steel skeleton and another across the street are included prominently in numerous shots. Even though this appears initially as a generic high-rise city, American audiences were very much aware from numerous painted signs across the street, including Bullock's 7th Street Building, Los Angeles Athletic Club, and Los Angeles Furniture, that Harold was situated in the middle of the downtown metropolis. A reviewer in *Motion Picture News* commented that "the spectator drinks in the sight of Los Angeles spread out in immediate vision."[24] Lloyd identified the site as the Ville de Paris department store, on top of which was a building under construction, which the studio regarded as "one of the most important 'props'" in the film.[25]

SAFETY LAST! (1923)

The seven-reel, full-length *Safety Last!* is the most useful of Lloyd's films for exploring in a comprehensive manner the relationship between skyscraper architecture and masculine identity, predicating Harold's manhood upon his conquest of the tall building. Released in April 1923, it continues the theme of an unintegrated masculine character, both ambitious and unrealized, who ultimately succeeds due to the melding of creative ingenuity and physical

Los Angeles signage in Never Weaken.

prowess, or brain and brawn. The film is more complex in its depiction of various paradigms of classed, raced, and ethnically inflected masculinity, which are seen in relation to "The Boy's" or Harold's white middle-class salesman. His pal and roommate Limpy Bill is a construction worker who represents the strength and fearless courage of working-class manhood. At the film's conclusion, his character is fused with Harold in a symbolic passing of the torch, providing the latter with the much needed encouragement and resolve to ascend the tall building. Other male characters include a greedy Jewish jeweler, a cross-eyed black porter, an effete supervisor, and a dissipated drunk, who were probably used by Lloyd for comedic purposes, but who also act as foils for the upstanding hero and buttress his middle-class whiteness.

Masculinity is also formulated in relation to femininity in *Safety Last!* In order for Harold to metaphorically begin his ascent, he must transcend the acquisitive, petty world of the department store's fabric counter, where a bevy of finicky female consumers threaten to deprive him of his already precarious manhood. Only when he renounces this world of feminine pretension and consumerism, located spatially on the ground floor, can Harold fully realize his masculine identity. The association of feminization with urban spaces and manly debility was introduced in 1869 by George M. Beard, who coined the term neurasthenia, linking the psychiatric condition to the rapid pace of urban life, which he termed "brain sprain."[26] According to experts, this malady was exacerbated by entrapment in stultifying offices and urban interiors in which men supposedly grew soft and effeminate. The preferred treatment for male sufferers recommended by physicians included physical activity and release in the out-of-doors, prompting an exercise craze and an interest in competitive sports such as football, baseball, rowing, and mountain climbing. Harold's escape from the department store to the performative spaces of working-class construction workers represents his break from the mental and physical constraints of feminization.

Harold's final rise to the skyscraper's crest also represents his business acumen and unbridled capitalist achievement, which ostensibly coincides with the success ethos of the 1920s. In a series of comedic maneuvers, he transforms himself from a salesman to a floorwalker, a general manager, an advertiser, and finally a performer. However, Lloyd's films possess a marked dialectical tension: although his characters appear to blindly clamor for achievement, they often subvert or transgress the very system they purport to uphold. In a 1968 interview, Lloyd admitted that he "meant to parody or genially poke fun at the American dream of success."[27] However, his numerous antics in *Safety Last!* seem more ironic than parodic, including the commandeering of numerous speeding vehicles in order to punch the bureaucratic time clock, representing his humorous undoing of modernity's strictures.

The plot concerns Harold's departure from the security of the Midwest to seek his fortune in the big city because his sweetheart will not marry him until he has made good. The film presents this interrupted heterosexual union so that Harold may prove his manhood, paving the way for marriage. As Mark Garrett Cooper has noted, love is often staged in Hollywood cinema as a visual problem beset with danger, which despite "spatial difference" and, I would argue, gender difference endures in the film's resolution.[28] In the case of *Safety Last!*, "The Girl" or Mildred stays at home while Harold braves the big city. Trains are implicated at the beginning of the tale as a means of separating the couple, but they are reunited through Harold's later mastery of the tall building.[29] So as to impress his fiancée Mildred, he sends her a letter in which he brags about his new position, accompanied by the gift of an expensive pendant. Wishing to share in his success, but sensing that he might be subject to urban temptations, she decides to visit him unannounced. Caught off guard, but hoping to maintain his position in her eyes, Harold assumes the role of the general manager, and even inhabits his office, one of many ingenious ruses that elevate his status, which he accomplishes performatively and spatially. A series of comedic mishaps-cum-opportunities ensues. For example, he rings a buzzer erroneously, which summons a row of subservient subordinates to his ersatz office, but he succeeds in maintaining the charade.

His big break occurs at a moment of cowardice, when he is forced to fetch Mildred's purse from the boss's office. Listening stealthily at the door, he overhears the manager say, "I'd give a thousand dollars to any man with a new idea that would attract thousands of people to the store." Harold jumps at the chance with a scheme to have his construction worker buddy, Limpy Bill, scale the skyscraper as a human fly, offering him half the proceeds. On the day of the event, a policeman (Noah Young), on whom the roommates had previously played a practical joke, pursues Bill like a Keystone Cop. The latter asks Harold to begin the climb instead and assures him that he will take over on the second floor. When Bill is unable to lose the officer, Harold is compelled to complete the publicity stunt himself. The task is replete with every imaginable side-splitting perilous obstacle and interruption, including pigeons landing on his head, a mouse climbing up his trousers, and a wayward beam that nearly knocks him unconscious. Virtually at the top of the tall building, Harold almost trips but catches himself by grabbing the hands of a large clock, while dangling precariously over the street far below. Ultimately, with his masculinity intact, Harold arrives at the pinnacle, where his soon-to-be bride meets him in full wedding regalia.

MASCULINITIES IN *SAFETY LAST!*

The film begins with Harold's masculinity in deficit due to his inability to provide for Mildred and continues with his failure to escape the feminized atmosphere of the department store where he is subjected to humiliating discipline by the officious floorwalker Mr. Stubbs (Westcott Clarke) and servitude by demanding female customers, a continuation of the gendered spatial division at the outset. Clean-cut, trim, and well-dressed, the character exudes an image of youthful efficiency and mobility favored by advertisers, yet his fashionable glasses and impeccable attire also suggest the foppish pretensions of aspiring city slicker.[30] To counter the latter perception, and convey the eventual redemption of Harold's masculinity, his lithe body is both compared to and conflated with the more ample body of Limpy Bill. Despite his seeming inability to measure up to Bill physically, the comparison of the two characters suggests that by borrowing the latter's resolute courage, he can combine his bookish demeanor with Bill's working-class instrumentality. In addition, Harold manages to transcend the role of mere sales clerk by recourse to initiative, becoming a temporary manager of the staff and an ersatz member of the advertising department with his climbing gambit.

The two needy confederates share an apartment and concoct multiple schemes to undermine authority, from evading the landlady to provoking a policeman. In spite of their spirited camaraderie, their jobs could not be more dissimilar. Early in the film, we glimpse Bill high atop a steel skeleton sporting an enormous grin; the viewpoint from below and the manner in which the construction worker dominates the frame enhance his monumentality and valorize his blue-collar masculinity. His commanding presence and his domination of lofty space convey a sense of unbounded freedom. Bill is also seen puffing cigarettes and sporting a pool stick, serving as phallic symbols and registering a devil-may-care attitude. A factory whistle sounds, which prompts the agile laborer to begin his descent from the steel scaffold to join Harold for lunch.

The freewheeling, lone image of Bill aloft is contrasted with Harold, who inhabits a crowded space far below, the ground level of the DeVore department store, where he must kowtow to hordes of wealthy female customers who shove him into submission. At the time this film was made, most department store salespeople and customers were women, locating Harold in a largely feminized profession and public sphere. Men employed in such positions viewed them as apprenticeships leading to bigger and better things.[31] Despite the fact that it is Saturday and the store is scheduled to close at 1:00 p.m., a demanding shopper forces Harold to remain and show her virtually every bolt of material on the shelves. After an hour of this humiliating servitude, the fussy customer decides that she wants the very first fabric presented. Adding insult to injury, the "hen-pecked" salesman is forced to clean up the entire store, which is now an unmitigated shambles. In another scene, the supposedly cultured clientele devolve into an orgy of grabbing and pushing at an "unmanned" counter and rip the clothes off Harold's back in search of bargain fabrics. The aggressiveness of the consuming feminized crowd is one of the many obstacles over which the salesman must prevail.

Limpy Bill in Safety Last!

An orgy of grabbing in the department store in Safety Last!

Lloyd's delineation of the department store is similar to that of French author Émile Zola in his novel *The Ladies Paradise* (1882), providing insight into the actor's cinematic depiction of the female crowd. Kristin Ross has noted that Zola's fictional department store, which served as an "allegory for bold new forms of capitalism," created the illusion of female omnipotence. Representing an escape from the routines of domesticity, these new democratic spaces of consumption catered to the whims of its shoppers. Zola's characterization of Parisian modernity and consumption is echoed in Benson's descriptions of American department stores, where women wielded power wholly disproportionate to their clout in society.[32] Zola described the store as a "vast feminine enterprise," in which "woman must be queen . . . she must feel it as a temple elevated to her glory, for her pleasure and triumph." This illusory power, as Ross points out, both elevates and manipulates the department store customer, creating a "public woman" who is "preyed upon by savage and violent impulses," which in the case of *Safety Last!* serves as a foil to Harold's resourcefulness. A description by the novel's main character, Denise Baudu, bears an uncanny resemblance to the film's DeVore department store and its driven customers:

> But the furnace-like glow which the house exhaled came above
> all from the sale, the crush at the counters, that could be felt
> behind the walls. There was the continual roaring of the machine
> at work, the marshalling of the customers, bewildered amidst the
> pile of goods, and finally pushed along to the pay desk.[33]

Hence, if the department store is viewed as women's temple, an illogical, mesmerizing space given over to a herd-like mentality and frenetic behavior, then the skyscraper in *Safety Last!* may be interpreted as the male tower, representative of rational achievement and ingenuity. Lloyd may have been aware of this dichotomy in attaching the skyscraper to the department store, antithetical gendered tropes of modernity.

Harold's emasculation in the department store is introduced in a previous scene, when he arrives to work ten minutes late, through no fault of his own. Overhearing the floor manager threatening to fire a tardy coworker, Harold spies several female mannequins and hatches a scheme. He dresses up as one of the dummies and is carted into the store by an unsuspecting black porter, under the very nose of his boss. Harold is so low in the office hierarchy that dissembling and cross-dressing are the only means to circumvent disciplinary action. Throughout the first third of the film, Harold is a feminized presence, a putative woman in a stifling environment from which he seeks release.

He is further emasculated by his immediate supervisor, the overbearing floor-walker who continuously reprimands him. Tall and lanky with long whiskers and a monocle from a bygone era, Mr. Stubbs may be viewed as one of the several

Cross-dressed Harold in Safety Last!

foils to Harold's middle-class manhood and modernity. Stubbs's clothing and demeanor characterize him as an old-fashioned fusspot, in contrast to Harold's youthfulness and quick-wittedness. Salesman Harold is thus engaged in a three-way struggle that is inflected by class and gender, caught between a demanding upscale manager on the one hand and irrational, upper-crust women on the other. In spite of the supervisor's nit-picking and tattletaling, Harold is able to supercede his authority by dissembling (dressing up as a female mannequin) and going over his head, by gaining access to the general manager who provides the opportunity for the climbing stunt.

Harold's masculinity is buttressed by his contrast with examples of marginalized ethnic and racial variants that enable him to retain his status. Even though his masculinity is temporarily destabilized, the ineluctable plot demands that Harold regain a fictional integration due, in part, to these juxtapositions. Richard Dyer has argued that white discourse reduces people of color to mere functions of whiteness, not allowing them the means of realizing autonomous identities.[34] Normative standards of physical perfection and health were proffered by advertisers in such magazines as *Saturday Evening Post,* which valorized Anglo-Saxons. These views were reinforced by governmental officials; in 1919,

Attorney General Mitchell Palmer identified the radical threat as "alien filth," with "sly and crafty eyes . . . lopsided faces, sloping brows, and misshapen features."[35] *Safety Last!* features both African Americans and Jews in relation to Harold in order to underscore his strengths and their putative weaknesses, assisting in the construction of Harold's whiteness and masculinity.

The black porter who unwittingly carries the cross-dressed Harold into the department store is meant to convey that he, too, is a dummy of sorts.[36] After Harold sneezes accidentally, the porter is so rattled that his eyes crisscross as he effects a frantic escape. Several scenes later, he is still shuddering high atop a ladder and refuses to be coaxed down by more reasonable white employees. His character is typical of earlier cinematic stereotypes of African Americans, coinciding with racist evolutionary theory, which defined white men as superior to women and children, and equated blacks with naive children and senile old men. According to film historian Donald Bogle, the most common stereotypes during the silent era were coons, toms, brutes, and tragic mulattoes.[37] Often presented on the silent screen to provide comic relief, blacks were "reduced to shivering wretchedness by thunderstorms, sliding panels, and ghost-like figures," whose eyes "seem to leap from their sockets."[38]

The porter's very dark skin is contrasted with Harold's exaggerated white makeup to further underscore racial difference. Their interaction echoes and reverses depictions of racial misrecognition in silent cinema, often found in so-called "baby switching" scenes in which white and black characters temporarily find themselves with the "wrong" child. Indeed, *Safety Last!* begins with Harold picking up a basket containing an African American baby instead of his suitcase before embarking on a speeding train en route to the big city, auguring the interaction between the two store employees and the impending, disorienting challenges of modernity. In the later scene, the porter's misrecognition is staged by Lloyd to highlight whites' anxieties about racial mixing and black mobility in urban environments in which they were more likely to see blacks, such as trains, department stores, and parks, after the postwar African American migration.[39] Harold is the one in the "know," who possesses the calculating agency to dissemble and thwart the time clock, while the porter is a naive victim of the cross-dressing ruse, encouraging audiences to assume the white, hence elevated, subject position. At a time when viewers occupied diverse class, gender, race, and ethnic positions, film producers were attempting to produce a standardized white viewer as a way to unify diverse immigrant audiences. Although blacks attended the movies, they were not addressed as audience members, except in disparaging terms. In spite of the porter's position as a store employee and a coworker of Harold, he is depicted as a synthesis of the coon and savage, an object of both amusement and superstition, in order to reinforce his subjugated status, thereby promoting an ideology of economic

Black porter shivering atop a ladder in Safety Last!

and spatial segregation. His naïveté and hasty ascent in *Safety Last!* are not simply used for laughs; they are meant as a premonition of and a spatial contrast to Harold's more purposeful ascent up the ladder of success symbolized by the skyscraper.

A Jewish jeweler likewise bolsters Lloyd's white manhood, and may have been employed to juxtapose two types of capitalist attainment; the latter is motivated by an honest desire for self-improvement and eventual middle-class family life, while the former is the sole product of avarice. Like earlier ghetto films, *Safety Last!* juxtaposes Old World customs and values with new American ways.[40] After Harold is finally released from the clutches of female acquisitiveness in the department store, on his way to lunch he is seduced by a "50% off" sign in the window of Silverstein's jewelry store, where he sees an opportunity to buy a chain for Mildred's pendant. Silverstein's clerk peeks out stealthily from behind the store window's darkened curtain, while the proprietor instructs his underling to lure Harold inside. The Jew's establishment is one of cloistered secretiveness, a sequestered, alien space hidden from view, in contrast to the upper sphere of Harold's eventual attainment. Its clandestine interior also contrasts with the public, democratic world of department stores, where women consumed openly with impunity and where "authentic" bargains could be had.

Dressed in Old World garb, the Jew is reminiscent of ghettoized Europe, a timeless image of the traditional in contrast to Harold's stylish modernity.[41] The hero's exaggerated whiteness and regular facial features are contrasted with the Jew's dark, hairy face, bulbous nose, and decaying teeth, suggesting disease and unclean practices. Sander Gilman has shown that Jewish physiognomy and skin was linked in anti-Semitic discourse to pathology, believed to be caused by inbreeding, which resulted in congenital nervousness and sexual ailments. According to Gilman, Jews had disease written on their skin, "the silent stigma of the black skin" or "the syphilitic *rupia.*" By the mid-nineteenth century, "being black, being Jewish, being diseased," and "being ugly" were inextricably linked.[42]

Jews, like blacks, were rendered as unfavorable types; the most common masculine stereotype was the clever and sneaky Semite, a trope that survives longer

Silverstein, the Jewish jeweler, in Safety Last!

in silent comedies than in melodramas. His most frequent occupation was pawn-shop owner, moneylender, tailor, or simple shop proprietor, who often achieved success "through devious and dishonest means."[43] *Safety Last!*'s stereotypical depiction of Silverstein borrowed from cinematic adaptations of Shakespeare's *Merchant of Venice* (1594–97) and Dickens's *Oliver Twist* (1837–39), both of which included depictions of shifty, dishonest Jews.[44] The widely successful film version of *Oliver Twist* (1922) featured Lon Chaney's bulbous-nosed, Jewish character Fagin rubbing his hands together every time money is mentioned, just like Silverstein.[45] Moreover, Silverstein also deprived Harold of the opportunity to eat lunch or nourish his body, symbolized by montage-like atmospheric inserts of Harold's food fantasy, which picture the disappearance of each course of a meal. With Shylockian disregard, Silverstein counts the money coin by coin, thereby symbolically exacting his pound of flesh.

Silverstein is depicted as a debased form of monetary accumulation in contrast to Harold's ambitious procurement of wealth. Heterogeneous audiences that included Jews and other immigrants were encouraged to identify with Harold rather than the jeweler, reinforcing Lloyd's valorization of white middle-class masculinity and its concomitant values. Although Jews viewing the film might have objected to the stereotype, they probably recognized that through humor and contrast, Lloyd was inadvertently pedaling an assimilationist message.

Further, a sauntering, slothful drunkard is introduced as a foil to Lloyd's teetotaling reputation put forth by the studio and the fan magazines. The inebriated fool is the informant who alerts the policeman that a daredevil is poised to climb the lofty Bolton Building at 2:00 p.m. Since Limpy Bill had previously escaped the policeman's clutches by hightailing up the side of a building, the cop's suspicions are piqued, and he prepares to arrest the construction worker; hence, the chase begins. Harold begins his ascent of the skyscraper shaft in place of Bill, while the latter clambers up the stairs to avoid being apprehended. On one floor, Harold is stymied by a falling tennis net, which is associated with leisure pursuits and gamesmanship, serving here as a symbol of folly. He struggles to disentangle himself as the drunk cheers him on from below. Finally, the net falls to the street and lands on the intoxicated man, who makes an aborted attempt to free himself. Subsequent to Harold's conquest of the skyscraper at the film's denouement, the camera shifts to the drunk who is on the ground, still wrestling with the net.

The resolution of his manhood occurs when Harold is symbolically fused with the virility of Limpy Bill, paving the way for his marriage to Mildred. After the climb has been successfully completed, the audience is encouraged to place Harold's face on the construction worker's body, in the space left blank in the tabloid advertisement, melding Harold's quick-wittedness and ingenuity with Bill's instrumental masculinity. Harold and Mildred are joined, and

Harold and Mildred at the top of the skyscraper in Safety Last!

adjacent to the couple is a cropped view of a testicular anemometer. Bill has provided Harold with requisite manhood to escape from the clutches of feminine acquisitiveness and emotionalism, Semitic greed, and primitive superstition, to a redeemed masculinity that is both cerebral and physical.

FROM INSECTS TO GODS: HUMAN FLIES, WORKING-CLASS MEN, AND MASCULINE AGENCY

According to Lloyd, the idea for *Safety Last!* originated from his experience watching a real human fly scale a skyscraper in downtown Los Angeles. He reported that, in 1922, he and producer Hal Roach were in the vicinity of the Roslyn Hotel when they spotted Bill Strothers climbing its forbidding granite walls.[46] Later, he recalled the incident a bit differently, stating that he saw an enormous crowd gather around the Brockman Building on 7th Avenue and noted the commercial potential attached to the escapade. He found the scene both frightening and compelling—every time he tried not to look, he was inexorably drawn to the dangerous stunt. The higher Strothers climbed, the more nervous he became. When the fly arrived at a precarious ledge on the twelfth floor, Lloyd was unable to watch for fear of an impending disaster, prompting him to rush around the corner to peek from a safe distance. At the end of the feat, he went up to the roof, introduced himself to Strothers, and invited him to visit the studio.

Lloyd recognized the potential for a thrill picture in the tradition of *High and Dizzy* and *Never Weaken,* while his publicists had already suggested the advertising potential of human flies as early as 1920. After meeting Strothers, he resolved to make a film centering on the climbing stunt, which would prompt audiences to vicariously experience a combination of thrill and dread, heir to the strong sensations and visceral emotions evoked in the early silent era's "cinema of attractions."[47] He also employed the feat as a prescriptive narrative device for how viewers, especially men, might overcome their fears by recourse to counterphobic strategies of risk taking in the service of achievement. Like Scottie Ferguson (James Stewart) in Alfred Hitchcock's *Vertigo* (1958), who has a fear of height but chases criminals over the roofs of San Francisco and who is seen dangling from a skyscraper ledge after failing to save a fallen policeman, Harold's films challenge fear by recourse to action. Thus, Strothers was engaged to play the role of the construction worker who climbs for both livelihood and sport, and provides Harold with the necessary courage to challenge his vertigo, even serving as his double in several scenes.[48]

Lloyd omitted an important portion of the film's origins, which deprived Strothers of credit in the plot's formulation and obfuscated the role of real human flies in the mythos of skyscraper climbing. He contended that the climb he witnessed in downtown Los Angeles provided the centerpiece for *Safety Last!*'s story, which, he claimed, was fleshed out by him and Roach with the help of his writing staff. This story was reiterated through the years in all of the descriptions of the film's thematic genesis. However, the events of Bill Strothers's own life bear an uncanny resemblance to those of the salesman in *Safety Last!* A North Carolina native, W. C. Strothers enjoyed a national reputation for his numerous climbs throughout the nation, even before his Los Angeles stunt. In accord with Harold in the film, he was not a climber by profession; rather, he worked in a clothing store, and his goal was to become a successful salesman. In 1915, while working in real estate, he witnessed a steeplejack climb a tall building and claimed that an idea began to take shape. One day, he was preparing for a property auction, for which he had designed numerous flyers. These advertisements for the sale were due to arrive by train, which was late. "Reckon I'll have to climb the courthouse," he remarked to a fellow drug store patron, who was also the editor of the daily newspaper. The next morning he discovered in the paper that he was scheduled to climb at 2:00 p.m., the same time as Harold ascended in *Safety Last!* eight years later. He rose to the occasion, and at the appointed time before an audience of 5,000 spectators, the accidental climber executed the exploit in a suit! As a result of his daring escapade, which was enhanced, no doubt, by his attire, he sold $35,000 worth of property. He continued to climb for the real estate firm to promote business for the next two years, before venturing out on his own as a professional human fly.[49] From 1920 to 1923, he was reported to have climbed the tallest buildings in many of the leading cities in the United States, often to benefit disabled war veterans.[50] It is uncertain if Strothers was that benevolent or was simply furnishing positive publicity to the press in order to promote the antics in *Safety Last!* as secure at a time when human flies were coming under renewed scrutiny because of their numerous accidents.

The meaning of *Safety Last!*'s plot is associated with actual skyscraper climbing and American notions of masculinity and achievement in the years preceding and following World War I. Perhaps the most famous "performer" was Theodore Roosevelt, who began as a bespectacled, debilitated youth and later advocated the "strenuous life" as a "revitalizing agent for the neurasthenic and dyspeptic American male."[51] His exploits received extended press, serving as a physical testament to self-creation through physical exertion. The working-class cowboys of the skies employed their bodily attributes and prowess in the service of a spectacle of manhood already in place, which they could capitalize on by the nature of their own dangerous work.[52]

The intrepid spirits and class affiliations of human flies were absorbed by the real and fictional flies, Strothers and Harold, respectively. These working-class men were willing to risk their lives in search of fame and fortune. Their death-defying exploits not only spawned *Safety Last!*, but the film continued an open-ended dialogue with actual human flies and the changing perceptions concerning their deeds. For example, the skyscraper scenes further prompted would-be climbers to imitate Harold, which unfortunately led several to meet untimely deaths, including the man hired by *Safety Last!*'s publicity crew to perform a climbing stunt for the film! Hence, we must be leery of the film's valorization of an escapade, ironically promoted by corporate interests, that threatened to turn lethal if replicated by desperate men seeking to improve their class status.

Skyscraper climbing for fun and profit was a popular nationwide interest in the postwar period. In 1918, the *Literary Digest* featured an article that proclaimed that now

> Atlanta has the climbing fever. Small boys are wearing out their parents, soda fountain clerks are discussing the fad with fair and ambitious customers, argumentative citizens are debating the merits of the toe-and-finger grips, while the local labor-union is considering whether or not to admit the "human spider" into the organization.[53]

Between 1918 and 1928, the *New York Times* published at least twelve articles on skyscraper climbing, including those concerning charity events, world records, and accidental deaths.[54] The craze was so popular that James Huneker,

Human fly from American Magazine *(March 1922): 30.*

one of the nation's most prominent art critics, entitled his two-volume memoirs *Steeplejack* (1920). He commenced his autobiographical account with a declaration that equated the profession with unparalleled aspiration and pointed to its class-inflected character:

> The avowals of a steeplejack! Why shouldn't a steeplejack make
> avowals? It is a dangerous occupation and, oddly enough, one
> in which the higher you mount the lower you fall socially. Yet
> a steeplejack, humble as his calling, may be a dreamer of daring
> dreams, a poet, even a hero.[55]

The sport was motivated by the public's fascination with the seemingly omnipresent construction workers and steeplejacks who could be seen atop the increasing number of skyscrapers around the country, but especially in America's metropolitan centers during the postwar building boom. These men, and a few women, performed a variety of jobs, including construction work, painting and repairing steeples and flagpoles, and putting up signs, among other tasks.[56] Sometimes these laborers were simply adventurers, which conflated them with other performing daredevils. Other flies or spiders such as Strothers realized the lucrative nature of these thrilling escapades for advertising purposes and as a profession akin to acting.

The nickname human fly or human spider not only refers to the skyscraper's capacity to reduce the climber to an infinitesimal speck, but also speaks to his skill in scaling a vertical wall like an insect. A large part of the stunt's thrilling character revolved around the climber's seeming ability to defy gravity while conquering vertigo and challenging fate from a death-defying distance. In order to insure both their well being and the positive outcome of their efforts, many flies wore special suction shoes and gloves, as did Lloyd, a fact that was largely unbeknownst to the public. This made the stunt seem even more astonishing as the flies seemed to dangle effortlessly from great heights without perceptible support.[57]

Many of these human flies enjoyed national reputations. In addition to Strothers, there was Harry H. Gardiner, Alfred Dow, Harry McLaughlin, and Fred Sutherland. Johnny Mercer, who dubbed himself "the human fly of America," had successfully scaled Cass Gilbert's Woolworth Building (1911–13), the tallest skyscraper in the world. He continued his exploits in Europe in a campaign to conquer "the tallest steeples and most difficult buildings."[58]

The press helped bolster these events by providing the requisite coverage and publicity, and by interviewing the performers in an effort to humanize them to their readership. Frequently, their articles contained salient insights into the lure of the profession and its impact upon public consciousness.

Contemporary journalists mythologized the flies as manly workers who courted danger. An article aptly titled "Adventures of a Steeplejack" (1922) chronicled the career of Alfred Dow, a twenty-four-year veteran who had been climbing since the days of the Spanish-American War. Dow and his confederates were depicted as urban pioneers or soldiers who had miraculously survived flashes of lightening, cannon balls, high winds, and nervous strain but who came out on top. In terms that conjure up both manly conquest and Manifest Destiny, Dow was described as having the same "calm, penetrating eyes" found in "seafaring men and North Country trappers." Instead of mastering the landscape horizontally, these new urban pioneers or cowboys were in pursuit of the urban mountain, the skyscraper, and the conquest of space. They described their profession as liberating, which ensured them a type of freedom and exhilaration that was unavailable to most city dwellers. When asked about the risks involved in his profession, Dow responded that he felt "sorry for the folks scurrying around like beetles in the street below . . . while he was above in the fresh air."[59] His lofty vantage point made him feel larger than life; he was akin to the skyscraper while the city dwellers were the ones reduced to dehumanizing, insect-like proportions. Dow believed that his job enabled him to escape the crushing effects of modernity and achieve a degree of liberation.

The need to achieve fame and fortune motivated other flies to ascend to loftier heights, much like the record setters of competitive sports. In accord with architects and their patrons who built taller, more distinguishable office buildings and sportsmen who wished to triumph, skyscraper climbers engaged in a competition with themselves and their peers in an effort to set new records, climb bigger structures, and invent novel exploits. For example, Fred Sutherland of Los Angeles began as a typical steeplejack but was prompted to achieve more dramatic records; reportedly, he climbed the 550-foot Washington Monument in two minutes, ascended a flagpole at the edge of the Grand Canyon, and ran up a tower in California.[60] Johnny Mercer, the fly who had scaled the Woolworth Building and was on his way to Europe, was convinced that he would become "world famous." He boasted, "I will return to New York, I will climb the Woolworth Building again, and everywhere I go people will point me out." Mercer was fully aware of the advertising potential in his numerous record-breaking achievements, reasoning that they would enable him to sell nerve tonic for the rest of his life.[61]

The quest for celebrity and accolades was not motivated solely by pecuniary interests, but was often prompted by the urban audience's enthusiastic response. *Safety Last!*'s Strothers exclaimed, "Of course, I'm out for the coin, but the real pleasure I get out of it is the crowd. It makes you swell inside when you look down and the crowd cheers. . . . I exult all over."[62] Other flies noted the spectators' reactions but in pessimistic terms, characterizing them as bloodthirsty and awaiting a tragedy. A steeplejack named Jack McCreary was repairing a church spire in Chicago before a crowd who "waited in the street below, apparently expecting him to tumble," which increasingly abraded his nerves. Sometimes the hazards of the job caused the crowd to feel mixed emotions, expecting an accident but fascinated and attentive nevertheless. McCreary responded to their rapt concentration by failing to return home after work: instead he hid in the belfry. He was found the next morning hanging from a beam, with a note that read, "I see nothing but my death will satisfy the public—so here goes."[63]

Spiderman Dow reported further on other men who succumbed to nervous strain, leading to mental decompensation, which was blamed on the job. A fly named Dan O'Brien challenged his partner Bob Merrill to a macabre race— "We'll both let go and the one that hits the floor first wins the drink." Recognizing his cohort's desperation, his partner tackled him, and both could be seen swinging from ropes high above the city. Finally, Merrill managed to fight off O'Brien's seemingly maniacal strength by knocking him out with a monkey wrench.[64]

For the majority of working-class men who chose to perform, skyscraper scaling was a lucrative means for distinguishing themselves in a competitive society that regarded achievement as the result of individual effort. Advice manuals exhorted men to make it on their own by differentiating themselves from their fellow workers, through a combination of mental acumen and bodily prowess. The physically challenging and nerve-wracking character of skyscraper scaling made it elusive to most, prompting Dow to summarize his companion's emotions, "I wouldn't swap it for any other trade in the world. And you will have to admit it's really one line of work where there really is room at the top."[65]

Journalist Bruce Bliven described the motivations of these working-class men, who were often inarticulate and indistinguishable from their peers, save for their daring exploits. Bliven claimed that climbing engendered the much sought-after respect they coveted:

> The rest of the crowd halts to view him who was a lowly member
> of it only a moment ago. While faces turn upward—hundreds of
> them. Admiration, wonder, friendly shouts of warning. In fact,
> you *are* the crowd, you see; in these moments, they live in you;
> you are the anointed torch bearer, carrying the flames of life up
> to the new heights, doing so in the eyes of all men.[66]

In spite of their quest for accolades and the journalist's romanticizing rhetoric, the majority of construction workers had to brave various occupational hazards, including physical strain, psychological stress, crippling falls, and even death. Strothers got his nickname Limpy Bill from the broken right foot he suffered during one of his climbing exploits in Santa Ana, California. As a result of this fall, he also sustained internal injuries that were rarely reported in the press during *Safety Last!*'s successful run.[67] Skyscraper work and stunts epitomized class liberation for the few and class exploitation for the majority. One third of the stories concerning flies that appeared in the *New York Times* from 1912 to 1939 concerned men who had either suffered serious injuries or had plunged to their deaths. Typical headlines read as follows: "'Human Fly' Falls as a Big Crowd Gasps," "'Human Fly' Stunt Kills," and "'Human' Fly Falls 10 Stories to Death."[68] Finally, in April 1923, the practice was outlawed in New York following the death of Harry F. Young, who was ironically climbing to help publicize Lloyd's *Safety Last!* Alderman Collins of New York characterized these men as "reckless individuals who for advertising purposes climb up the sides of large buildings, endangering their own lives and the lives of others and block traffic." The alderman made specific reference to the death of Young, "who lost his foothold while scaling the Martinique Hotel."[69] A criticism of these risky stunts was explored further in the silent film *Skyscraper* (1928), in which a young construction worker plummets to his death after trying to imitate the rope-swinging tricks performed by such daredevils as Harold in *Safety Last!*

Construction workers, flies, and their families enjoyed no monetary compensation for accidents or fatalities. Fred Sutherland recounted that when he was given a job, he was required to sign a written contract with his employer that precluded all legal claims against the latter in case of injury or death.[70] Even Lloyd's own promoters told theater proprietors that when they acquired a fly to promote the film, to make sure that "he has a police permit and that he signs a waiver making himself and no one else, responsible in case of accident."[71]

The exploitation of human flies was explored in the *New Republic,* following the demise of *Safety Last!*'s publicity fly, Harry F. Young. "Why do you inquire, should a sober human being with warm blood coursing through his veins go out and risk a hundred deaths to climb the side of a building?" Bruce Bliven asked rhetorically. He began his exposé by delving into the working-class man's quest for glory and acknowledgement, but quickly turned his attention to their misuse by promoters who could buy a man's life for the paltry sum of one hundred dollars. Why wouldn't an aspiring fellow who knew the risks, and was obligated to support his family, put more value on his efforts? Bliven inquired. His answer was steeped in issues of class exploitation, taking particular aim at Lloyd and his publicity apparatus—"You feel so insignificant somehow, sitting there with a press agent in tortoise shell rims."[72] Lloyd's white-collar agent, who was clearly a stand-in for the actor, was held inadvertently culpable in Bliven's estimation. Fly Harry Young could transiently share in the celebrity accorded the wealthy Lloyd, without the concomitant benefits of either adequate monetary remuneration or insurance.

Bliven's indictment of Lloyd is borne out by the record. Lloyd himself had the benefit of life insurance for his carefully choreographed climb in *Safety*

Last!, with the additional advantage of supporting platforms and safety nets in case of accident. Even though Lloyd appeared to hover precariously from great heights, he was little more than three stories from the ground. When he was asked to climb Chicago's tallest building, Graham, Anderson, Probst, and White's Wrigley Tower (1920–24), to christen its clock during the film's promotional tour of the city, the actor adamantly refused. Unbeknownst to Lloyd, city dignitaries had hired a professional human fly who was waiting in the wings dressed like Harold should the film star decline. In defiance of the greedy civic boosters, the working-class understudy recognized that the windy conditions around the skyscraper rendered the stunt too dangerous and walked off the job. His assertion served as a resounding rejoinder to Bliven's queries.[73]

In addition to the acquisition of a real human fly to accompany the film's run, a multitude of other risky stunts were proposed to hype up the audience. The press book dubbed Stunt No. 5 "'Human Fly' Mystery Man Climbing Department Store Building." Theater owners were told to "secure the services of a human fly. As an ad for a local department store, have him climb the side of their building." Billboard advertising would augment the stunt with the name Harold Lloyd clearly legible on the building's crest. Even the fly would be provided with a sign with *Safety Last* emblazoned on his back, rendering him a mobile billboard. The press book recommended additional ploys, such as having the fly affix letters to the side of the skyscraper in the course of his climb, so that when he reached the summit, the film's title could be read vertically, doubling as an enormous theater marquee.[74]

In view of the immense dangers of skyscraper scaling, perhaps the ultimate irony is that the promoters took advantage of the film's thrilling character while associating it with safety and precautionary measures. The title *Safety Last!* reinforced the double entendre: it referred simultaneously to the exercise of security at all costs and to safety as the ultimate resort. Stunts 1 and 2 were titled "Safety First and Traffic Tie-Up" and "Tie-Up with Safety Articles for Window Display," respectively, linking them to the national safety movement to prevent industrial accidents and ensure workers' well-being.[75] Theater owners were advised to contact their local safety councils and plan a "Safety Week," and distribute window cards to ensure that viewers associated the film with civic virtues. Firemen and policemen were to be included in the advertising campaign since they frequently "control the 'Safety First' movement."[76] At the same time, real flies were praised as courageous and their daredevilry championed as hypermasculine, their deeds equated with those of policemen, arctic explorers, and African hunters.[77] The promoters wanted it both ways, hoping to appeal to diverse audiences; women were the designated targets for the safety angle while men were encouraged to identify with the action hero.

Lloyd's desire to vicariously create the psychological tension of the human fly's ascent formed the impetus for the film. However, the selection of a real fly,

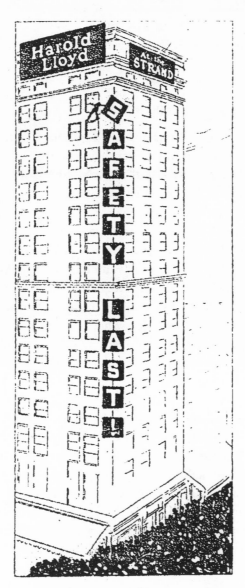

Stunt No. 5. Human Fly Mystery Man Climbing Department Store Building.

Human fly tie-in, Safety Last! *press book.*

Bill Strothers, provided the requisite instrumental masculinity, which could be conflated with Harold's bookish persona. Harold's climb may also be viewed in light of the quest for instant fame that characterized real climbers' motivations. Although comedically rendered, the climb was not represented as a facile endeavor, but one beset with risks and near fatal scrapes, which paralleled actual stunts. Stuart Kaminsky has even interpreted Harold's hanging from the clock's hands as a huge *vanitas* image, a symbol that time was running out for the hero.[78] The audience's conflicted responses to *Safety Last!* echo the reports of real flies, who claimed that crowds often devolved into an irrational mass that seemed to perversely wish for a tragedy, which unfortunately occurred too frequently.

URBAN MODERNITY AND THE SKYSCRAPER

Harold's masculine subjectivity is produced by Lloyd in relation to the urban spaces and tropes of early twentieth-century modernity in America, of which the skyscraper is the major icon. Tall office buildings in Lloyd's films are not simply singular entities, but are seen as aggregates and in relation to other manifestations of urban modernity. Like the later location-shot city films of Europeans such as René Clair, Fernand Léger, Dziga Vertov, and Walter Ruttmann, Lloyd's skyscraper films serve, in part, as symphonies to metropolitan Los Angeles. Although less celebratory and experimental in the use of formal devices (e.g., montage, split screen, etc.), they create a vicarious feeling of being in the American metropolis while critiquing and triumphing over the rush for achievement.[79] Both the actor, whose offscreen nickname was Speedy, and his filmic counterpart were fashioned in response to the accelerated pace of modern life. The careening cars, the all-pervasive mechanical office equipment, the urban crowds, and the numerous skyscrapers in all stages of development included in *Safety Last!* are meant to underscore Harold's confrontation with the seemingly omnipresent machine culture of America in general and Los Angeles in particular, which serves as a challenge to his masculinity. As Stuart Kaminsky observed, "Harold's frustrations arise in the physical problem of urban existence. The daily task of getting up and going to work becomes a chore of monumental dimensions," which are indicative of "the psychological traumas of American industrial living."[80] The hero is poised to engage it in an actual and metaphorical duel in order to effect a triumph, literally outdo it at its own game. On the ground level of the DeVore department store, he partakes in the first of many actual and metaphorical battles with a demanding, umbrella-wielding female customer.

Lloyd's depiction of the harried Harold and his environs must be viewed in light of early twentieth-century notions of modernity.[81] The concept of modernity has neither fixed chronological boundaries nor thematic parameters; like gender, it must be both problematized and historicized. Harold's confrontation with and reaction to modernity is informed by past conceptions, an amalgamation of the views of Parisian Charles Baudelaire and Berliner Siegfried Kracauer. Diverse scholars generally agree that the character of human existence in cities from the mid-nineteenth century on has been characterized by fragmentation. Ben Singer has differentiated three types of modernity—moral and political, cognitive and socioeconomic, and neurological. According to Singer, the socioeconomic occurred in the area of material culture in the last two centuries with the rise of rapid industrialization, urbanization, mass consumerism, and the proliferation of new technologies and transportation. This gave rise, in turn, to modernity as a neurological concept, whereby the urban inhabitant is subjected to a multiplicity of physical and mental shocks occasioned by the accelerated pace of the environment, its machines and the omnipresent crowds.[82] Baudelaire, who coined the term "modernity" in the 1860s, viewed city life served as an intoxicant; immersion in the urban crowd provided the artist/flaneur with novel creative stimuli, at once electrifying and replete with energy.[83] For others such as German sociologist Georg Simmel and Siegfried Kracauer, urban shocks had a direct effect on the nervous system; the former claimed that overstimulation caused the individual to develop a "protective organ for itself against the profound disruptions with which the fluctuations and discontinuities of the external milieu threaten it," leading to both a "matter-of-fact" and a "blasé metropolitan attitude," while the latter argued, in contrast, that these shocks prompted a need for heightened stimulation, which explained the development of sensationalism.[84] The depiction of Harold and his metropolitan setting has elements in common with Baudelaire's notion of the vigorous effects of modernity, melded with Kracauer's belief that city dwellers required heightened sensations because of overstimulation. These included the hero's continual confrontation with the machine, his invention of a hair-raising stunt to promote consumerism, and his company's promotional article in a tabloid newspaper.

Modernity and its icon the skyscraper are set up as foils that Harold must overcome in the narrative. At first, he is muddled by the mechanical assault, the female crowds, and the conformist regime of time clocks and overbearing managers, but it is not long before he devises a myriad of strategies to undermine its all-consuming presence. Harold is dialectically related to modernity; he is not simply acted upon like Charlie Chaplin's lowbrow tramp who inadvertently manages to gum up the works (e.g., *Modern Times*); rather, the quick-witted, middle-class salesman is an instrumental agent who temporarily thwarts mechanical efficiency, authoritarian practices, and bureaucratic supervision in the service of his own success.[85] For example, he undercuts consistently the regimentation of time and turns the work-a-day world into one of entertainment and leisure, literally liberating workers spatially from the interior confines of the skyscraper, often by recourse to distraction.[86] His urban theatrics and slapstick devices create a sense of estrangement or interruption for office denizens, who gaze out of office windows in pleasurable release, while an urban crowd seeks respite in the street turned outdoor theater. Kracauer was the first to identify American slapstick as a genre that subverted modernity's often overwhelming regime through parody and confusion in 1926: "One has to hand it to the Americans: with slapstick films they have created a form that offers a counterweight to an often unbeatable discipline, the film itself dismantles this self-imposed order quite forcibly."[87]

Harold's transitory challenges to modernity may also be explained in part by Russian literary theorist Mikhail Bakhtin's discussion of the bawdy laughter and excesses of medieval carnivals. Bakhtin argued that these earlier lowbrow "comic shows of the marketplace" provided both performers and spectators with a form of release from the strictures of officialdom through humor. He characterizes these presentations as essentially ambivalent, both a challenge to and an affirmation of the power structure, a safety valve of sorts. Enacting these in bodily form allowed actors and audiences a type of ribald expression in otherwise repressed, institutional spaces, much like Harold and his urban audiences in the regimented spaces of office buildings and bureaucratic labor.[88] Lloyd's performances seem all the more rebellious and absurd precisely because he accomplishes his athletic feats in formal work attire, providing his audiences with a vicarious rebellion from their own work-a-day lives.

French theorist Gilles Deleuze provides additional insight into Lloyd's use of visual dialectics, characterizing the devices employed by both Chaplin and Lloyd as burlesque. These actors create in their films visual analogues that look similar but have opposing meanings, thereby critiquing through comedy. As Deleuze points out, when Harold sets out for the big city at the beginning of *Safety Last!,* we see bars, a dangling slip-knot that looks like a noose, a woman crying, and a priest. We soon discover that all of these images are part of the train station platform.[89] Yet by conflating these images, Lloyd augurs the imminent threats of the city and the "deathly" challenges occasioned by modernity that he manages to circumvent.

Lloyd's quickness and agility in confronting the vagaries of modernity, from dangerous speeding cars to mechanical devices in *Safety Last!,* was meant to underscore the accelerated pace of American life, which was referred to as the "age of hurry." The prevailing attitude was that aspiring men were expected to keep up and even relish the challenge, thereby dominating space and time.[90] Car manufacturer Henry Ford praised the young man who "hops across the continent in a day" because he is "marching the way progress is going." The journalist Mark Sullivan explained that the new manly American hero was dubbed a "go-getter," and he was prompted to move more rapidly as a result of the speeding up of industry.[91] Salesmen like Harold were required to exceed expectations, not simply keep up with past sales and profits. Contemporary journalist Frederick Lewis Allen noted that salesmen in the 1920s were pressured more than ever before to measure up to a quota system, which was increased yearly. "A man should always be reaching out for larger work, grander results, always aiming to beat his own record," a company manual for the insurance industry exhorted.[92] Contests and ingenious ploys were used to stimulate the sales force to reach greater and greater production feats, much like Harold's publicity gambit to attract customers. As historian Susan Porter Benson reported, "department-store publicity of all types tended toward the grandiose; 'showmanship' and 'dramatization' became advertising-department watchwords," which ironically competed for the customer's attention.[93]

In *Safety Last!,* when we first meet Harold in rural Great Bend, Indiana, he mistakenly jumps on a horse-drawn cart as a speeding train, which he eventually catches, departs from the station. This scene points to his small town inexperience and portends his subsequent entanglements with the vagaries of urban transportation; he begins as the proverbial rube in the city.[94] In spite of his early arrival to his first day of work, he is mistakenly whisked away to the other side of town in the back of a delivery truck because he took a few minutes to relax. However, the enterprising Harold will not be undone. After he is thrown from an overcrowded streetcar and fails at two hitchhiking opportunities, he feigns illness and commandeers an ambulance by using it as a taxi. Harold recovers just in time to tell the driver through a voice tube to let him out at the next corner, the location of the DeVore department store.

In spite of near record-breaking speed in hijacking the ambulance, the go-getter Harold still arrives two minutes late for work, which could result in his dismissal. He sneaks in undetected and turns back the hands of an electronic time clock before punching in. These punch clocks, which were ushered in by Taylorism, effected a further erosion of masculine autonomy and an increased dependency upon machines and a new class of managers.[95] William Henry Leffingwell extended Taylorism from the factory to the corporate business environment with the introduction of scientific office management in the 1910s, leading to the bureaucratization and routinization of office work. He introduced Taylorist principles in the form of efficiency studies and a new cadre of supervisors to ensure production.[96] Harold's initial experience thwarting the bureaucratic, mechanical rationing of time portends his later encounter with the huge skyscraper clock. Not only is Harold prompted to harness the city's mechanical transports, but he also possesses the requisite mental acuity to outwit the skyscraper's new machines.

Authoritarian supervisors are further impediments to the acquisition of his masculinity and must be outsmarted. The DeVore department store demands a strict dress code, enforced by the fastidious floorwalker, Mr. Stubbs. He reports Harold to the general manager for an infraction, after the erstwhile subordinate has his overcoat ripped from his person by the aggressive female customers. During Harold's subsequent impersonation of the boss, one of his first actions is to take Stubbs down a few pegs by instructing him to curtail his petty behavior. "You're no collar ad yourself," he chastises Stubbs, pointing to the standards exacted by advertising in concert with corporate values.

Urban modernity in the form of electronic gadgetry is also the cause of Harold's disorientation, a further illustration of the bombardment of stimuli or shocks, which were noted by Simmel and Kracauer. Christened the Machine Age in America, the 1920s witnessed a rapid increase in supposedly laborsaving mechanical devices, which also permeated the business office.[97] Supporters of the new mechanical era believed that an acceptance of technology would engender a better, more efficient way of doing business, thereby increasing productivity. Henry Ford proclaimed, "for the most part a man with a machine is better than a man without a machine."[98] Other American contemporaries were less sanguine concerning the advantages of the machine and its accompanying ethos. A tireless critic of mechanization and urbanization throughout the decade, Lewis Mumford regarded the new skyscraper office as dehumanizing and its employees little more than automatons. In "The Intolerable City" (1926), he traced the daily schedule of a lowly office functionary, who worked in an up-to-date skyscraper office steeped in machinery and traveled in a crowded subway before returning "home to four cubicles," underscoring his wholesale containment.[99] Mumford was not the only critic of skyscrapers and machine culture; echoing Simmel, urban sociologists Nels Anderson and Maurice Davie argued that the rapid pace and demands of modern life led to a "standardization of the personality," irrational behavior, and even nervous breakdowns.[100] Interestingly, these critiques are similar to Kracauer's diatribes against Weimar Berlin's cinematic rather than real skyscraper architecture, which he accused of creating mesmerizing monumental spectacles, thereby fetishizing American Fordist Taylorism. He, too, believed that machine culture did not foster a sense of organic community; rather it reduced individuals to a "tiny piece of the mass."[101]

Safety Last! must be evaluated in the context of changes wrought by modernity in America and the concomitant debates that accompanied these transformations, which were explored by Lloyd. The film represents his effort to re-create vicariously the trials and tribulations of a rural dweller or rube who must contend with the disorienting effects of office machinery and learn how to harness it to his advantage. When the unannounced Mildred insists on seeing the general manager's office, which she mistakenly takes for Harold's, the latter is launched into a mechanical world in which he can barely maintain control. He sits on the boss's desk in a casual, proprietary manner to underscore his elevated status, but he unintentionally presses a set of remote control buzzers, which summon a bevy of subordinates. They assume a linear formation as if performing a military exercise, perhaps a commentary on the new regimentation of staff members for maximum order and productivity, which was a characteristic of scientific office management. Harold protects his assumed identity by employing his rapid reflexes and wits to extricate himself, falling in line with the others to evade discovery. Everyone looks confused, deciding that the buzzer must have sounded a false alarm. Harold explains to Mildred that he has his workers practice this fire drill regularly to test their preparedness. Even though he is a subordinate, he demonstrates that he is resourceful enough to think on his feet when faced with technology's unpredictable, defamilarizing character.

Harold's skyscraper climb comprises nearly one quarter of the film and represents his ultimate confrontation with the challenges of modernity and his acquisition of masculinity. Although he commences the ascent up the skyscraper shaft in a dapper business suit, he ironically transforms the building into a site of leisure and entertainment, albeit only for a short time. The necessity to distinguish himself in the city by increasingly more dramatic gambits and publicity, which is reinforced by the use of tabloid journalism, is also communicated by his juxtaposition with the urban audience, who demand more exciting sensations. These scenes are also a commentary on the star-making apparatus and its attendant publicity machine that began to characterize Hollywood's moviemaking industry. A flock of admiring women greets him on the third floor and applauds his gambit, signifying the manner in which stars are publicized and fans are produced. Harold is clearly the star of this show.

The effects of Harold's antics on bureaucratic office labor are underscored by the wholesale diversion of the employees, who gaze eagerly out the window from every floor of the tall building. In accord with Hollywood cinema, which provided entertainment value to the masses, Harold supplies the urban audience and himself relief from conformity and the hegemony of punctuality and efficiency. His ironic undermining of capitalism's production ethos paves the

Employee line-up after Harold presses the buzzer in Safety Last!

way for his own reemasculation and acceptance of its very premises: individual initiative, risk taking, and success at the film's conclusion. At the same time, his gambit diverts the urban audience from the corporation's ultimate goal, which is to prompt consumption in the DeVore department store. Several scenes serve to illustrate his wholesale amusement of both the pedestrian crowd and office workers alike. When Harold is in danger of losing his balance, Bill throws him a rope and he swings through the air like a trapeze artist performing a high wire act, to the accompaniment of circus music.

Harold's final, albeit temporary, subversion of bureaucratic conformity occurs in his confrontation with an enormous clock that crowns the skyscraper, a continuation of his previous run-in with electronic time maintenance. These skyscraper clocks were heir to medieval bell tower clocks, which originated in monasteries and spread to the city square. According to Mumford, "Time-keeping passed into time serving and time accounting and time rationing," virtually defining urban existence.[102] When Harold just about reaches the skyscraper's summit, Bill opens an office window to offer him a plank, but succeeds in knocking him on the head instead. In a gesture of desperation, Harold grabs onto the hands of the huge timepiece. This misguided gesture causes the clock's enormous face to detach, which results in Harold's precarious dangling from its bent and damaged extremities. In spite of his momentary setback, he succeeds in literally and figuratively stopping time, thereby thwarting modernity's regulation of urban life, where workers are engaged in office labor despite the fact that it is a Saturday. One is reminded of Simmel's claim in "The Metropolis and Mental Life" of the inextricable chaos and waste of time that would ensue if "all the watches in Berlin went wrong in different ways," much like *Safety Last!*'s enormous skyscraper clock, which regularizes urban time and space.[103] Perhaps that is why Harold is briefly punished for his transgression. Confronted by a threatening dog at another window, he lunges for a flagpole, which also breaks, causing him to suffer an electric shock while enmeshed in the clock's innards. This scene reinforces Harold's dialectical relationship with modernity: the disciplining, mechanical apparatus impedes his progress, and he, in turn, thwarts its regime, before his ultimate conformity and tacit support of its precepts.

Lloyd's dependence on the urban crowd as a necessary component for his feat reflects the metamorphosis of Los Angeles into a major metropolis, with most of the population density in the city's downtown region. The scene underscores further that Hollywood actors require a crowd or a mass audience to ensure their star power. Beginning in the 1870s, a series of land booms, which were orchestrated by the major railroad companies who acted as the city's first boosters, promoted Los Angeles as a healthful, subtropical paradise. By the 1920s, due to the increase in employment occasioned by "green and black gold" and the motion picture industry, the city experienced the most dramatic growth in its history.[104] Over two million people moved into the state, while Los Angeles alone gained 272,037 denizens, prompting urban historian Carey McWilliams to characterize this period as "the largest internal migration in the history of the American people."[105] *Safety Last!* utilizes the skyscraper either alone or en masse to highlight Los Angeles's metamorphosis into a major metropolis, underscored by the numerous shots of tightly packed buildings, numerous advertisements, and the perpetual parade of vehicular traffic, which spell urban congestion. The film's skyscraper scenes were shot on location on several streets and tall buildings in downtown Los Angeles, and the long shots of Harold's climb (performed by Strothers) occurred on the exterior of the International Bank Building on Temple and Spring Streets. According to producer Hal Roach, at least four tall buildings were employed for publicity stills, including the Los Angeles Investment Company, the Western Costume Building, the Merchant's National Bank Building, and the "whopping 13-story" Washington Building.[106] Several of these new skyscrapers were located on Spring Street, which was known as the "Wall Street of the west."[107] A tourist postcard of 1914 with the title "A Few of Our New Skyscrapers" announces that the city was proud to show off its burgeoning new heights. *Safety Last!* may thus be viewed as one of the first full-length urban films in the United States that featured Los Angeles, not New York, as a site of commerce and modernity.

Postcard: "A Few of Our New Skyscrapers, Los Angeles, Cal," 1914.

In addition to exploring the crowd as a material fact, *Safety Last!* plumbed the meaning of the crowd as a psychological trope of modernity, particularly the individual's relationship to the mass. In an era of shrinking personal autonomy due to the rise of corporate capitalism and the concomitant pressure to succeed by recourse to one's own initiative, it was also necessary to separate oneself from the group. According to Simmel, the urban denizen had a need to distinguish himself from the crowd, which demonstrated his sophisticated intelligence and greater nervous energy.[108] One method to seek removal and distinction was to inhabit the various skyward roof gardens or observation decks that provided a magisterial gaze for visitors. Yet, it is important to note that the acquisition of novel ways of perceiving the city was conditioned by one's class and gender position.[109] Harold achieves the distinction recommended by Simmel both spatially and economically with his rise to the top of the office building, while simultaneously claiming his masculinity. The acquisition of his manhood is also accomplished by his detachment from the emotional feminized crowd, both in and out of the department store, who represent mass consumption and acquisitiveness. Yet his character never achieves complete autonomy; rather, he is dialectically related to the mob throughout the skyscraper sequence; he needs the mass audience for his star power and validation and seeks disengagement from it in the attainment of an elevated class status and an integrated gender identity.

The urban audience who has gathered below to cheer him is an integral part of the feat, which is underscored by the use of repeated crosscutting shots from the crowd to the performer above. They respond with uniform admiration and amusement to Harold, who is either oblivious to or unconcerned with the implicit danger of his performative. For example, a mouse crawls up his trouser leg, prompting the actor to shake spasmodically in order to relieve the discomfort and dislodge the intruder, a gesture that doubles as a jazzy tap dance. Even though Harold is precariously teeter-tottering on the precipice of a window ledge far above the street, the crowd continues to cheer and applaud, thirsty for sensational thrills even if it means the performer's demise.

Safety Last!'s designation of the crowd as singular entity that responds uniformly and unthinkingly to Harold's death-defying antics is a selective depiction of crowd psychology.[110] The most popular disseminator of this perspective was the Frenchman Gustav Le Bon, whose *The Crowd: A Study of the Popular Mind* (1895) exerted a far-reaching influence on subsequent writings in group psychology and collective behavior. Characterizing the age as "the era of the crowd," Le Bon differentiated between the anonymous, homogeneous crowd (e.g., caste, class) and the heterogeneous crowd (e.g., street crowds). According to Le Bon, the urban crowd served as a great leveler, temporarily erasing the differences between classes. He recognized that although a vast chasm may exist intellectually between a great mathematician and a boot maker, in a crowd

Crowd scene in Safety Last!

this difference is obliterated in favor of "the unconscious qualities" that gain the "upper hand."[111] Harold's desire to differentiate himself from the leveling character of the crowd in the film is the only way to achieve fame and fortune, while triumphing over modernity's all-pervasive character.

Le Bon was not optimistic about the crowd's potential democratic spirit as were later writers such as Kracauer and Benjamin; rather, he viewed them as highly suggestible conglomerates that operated irrationally, as if in a state of hypnosis, linking them to the feminine. They were frequently given over to violent sentiments, which increased "especially in heterogeneous crowds, by the absence of responsibility." Thus, the individual in a crowd was subsumed by intemperate, collective feelings, divorced from the consequences of his or her reactions. Le Bon supposed that the crowd's imagination was most forcibly stimulated by theatrical representations, in which the group experienced the same emotions.[112] In accord with Le Bon's assessment of the crowd's latent aggression, Harold's urban spectators clamor for more imminently dangerous stunts. In order to detach himself from their feminized emotionalism, he separates himself spatially and metaphorically in the acquisition of his manhood.

The mob's demand for more stimulating entertainments was both inspired and reinforced by the rise of tabloid journalism, which is used in the film as a ploy to attract the urban audience.[113] They are prompted to attend the event by the placement of a front-page story in a big city newspaper that sported a captivating headline, mimicking the look of such papers as *The Daily News,* which commenced publication in 1919 and was selling one million copies by 1925. Echoing Kracauer, historian Roland Marchand asserted that the term tabloid came to increasingly suggest "a certain style and a sensational mode of appeal," which, in turn, created a "tabloid audience."[114] Front pages were used to capture the potential buyer's attention with a single, bold title that was accompanied by a few dramatic photographs. This was the strategy employed in *Safety Last!,* augmented by the use of the word "mystery" and a photograph of a faceless adventurer, which was meant to stimulate further curiosity, hence participation in the street theater.

In concert with the newspaper's sensational publicity, the DeVore department store produced a placard displaying a large graphic image of the fictional Bolton Building, the site of the stunt.[115] An entire frame of the film is given over to the skyscraper advertisement. It is unclear whether the filmmakers used the pictorial illustration to highlight the tall building, or whether the image was meant as a souvenir for the event's attendees. Both interpretations are in concert with the function of early skyscraper postcards and visual souvenirs, which were produced since the late nineteenth century for tourists. These ennobling images of tall buildings were designed to encourage visitors to appreciate the wonders of technology and, at the same time, garner business for the owners.

It is appropriate that tabloid-advertising strategies are employed to sell the skyscraper performative in the film, since tall buildings have served as advertising icons for business interests. Architectural historian Katherine Solomonson and historian William R. Taylor have demonstrated that corporate America wanted their skyscrapers to have appeal as advertisements, to serve as "continuous beacons of publicity" for the company image.[116] As I have shown elsewhere, this strategy was employed successfully in the promotion of New York's famed Woolworth Building, which was dubbed the "cathedral of commerce," suggesting that the dime-store magnate possessed lofty values and civic responsibility.[117] A skyscraper's preeminence was used as a publicity ploy to imply that bigger was better and hence more profitable, resulting in a height mania that still survives to this day. Solomonson argues further that skyscrapers served "a function akin to trademarks that were increasingly being developed to produce a rapidly recognizable identity for corporations and their brand name products."[118] Lloyd, too, referred to his glasses as a trademark and his character as a type, which could also sell as a commodity. Thus, Lloyd's publicity stunt up a skyscraper served to advertise the DeVore department store by depicting the touristic appeal of the Bolton Building as a monument.

To underscore the advertising mania that characterized the era, as Harold

Bolton Building advertisement in Safety Last!

climbs, the camera pans the surrounding buildings, situating the viewer on eye level with the numerous painted signs or billboards, such as Bullock's Department Store and the Los Angeles Stock Exchange, that were affixed to lofty skyscrapers. Like tabloid headlines, billboards were increasingly rendered in more simplistic, eye-catching terms to distinguish them from the abundance of visual stimuli, encouraging the urban dwellers to direct their gaze upward. Formerly situated on street level in the early years of the century, signs with bold graphics were increasingly placed on tall buildings to attract the gaze of a mobile, ambulatory spectator, or "a citizen on wheels."[119] These signs also served as an architectural accompaniment to the skyscraper itself, positioned to encompass the lofty vantage point of office workers, high-rise apartment dwellers, and roof garden enthusiasts. Harold's stunt, which is tracked by the camera, also prompts the crowd below to notice the advertisements that surround him, rendering him as an advertisement among many.

Skeletons of emergent buildings are interspersed in the crowded urban landscape with its numerous buildings and conspicuous signs and serve as a further backdrop for Harold's climb. Steel frames replaced load-bearing post-and-lintel construction as the structural components that enabled skyscrapers to soar limitlessly. In accord with the Eiffel Tower (1887–89), these naked frames may be viewed as icons or monuments of modernity, the products of engineering prowess and an unequivocal belief in progress. The camera is employed to highlight the skyscraper's physical properties, particularly its lofty presence and gargantuan size in relation to Harold's. Before he begins, the camera pans the building from bottom to top to underscore the imminent dangers that he faces. Frequently, the camera shifts from lofty pinnacle to the street below, which creates a vicarious feeling of vertigo and differentiates Harold's elevated position from the crowd's lowly status. The building's height is further communicated by the enumeration of each floor that must be surmounted in order to reach the top both spatially and symbolically. However, a long shot is employed that shows the hero (played by a double) clinging to the side of the building to highlight the skyscraper's girth and monumentality, which renders Harold an infinitesimal speck. This dramatic discrepancy in size between the architecture of modernity and the urban denizen prompted commentators, as early as 1905, to bemoan the skyscraper's dehumanizing presence, which rendered human beings the size of mere insects.[120] This rooftop perspective emerged with the joint birth of the camera and the Parisian metropolis and may be seen in both the early photographic experiments of Nadar and the paintings of the French Impressionists.[121] The contrast in magnitude may have inspired the appellations human flies or spiders to daredevils who scaled skyscrapers.

When Harold finally arrives at the top, he overcomes his small stature in relation to the tall building by metaphorically fusing with it. A space formerly inhabited by the intrepid construction workers or successful businessmen who commanded magisterial perspectives of the city now belongs to Harold. Despite his collusion with modernity's stratagems, seen in his adoption of the sensational publicity tactics of tabloidism, that rendered him a human billboard, Harold has effected a victory of sorts, which resulted in his separation from the multitude of pedestrians below. In *The Practice of Everyday Life* (1984), French theorist Michel de Certeau explained his sensations from atop the 110th story of the now defunct World Trade Center, an experience that transformed him from a walker into a voyeur. Viewing the city from this lofty vantage point like a flying Icarus enabled him to "leave behind the mass," the crowds, and the "nervousness of New York traffic," to virtually triumph over modernity itself. From the skyscraper crest, de Certeau noted a feeling of omnipotence, allowing one "to read it [the city], to be a solar Eye, looking down like a god," much like that noted earlier by real human flies and enacted by Harold.[122]

HAROLD LLOYD'S MASCULINITY: SELF-HELP AND SELF-PROMOTION

There has been no sustained effort to explore the construction of gender in Lloyd's films, the presentation of his star persona, or the relationship between the two. It is difficult to discern the differences between the film character, the actor's guise, and the actual person, if indeed one ever existed. Since Lloyd and movie critics often referred to most of his characters as Harold, the actor's three personas were in continual relay, with often no clearly delineated boundaries between them. Lloyd's tripartite masculine identity was developed in the 1910s, at a time when the production of Hollywood stars became an integral part of the selling of a movie. As film historian Richard de Cordova and others have argued, a star's often multifaceted personality was forged across a number of films and embossed by Hollywood's publicity apparatus.[123] Extrafilmic sources such as fan magazines, press books, film trailers, and the like helped construct the star. These, in turn, were in a perpetual dialogue with a host of cultural discourses disseminated in the mass media, including popular advertising, pulp fiction, and advice literature, which helped flesh out an actor's gender identity.

Lloyd himself was an active participant in the forging of his gendered star persona; he granted numerous interviews to fan magazines and popular journals, and even completed the full-length biography *An American Comedy* (1928) at the height of his fame and box-office success. Lloyd selected specific events in his life in an effort to shape public perceptions of him and his characters, resulting in a gendered self that is less an accurate reconstitution of the "real" Harold than a reflection of what it meant to be a certain type of man in the first two decades of the twentieth century. At any given moment in history, masculinity itself is a fluid or what Martin Berger calls a "supple" notion; several types of masculinity coexist and aspects of one or the other often make their appearance in a single individual.[124] Masculinity is never a stable or fixed concept but is always a negotiation between a person and the cultural setting in which he resides; each mediates the other. Any effort to understand the multifaceted Lloyd, and by extension the character of Harold in his skyscraper films, requires one to situate his story within the context of then-current views on masculinity and success.

Born in Burchard, Nebraska, in 1893, Lloyd depicted his childhood as average, referring to himself as "a plain freckled kid from middle America," who, like his characters, made good because of his industriousness and love of challenges.[125] Biographers echoed Lloyd's perspective of himself: Annette D'Agostino claimed that, as a child, Lloyd was a telegraph messenger, a stockroom boy, a snack vendor in a baseball park, and an apprentice in a blueprint shop, among other youthful employments.[126] *Motion Picture Magazine* reported in 1927 that Lloyd was a modern version of a typical Horatio Alger character who "worked hard, helped his family, refused to be discouraged by defeat, and finally became a millionaire. . . . Alger himself might have written the story of this young man. He might have called it 'Harold the Hustler, or From Rags to Riches.'"[127] As Harold and the fan magazines would have it, he resembled heroes like Luke Lark of Horatio Alger's *Struggling Upward,* who came from humble origins, were loyal to their mothers, and were seemingly free of vices.[128] The moral of the manufactured tale was that individual initiative would triumph over class origins and corporate surroundings, a message that was reiterated again and again in Lloyd's films.

Central to the Lloyd myth and his characters' accomplishments was that achievement was predicated on overcoming obstacles and adversity with an intrepid spirit, that it was necessary to test one's manly mettle for true success to ensue. This was only possible through abstinence and wholesome living and the rejection of the wastrel's life, which was equated with feminized masculinity. Many of Alger's stories likewise feature a stalwart, resolute hero who is juxtaposed with an effeminate, indolent male counterpart, serving as the antihero, whose dissolute habits lead to defeat. In *Making His Way,* the manly main character, Frank Courtney, is contrasted with his swindling stepfather, who dressed in "a flowered dressing gown" and whose dissipated, lazy son spent "no little time on personal adornments."[129]

Harold's chaste and upstanding masculinity is formulated in relational terms in *Safety Last!,* in which a drunkard is employed both for comedic effect and as a foil. Lloyd recounted in his autobiography how he accompanied an alcoholic family friend on a journey to regain his physical stamina after a bout of dissipation. After the man completed the putative rest cure, the young Lloyd's job was to keep the man from falling off the wagon. To his chagrin, he discovered that the drunkard was far from rehabilitated and continually devised various gambits to subvert his youthful supervisor. Lloyd reported in the spirit of one of his filmic counterparts, "It never was needful to ward me away from the flying hoofs of the Brewer's big horses."[130]

The studio's publicity apparatus echoed Lloyd's claims of purity and abstinence by countering the image of a rare, inebriated Harold in the film *High and Dizzy.* Originally titled *High and Dry,* the film's name was changed by producer Hal Roach to dispel any potential associations with disappointment due to alcohol deprivation.[131] The press book maintained in a rather defensive tone that Lloyd himself was a "total abstainer" and that his favorite indulgence consisted of ice cream, while referring to the film, somewhat hypocritically, as "a sparkling comedy cocktail."[132] A contemporary reviewer of *Feet First* echoed this characterization of his pictures when he stated that "all of them" were "clean."[133] Later commentators reiterated the image of a wholesome Lloyd, even contrasting him with his scandal-ridden contemporaries such as Chaplin, Arbuckle, and Keaton.[134]

Lloyd's and Harold's masculinity is also understood in the context of notions of the self-made man, a term originally coined by Henry Clay in 1832 to describe someone with a patient but ambitious temperament and an entrepreneurial spirit. A man's success was based on his own initiative and will, and "the individual who failed had only himself to blame."[135] As sociologist Michael Kimmel has argued, what defined the nineteenth-century man was "success in the market, individual achievement, mobility," and "economic autonomy.

This was the manhood of the rising middle class. . . . Success must be earned, manhood must be proved—and proved constantly."[136] Self-made also implied that achievement was measured not in relation to others or by cooperation, but solely through one's efforts to fabricate an individual identity. According to Reverend Calvin Colton, who wrote in 1844, American men often begin from modest circumstances, but "rise in the world, as the reward of merit and industry" and "personal exertions."[137]

Self-made signified not simply hard work and initiative, but also individual material achievement in an urban context. Historian John Cawelti asserts that "in the cities and especially among the younger generation self-improvement meant moving in the new world of industry and business."[138] The focus was not on gender, race, and class barriers; it was assumed that success was within the reach of anyone who exerted the effort. Men no longer saw themselves as part of a larger community, or even a cosmic order, but as isolated selves whose own deeds determined their destinies.

The term self-made had clear architectural analogies, implying that one began from scratch and created oneself as if building an edifice, or in the case of Harold, climbing one. In the construction process, one ascended higher and higher, until the building was complete, thus implying upward mobility. Orison Swett Marden, one of the most influential self-help writers of his generation, featured the following poem on the frontispiece of his book *Success* (1897):

> Build it well, what 'er you do;
> Build it straight and build it true;
> Build it clean and high and broad;
> Build it for the eye of God.[139]

Numerous self-help writers, whose own rags-to-riches sagas served as corroborative evidence of the soundness of their advice, preached the gospel of individual masculine achievement through private initiative and exertion. Marden's books sold twenty million copies worldwide and were translated into twenty-five languages. He disseminated these ideas in his widely read periodical *New Success* (1918–28). Inspirational titles, such as *Rising in the World Or, Architects of Fate* (1895), *Success* (1897), *The Secret of Achievement* (1898), *The Young Man Entering Business* (1903), *He Can Who Thinks He Can* (1908), and *How to Get What You Want* (1917), attested to the dual mantra of personal responsibility and material acquisition.[140] In his numerous books written between 1895 and 1917, Marden often spoke to the up-and-coming clerk or salesman, similar to Lloyd's fictional counterparts, who "can live in a store of his own which his imagination builds . . . the humblest dreams of power."[141]

It not known whether Lloyd read Marden's highly influential self-help books, but the latter's ideas were woven into the very fabric of popular views on masculinity, promoted in *New Success* and several other periodicals such as *American Magazine* and *Collier's*.[142] This message seemed to have resonated with the young Lloyd, who proudly claimed that he worked indefatigably at any job offered to him, but who had a dream since childhood, an abiding desire to be an actor. In *Girl Shy* (1924), the stuttering protagonist is engaged in writing his own self-help guide, which results in his finally consummating a relationship. *Feet First* features Harold enrolling in the so-called Personality Plus program, which he discovers in a popular magazine. The mail-order course, a parody on the facile craze, assists him with his elocution skills, which in turn help him sell himself in an efficacious, manly style to his overbearing boss and to his abiding love interest.

The rhetoric of self-made masculinity began to shift in the years 1895–1915 from a concern with perseverance, patience, and prudence in favor of perfecting oneself through the development of personality, which could be molded through mental initiative or the power of positive thinking.[143] Pathé Exchange claimed that Lloyd was motivated to be "braver and braver" in the performance of his hair-raising stunts by the theories of French psychiatrist Dr. Émile Coué, whose autosuggestion served as a prelude to achievement.[144] Lloyd reported in his autobiography that he employed Coué's ideas in the formulation of the character Harold in *Why Worry* (1923), a film that was made just prior to *Safety Last!*[145] Widely read in the United States beginning in the 1920s, Dr. Coué's book *Better and Better* (1921) prescribed autosuggestion to the masses as a sure-fire strategy for self-fulfillment and achievement.[146] Similar in spirit to Marden's earlier *He Can Who Thinks He Can,* Coué claimed that exercising mental energy in the service of instrumental deeds would insure success.

The prescriptions for achievement offered in Marden's voluminous oeuvre read like a manifesto for an understanding of Harold's masculinity. In accord with Coué, Marden emphasized the importance of will power and mental energy in the realization of one's objectives. Pithy quotations from the rich and famous or those that had attained their goals introduce a good number of Marden's chapters. Joseph Kossuth's dictum "Nothing is impossible to him who wills" appeared in *The Secret of Achievement* and pointed to the synthesis of mental energy with instrumental actualization.[147] Marden supposed that inchoate thoughts must be harnessed into a monolithic aim that could define one's life purpose, much like Lloyd's self-proclaimed drive to become an actor, or Harold's serendipitous idea to scale the Bolton Building.[148] This all-defining vision, the author asserted, was a characteristic of all great men and resulted in civilization's innovations. Marden's philosophy was predicated on a confidence in the benefits of progress, which was equated with technological advancement. In *He Can Who Thinks He Can,* Marden disclosed that singular masculine agency produced the marvels of modernity: "Our great ocean liners, our marvelous tunnels, our magnificent bridges, our schools, our universities, our libraries, our cosmopolitan cities are all the result of somebody's dreams."[149]

Marden's purported goal was to impart hope and instill motivation in his young middle-class audience, much like Lloyd's department store clerks, office employees, and shoe salesmen. He pitched his appeal to those who aspired to be better and who equated success with the acquisition of wealth. Lauding the accomplishments of Carnegie or Schwab, Marden likened their visionary drive with that of the average man, thereby asserting that success was within anyone's grasp. He claimed that Americans were already fertile ground for his message because of their native temperament: "Dreaming is especially characteristic of the typical American. No matter how poor, or what his misfortune, he is confident, self-reliant, even defiant at fate; because he believes better days are coming."[150] In order to distinguish himself, it was imperative to avoid becoming a mere cog in a wheel or a slave of modernity; rather, the man with original ideas who attracted attention served as the best advertisement for himself.

Mental acumen and novel ideas must be accompanied by vigorous action. "A little more persistence, courage, vim! Success will dawn o'er fortune's cloudy rim," introduced a chapter titled "The City of Purpose" in *The Secret of Achievement*.[151] The maniacal energy of Thomas Edison, who claimed to work twenty-one hours per day, was offered as a model to emulate. Yet even the combination of a visionary spirit, novel schemes, and tireless energy did not guarantee achievement. Men must be prepared to encounter numerous setbacks and misfortunes before acquiring the prize. Indeed these very difficulties were essential to masculine character development, to testing men's determination. Prefiguring Lloyd's actual and metaphorical climb up the skyscraper in *Safety Last!,* Marden employed architectural language to depict aspiration under adverse conditions: to "make stepping stones of our stumbling blocks, is the secret of success."[152]

A telling passage in his book *Success* concerned the burgeoning skyscrapers in his midst. He reported on a man who wished to go to the top of a tall building, only to find the elevator broken. Mounting the stairs, the man realized that although the elevator may have facilitated the ascent, there were no symbolic elevators in life. "I've had to climb every place worth reaching," he claimed, and wished that everyone was compelled to attain his status in life without recourse to elevators. Even though the man concluded that he may have taken the elevator if it had been operational, he was, nevertheless, gratified that "we have to climb" or exert ourselves "to rise in the world."[153]

The benefits of individual achievement in the face of hardship were being touted at a time when men were facing a loss of autonomy in the workplace. At the beginning of the nineteenth century, four out of five men were self-employed, but by 1870, this number had dropped to one third.[154] Wage earners in large factories produced goods, and a cadre of clerks and low-level salesmen pedaled them to the public, often under the supervision of a new class of managers and supervisors. Nevertheless, self-help books continued to put the onus of achievement on the individual rather than on the corporation in an ever more competitive marketplace. T. J. Jackson Lears claims that advertising reinforced the ethos of corporate management, resulting in a novel and demanding notion of individual well-being, or "personal efficiency," which signified a coalescence of "the supposedly private realm of physical or emotional wealth and the public world of organized competition for success," creating a new subjectivity.[155] A similar assertion may be made about self-improvement literature, which melded the public and private realms and promulgated the conformist and competitive values of corporate management.

In response to the self-help literature that emphasized new ideas and ingenuity, Lloyd created Harold, a young middle-class man who reflected the current interest in youth culture that characterized the post–World War I era, complete with appropriate attire, glasses, and a spunky attitude. In demeanor, he was closest to the silent film actor Douglas Fairbanks, who, as Gaylin Studlar points out, exuded an air of "idealized boyish masculinity."[156] Lloyd the businessman consciously selected a persona for an emerging mass audience who seemed, more than ever before, obsessed with the "behavior, interests, and amusements" of the college-age population, which had increased dramatically in the years 1900–1930 and would be more apt to identify with his character, and hence increase box office receipts.[157] The appeal of youth in the 1920s went beyond the campus, creating a virtual "filiarchy" in the United States that threatened to overturn tradition, promoting "malleability and individualism" as positive values, according to Stuart Ewen.[158] Historian Paula Fass asserted, "Youthfulness became synonymous with smartness, and young and old were beginning to look upon youth as models for fashion, dress, music and language. . . . Between the realities of youth behavior and youth societies, and the excitement of a rapidly changing world, the young had come to represent modernity."[159] Lloyd stated, "I had been feeling around for youth, possibly a boy who could be carried through a college series."[160]

Lloyd's appropriation of his trademark faux tortoise-shell horn-rimmed glasses for his character sometime around 1917 was prompted by a collegiate preference and subsequently became a fad among the young due to his further popularization of the style.[161] In the United States, round lenses with tortoise-shell frames had been in fashion since 1913, shortly after they were imported from Vienna. As the *Kansas City Star* reported in 1913, they were initially looked upon as "an affectation and ridiculed in public." Prior to the 1890s, glasses were still associated with old age and infirmity, and were prohibitively expensive. This began to change. The *Star* continued:

> And now comes an age of glory in infirmity. The average human
> person, instead of being ashamed that his eyes are on the blink,
> actually seemed to be proud of it. He gets his prescription done
> up in owl-like round lenses the size of twin motor lamps. And he
> has these framed in bulky tortoise shell, imitated in celluloid.[162]

Lloyd's decision to replace his earlier characters, Willy Work and the Chaplin-esque Lonesome Luke, with the "College Kid look," a new mutable, middle-class youth who wore spectacles, was an attempt to distance him from the low comedy genre by adopting a signifier of intellectual acumen and modernity.[163] As fashion designer Samuele Mazza has pointed out, "at least since the beginning of modern history, glasses had still partly retained a trace of symbolism, if only because they served to identify not the wise man, but at least the cultivated one, the intellectual, somebody who had something to do with reading."[164] In contrast to the pince-nez or lorgnette still worn by older professionals or the wealthy, Harold's light-weight celluloid glasses were associated with the mobility of speeding cars and the freshness of an educated, albeit sometimes awkward young adult.

The glasses also served the function of forging an image of a man who was unlikely to assume an assertive stance, unless pressed, a nerd in need of courage. There is some controversy as to who originated the idea for the bespectacled youth, his producer Hal Roach or he himself.[165] Most Lloyd biographers agree that the character's full identity was fleshed out after he saw a film about a meek parson who wore glasses.[166] In his autobiography, Lloyd recalled that the unassuming man of the cloth was tolerant and peaceful with glasses on, but when injustice ensued, he was catapulted into aggressive action. After subduing a villain who had abducted a young woman, he calmly dusted off his clothing and reassumed his judicious deportment.[167] In 1962, film critic Nelson Garringer recognized that this character was an amalgamation of two types of American manhood, one brash and breezy, who exuded optimism, and the other a "shy awkward fellow who at first seems unable to cope with life," a characteristic reinforced by the glasses.[168] This dual persona served Lloyd well: he elicited audience sympathy and prompted identification with the underdog's plight.

Glasses, a neat three-piece suit, and a straw hat identified him as a fashionable, well-dressed youth. Lloyd claimed later, "there was a fundamental basic idea with my character in that he more or less represented the young man who was a clerk in a store, someone in what the British call the 'middle class,' always struggling against the bigger man."[169] The suit also coincided with the middle-class uniform pedaled by advertisers to designate the new generic businessman, stockbroker, or up-and-coming salesman. As historian Roland Marchand has suggested, working-class men rarely appeared in marketing vignettes; rather, the advertiser's hero was well appareled in a suit, tie, and hat or upscale leisure attire. When young men were featured, they "were often salesmen, aspiring to the popular intermediate step of sales manager or a stereotypical business ladder."[170] These costumes were promoted also by Marden, in the pages of *New Success,* who persuaded his readers to devote serious attention to their exterior selves, which could also determine their upward trajectory:

> Your personal appearance, your dress, your manner, everything
> about you, the way you keep yourself groomed, how you carry
> yourself, what you say, . . . all these things are to you what the
> show windows of a merchant's store are to his business. . . . Your
> appearance will be taken as an advertisement of what you are. It is
> constantly telling people whether you are a success or a failure.[171]

Suits and masculine professionalism have been inextricably linked since the seventeenth century, when they came to signify simplicity and sobriety. Citizens of the professional classes in Protestant countries wore dark suits and white linen shirts, which communicated both clerical intelligence and military readiness and served as an antidote to courtly elegance.[172] Following in this tradition, Harold the go-getter, defined by his trademark glasses and neat ensemble that characterized him as a new middle-class Everyman, was poised to enact the competitive corporate ethos for the new mass-consuming youthful audience.

INTREPID MEN AND NERVOUS WOMEN: CONSTRUCTING THE AUDIENCE

The publicity campaign launched by Lloyd and Pathé Exchange recapitulated the gendered and class-inflected constructions of Harold in the film. Audiences were instructed to ignore his feminization in the DeVore department store in favor of a fearless man who was not afraid to tangle with tall buildings. Lloyd was described as both hardy and cerebral, a friend of construction workers and a devotee of the self-help psychiatrist Dr. Émile Coué. Male viewers were especially persuaded to identify with the character's audacity and, like Harold, encouraged to "beard the lion" in their respective professions.[173] One reviewer agreed with this strategy, stating that "thrill movies generally are of more interest to men than to women. They present physical courage that all men think they have, but haven't."[174] Female viewers, in contrast, were depicted as nervous and potentially hysterical, in need of precautionary measures to help stem their emotions, a ploy to enhance the film's thrill potential. They serve to augment the female department store consumers in the film, who are reduced to an irrational mob-like frenzy in search of bargains.

Unlike typical publicity concerning Lloyd, which rendered him as an all-American boy with a youthful spirit, *Safety Last!*'s promoters compared him to a hard-working manual laborer. It was reported that he injured his shoulder during the clock sequence, to give the appearance that he performed all his own stunts, which he didn't. To counteract his sometimes awkward film persona, his publicists claimed that he was a dedicated and diligent laborer: "The life of more people has been rose-tinted in the press, but no steel construction worker has ever toiled harder than Harold Lloyd and company in the making of this picture."[175] This characterization was echoed by Lloyd, who repeatedly told interviewers that when he visited a fortuneteller after shooting the film, she felt the calluses on his hands and surmised that he earned his living at manual labor.[176] Lloyd's putative working-class sympathies were extended to his inclusion of workers' opinions in the marketing of his films, an indication of his democratic spirit, according to the studio. He reportedly previewed his films prior to their release before diverse audiences, including office staff, "laborers, plumbers, plasterers, electricians, painters, masons, and mechanics."[177] The studio's overly compensatory description of Lloyd was supposedly written in response to a typical conversation overheard in a theater lobby after the screening of *Safety Last!* A patron was said to have griped about Lloyd's privileged economic position in Hollywood: "Pretty soft for Harold Lloyd, eh? Just having the fun of making comedies to make people laugh and getting paid for it. Yep, pretty soft. I'd like to be in his boots."[178] In order to make the character more palatable and to obfuscate his upper-class affiliations, which prompted resentment, the studio sought to bolster the physical, instrumental side of Harold's masculinity.

Promoters augmented the reports on Lloyd's working-class sympathies with information on the strength of his mental determination, creating an image of brawn and brain that was consonant with Harold's character in *Safety Last!* A bold headline in the press book, "Lloyd Uses Coue Theory Filming 'Thrill' Comedy," asserted that the actor was an ardent devotee of Coué.[179] Historian Paula Fass identified Coué's teachings as the basis of a "short-lived and telling infatuation with self-improvement by way of self-hypnosis." The psychiatrist's popular phrase to initiate his autosuggestion technique—"everyday in every way, I'm getting better and better"—became a popular slogan of the nation's collegiate population.[180] Lloyd substituted Coué's verbal prompt with the more applicable, "day by day in every way I'm getting braver and braver," which he supposedly employed to arouse the requisite courage to perform his skyscraper stunts.[181] The actor reasoned that while it was a cinch to walk across a ground-level plank, elevating it to the top of a building resulted in immeasurable fear. Over a series of weeks, by repeating the phrase and gradually raising the plank, Lloyd claimed that his trepidations were minimized. This rationale was taken almost verbatim from Coué's *Self Mastery through Autosuggestion*:

> Suppose that we place on the ground a plank 30 feet long by 1 foot wide. It is evident that everyone will be capable of going from one end to the other of the plank without stepping over the edge. But now change the conditions of the experiment, and imagine the plank placed at the height of the towers of a cathedral. . . . Before you had taken two steps, you would begin to tremble . . . certain to fall on the ground.[182]

Coué believed that the feeling of vertigo was caused by the mental picture of falling, in spite of the efforts of the will to curb these morbid fantasies. Only by "training the imagination" by consciously offering it alternate suggestions could one counter the fear and succeed in the seemingly impossible task at hand. Within reason, a person was capable of accomplishing all that he desired by simply mastering his thoughts. Echoing the popular self-help writers of the day, Coué asserted that "We are what we make ourselves and not what circumstances make us."[183]

Lloyd and his publicists invoked these psychiatric nostrums to attract not only the nation's youth, but the general population, who were also swept up in the Coué craze. Although Lloyd may have honestly benefited from the Frenchman's teachings, Pathé Exchange recognized that simply invoking the name Coué served as a strategic ploy, resulting in the rise of box office receipts. The popular psychiatrist enjoyed both attention and praise as a result of a successful American tour. In March of 1923, Coué visited several cities to promote his theories of auto-suggestion, which resulted in the opening of his institutes in New York and other venues. As *Current Opinion* reported, "Tributes paid to him by Edison, Henry Ford and Mary Garden have been more prominent, but no less significant, than testimonies of unknown men and women who have derived benefit from his ministrations."[184] This was one of numerous articles that appeared in the press for several months after his visit, and concurrent with the release of *Safety Last!*

At the same time that Pathé and Lloyd were trumpeting the therapeutic benefits of Coué's technique, they were constructing female audiences as emotionally weak, with nervous systems too fragile for the film's jarring scenes. This was obviously a tactic to intensify the general audience's anticipatory anxiety levels. During the course of the film's run, owners were instructed to have a big white ambulance standing in front of their theaters with a bold red sign that read, "For Hysterical Patients Who Laugh Too Much at 'Safety Last.'"[185] To augment the appearance of female mental instability allegedly provoked by the film, proprietors were further persuaded to plant a young woman in the audience who would go into hysterics, and have her collected onto a stretcher and carted away by attendants to the awaiting ambulance. A throng of reporters on hand would insure the believability of the choreographed scene. The publicity stunt had its intended effect. Many reviewers pointed to *Safety Last!*'s ability to create a vicarious feeling of dizziness.[186] One even cautioned those "people afflicted with nervous disorders or women to whom shock of any kind would be dangerous" to avoid the film.[187]

Female audience members were further encouraged to identify with Mildred, Harold's love interest, for whom he braves the skyscraper shaft. According to the promoters, the hero's desire to make good was prompted by his sweetheart: "Mildred is the cause of everything as has been with women throughout the ages." He is willing to go through various trials and tribulations to attain one of his prizes, "the pretty little leading lady," who simply awaits his arrival at the top of the building dressed in fashionable wedding attire.[188] Yet, the studio wished to construct Mildred as a modern woman who, in accord with Harold's dapper glasses character, is cognizant of new fashion trends. She rejected Parisian fashions in favor of short dresses, "which are as typically American as the 'flapper.'"[189] In accord with Harold, she was depicted as a symbol of youthful modernity, and their fictional union was echoed in their real life marriage—the two had recently wed, shortly after the completion of the film. Audience members were told that they could meet the happy couple at participating theaters and vicariously share in their nuptial bliss.

An evaluation of audience reception during the silent era is difficult due to the paucity of available documents. Lloyd saved both fan mail and press clippings, which provide a partial glimpse of how male and female viewers responded to Pathé Exchange's efforts to circumscribe and mold gendered reactions to Harold's thrill pictures. When *Safety Last!* played in Chicago, the branch manager of the studio felt compelled to confess to Lloyd that he and his buddies responded in a less than manly fashion, perhaps aware that they had not conformed to the publicity campaign's expectations. "I wish you could have been here to see a bunch of 'roughnecks' who were unable to control themselves in expressing their feelings during the entire seven reels." In the last two, we "begged you out loud to be careful," he reported.[190] A similar anecdote was recounted by a journalist writing for the *Milwaukee Journal* when the film opened in that city. Theodore Stevens, the guest of honor at the event, was forced to remove the cigar from his mouth to allow himself to express his amusement and fear. Apparently, "Mr. Roberts" and others "screamed with the rest of the feminine contingent."[191] Women and children screamed too, as Miss Hilda Lippertz of Honolulu informed Lloyd; but in spite of her inability to contain herself, she felt obliged to protect Lloyd by exclaiming, "Get down, or you'll fall."[192] The sparse fan mail that specifically refers to this issue nevertheless indicates an awareness of the studio's gendered expectations, but suggests that there was very little difference in the responses of male and female audience members to Lloyd's fictional yet somewhat convincing death-defying antics.

Fan magazines claimed that audiences in general were obsessed with plumbing the mysteries of Lloyd's stunts. To satisfy the devotees's curiosities, at least two journalists provided in-depth accounts of the actor's climbing stunts and, in doing so, compromised the image of dauntless masculinity proffered by Pathé Exchange's publicity department.[193] By deconstructing Lloyd's physical relationship to the skyscraper, and his incapacity to fully master the building, he was deprived of his sought-after working-class affiliations. Both reporters concurred that false building fronts were employed that raised the actor only two stories above the street but that created an illusion that he was at the skyscraper pinnacle. In order to craft the impression of lofty distances, the false fronts were interspersed with long shots of adjacent streets, producing the fiction of a limitless downward plunge. Cameramen were placed on high scaffolds several feet from the set to capture the requisite distance required to reinforce the feeling of scale. It was further reported that Lloyd did not perform all of his stunts,

From the documentary film Harold Lloyd: The Third Genius, *1989.*

as had been asserted in the press book; on at least two occasions, doubles were employed. Lloyd may have contributed to his compromised masculine image by his own declaration—"No more thrill pictures. My wife won't let me."[194]

Lloyd's skyscraper films may be viewed as heirs to the nineteenth-century capitalist-inspired belief that success was attainable by one's individual efforts and creative agency, which could be realized if only one tried hard enough. Skyscrapers were seen as the material incarnation of inventiveness and aspiration, the counterparts or analogues of inventors, builders, and the entrepreneurs who inhabited them. Climbing skyscrapers for fun and profit, a feat first invented by working-class men as their only hope of reaching the top, hence attaining success, echoed the era's desire for greater entertainment spectacles as tabloid journalism and the mass media created a more public masculine subjectivity. Even though Lloyd performed these working-class quests with irony and to temporarily undermine the work-a-day world, he seemed to ultimately subscribe to corporate ideology. In order to be a fully integrated, middle-class man, he battled the era's monument to modernity, the skyscraper, and won. Only when Harold arrives at the tall building's pinnacle, could he claim the prizes—money, fame, and the "girl."

TWO

Icons of Exploitation:
Gender and Class Disharmony
in the Depression-Era Skyscraper Office

In a scene from the film *Baby Face* (1933), Lily Powers (Barbara Stanwyck) and her sidekick Chico (Theresa Harris) have just distinguished themselves from the undifferentiated stream of urban workers who maintain a relentless pace. Anonymous bodies and feet move in accelerated synchronous motion in contrast to Powers and Chico, who stop momentarily to take stock of the unfamiliar metropolis, having just arrived from a smaller city. The camera pauses at the majestic, multistoried entrance of a towering skyscraper, before panning the building's full girth from floor to pinnacle. Powers looks up expectantly at the "gigantic forty-story skyscraper," then at "a hurrying crowd of well-dressed people coming and going through its gilt bronze doors." To her, it symbolizes wealth and power, which is reflected in her eyes and which she hopes to attain. Chico's eyes remain downcast, deprived of the ability to dream of upward mobility through her own agency. Surveying the skyscraper in this manner served as a rhetorical filmic device during the Depression to emphasize the disparity between the diminished woman or man and the towering edifice, which portends the subsequent challenges and short-lived triumphs in the metropolis.[1]

Henri Lefebvre provides a useful paradigm for understanding such cinematic depictions of the skyscraper in his seminal book *The Production of Space* (1974), arguing that architectural space implies a "logic of visualization," embodying its intentions. The "arrogant verticality" or "phallocentric" character of skyscrapers is meant to impress spectators and connote power, which Lefebvre believes is often coercive. Skyscrapers also imply a twofold stratagem with regard to both urban inhabitants and, by implication, film viewers, which includes a dialogic movement between a building's massive whole and its parts, which are often small or contained.[2] Skyscraper films of the 1930s explore the discrepancy between the skyscraper's outward magnitude and its innards, frequently employed as a critique of claustrophobia and sexual predation. Spatial

Lily Powers (and Chico) looking up at the skyscraper in Baby Face.

ideology in the form of grand skyscrapers that are but a veneer to oppressive interiors is embedded in the films to insure the expulsion of menacing corporate bigwigs while ushering women back to the domestic sphere or their class roots. The contrast is also offered to highlight the distinction between the seemingly inanimate impersonal facade and the inner workings or lives of the tall building's inhabitants. Entire buildings serve as parentheses that are meant to frame a cross section or microcosm of urban life and its diverse classes during the Depression, a convention borrowed from Henry Blake Fuller's pioneer skyscraper novel *The Cliff-Dwellers* (1893).[3]

Once inside the cinematic skyscraper, the strategy of dissection is continued in the delineation of the architecture's component parts. The tall building is not merely a monolithic shaft scanned significantly by the camera; it is a multifaceted universe unto itself, comprising portal, lobby, elevator, identical stories, private office, boardroom, penthouse, and recreation area, each of which is invested with meaning. This expanded portrayal is due, in part, to the increasing complexity of the new, more elaborate, multipurpose office building, which was becoming a material reality by 1929, prompting architect Raymond M. Hood to refer to it as "a city under a single roof." Hood called for a greater application of this principle, with shops, stores, theaters, clubs, and restaurants located in a single megastructure.[4]

Films such as *Big Business Girl* (1931), *Under Eighteen* (1931), *Skyscraper Souls* (1932), *Counsellor at Law* (1933), *Baby Face* (1933), and *Wife vs. Secretary* (1936), among others, explore the entire skyscraper and its component parts in an effort to prescribe class-inflected and gendered identities in the service of a redeemed patriarchal capitalism fueled by the activities of workers. The sky-scraper office building suffered a fall from grace during the Depression, from a proud and soaring symbol of individual achievement to a debased tower of exploitation, associated with the profligate speculation that characterized the Harding, Coolidge, and Hoover administrations. Their newly maligned reputations were accompanied by a sharp decrease in actual construction due to the economic debacle; for example, only seven skyscrapers were built in New York City from 1934 to 1946, while 138 structures were erected from 1925 to 1933.[5] As a result, scores of construction and office workers alike found themselves newly unemployed; following the completion of the Shreve, Lamb, and Harmon's Empire State Building (1931), over 3,500 of the former lost their jobs. Many reminisced about feeling on top of the world, their heroism captured in the photographs of Lewis Hine (see chapter 3), only to be cast aside, the Depression's forgotten heroes. Hence, the go-getters fashioned by Lloyd in the 1910s and 1920s, in which a typical white Anglo-Saxon aspirant succeeds by scaling the skyscraper, the metaphorical ladder of success, quickly fell out of favor. Sky-scrapers in Depression-era cinema are frequently rendered as sites of charged eroticism and class tensions, where rapacious businessmen prey on their male and female subordinates with equal gusto, and where suicide and murder, occasioned by financial ruin and betrayal, lurk. Among the prescriptive moral messages recommended by the studios was that happiness could be achieved by exiting these dens of iniquity or supplementing them with a more integrated, gratifying private life. Luxury and pleasure were also portrayed for their entertainment value or the audience's vicarious enjoyment before characters are ushered back to their predetermined, more modest spheres.

Previous scholars have viewed the construction of gender in Depression-era films largely in the context of domineering studio magnates or the negotiations between the studios and the newly empowered Production Code Administration (PCA) of the Motion Picture Producers and Distributors of America (MPPDA). Although censorship is crucial for exploring cinema's repressions during the Depression, as most scholars agree, the formation of the PCA, which called for the mandatory expurgation of salacious dialogue and graphic sexual or violent details, in 1934 (formerly the Studio Relations Committee that had attempted unsuccessfully to enforce the Production Code since 1930) must be broadened to include the studio's own ideological interventions.[6] A more covert series of negotiations often began at the level of adaptation from short stories and novels to final scripts. Many of the aforementioned films were based on women's popular fiction, most notably the work of the best-selling author Faith Baldwin, whose serials and books served as springboards for *Skyscraper Souls* and *Wife vs. Secretary*, among others. The alteration of Baldwin's text, and particularly her empowerment of women in the business world, illuminates the manner in which alternative voices were suppressed in favor of a return to traditional gender roles and class affiliations.

SKYSCRAPER SOULS: ATOMIZED AND SEXUALLY CHARGED SPACES

A conscientious, upwardly mobile woman seeks the challenges of the work-a-day world but is stymied by a predatory male boss who views her as handy amanuensis and potential bed partner.[7] Lynn Harding (Maureen O'Sullivan) is the perky go-getter of *Skyscraper Souls* who, upon entry into the world of business, must immediately fend off both the overzealous advances of a fellow worker and the premeditated, more predatory designs of skyscraper owner David Dwight (Warren William). Likewise, college-educated Claire McIntyre (Loretta Young) of *Big Business Girl* arrives in the big city to embark upon a career at a prestigious advertising agency. She is met by the brash, cigar-smoking boss Mr. Clayton (Ricardo Cortez), who assumes that she is already an employee and begins to bark orders such as, "Take off that hat." After she introduces herself, he quips, "I was married once to a girl named Claire, one of my follies of 1920," asserting his power sexually while staring salaciously at her legs. Clayton delivers his tirade while pacing the full length of the office in a domineering manner, dictating a letter to her while continuing to admire her attributes. Learning that she is not his employee after all, he commands, "You are not looking for a job around here. You are working here."[8] The scene underscores that Ms. McIntyre has been hired rather capriciously by a superior who is as much interested in her legs as her capabilities and augurs his subsequent effort to seduce her.

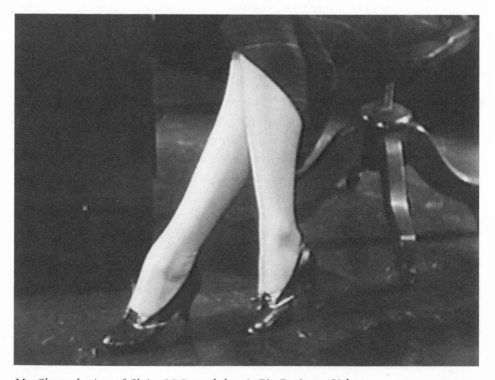

Mr. Clayton's view of Claire McIntyre's legs in Big Business Girl.

Both scenes rehearse the view that women's entry in the business world in increasing numbers, beginning at the end of the nineteenth century when separate-sphere ideology was still prevalent, eroticized commercial space. Even social reformer Jane Addams was concerned that offices of men and women coupled with women's lower wages served as a temptation to "fall into a vicious life from the sheer lack of social restraint."[9] By 1920, office buildings were often depicted in fiction as the sexually charged sites of amorous trysts between powerful older bosses and their younger female subordinates.[10] Earlier stories about female skyscraper labor suggested that through a combination of feminine charm and diligence, working women could gain the attention of their male superiors, resulting in their Cinderella-like rise from office wife to boss's wife. Although these potential office romances were initially rendered as titillating, Depression-era films encouraged an alternative: if one sought romance in the skyscraper office, it was to be realized with a class confederate rather than a superior. Faith Baldwin observed in the foreword of her novel *The Office Wife* (1929), which was later adapted to the screen:

> The young business woman of today often falls in love, whether consciously or not, with her employer, thereafter measuring the men she meets by the yardstick of the man who has already arrived. This is distinctly a modern problem. It will continue to be so until girls marry the men who are, like themselves, on the lower rungs of the ladder.[11]

While flirtations between male superiors and female clerical workers were provisionally permissible for entertainment value, gold digging, predation, and status seeking were more often considered morally reprehensible.

Lynn Harding of *Skyscraper Souls* has recently arrived in New York to pursue a career as a secretary in the famed Dwight Building, the tallest building in the world. Her initial encounters with the clumsy bank teller Tom Shepherd (Norman Foster) and the predatory owner of the skyscraper David Dwight identify the mammoth structure as a site of sexual conquest, financial impropriety, and danger. The story centers on the machinations of Dwight who aims to own the preeminent skyscraper outright as a testament to his ego. However, he still owes thirty million dollars on the mortgage, which he has borrowed illegally from the Seacoast National Bank's depositors. When his debt comes due, he asks his board to front the money so as to avoid the penitentiary, but they decline. He acquires some of the funds from the gullible bigwig Charlie Norton (George Barbier), and the remainder by driving up the price of Seacoast stock before selling short. All the little people in the building think that Seacoast is a good bet, and most buy stock frantically, which leads to their financial ruin. While he is manipulating events on the financial front, the married Dwight tries to seduce Harding. Dwight's former mistress Sarah Dennis (Verree Teasdale) warns him not to proceed, but when he declines to heed her warnings, she shoots him in an act of desperation before leaping from the skyscraper pinnacle to the horror of pedestrians below. These two morally compromised characters make way for Harding and Shepherd to pursue their relationship, heralding a new beginning. The skyscraper's redemption lies with its office denizens whose collective labors will continue to keep the building in operation.

The establishing shot of *Skyscraper Souls* is a fictional bird's-eye view of the slab-like Dwight Building and a dwarfed Empire State Building. The contrast of these two lofty edifices underscores the degree to which the film was informed by developments in material culture and the debates swirling around speculative skyscrapers, here used as a way to warn of the perils of constant upward striving. In 1932, when the film was released, the 1,248-foot Empire State Building was the world's preeminent office building, and the juxtaposition of the two structures acknowledges the height mania that had gripped the architectural community and tabloid headlines. Would it be the Chrysler or the Empire State, or would the Bank of New York Building really reach 1,600 feet as reported in the newspapers?[12] The blocky, monolithic shape of the stony

View of the Dwight and Empire State Buildings in Skyscraper Souls.

Dwight Building, which mimicked the popular stylistic preference for slab-like skyscrapers that emerged in the late twenties, resembles an enormous tomb-stone and portends the tragedies that haunt its interior, including the interment of an employee-turned-thief in a jeweler's vault, a murder, and two suicides.[13] The view from above both suggests an omniscient spectator who evaluates the exterior architecture and foreshadows the downward spiral or plummeting of its inhabitants' fortunes. Unchecked height, relentless striving, and ineluctable death are inserted at the outset.

The comprehensive external view of the building announces it as a major player in the drama, employed throughout the film in various seasons and weather conditions to show the passage of time and as a reminder of its central-ity. The film's press book underscores its role as a primary character:

> And then there is the skyscraper. Always it looms forth as an important figure in the drama . . . over the lives of all; this build-ing spreads its shadows. In their mad pursuit of love and lucre the thousands of workers in the skyscraper are so many prisoners in the steel cells they call their offices.[14]

A catch line suggested to theater owners further underlined its meaning as a ne-farious presence: "There it stood, steel pillar soaring 102 stories into the skies . . . a cold lifeless thing—but in this strange mighty drama it lives and breathes and wreaks destruction on those who would seek to occupy it . . . the skyscraper."[15] Several of the films' reviewers echoed the opinion that skyscrapers were the evil culprits of the misfortunes that befell its denizens. Richard Watts Jr. in the *New York Tribune* referred to them thus: "Modern towers of Babel, they drive their builders into excesses of godless arrogance, which even results in the destruc-tion of those responsible for these evil monuments to man's pride."[16]

As the action shifts from the building's exterior to its interior, the story changes from a concern for the skyscraper's effect on the masses to its impact on various individuals, who are meant to serve as examples of different class and gender positions. Depression-era cinematic skyscraper interiors are often stu-dio fabrications with elements borrowed from an array of real skyscrapers and other types of buildings to underscore each space's symbolic intent and spatial practices. Its multifaceted character becomes a microcosm of urban life, and its various parts, from lobby to penthouse, serve as poignant characters. Film critic Rose Pelswick noted that the Dwight Building "houses everything from a bank to Turkish baths" and that both lobby and elevator featured the frenetic rushing of the crowd before the camera's concentration on the film's individual protagonists.[17] In a preliminary script, screenwriter Edith Fitzgerald recom-mended that different portions of the building be used to punctuate aspects of the story.[18] Director Edgar Selwyn concurred; likening the film to *Grand Hotel*

(1932), he explained that architectural parts and wholes were purposely high-lighted to underscore meaning:

> Instead of taking a single drama of an individual, we have taken
> the drama of thousands of persons and united them through the
> background, which in this case is a New York skyscraper. We
> show bits of the incidents in the lives of these "skyscraper souls,"
> then unite them in one grand cataclysm.[19]

A view of the lofty entry that is shot from above reduces the workers to an anonymous silhouetted mass before shifting to the skyscraper lobby, which is teeming with humanity. The entrance is employed to suggest frenzied moder-nity, where the urban crowd moves in a relentless stream, as so many cogs in the office assembly line, their animated pace augmented by a rapid jazzy score. A preliminary script described this scene in the following terms:

> We dissolve to the sidewalks which lead to the building. There
> are many persons on the sidewalk . . . men and women, moving
> to their daily tasks. They are the robots of the building, its slaves.
> They hurry. They have to hurry. If they stopped to think, civili-
> zation would crash.[20]

Across the threshold, the cinematic skyscraper lobby assumes the role of the town square or metropolitan thoroughfare, where different classes and sexes mingle. Tom Shepherd runs into Harding's friend Myra (Helen Coburn), before colliding slapstick style with a larger, more successful fellow who threatens to pick a fight in the dog-eat-dog world of high finance. The skyscraper office workers' bustling demeanor and the rapid tracking of their movements sug-gest that their identities are mutable, mediated by the technologically advanced space they inhabit and the multiplicity of their encounters.[21] An ersatz egalitar-ian space, the lobby is rendered as a place where bosses meet secretaries and office boys alike, prior to conforming to the class and gender stratification in the offices above.

The Dwight Building's commodious imaginary lobby is elegant, its glisten-ing stone floor decorated with modernist chevron patterns that echo the crowd's rapid, directional motion. Both skyscraper portals and lobbies assumed a more theatrical character in skyscraper design in the late 1920s and early 1930s and contributed to the appearance of their cinematic counterparts. Many new of-fice buildings in New York City such as William Van Alen's Chrysler Building (1930), Raymond M. Hood's Daily News Building (1931), and the Empire State Building (1931) featured majestic entranceways and dramatic lobbies that were designed in part to lure potential tenants and customers. For example, the main

The lobby in Skyscraper Souls.

entrance of the Empire State Building on Fifth Avenue includes a thirty-foot portal, which was "defined by a diamond-shaped grille framing the glass" creating a "solid, substantial and dignified" appearance.[22] The entrance is augmented by columns that are crowned by soaring eagles, which suggest an image of enduring power. An imposing three stories high and one hundred feet long, the lobby is designed to accommodate the thousands of workers and customers who crossed its threshold, rendering it a veritable city square. Architectural historian Kim Dovey claims that a client's first impression of a business's success is molded by a building's foyer; hence the architect's aim is "quite literally to 'entrance' through impression management." These lofty interior showcases are often rendered in ersatz marble to augment the idea of wealth, echoing the soaring building's outward grandeur. "In the foyer, the triumph of surface reaches its peak as a spectacle of art, space, and light."[23]

The lobby also doubles in the film as a meeting place for charged heterosexual encounters and amorous trysts, where bodies collide like atomic particles and produce metaphorical sparks. In the class- and gender-segregated office building, the lobby is often designated for romantic initiation or pursuit. Harding and Shepherd meet in the lobby, in front of an indoor newsstand heaped with products. He drops a coin and encounters Harding's attractive ankle, which he grabs, feigning the retrieval of his nickel as the camera zooms in. Shepherd's gesture focuses attention on her atomized bodily part as a commodity and the skyscraper as a site of pecuniary and sexual acquisition. The cinematic lobby repeats the character of real lobbies of new multipurpose skyscrapers, which featured stores with seductive display windows where goods were offered up and consumed, thereby conflating work and leisure space and the spaces of production and consumption. One of the promotional strategies offered by the film's publicists was to place advertisements for the film in "Lingerie Shops in Office Blgs. [sic]," identifying the real and fictional skyscraper lobby as site of the eroticized pursuit of goods and women as consumable consumers.[24]

Benjamin's discussion of early nineteenth-century Parisian arcades, glass-enclosed structures replete with commercial establishments, provides insight into the workings of skyscraper lobbies in general and Harding and Shepherd's encounter in particular. Both arcade and skyscraper lobby are indoor commercial spaces where the vagaries of weather do not impede the controlled environment's luxurious comforts, prompting a relaxed demeanor and social engagement. One is also reminded of Kracauer's discussion of "The Hotel Lobby" (1922), which he categorizes as a luxurious space given over to leisurely reflection, fragmentation, and mask-like anonymity.[25] Unlike Kracauer's delineation of the hotel lobby as a space given over to passivity, both arcade and skyscraper lobby are spaces designed for the mobile, engaged consumer, set in motion by a strategy of visual display that includes eye-catching signboards, the aesthetic presentation of merchandise, and pleasing architecture that creates desire in potential customers, thus equating buying with entertainment and pleasure. In addition, the parade of fashionable women in this public/private realm, and the employment of seductive sales personnel, renders the space an optimal setting for the amorous rendezvous.[26]

Depression-era skyscraper cinema visualizes the elevator as a continuation of the lobby, where the crush and containment of bodies breeds familiarity and charged romantic encounters. Physical proximity and the elevator's rapid upward thrust are meant to augur the heterosexual liaisons to follow. Close-up shots of elevator interiors are employed to underscore its congested character, which is again felt vicariously by the viewer. These scenes were prompted, in part, by the changing nature of elevator travel in the new multipurpose skyscrapers; high speed and efficiency were needed to move the mass of workers in these new megalopolitan structures. The Empire State Building boasted elevators that could catapult passengers to the top floor in two minutes, thereby creating a physical rush or possible discomfort.[27] Moreover, there were multiple elevators in the super skyscrapers' extended elevator banks, which resembled major thoroughfares; the Empire State Building sported sixty-two passenger elevators while the Chrysler boasted twenty-eight. Often the compression of bodies in these skyscraper lifts resembled the crowded character of a subway car during rush hour, except the journey was vertical rather than horizontal. In *Skyscraper Souls,* Miss Dennis articulates her view of elevators, which demonstrates an awareness of new elevator sensations occasioned by technological advances and her desire to protect its passengers from overstimulation and potential accidents. In a memo that she dictates to Harding, she states, "Referring to your ad in the commercial journal, I feel that you lay too much stress on the speed of our express elevator system, causing a certain timidity on the part of the public. More emphasis should be put on the element of absolute safety."

In accord with the lobby, the elevator is also rendered as a democratized public space where bigwig and clerk alike meet on the same plane and jostle one another with impunity. Shepherd continues his seduction of Harding in the fast-moving elevator, an almost wholly male homosocial space, where he shoves an older cigar-smoking superior in order to make time with the object of his desire. Someone inadvertently pushes Shepherd virtually on top of her, prompting Harding to slap him and storm out just as the elevator comes to a stop, a case of elevator interruptus. Both lobby and elevator space construct women as objects of desire and predation, where they resist the forced proximity occasioned by modernity. One is reminded of Fran Kubelik (Shirley MacLaine) in Billy Wilder's *The Apartment* (1960) quipping, "Something happens to men in elevators. Must be the change in altitude—the blood rushes to their head, or something."[28] *Skyscraper Souls*'s publicity apparatus attempted to capitalize on the thrill of the elevator ride. One of the catch lines that was recommended to distributors pointed to the sensations afforded by the viewer's vicarious elevator trip: "To the top and bottom of the world's largest building at express elevator speed . . . with Life, Love, Hate, and Death as passengers . . . 102 floors and a thrill at every floor."[29]

Elevator groping was employed for titillating entertainment value and identified female refusal as the appropriate response of the virtuous protagonist.[30] Female office workers such as Harding frequently end up with male middle-class equals such as Shepherd, whom they initially tried to fend off, thereby promoting elevator antics as a permissible, albeit annoying form of heterosexual, class-inflected behavior. In a preliminary script, Shepherd is described as an ebullient, enthusiastic youth who means no harm. "He's inclined to treat life as if it were a football game. . . . He's one of the few survivors of the age of eagerness. And he's wholesome."[31] Although faces might be slapped and advances rebuffed, elevators—in contrast to penthouses, for example—were rendered as appropriate sites of pleasure where class reintegration often commenced.

Opulent penthouses and rooftop pleasure gardens located high atop skyscraper pinnacles are the purview of upper-class bosses and corporate board members who command magisterial perspectives over the city, representing

Elevator antics in Skyscraper Souls.

their visual ownership of the urban sphere. Historian Roland Marchand noted that American advertising during this period, an observation that one may readily apply to film, likened a commanding view with high status in the firm, while conjuring up "that ineffable sense of domain gained from looking out and down over broad expanses . . . best epitomized by the phrase, 'master of all he surveys.'"[32]

Penthouses were featured in the luxurious apartment and residence hotels that proliferated in New York City in the mid-1920s, the product of a building boom in high-rise residential architecture resulting from recent ordinances that temporarily exempted these new buildings from real estate taxes. A flurry of building occurred in midtown Manhattan, with both Park and Fifth Avenues serving as the prestigious new addresses of opulent skyscraper apartments. The wealthy were prompted to relinquish their private palatial residences due to rising taxes and the paucity of servants in favor of these new "mansions in the clouds," which included maid services, private dining rooms, beauty shops, and a host of other amenities.[33] This way of life was also associated with the American businessman, who often lived like a nomad and required all the comforts of home in his new skyscraper dwelling. Luxury high-rises and apartment hotels such as Emery Roth's Fifth Avenue Hotel (1926) included commodious penthouse suites with multiple stories and roof gardens to satisfy both Old World money and the new titans of finance.

Penthouses appeared with increasing frequency in cinema to signify simultaneously the glamour and decadence of skyscraper living, often elaborately rendered in the moderne style by art directors such as Cedric Gibbons at Metro-Goldwyn-Mayer.[34] The display of architectural opulence was included for entertainment value, often at odds with a film's overarching message of the renunciation of materialism. Bosses with penthouses in skyscraper films signified a debased form of masculinity, in synchrony with the despoiled buildings they inhabited. They are depicted as wolves who are poised to annex women and men alike in their spaces of leisure, which are frequently located in the same building in which they do business. More often associated with luxurious residential apartment buildings, office building penthouses are employed in films to serve specific ends: to illustrate how opulent privatized space that had infiltrated the public domain was used as a tool of predation and seduction by mercenary bosses.

Dwight inhabits a penthouse apartment at the crest of his building, where he maintains his illicit affair with Miss Dennis, his office wife. He also employs the penthouse's spacious rooms and ample terrace to manipulate the gullible financier Norton to help him pay off an illegal loan at a contrived party and as the stage for his attempted seduction of the unsuspecting Lynn Harding. A full band, seductive women in lavish finery, and expensive champagne abound in the majestic setting, which is crowned by a glittering nocturnal skyline that exudes luxury. The debonair, crafty Dwight exploits the bloated, buffoon-like Norton by recourse to illicit activity on two fronts. He first plies him with bootleg alcohol and then foists him upon a professional gold digger, gambits that are intended to soften him up before Dwight swoops down for the kill.

Harding is lured up to the penthouse with the assignment of a fake business report that is manufactured for the occasion, which she must deliver to Dwight after hours, a risky time for female employees. Upon her arrival, she is preyed upon by both Dwight and Norton, who vie for her attention by supplying her with illegal champagne, to which she is unaccustomed. Norton inquires tellingly, "Are you a good chicken?" pointing to her role as a fresh, innocent victim. Before long, she is tipsy and ripe for exploitation. In the novel *Skyscraper*, which served as the springboard for the film, Harding is more careful, but intuits that penthouses are fraught with menace:

> She felt, very dimly, wordlessly, that there was danger in terraces above a city, in the anachronistic blooming of spring flowers from soil scattered in cement and set upon steel, danger in dreaming

David Dwight's penthouse in Skyscraper Souls.

lights, in distant streets, the ugliness veiled and softened, danger
in voices speaking precisely patterned words.[35]

The inebriated Harding of the film is led out to the terrace by Norton for the
proverbial view and to dance the rumba. The disorienting, destabilizing character of the penthouse is emphasized by her comment, "The Dwight Building's
done a somersault." Before long, she is spirited away by the gold digger to
Dwight's private bedroom, where she falls asleep. A priapic sculpture and a
salacious painting of a woman's buttocks, which decorate the bedroom, signal
bigger peril for the youthful amateur. Later that evening after the successful
manipulation of Norton, Dwight discovers her in his bed. He offers her material
comforts in exchange for sexual favors, which she declines. By the skin of her
teeth and Dwight's temporary magnanimity, she escapes his rapacious clutches
with her virtue preserved.

In the film *Baby Face,* the penthouse suite is the ultimate prize of the mercenary Lily Powers, who literally and figuratively sleeps her way to the top,
from lowly office boy to company president.[36] A panning shot up the immense
shaft of the Gotham Trust Company Building chronicles her meteoric rise from

Lily Powers's rise upward in Baby Face.

the personnel department, to accounting, and finally to the penthouse, which is dripping in preciosity and wealth, signifying her class rise. She is one of the few female characters who are allowed entry to the corporate board room, where she attempts to manipulate the bank's board of directors to pay fifteen thousand dollars to avert a sex scandal. When women enter the boardroom in Depression-era cinema they are frequently debased, much like corrupt bosses such as David Dwight in *Skyscraper Souls*. They are willing to sexually or economically exploit others if it serves as a stepping stone to their own success. The penthouse's material plentitude shields a world of emotional and ethical bankruptcy, often a prelude to the demise of one or more of its inhabitants, which includes suicide or murder. Powers's husband Courtland Trenholm (George Brent) begs his new bride to lend him a half million dollars to ward off financial ruin, which she refuses. She reconsiders, but almost before it is too late; in his office below the penthouse, he has already shot himself. Trenholm survives the self-inflicted wound, but redemption for the couple is only possible through their joint renunciation of opulent penthouses and all that they signify in favor of a new beginning in the working-class environs of Pittsburgh, Pennsylvania.

The seductions of the penthouse are also seen in *Under Eighteen,* which features a rooftop pool where scantily dressed couples dance and drink with abandon.[37] Warren William, who played David Dwight in *Skyscraper Souls,* is cast as a wolf whose goal is to seduce an innocent, working-class minor who has fallen on hard times and is tempted to leave her upstanding boyfriend. The predator's power over the crowd is underscored by his flinging of a diamond ring into the rooftop pool, prompting a feeding frenzy by bathing beauties who dive in after it. Scintillating jewels, theatrical nocturnal illumination, and seminude bodies create the entertainment spectacle, which is at odds with the moral message of thwarted temptation and preserved innocence, which is also featured in *Skyscraper Souls.* The Depression audience is encouraged to vicariously consume and indulge in free sexual expression with a multitude of partners and imbibe the pleasures of a wanton, upper-class life, while identifying with the virtuous renunciations of the film's working-class couple.

Dwight's penthouse suite is adjacent to his own office at the skyscraper's crest in *Skyscraper Souls.* His taste for acquisition is echoed in the room's studied sumptuousness and accoutrements, which include a sleek primitivist sculpture, enforcing his colonialist intentions. In contrast to Harold Lloyd's earlier films in which the tall office building's crest is synonymous with hard-won success, the thirties cinematic skyscraper pinnacle is frequently the scene of corrupt deals and tragedy, including murder and suicide. Here, Dwight manipulates the board to bail him out of an illegal loan and plots to bilk unsuspecting shareholders of millions of dollars so he can own the Dwight Building outright. In his private office, he delivers a monologue of pharaoh-like grandeur, praising his lofty monument, while rationalizing the deaths of those who built it: "A million men sweated to build it. Mines—quarries—forests—factories. Men gave their lives for it. I'd hate to tell you how many men dropped off these girders as they were going up. But it was worth it!" Dwight's lack of conscience results in his own murder by Dennis in his well-appointed office, which will immortalize him in steel and stone.

The skyscraper's debased pinnacle is also the site of the suicide of Dennis, the third death occasioned by Dwight's egotistical and greedy double-dealing. The first is Dwight's most loyal board member, Harrington Brewster, who loses everything, and whose death earns him a tabloid headline. The same is true in *Baby Face,* in which the skyscraper is directly implicated in the deaths of Powers's sexual conquests. Before jumping, *Skyscraper Soul's* Dennis surveys the cityscape from the highest promontory with a full view of the Chrysler Building in the distance, her only opportunity to achieve ocular possession of the city before her demise. Dressed in funereal black, she extends her arms in a cruciform pose, implying her martyrdom at the hands of the towering Dwight Building. Plummeting fortunes and bodies, both real and imagined, of Depression-era skyscraper films served to remind the viewer of the ineluc-

Newspaper headline of skyscraper suicide and murder in Baby Face.

table consequences of upward mobility predicated on immoral activities, either sexual or financial. In contrast to the camera's previous upward panning of the seemingly limitless edifice, the street is now viewed from above, presaged at the film's outset, creating a vicarious feeling of vertigo and dread.

If the egalitarian lobby is the spatial and metaphorical class-inflected counterpart of the penthouse and the private office, the skyscraper bathhouse or steam room is the penthouse's homoerotic mirror. This artificially fabricated space is located in the building's subterranean realm in *Skyscraper Souls* and is the repository of suggested illicit eroticism and secret manipulations, echoing Gaston Bachelard's designation of underground cellars as a house's dark unconscious or repressed underbelly.[38] It also bears a resemblance to Michel Foucault's heterotopia, a place of deviance or "otherness," often inserted into an incongruous space, much like this site of leisure located in a building otherwise given over to business. Heterotopias also presuppose a "system of opening and closing that isolates them and makes them penetrable."[39] Dwight's seduction of Norton, which began in the penthouse with bootleg alcohol and an illegitimate heterosexual encounter, continues in the homosocial gymnasium, pool, and bathhouse, where the latter's fleshy, recumbent body is sprayed, massaged, slapped, and simultaneously cajoled into capitulating to Dwight's subterfuge. The final script advises, "Close shot of attendant yanking Norton's leg. He's about to be had."[40] The yanking of his leg that serves as a genital substitute serves to underline this manipulation, or "jerking off." Even though the act is not blatantly shown, Norton's passivity, the seminaked bodies, and the aggressive handling of Norton by both Dwight and a beefy attendant suggest an "encoded ambiguity" with regard to sexual identities.[41] Norton's question, "What about a merger Dave?" refers to the partners' future financial arrangement and serves as a covert homoerotic reference. As Eve Kosofsky Sedgwick has pointed out, homosocial bonding rituals with decidedly homoerotic overtones became part of institutional practice in Europe and America in order to preserve patriarchy.[42] One might infer that the implied homoerotic seduction of Norton is also employed for the purpose of securing Dwight's preeminent power.

The post-Code *Wife vs. Secretary* also includes a homosocial steam room scene, which is sanitized and transferred to the baronial private dwelling of a private publisher. Embellished with numerous stained glass windows, the gothic dwelling lends the scene an air of propriety and covert religiosity. George Barbier, who played Norton in *Skyscraper Souls*, serves again as the object of

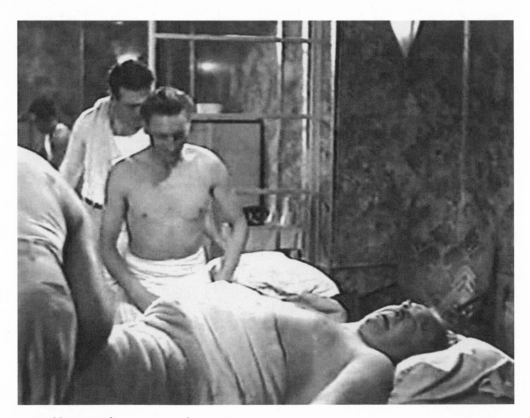

Bathhouse in Skyscraper Souls.

manipulation by financier Van Stanhope (Clark Gable), illustrating the manner in which casting provides the necessary subliminal suggestion for reading sexual innuendos after the enforcement of the Code. Gable's and Barbier's naked bodies are hidden under a steam cabinet with their heads exposed, no doubt to appease the censors who made it patently clear that "certain locations are so closely and thoroughly associated with sexual life or sin that their use must be carefully limited."[43] The appearance of the previously manipulated Barbier in the suggestive bathhouse left audiences to wonder about the covert activities behind the actual and symbolic closet. Buckets of cold water are thrown over their heads, which play as both slapstick and the dampening of their physical ardor. A preliminary deal is clinched in the steam room, in the private company of undressed men, instructing the audience that successful businessmen were adept seducers of both men and women.

Bathhouses have long been associated with homosexual activity, in part because they were one of the few public places where gay men could gather when their activities were criminalized. There were several types of facilities available to New Yorkers at the turn of the century. Tenement dwellers with limited access to washing facilities and dependable plumbing frequented the

Steam room in Wife vs. Secretary.

numerous public bathhouses designated for the poor. In contrast, wealthy New Yorkers sought refuge in the numerous Roman and Turkish baths, the former historically associated with the decline and decadence of a failing empire, while the latter were associated with oriental exoticism and profligate sexuality in the western imagination.[44] Those in the "know" recognized that other designated bathhouses were homosexual gathering places.[45] Even though sexual activity might not occur on the premises, they often served as meeting grounds for future liaisons. For example, New York's Lafayette Baths was a recognized location of such encounters in the early years of the twentieth century and was subject to a police raid in 1929.

The appearance of bathhouses in the cinematic skyscraper, a building type that has been traditionally associated with business activity, did not simply represent the superimposition of an outwardly incongruous architectural trope; rather, bathhouses, pools, and recreational facilities began to appear in new multipurpose office buildings to decrease urban congestion by situating dwellers' multiple needs under one roof. Perhaps the most blatant example of the conflation of two seemingly incongruous architectural types, the skyscraper and the bathhouse, occurred in Goldwin Starrett and Ernest Allen Van Vleck's Downtown Athletic Club (1930), which Rem Koolhaas has categorized as "the complete conquest—floor by floor—of the Skyscraper by social activity."[46] The thirty-five-story building featured everything in the way of manly exercise, recreation, and physical renewal, including a poolroom, boxing facilities, a swimming pool, restaurants, a bowling alley, a golf course, and a medical facility devoted to colonic irrigation. From the twentieth to the thirty-fifth floor, bedrooms were included for those who wished to reside in the building. On the tenth floor, dressing rooms were "arranged around a Turkish bath; sections for massage and rubbing, an eight-bed station for artificial sunbathing, a ten-bed resting area."[47] The homosocial nature of the majority of the Downtown Athletic Club's activities was also conducive to both the relaxing consummation of business deals and the pursuit of homoerotic liaisons in a private atmosphere, where paying club members would not be subject to the type of harassment formerly found in public baths. However, homosocial bathhouse bonding or otherwise was still interpreted through the lens of 1930s cinema as a corrupt mercenary practice; hence the cinematic depictions may be seen as analogues to the actual police raids, which sought to discredit or rout out homosexual behavior.

The Dwight Building also houses a fashion house that is linked conceptually to the seductive presentation of commodities in the skyscraper lobby, and it is inhabited by loose women in lingerie and two dissembling Jews with thick foreign accents. The inclusion of fashion establishments served a dual purpose in Depression-era cinema, where entertainment values were often at odds with the film's overriding prescriptive message.[48] These scenes provided both male and female viewers with the voyeuristic pleasure of viewing fashionable, often luxurious attire and scantily clad women, coupled with the implicit consump-tion of such goods. Female viewers would subsequently be doubly seduced by studio advertising tie-ins of their favorite stars wearing the featured clothes, in which they were encouraged to purchase less expensive versions of the gar-ments.[49] However, these fashion houses were also depicted as dens of vice, where wealthy men cruised for potential mistresses and innocent female em-ployees guarded their virtue in troubled economic times when temptation was at its peak.

In *Skyscraper Souls,* Lynn enters the fashion house in search of her friend Jenny LeGrande (Anita Page), a wise-cracking Harlow look-alike with a Brook-lyn accent. In a case of mistaken identity, the owner Vinmont (Gregory Ratoff) believes Harding to be an important buyer from Kansas City and tries to sell her merchandise. He confides to his sidekick that in order to be successful, it is nec-essary to "pull the wool on the eyes of some greenhorn." In the film's shooting script, Vinmont reveals to his friend Jake Sorenson (Jean Hersholt) that it was necessary to change his name from Weinberg to insure his success.[50] The fash-ion house that is peopled by the Jewish Vinmont and Sorensen and undressed models such as LeGrande, who admit to supplementing their incomes with pri-vate activities, identify it as a site of deceit. Vinmont is a dishonest, calculating Jew, a carryover from stereotypes found in films of the silent era. This scene, which directly follows the lobby and elevator scenes at the film's outset, also announces that the skyscraper is a place where duplicity and dissembling are normative activities. No one save perhaps Harding and Shepherd are who they appear to be.

MACULINITIES AND FEMININITIES IN DEPRESSION-ERA CINEMATIC SKYSCRAPERS

The titillating penthouses, bathhouses, and fashion establishments peopled by scantily clad, dissembling characters offered up in Depression-era skyscraper films are meant as foils for the films' overriding prescriptive messages—the celebration of loyalty, honesty, and an allegiance to one's class confederates. Morally debased characters are ultimately marginalized or killed off in favor of the virtuous New Woman and her aspiring middle-class Joe, who must either recast the skyscraper in their own image or extricate themselves either symboli-cally or physically from its premises. The final scene of *Skyscraper Souls* shows Harding and Shepherd exiting the lobby together, resolved to get married and have babies, even if it means starting out with only Shepherd's fifty-dollar-a-week salary, which had previously seemed inadequate to Harding. These values are further promoted through the formulation of various paradigms of mascu-linity and femininity, which are fleshed out in the characters' personality, body type, mode of dress, and the manner in which they inhabit architectural space.

Masculinity and femininity are constructed relationally in accord with the structural model put forth by Robert Connell, in which various gender types are mutually dependent upon one another for their legitimacy. In 1930s skyscraper films, masculinity is often constructed in hierarchical terms, both spatially and symbolically. Bosses occupy skyscraper pinnacles while their male and female underlings inhabit the lower stories and collective spaces, echoing the spatial politics of actual office buildings. Each kind of masculinity inhabits and negotiates space in a different manner, depending on the status of the man in the office hierarchy. Inferior office boys, obsequious yes-men, average clerks, dishonest con men, dissemblers, and acquisitive superiors are depicted in a pecking order where big fish eat little fish, before the designated hero, usually an ordinary clerk, comes to his senses and renounces the values of predatory patriarchal capitalism in favor of an "improved" New Deal–inspired variation, hence displacing the businessman as the ideal form of masculinity.

Near the very bottom of the hierarchy are youthful office boys with slight or fleshy, characterless bodies who exert their meager influence by flirting or attempting to acquire sexual favors in imitation of the boss's privileges. They are preceded only by the occasional African American janitor who is infrequently seen mopping the floor or greeting the boss as he disembarks from the elevator, never inhabiting inner office space. The young white gofers or underlings inhabit feminized or public space in the skyscraper office, where spatial allotments are correlated with power. Despite their meager allocations, these brash youth try to dominate their surroundings to compensate for their lowly standing.

Counsellor at Law includes two office clerks or messengers whose major occupation is to play up to the brassy switchboard operator who answers calls in the reception area. The desk of Henry Susskind (Bobby Gordon) is near that of Bessie Green (Isabel Jewell), which he assumes gives him license to continuously intrude on her conversations, which are often of a social rather than business nature. A similar messenger from an adjacent office who resembles the first in his slim demeanor and forward personality leans over her desk to admire her legs and quips, "Say kid, that's some run you have in your stocking." When she expresses disappointment over her compromised appearance, he leers over her desk and continues suggestively, "I'll buy you a new pair if you let me put them on for you."[51]

Lily Powers and the Gotham Trust Company's male personnel department receptionist (Maynard Holmes) use each other for their own mutual benefit in *Baby Face*. Plump with a cherubic face and a boyish southern drawl, he drips with obsequious charm, which Lily employs to her advantage. His soft body and affected mannerisms suggest a feminized masculinity rather than the stalwart variety seen in his superiors. "Do you have any experience?" he inquires knowingly, moving closer to her, to which she replies, "plenty," resulting in their retreat to an inner office to test her claims. He is the lowliest in a series of men she sleeps with on her way to the top of the architectural and economic pyramid.

Personnel Department receptionist in Baby Face.

Not far behind the office boys are the fawning yes-men who either fa-cilitate the boss's nefarious practices or are subservient to his every whim, the enablers in Connell's structural model. They are usually played by older, grey-haired men, whose looks and demeanors suggest that years of domina-tion have rendered them bland and intimidated, wholly impotent in the face of strength, the male counterparts of secretaries. *Skyscraper Souls*'s board of directors represents a collective of such types, who try ineffectually to resist Dwight's unlawful use of bank depositors' monies to advance his own interests, but who capitulate once he calls their bluff and threatens to resign. Dwight rises from his seat aggressively and towers over them in stature in his well-appointed private office replete with signifiers of possession. They learn that Dwight is planning a merger between Seacoast National Bank and Hamilton Interstate, which will enhance their assets, and so they are willing to overlook his illegal activities. "If you can tie us up with the Interstate, we'll be sitting on top of the world," one declares excitedly, illustrating his desire to conquer space as Dwight and his skyscraper already have. In the meantime, they hover around Dwight in a circular group, unable to differentiate themselves. Dwight's own private secretary or yes-man, Johnson (Harry C. Bradley), an elderly be-spectacled fellow with a tiny voice, observes the meeting in silence. When the spineless board members leave, he says almost breathlessly, "My heart stood

Yes-man in Big Business Girl.

still for a minute there, Mr. Dwight. What would you have done if they had accepted your resignation?" "I knew they wouldn't, Johnson," Dwight replies with assurance.

The fiftyish Luke Winters (Frank Darien) of *Big Business Girl,* a slightly built man with flattened, pomaded hair, is perhaps the most caricatured version of the boss's lackey. He sports a derby and cane and speaks in an affected voice, signifying effete masculinity and class pretension. When the enthusiastic Claire McIntyre applies for a position at the Clayton Advertising Agency, he wards her off dismissively, eager to extricate himself since the boss is away. He has failed to open an important cable sent by Clayton, which highlights his incompetence, stupidity, and lack of drive. Yet, after Clayton returns and hires Miss McIntyre, the decision suddenly looks good to the chameleon-like Winters. She enters her superior's office and finds Clayton reading her advertising copy, with Winters seated in an identical posture. She addresses them both.

> MISS MCINTYRE: How did you like it?
> CLAYTON: Rather childish.
> WINTERS: Very bad.

"Yes, indeed, R.J." and "Absolutely, R.J." are Winters's favorite toadying phrases. Subsequent to Miss McIntyre's departure, Clayton admits to Winters that her copy was nearly perfect. He confides that his decision to undermine her was purposely designed to make her feel less competent and more compliant, adding that he would have had to pay a man with her talent four times as much. The unctuous Winters is in on the subterfuge, but since his major role is to please the boss, he will do and say anything.

Bosses are at the top of the precarious skyscraper office hierarchy, often positioned as such in order to be taken down or taught a lesson. Their mercenary behavior characterizes them as "fallen men," representing a debased form of manhood, occasioned by their dubious dealings and illicit behavior. During the previous decade, businessmen were rendered as ideal American heroes or hegemonic models of masculinity; after the Great Crash, they were suspected of illegal maneuvering and financial misconduct. Lary May has demonstrated that films that feature "big business villains, who are associated with crime, threatened foreclosures, and corrupt practices" increased markedly in number during the Depression.[52] Previous go-getters such as Harold Lloyd and Douglas Fairbanks who were celebrated for their aggressiveness or business acumen in the films of the 1910s and 1920s are now depicted as exemplars of dishonesty in the newly compromised office building, often rendered as dens of iniquity rather than towers of progress.[53] Impeccably dressed and good looking, the Depression-era boss runs the gamut from the rugged charm of Stanhope in *Wife vs. Secretary* to the sinister smoothness of Dwight in *Skyscraper Souls* and Clayton in *Big Business Girl*. The actor Warren William, who played Dwight, was frequently cast as a suave but pernicious rogue, described as "the era's most indelible portrait of the big businessman."[54] Tall and well built, William and other cinematic bosses commanded cinematic spaces by their stature and the manner in which they advanced assertively through the skyscraper's interior. When Dwight describes his towering building as traversing space "halfway to hell and right up to heaven," he is also commenting on his ability to control bathhouse, private office, and penthouse alike.

In contrast to their underlings, bosses bark orders with impunity or assume that their subordinates' free time is an extension of their own business interests. Stanhope, Clayton, and Dwight often require their secretaries and male office assistants to work well after dark, entertaining and, in the case of secretaries, flirting with potential customers. Dwight steps into Miss Dennis's office and finds Lynn Harding trying on a dress and decides she is fair game. Clayton paces aggressively up and down the outer office shouting orders at Miss McIntyre, who doesn't even work for him yet, so accustomed is he to commanding anyone he chooses. In both cases, these bosses believe it is within their purview to demand sexual favors from their female charges, even if it means interfering in their relationships with their boyfriends or husbands. Indeed Clayton concocts an elaborate scheme to have the married McIntyre discover her husband Johnny Saunders (Frank Albertson) in the arms of another woman, a plot that must fail so as to ensure the triumph of virtue over vice. In Depression-era cinema, these bosses signify upper-class advantage that is inherently mercenary and is ultimately revoked.

The ideal of masculinity in the cinematic tall building is the average working Joe, the loyal mid-level office employee who often imparts the film's prescriptive message to the audience. He is meant to serve as the moral compass, articulating the position that an adherence to one's class and traditional gender position is the preferred strategy in hard times. This up-and-coming hero is awarded raises for his gumption and conscientiousness, while his female counterpart is preyed upon or shuttled off for hers. Often as tall as the boss, he dresses neatly and professionally much like Tom Shepherd in *Skyscraper Souls,* who is also known to topple the proverbial apple cart. In scene after scene, which double as comic relief and an audacious challenge of authority, echoing Harold's ironic duels, Shepherd runs into objects and people alike, especially big men or those in power. Forced to wait for Lynn until 3:00 a.m. during her late-night encounter with Dwight and Norton, he confronts her inappropriate behavior. He storms away and bumps into Dwight before completely upsetting an elaborate, strategically arranged lobby display in the shape of a skyscraper, which collapses like a house of cards. Following this telling disturbance, Dwight is seen headed into the elevator that is, not coincidentally, going down, signaling his subsequent demise and auguring Tom's rise.

Prior to their altercation, the faithful Shepherd sticks by Harding while she is writing the after-hours report requested by Dwight. In Harding's nondescript office, they share a sandwich and a wholesome bottle of milk, and Shepherd inquires, "How do you like living out of a paper bag, eh?" Harding expresses her disappointment and unwillingness to live a life of privation having glimpsed the life afforded by Dwight. "I could never marry a poor man," she concedes. When he assures her that he is "knocking down fifty dollars a week" with eighteen hundred in the bank, Lynn rejects his offer. "That wouldn't be enough for two people living in New York to have babies and everything. You wouldn't expect me to marry and not have them," Harding says. His pride wounded, Shepherd replies in a bullying manner, "When you're my wife, you're going to quit working." At the end of the film, after Shepherd and all the little people have lost all their savings in a frenzy of wild speculation on Seacoast stock, which Dwight had manipulated, the couple is seen leaving the skyscraper together, a realization of Shepherd's class-inflected paternalistic advice. In a reversal of the power dynamic, she is now chasing him. It is unclear whether she has capitulated to Shepherd's viewpoint or whether she will quit because of the vagaries of the economy. "I haven't got any money. . . . All I got is fifty dollars a week," Shepherd announces. To which Harding answers, "People get

Tom Shepherd upsetting a store display in Skyscraper Souls.

married on less than that." "I guess I have to if you're going to have all those babies," Shepherd replies. Harding's virtue has been saved, in part, by Shepherd's
steadfast persistence and traditional values; the nuclear family is reinstated as
the preferred bastion of economic relations, temporarily under siege by wolves
and libertines with money; the man is restored as the breadwinner while the
woman eventually assumes her role as homemaker, leaving the corrupt work-a-
day world of finance and business.

The realignment of class equals also occurs in *Wife vs. Secretary,* but not
before similar temptations and altercations ensue. Dave (James Stewart), who
serves a similar function to Tom, is the promising boyfriend of Helen "Whitey"
Wilson (Jean Harlow) and offers her all the comforts of a middle-class life and
its concomitant stability.[55] In one scene, Whitey and Dave are having dinner
in the crowded flat of her older sibling and spouse, where she resides, before
going out for a night on the town. Their bickering and talk of a divorce are
meant to caution Whitey against the pressures of marriage in troubled economic
times. Boss Stanhope telephones and summons her to his private penthouse
party to deliver documents, which are needed to clinch a deal. Leaving Dave in
the lurch, she complies unquestioningly. The occasion is Stanhope's wedding

anniversary, but he invites her upstairs nevertheless to his personal office suite, freighted with class privilege and corruption from such films as *Skyscraper Souls* and *Under Eighteen,* much to the suspicion of several guests who stare and gossip on the sidelines. The sumptuous setting and array of prominent guests act as a temptation to Whitey, seen by the camera's tracking of her upward ascension via a majestic staircase to the second story of his penthouse apartment. When she returns home at 2:00 a.m. after mingling business and pleasure, she finds the steadfast Dave asleep in his car. Hoping to win her back, he tells her about his raise and implores her to hand in her resignation, which she refuses to do. "We want to have a home and kids like everyone else. You have this good job you're getting used to everyday. You meet men like Stanhope—millionaires. You'll get used to it and won't want to get married." Dave serves as the voice to delimit female ambition, viewed as a displacement of women's putatively natural desire for security and love.[56] The final scene of the film shows the vindication of Dave's values and Whitey's final capitulation. A long shot of a nocturnal skyscraper that signifies the workday's end, or perhaps the imminent demise of Whitey's career, features the newly reconciled lovers riding off to embark on their future

Van Stanhope and Helen "Whitey" Wilson ascend the penthouse stairway in Wife vs. Secretary.

together. Escape from the corrupt clutches of the skyscraper that is a symbol of exploitation and economic adversity is necessary for their success.

Masculinities are also constructed in relation to femininities, yet it would be incorrect to suggest that gender is constructed according to a simple binary model (i.e., masculinity vs. femininity). In order to achieve the desired prescriptive resolution, 1930s skyscraper films formulate a new ternary construction, dubbed the "office triangle," which consisted of boss, wife, and secretary.[57] This formula delineated the skyscraper as inherently erotically charged and its gendered and class-inflected relationships as problematic. In 1936, *New York Times* critic Frank Nugent noted, concerning *Wife vs. Secretary*, that "Faith Baldwin looks slant-eyed at the world and finds it triangular. Out of this little triangle, she has fashioned 'Office Wife' and a host of other popular novels" and "superficial and handsomely produced pictures."[58] The formulaic office triangle is augmented by different types of femininity, which are also seen in relation to one another and employed to achieve the desired cinematic resolution. The New Woman, the fallen woman, the old maid, and the upper-class doyenne, among others, are fashioned in comparative terms and in relation to the skyscraper spaces they occupy or choose to avoid. Rather than analyzing the depiction of each of these types of femininity separately across films, it is instructive to examine how they interact with one another in the same and similar films.

Whitey and Dave leaving the city in Wife vs. Secretary.

The office triangle is the perfect structural metaphor for the skyscraper's hierarchical space; in accord with his status in the masculine pecking order, the boss occupies the pinnacle of the triangle in relation to femininity. His upper-class wife and his untiring secretary reside at opposite ends of the base, showing their subordinate status and their competition with one another; the former vies for his attention, which is taken up with business concerns, while his handy sidekick secretly wishes that he would regard her as a woman. Sometimes the boss takes a more personal interest in his secretary, which identifies skyscraper space as sexually charged and conflicted. Part of Metro-Goldwyn-Mayer's publicity campaign for *Wife vs. Secretary* included a smiling Clark Gable at the triangle's apex, with Jean Harlow and Myrna Loy below.[59] The title of the film, which was taken from a story by Faith Baldwin, underscores the inherent tension that such a configuration generates.

Different versions of femininity are juxtaposed to teach a moral lesson, and to buttress the preferred or hegemonic type sanctioned by the film. In the skyscraper office film, femininity is frequently problematized, or more in need of rehabilitation than its masculine counterpart, for which an ideal (e.g., mid-level office clerk) is provided. Perhaps the closest to the ideal type is the New Woman exemplified by Lynn Harding in *Skyscraper Souls,* Claire McIntyre in *Big Business Girl,* and Whitey Wilson in *Wife vs. Secretary.* Conscientious and dependable, they serve as the boss's right-hand woman and are indispensable to the successful functioning of the office. Yet their domination of his time and their habitation of business space are also seen as a handicap that creates the boss's unwelcome dependence and interferes with their private lives. Their seeming omnipresence is exacerbated by their youthful attractiveness, which acts as a distraction and a threat to present and future marital felicity for the boss and for themselves. This New Woman is lauded for her skills and admired for her looks, but she is employed in thirties cinema to ultimately renounce her career for a heterosexual dyad between class equals and the survival of the nuclear family.

The concept of a New Woman who was distinguishable from her cloistered, domesticated counterpart entered popular cultural discourse at the beginning of the twentieth century. She signified a wide array of behaviors that included financial and professional independence, sexual freedom, political activism, and feminism, among others.[60] Prior to the Depression, the New Woman in cinema was often a sexual libertine who sought gratification in acquisition of commodities or in the narcissistic beautification of her own person.[61] In thirties cinematic skyscraper space, the New Woman is rendered as someone who enjoys her work and its concomitant professional challenges but is diverted by husbands or indefatigable suitors who convince her that her ambitions are impractical or abnormal. She is attractive and well-dressed, but her desire for material goods is part of a long-term plan to establish a firm financial base for her future. At the same time, this cinematic New Woman is the subject of sexual scrutiny by a host of men, particularly those in power, which leads her to the arms of loyal boyfriends and results in the implied renunciation of her ambitions. What begins as a potentially companionate relationship leads inexorably to the domestic sphere. Skyscraper space is staged as a place beset with evils and pitfalls, and work is rendered only as a temporary way station on the road to feminine fulfillment.

The sartorial presentation of the New Woman runs the gamut from slinky evening wear to stark professional attire, often sending mixed signals that are meant to illustrate their problematic gender adaptations. Lynn Harding wears a conservative, dark dress and even sports a blouse and a tie, markers of the new professional woman with so-called masculine ambitions. When trying on a fancy dress for Miss Dennis, she is spied by Dwight, which strips her of professional identity in the office. The college-educated Claire McIntyre is appointed with an austere, yet fashionable dress, replete with sharp angles and zigzag motifs, which echo the functional modernity of the office space. When she is required to entertain an important client at a sumptuous party, she is seen sporting a seductive backless gown, bent on employing her sexuality to her own advantage.

The gender confusion hinted at by clothing is reinforced by the use of nicknames: Whitey in *Wife vs. Secretary,* Rexy in *Counsellor at Law,* and Mac in *Big Business Girl.* These androgynous names imply that they will never be regarded as complete women as long as they occupy business space where their choices are either sexualized object or diminutive buddy. Nicknames suggest further that the boss has assumed a degree of unprofessional familiarity that is a prelude to future physical advances.

More frequently, secretaries in these films are valued as office ornaments despite their competence, a characterization that McIntyre decides to exploit to her advantage. Overhearing her boss's private conversation concerning her proficiency and realizing his amorous intentions, she decides to play the flirtation card for everything it's worth, save compromising her morality, if it means landing an important account. The publicity kit for the film, which included lobby cards, press clippings, and suggestions for advertising, exaggerated the sexual activities of these secretaries, instructing audiences that the only way a woman could succeed in business was through personal charm, glamorous clothes, and after-hours pursuits rather than competence. Even if they possessed the requisite skills, they were sure to be exploited. "'Big Business Girls Make It Their Business to Be Attractive,' 'She Was Great at Her Desk, But You Should See Her on the Dance Floor with a Big Buyer,' 'What She Does after 5:00 p.m. Is Nobody's Business,'" the ad copy read.[62]

Office wives and boss's wives are dialectically related to one another; both derive their identities, in part, from the boss's accomplishments, and both are rendered as appendages to his business and emotional demands. The real wife is separated from the secretary spatially and by class, identifying their roles as both similar and mutually exclusive. She is an inhabitant of the private realm and the world of leisure, with servants and the financial means to satisfy her whims. Wives are frequently rendered as society matrons or dilettantes, often decked out in furs, with affected speech, in contrast to the brassy or matter-of-fact delivery of their office counterparts. Their major activities include shopping, planning parties, vacationing, and lunching with friends, showing their ignorance in the ways of business. They enjoy unrestrained spare time as consumers rather than producers in contrast to their hardworking female counterparts.

Linda Stanhope of *Wife vs. Secretary* inhabits a luxurious penthouse apartment and is rarely seen in Stanhope's high-pressure advertising agency. When she appears unannounced at his business office with her mother-in-law Mimi, she finds her husband lodged suggestively in a phone booth with Whitey, underscoring that the skyscraper is a hotbed of enticement. Mimi advises her to get rid of that secretary at once, convinced that the temptation of a beautiful assistant will undermine the marriage. Linda articulates her role as the keeper of the domestic hearth, "I try to make his life smooth and pleasant. . . . I want to be a refuge from all that." Stanhope fails to tell her about an imminent deal

Whitey and Stanhope in the phone booth in Wife vs. Secretary.

that must be kept secret, because of her failure to understand financial matters and her tendency to gossip, which is depicted as a feminine trait and the primary cause of their marital discord, rather than his flirtation with Whitey. The boss's wife represents a renewed version of upper-class Victorian femininity, as described by sociologist and economist Thorstein Veblen, an icon of display or conspicuous consumption provided by her husband's wealth and status, whose role is to inhabit the domestic sphere and provide a haven from the world of commerce.[63]

The fallen woman provides an additional foil to the ambitious New Woman, serving as an object lesson in behavior to avoid. *Skyscraper Souls* features several such types. Perhaps the most troubling is the well-meaning, once virtuous Dennis, who remains a paragon of competence and maternal supervision but is spoiled by her capitulation to Dwight's sexual advances. She is heir to the nineteenth-century variant of the fallen woman, a character who earns the audience's sympathy precisely because of her victimization and decline.[64] Sarah Dennis has been with Seacoast National Bank and Dwight's mistress for fifteen years with little to show but a comprehensive knowledge of elevators and the continued promise of being a kept woman. She is elegant and professional but getting older, which prompts Dwight to try to pension her off in favor of the younger Harding. She is frequently seen in Dwight's private office and penthouse suite, and on one occasion, she is late to work because she is breakfasting there in nothing more than flimsy black lingerie. Her death and redemption results from her desire to protect Lynn from Dwight's overtures; she shoots him in a final self-abnegating act of virtue, and she is martyred. The death of the fallen woman who literally and figuratively plummets from the skyscraper is not only meant as a caveat to those who would be tempted to exchange sex for upward mobility, it also serves as a warning to working women who stay at their jobs too long.

Fallen women may save themselves from the ineluctable journey downward if they renounce their prior ways for the sanctity of heterosexual matrimony. *Skyscraper Souls*'s Harlow look-alike, Jenny LeGrande, is a fashion model with a checkered past, who combines the class aspirations of the acquisitive gold digger with the redemptive possibilities occasioned by the renunciation of vice. In accord with Dennis, LeGrande is exposed in transparent black undergarments to men who traipse through Vinmont's fashion house with impunity; she is simultaneously a consumer, an erotic spectacle, and an object of consumption. One such habitué is Jacob Sorenson or Jake the jeweler, a Jew with a heart of gold who is willing to overlook LeGrande's prior dalliances. To her disbelief, he offers her his hand, well aware of and unperturbed by her checkered past. "You want to marry me? Do you know what kind of girl I've been?" LeGrande inquires incredulously. "We don't have to worry about the past," Sorensen assures her. "We start from here together." Sorensen is short and stocky with a

Sarah Dennis jumps from the skyscraper pinnacle in Skyscraper Souls.

heavy accent and, in spite of his sizable wealth, is not accorded the same social standing as his Christian peers, symbolically and spatially excluded from the skyscraper boardroom. LeGrande's blonde good looks provide him with an assimilation strategy that will assure his salvation, while he offers her class privilege within the inviolable bond of marriage.

An unusual variation of the so-called fallen woman type is *Baby Face*'s Lily Powers, who is allowed entrée to all facets of the skyscraper's hierarchical and gender-segregated space, but is punished and redeemed, as is the case with many working-class women in thirties cinema, by an adherence to her original class and gender position. Building upon the delineations of Powers put forth by previous scholars such as Richard Maltby and Lea Jacobs who view her as a gold digger who ultimately falls, I would like to suggest that she is constructed as an amalgam of three paradigms of femininity: the gold digger, the fallen woman, and a callous, masculinized working-class version of the New Woman.[65] Her behavior is as much related to the predatory boss trope found in many Depression-era skyscraper films as she is to her female gold-digging counterparts. Indeed she learns how to prey on men from the manner in which they have preyed on her in the sordid speakeasy where she was raised by her father, who had no compunction about pawning her off to coarse, burly steel mill workers and ward bosses alike. This squalid homosocial setting prepares her for the skyscrapers' equally mercenary, gender-segregated space, which is delineated as the speakeasy's counterpart. Indeed one of her worst transgressions is to insert herself in spaces previously reserved for privileged men, from small-time managers to supervisors, and ultimately the bank's president, Courtland Trenholm. Her mentor, the cobbler Adolf Cragg (Alphonse Ethier), informs her, "just as a man can make use of men to rise in the world—even more easily can she."[66]

Powers exerts her authority by a combination of mental acumen and sexual exploitation, in accord with male bosses of thirties' cinema such as David Dwight of *Skyscraper Souls*. Her character is formulated in part by the subtle negotiations of Warner Bros. and the newly founded Production Code Administration; however, the delineation of her femininity was in place before the interference. Although Warner Bros. was required to expunge salacious dialogue and activities, change the Nietzschean character of Cragg (Kragg in the script), who promoted a "survival of the fittest" credo, and return her to the steel mills from whence she came, Lily still suffered the loss of her material comforts and castigation for her deeds. Maltby points out:

> The narrative always presented a patriarchal moral, in which
> Lily's aberrant expression of her sexuality resulted in her pun-
> ishment. The crime of which the narrative found her guilty was
> patricide, but the form of her punishment changed . . . to a more
> inclusive and perverse form of patriarchal revenge, by which
> she was returned to the world from which she had attempted
> to escape.[67]

In the original version, she simply loses boss Trenholm to suicide whereas in the film he survives and is reduced to a manual laborer. Powers's class demotion and excommunication from the skyscraper's boardroom, penthouse, and private suite was as much a critique of her sexual prowess as it was of her inappropriate class aspirations and transgression of gender boundaries. She is poised to assume a masculinized feminine identity, seizing the power, money, and spatial prerogatives formerly reserved for men, thereby temporarily subverting the male hierarchy. The press book even characterized Powers's behavior as bellicose: "Lily invades New York and the world of business."[68]

Powers begins her spatial ascent from her father's lowly speakeasy, a primitive world of vice and corruption. Her squalid rickety shack, situated in a dystopian landscape darkened by belching smokestacks, is Lily's private hell, which is appropriately destroyed in a fiery blaze. Despite her corrupt origins, she has ambitions, signified by her symbolic adoption of the curmudgeonly cobbler Cragg, both surrogate father and mentor, who instructs her to better herself through his dissemination of advice and reading materials. In accord with Harold Lloyd's male characters of a decade earlier, she is educated in the ways of go-getting and self-betterment, albeit with a ruthless, social Darwinist twist. In the original script, her teacher echoes Nietzsche, "You must *use* men, not let them use *you!* You must be a *master,* not a *slave! . . .* Exploit yourself! Go to some big city where you can find opportunities. . . . Be strong—Defiant! *Use men—to get the things you want!*"[69] In the final script, which adheres to the recommendations of the Production Code Administration, Cragg differentiates between the right and wrong way to achieve these aims, but still encourages her to seek control over her fate: "Go to some big city where you will find opportunities. But don't let people mislead you; you must be a *master,* not a *slave.* Keep clean, be strong—defiant! And you will be a success."[70]

Powers is a suave dissembler who assumes a sweet demeanor, hence the appellation Baby Face, that masks predatory motives, much like David Dwight or the very men that she vamps. Capable and ambitious, she is a New Woman gone wrong who will use both her mental skills and her feminine wiles to get ahead. We learn early on that she's both efficient and resourceful. When the clerk Jimmy McCoy (John Wayne) informs the assistant bank manager about Powers's smarts—"She's very intelligent. She's head and shoulders above any girl in the place"—Brody (Douglass Dumbrille) doesn't seem interested until he sees Powers, who goes out of her way to simultaneously showcase her competence and her sexual charms. She learns how to get ahead by mimicking the dress and behavior of her attractive female cohorts, even reading a book on etiquette by Emily Post. She is soon promoted to Brody's department and his care and begins her upward spatial and class rise. Later, when she is transferred to the bank's Paris branch to avoid negative publicity after her penultimate affair with the recently murdered bank's vice president J. P. Carter (Henry Kolker), she assumes a polished demeanor and the requisite business skill for a successful career. When Trenholm arrives in Paris, he is informed by the branch manager that Powers, who has changed her name to Mary Allen, is excelling in business:

> MANAGER: Miss Allen has done very well. We've put her in charge
> of our Travel Bureau.
> TRENHOLM: Really? I'm glad to hear it.
> MANAGER'S VOICE: By the way, this department has increased its
> business forty percent since the first of the year.[71]

The scene suggests that this mercenary, albeit pragmatic New Woman had formerly chosen seduction as the primary road to class ascension, the true badge of the gold digger, cognizant of the fact that it is her only entrée to the boardroom and penthouse, or the upper reaches of privilege. "What chance has a woman got?" she asks the old cobbler early on.[72] In the foreign environs of Paris, she proves herself, but with little guarantee that she will advance much further.

After a requisite murder/suicide and attempted suicide occur within the speculative world of skyscraper space and mercenary capitalist practices (Maltby attributes the Crash to her deeds), the New Woman is deprived of her professional identity, which is replaced by marriage, a restoration of her appropriate gender position in patriarchy. This does not occur without her class demotion, which represents the consequences of her acquisitive behavior. James Wingate of the Production Code Administration advised Warner Bros. to construct an ending "to indicate that Lily disregarded the cobbler's advice, and in the end, show her stripped of her social standing, and thus drive home the point . . . 'use your body for material advancement' has been entirely discredited."[73] Her fall from grace is redeemed by her analogous descent in the economic hierarchy, which she chooses altruistically by returning Trenholm's money in order to save the bank. Although the film implies that the scandal occasioned by her behavior was the original cause of the bank's near failure, it is her final act of generosity and material renunciation that saves it. Unlike Dave and Whitey or Lynn and Tom, she does not marry a class confederate; rather, the now penniless Mr. and Mrs. Trenholm are ultimately demoted to the same lowly class position in the steel mills of Pittsburgh, similar to the place from whence she came.

The film supports the idea that a woman's adherence to a prescribed gender and class position represents a way out of the Depression. Although it fashions the New Woman as a working-class sexual predator rather than sexual victim, the implications are clear, that female professional identity is either elusive or impossible. Happiness for women is found in their removal from skyscraper space and nefarious urban influences in favor of a return to domesticity and, in the case of Powers, hard labor. To underscore the hope that women would renounce the business world, and to offset the potentially damaging effect on Barbara Stanwyck's reputation, the press book described her as "Mrs. Frank Fay, with a reputation of being an ideal wife, housekeeper, hostess, and screen star of ability."[74]

In accord with the fallen woman, the old maid or female office drone is also presented as a testament to what happens to professional women who decide to remain in the skyscraper office too long. Homely in appearance, with dark hair either tightly pulled back or in a bun, and wearing large-framed glasses, they are juxtaposed with their more glamorous counterparts in *Baby Face, Skyscraper Souls,* and *Big Business Girl,* among others. They conform most closely to the cinematic stereotype of librarians, who are usually older women, who sport glasses, modest clothing, and a bun hairdo.[75] Lily Powers is dressed in frills and ruffles and sports a new marcelled hairdo in an effort to get noticed by assistant bank manager Brody, the first man in the skyscraper food chain with real stature. She and the "homely, efficient-looking girl," as she is described in the script, who is wearing a dark dress and owlish glasses, are placed in close proximity to one another, underscoring the physical differences between them.[76] Both are situated in a large, nondescript office filled with female clerical staff, suggesting that the scene's intent is meant to pose the question, whose talents will be noticed in the anonymous world of female clerical labor? The plain woman is reading off figures to Powers in a nervous robotic manner, but the latter is barely listening. When she spots an opportunity to elicit Brody's attention, Powers quickly disengages and cuts across the room, leaving her unattractive counterpart in the lurch. She practically snuggles up to him as she showcases her business efficiency, a strategy rewarded by a promotion. The message is clear: homely women finish last no matter how competent they are.

Claire McIntyre of *Big Business Girl* paces nervously in the company of the office factotum Sally Curtin while awaiting her appointment with Clayton. Curtin is a gaunt middle-aged woman with a sallow complexion, a tightly wrapped bun, and unremarkable attire, contrasting markedly with McIntyre's spunky youth and jazzy appearance. McIntyre confides to her that she has barely slept because she is excited about the opportunity to write advertising copy for the company. "Wait until you've been around here as long as I have, you'll get used to insomnia," Curtin commiserates. "I used to be terribly ambitious myself, getting a job at a man's salary. I used to try to write copy," she adds dejectedly. When McIntyre responds that she will succeed or "bust a lung trying," Curtin

Lily Powers and the office drone in Baby Face.

counsels, "It takes more than a successful career to keep a girl warm at night." Drab, dyspeptic characters like Curtin are meant to warn up-and-coming professional women to avoid ambition, which will ultimately fail, in favor of the safety of domestic space and matrimony. Those that do remain are either tarts or dissatisfied old maids without a future. It is significant to note that the frustrated Curtin was a Hollywood invention, not present in the original short story.

The adverse effects of choosing a profession over marriage were articulated by women's organizations and presented in advice literature for women seeking employment. According to Frances Maule in *She Strives to Conquer* (1934), the National Federation of Business and Professional Women's Clubs were opposed to the "frustrated spinster in business," in favor of the "married woman worker." Maule advised:

> For the average normal woman, a husband, home and children
> are necessary to complete and harmonious development. The
> successful business woman of the future will not only want to do
> her job well, but to reach this full development by leading a well-
> rounded personal life.[77]

The lowest in the female office hierarchy are African American women, who are rarely shown in skyscraper films and are rarely permitted in office interiors, relegated rather to hallways and lobbies. Lily Powers's sidekick and maid Chico accompanies her to the Big Apple and watches her flirt with a doorman at a huge skyscraper entrance. When Lily seeks an office job, Chico is stationed in an outer corridor, with the tacit understanding that she would not even be considered for such a position. Her plight paralleled actual conditions for African American women in the skyscraper office in the 1930s, when the majority of female clerical workers were white, middle-class, and unmarried.[78] Chico's only hope of material advancement is as Lily's maid; she finally gets a fancy new uniform only when Lily has moved uptown to a luxurious new apartment, her class rise wholly dependent on Lily's advancement, not her own efforts. Chico's character suffers from what Deborah King calls "triple jeopardy," barred from the business sphere by race, class, and gender.[79] As a *doppelgänger* to Lily, she represents a more blatant example of female enslavement.

The secondary status afforded to women of color is examined in *Skyscraper Souls*. Several scenes picture scores of anonymous working-class women down on all fours, methodically and endlessly scrubbing the lobby floor to a high polish. They are the skyscraper's nocturnal denizens who occupy deserted space, separated from the hustle-bustle of the daytime crowds, and rendered mute and invisible. Harding and Dwight encounter them after disembarking from the elevator after his attempted seduction, but neither acknowledges their presence; rather, the scores of women are employed as background furniture. Dwight has

Hobbled female workers in Skyscraper Souls.

just offered Harding the material comforts of being a kept woman, which she refuses. He replies, "So you would rather go on working?" The camera surveys the regal couple from above parading through the palatial lobby in contrast to the hobbled women who toil ceaselessly, serving as a visual analogue to Dwight's juxtaposition of labor with the benefits of leisure. Seen in faceless silhouette, these female beasts of burden are images of working-class labor and coded blackness, the absent presences that keep the building running.

FROM STORIES TO SCRIPTS: THE DELIMITING OF FEMALE AMBITION

Skyscraper office films of the Depression era were often adaptations of serialized short stories and pulp-fiction novels by female writers who sought to explore the dilemmas of professional women who were seeking to balance their careers and private lives, which encompassed romance, sexuality, marriage, and family. Beneath the visual and written cinematic text comprising numerous preliminary scripts, a final version, and visual interpretations by directors and set designers, there is often a female-authored short story or novel that requires restoration. In doing so, one discovers that the overarching prescriptive messages proffered in the films did not coincide with their original authors' primary intentions. In terms of the construction of gender, the films were often decidedly more conservative than the stories on which they were supposedly based. By engaging in a close reading of these pulp-fiction variants and contrasting them with their cinematic counterparts, a virtual reconstitution of repressed gender types and their concomitant spaces is allowed. A phantasmic space is created by these formative texts, a cinematic space that might have been, which serves as an implicit critique of its distorted counterpart. This phantasmic space is fleshed out by actual secretaries who spoke out, in self-help books and articles aimed at female office workers, against the tabloid-like depiction of themselves, challenging the notion that these films were produced to satisfy a uniform female audience who simply "liked dirt," as film historian Thomas Doherty claims.[80]

Film historians concur generally on a pre-Code (1930-34) and post-Code (1934 on) chronology when assessing Depression-era censorship, yet all caution that there needs to be a close examination of the negotiations between the PCA and the studios in assessing the Code's impact on the exclusion of sensational and racy details and the ways in which narrative structure and meaning were altered by either prudish, bureaucratic interlopers or well-meaning idealists.[81] Yet Richard Maltby has shown that the negotiations of Warner Bros. and the PCA in the making of *Baby Face* illustrate that in spite of the removal of blatant eroticism and even the alteration of both dialogue and ending, Lily Powers is still punished for her mercenary deeds by the same patriarchal forces that occasioned her victimization in the first place. This points to the Code's success in eliminating one set of moral strictures while preserving others, which helped to fashion her gender identity.[82]

Any assessment of Depression-era censorship must commence with the series of covert alterations that began at the level of the adaptation from story to script, which preceded both an adherence to the 1930 voluntary pre-Code recommendations and the mandatory 1934 post-Code strictures. These changes were not always made as a way to dilute the meaning of elite literary texts nor were they transformed only for the purpose of conforming to current mores.[83] Baldwin's fiction was as pulp as its filmic counterparts and as wholesome as the Code demanded. Her fiction was modified in the formulation of both film's architectural space and the gendered identities for the purpose of warning women away from metropolitan settings, which were considered antithetical to their natures. Baldwin's novel *Skyscraper* (1931) and her story "Wife versus Secretary" of 1935, which formed the basis for the pre-Code *Skyscraper Souls* and the post-Code *Wife vs. Secretary* films, respectively, are virtual case studies in the ways that female ambition and professional aspiration were misrepresented in favor of a prescriptive ideology that discouraged women from working in the supposedly sexually charged and mercenary world of skyscraper space.

Faith Baldwin (1893–1978) was one of the pulp-fiction writers who was the most highly paid and sought after by the studios during the Depression, the recipient of large sums for her motion picture rights. Her numerous books and serialized short stories, which concerned the challenges faced by working women in tall office buildings, included *The Office Wife* (1929), *Skyscraper* (1931), *Self-Made Woman* (1932), and "Wife versus Secretary" (1935).[84] As Laura Hapke noted in the recently rereleased version of *Skyscraper,* Baldwin's novels "negotiated the tensions between emancipation and conformity; modern and traditional womanhood; vocation and marriage."[85] Paraphrasing the author, a contemporary of Baldwin summarized her plot lines in the following terms:

> Her women are not concerned "with large problems discussed in large clubrooms filled with large ladies," discussing whether or not a woman can have a career and a husband. They are busy trying to untangle their own problems of love and work, jobs and marriage that are peculiar to this skyscraper age.[86]

Baldwin supplemented her stories of skyscraper office labor with an examination of the difficulties of mediating these multiple female identities against the backdrop of the Depression, which added further privation and stress to their lives. Several commentators noted that Baldwin's fictional depictions of women's labor in office space that were adapted in cinema represented a misrepresentation of her intentions and of the nature of female office work. In doing so, the studios altered the delineation of skyscraper space and women's capacity to produce it other than through sexual means. An anonymous reviewer of *Skyscraper Souls* who praised the lavishness of the stage sets recognized, "Yet to make the picture in its present form, plenty of liberties have been taken with Faith Baldwin's story, 'Skyscraper,' that ran in *Cosmopolitan* about a year ago."[87] Another reviewer, Richard Dana Skinner, noted that the film lacked any semblance to actual office employment, which he blamed on "the race for sensation." "In the process," he complained, "good ideas are spoiled. They are twisted out of semblance to life in order to serve the dominating purpose of the Hollywood magnates."[88]

The distortion of Baldwin's fiction and indeed her very person began egregiously in the film adaptation of her novel *The Office Wife* (1930), in which a fictionalized version of the author appeared. Baldwin's stand in, Kate Halsey (Blanche Friderici), is introduced early on as the mannish author of successful serials and books.[89] Short cropped hair, a man's suit, and a cigar identify her as a commonplace caricature of a suffragist or lesbian, introducing the taint of masculinization and abnormality to female professionalism.[90] Frustrated at being pigeon-holed as an author of trite women's fiction, Halsey asserts that she would prefer to write on the caliber of a "Jack London, Jim Tully, Ernest

Hemingway," or herself, but is given stories on "baby rates" instead. The head of the successful Fellows publishing company offers her a story idea and generous monetary compensation, the opportunity to write a novel called "The Office Wife." Depriving Baldwin of creative agency, the film depicts Lawrence Fellows (Lewis Stone) as the originator of the story idea. However, the fictional Baldwin is vindicated, in part, when a debate with Fellows ensues, concerning whether a boss selects a secretary for her looks or competence. Halsey insists on the former; and in the end, she prevails when the incongruous marriage of the elderly Mr. Fellows and his youthful office wife occurs.

Baldwin's novel *Skyscraper* pictures New York's 840-foot Seacoast Building as a monument to human achievement or a "concrete manifestation of man's upward striving" for those who dare to dream, and a trap for those with pernicious intentions.[91] In contrast to the depiction in the film, this preeminent Manhattan skyscraper is not a monument to David Dwight's ego or his greed but belongs to all those that occupy it, their views mediated by their class affiliation, their moral fiber, and their gender position within the office hierarchy. For Lynn Harding, it is a space that offers exciting professional opportunities; for Tom Shepherd, it is a skyward voyage to the radio tower that presents limitless possibilities; to Jenny LeGrande, it is both a boring bureaucracy and a way station to material comfort; and to David Dwight, it is a nefarious trap of his own making.

Lynn Harding is the main protagonist of the novel rather than David Dwight. It is a story that concerns women's quest for professional identity rather than one about a megalomaniac male entrepreneur whose goal is to own the tallest building in the world and who will destroy anyone who impedes him. Baldwin explores the challenges that faced working women in the modern age, such as the dilemma of balancing their careers and their personal lives, with the hope that both may be rewarding. These issues are investigated against the backdrop of the physical proximity of bodies in urban space and the liaisons that ensue. The Depression is examined as a variable that complicated women's lives, which often prompted them to consider unsavory choices because of economic privation. There are no salacious bathhouse scenes, attempted jewel heists, suicides, or murders. Miss Dennet (Dennis in the film) does not shoot Dwight and subsequently leap to her death; instead she saves Harding from Dwight's attempted seductions. The older female superior is not his office wife but a successful supervisor who is poised for a promotion. Although she had a relationship with him twenty years prior, her career has flourished at the expense of her personal life. For his part, Dwight is a prominent, albeit shady lawyer who does not even work in the building. The wheedling, upper-crust Mrs. Dwight who materializes only to request money does not exist in the novel, hence the absence of the formulaic office triangle. Details of the story are exaggerated, and scenes are manufactured in the film to enhance the titillation and sensational appeal, thereby distorting Baldwin's protofeminist intentions.

The director of the film, Edgar Selwyn, blamed the misrepresentation on the film industry's need to compete with the tabloid press, forced to cultivate a jaded audience that was used to heightened thrills. "Murder, robbery, intrigues of all kinds have become commonplace through continual repetition in the press. Ten years ago these would have caused civic upheavals; today they are read with complacence," he complained. The "life dramas" have thus been relegated to the inside pages. "We have to top the newspapers, which have the advantage of freedom from censorship restrictions."[92] Even if the director's appraisal of audience response was accurate, it does little to clarify the nature of the sensationalist inclusions and the demotion of Harding to a secondary role in the film's plot.

Fifteen scripts and partial scripts were written by at least seven different writers in preparation for the film, dating from August of 1931 until May of 1932.[93] The first, by John Lynch, which was dated 1 August 1931, introduces the distortion and tabloidization of Baldwin's original story. The camera commences with a panning shot of the impressive Hudson Building, moves to the mechanical synchronization of the elevators, proceeds to the rushing pedestrians on the sidewalk, and tracks them through the entranceway to the elevators. Lynn Harding is differentiated from the others, and so is David Dwight, who notices Harding and decides to take the elevator, establishing the skyscraper as a site of regimentation and sexual predation. The denouement of this version features the hero Dwight jumping from the pinnacle of the massive office building. By 14 December, screenwriter Edgar Allen Woolf has Miss Dennis kill Dwight before leaping to her death.

Elmer Harris, who completed the shooting script on 3 May 1932, begins his version with an airplane circling the eponymous Dwight Building (changed from the Hudson Building) to the skyscraper cupola, where a flock of pigeons is seen cooing and mating, reinforcing the romantic nature of the tale. A married couple, Mara and Bill, are fighting because he is unemployed, which establishes the Depression as an important element of the tale. Various characters collide and the scene changes to Vinmont's fashion establishment. Although a few details change in the film's opening—cooing pigeons are replaced with Shepherd grabbing Harding's ankle—themes of mechanization and sexuality are underscored, while suicide and murder are continued, developments contradicting Baldwin's intent.

In her book, Baldwin depicted Lynn Harding as an aspiring New Woman or "bachelor girl," with a college education and professional ambitions, rather than the secretary of the film. She has an important job as a sales researcher in the trust department, a testament to her sense of responsibility. Miss Dennet is her immediate supervisor and surrogate mother, who is grooming her for a promotion. Harding is not simply a cute office assistant, but an attractive professional woman, a robust "blue-eyed pioneer to new lands," who reads books such as *Financial Systems,* augmented by evening courses in business at Columbia University to improve her skills. She enters into an egalitarian relationship with Tom Shepherd early in the novel, always insisting on paying her own way, declaring to a coworker that marriage should be "on a fifty-fifty basis, a partnership." Soon after her romance with Shepherd gets serious, she thinks to herself, "I don't want to marry anyone. It's too much of a risk. And I'm getting somewhere with my job." Later, when marriage is discussed, and Shepherd pressures her to leave work after the wedding, Harding rebels. "You haven't thought of me at all—of how much I like my work, how anxious I am to get on with it." After a fitful interchange, she finally bursts out, "No, I won't marry you and give up my job."[94] In contrast, the film renders Harding's postponement of marriage as the result of the inadequacy of Shepherd's salary to start a family. The only similarity between the novel and the film is Harding's desire to have a sound financial foundation before they tie the knot. Baldwin's novel makes no mention of Harding's desire for children; instead she is rendered as a go-getter with a desire for a balanced life that includes a career and a relationship. One reviewer of the book noted,

> Office girls who waver between deserving young men and slightly worn but predatory big businessmen threaten to become a drug on the fiction market. Their mental and emotional reactions have been charted in so many forms that it is easily possible to compute the number of chapters in which they will waver, the precise point at which their eyes will be opened to the truth, and the ensuing point at which their arms will be opened to the right— usually—the younger man.[95]

Harding's upstanding virtue and sense of purpose is contrasted with the compromised morals and indolence of Jenny LeGrande, born Alice Smith in Brooklyn. In accord with her cinematic counterpart, she works as a model, but not in an establishment owned by two dissembling Jews sporting absurd berets; rather, she is employed in a fashion house belonging to Madame Fanchon. Her boss is a serious woman who frowns upon her charges' dalliances with buyers for extra cash, which had become endemic to the industry during hard times. Just like Miss Dennet, who is robbed of the full scope of her professional identity in the film, Fanchon is simply written out of the film's script.

Harding's industriousness is matched equally in the book by LeGrande's disinterest in the world of business and its oppressive bureaucratic space. When visiting Harding's office, she cast a "curious glance at the filing cabinets, which repelled her slightly, as did the clicking of typewriters, the efficient mechanism of the place." She preferred "sliding in and out of gowns, made meticulously to her measure . . . liked sitting for an hour at a dressing table smoothing unguents over her face, painting her lips with scarlet" because "it called for no effort of the mind." She is pursued romantically by Slim, a regular guy, but prefers to be kept by an older Jewish sales representative, Meyer, who provides her with an uptown apartment and a maid. In spite of her shortcomings, this kept woman is a loyal friend who falls victim to the Depression and the sometimes ruthless world of the skyscraper. Harding muses on LeGrande's predicament, "It's economic: it has to do, somehow, with the entire economic system. . . . It seemed to her as she bent over her desk that the entire weight of the massive building was upon it, that she was oppressed, burdened, hemmed in."[96] Unlike the novel, the film renders the morally compromised LeGrande as simply a tart whose only hope of redemption is through the intervention of Sorensen the jeweler who is willing to overlook her past; the novel shows her as a victim of economic forces seemingly out of her control. In the latter, LeGrande decides to extricate herself rather than to continue her two-timing of Slim and Meyer, thereby introducing the possibility of her own salvation.

The adverse effects of the Depression on working women's relationships with significant others are explored in Baldwin's account via the characters of Mara and Bill, a couple who are experiencing marital difficulties. Mara holds a job in the bank, but Bill is out of work. They are also under harsh financial strain, which causes Mara to blame Bill for their hardships and to conclude that vamping the boss is necessary to keep her job. The author intimates that the only reason she is working is to keep the couple afloat, warning Lynn, "A girl who marries and goes on working is a fool: and a man who agrees to the arrangement is a worse one."[97] Her glum and dejected husband Bill proves her point; with too much time on his hands, and because of his implied emasculation by his frustrated wife, he begins an affair with a beautician. He finally regains his manhood by confronting the interloping boss, finding a job out of state, and giving Mara an ultimatum. Mara loses her job because of Bill's outburst, and they end up reconciling. Baldwin suggests through the delineation of these characters that it is acceptable for married women to work as long as their husbands are employed; otherwise a crisis in masculine identity will ensue, and women and men alike will be tempted to seek romance and financial benefits elsewhere. These caveats to married women who work are entirely omitted from the script and film. Mara becomes the minor unmarried character Myra, who is always borrowing money from either LeGrande or Harding. She solves her financial dilemma by plotting with her boyfriend Slim to rob Sorensen's jewelry store, a plan that backfires when Slim (Wallace Ford) is accidentally interred in the vault.

Baldwin blamed the Depression era's so-called marriage bar that was instituted by the bank for adversely affecting Harding and Shepherd's relationship. After they decide finally to wed, Harding breaks the news to Miss Dennet, who is initially none too keen on the idea, preferring that Harding reach her full career potential. Yet there is another obstacle that prevents Harding from having both a job and a husband; Miss Dennet informs her that the bank is firing married women whose husbands also work for the company. In Baldwin's estimation, these are the factors that render Harding ripe for temptation and David Dwight's overtures, rather than the removal of her dress in an inner office seen in the film.

Tom Shepherd is depicted in the novel as a wholesome type, not the bumbling and aggressive bank teller of the film. He starts with traditional ideas concerning a woman's place in the office, chagrined that his girlfriend is choosing a career over domesticity. "I'm always sorry when I see a girl slaving her life away in the toils of a soulless corporation," Shepherd informs Harding, while he thinks, "It's a damn shame that pretty women have to work." As their relationship develops and they begin to plan their future, he becomes more resistant to the idea: "Do you think I'd let my wife keep on working?" he bullies. In terms of his own professional identity, he is as conflicted as Harding; although he is working as Mr. Norton's private confidential secretary, he has no interest in business. Instead, he dreams of becoming an engineer or an inventor and working in the skyscraper's uppermost radio tower. By the middle of the novel, Shepherd begins to empathize with Harding's desire for a satisfying career: "Because of his own dissatisfaction with his job and his longing growing stronger daily, to be somewhere he would feel perfectly at home, doing something he believed to be important and constructive, he was beginning to understand Lynn's attachment to her own work."[98] Shepherd's new headquarters are devoted to the dissemination of information, a redeemed version of the skyscraper pinnacle, which points to the promise of the future.

Baldwin's readers are introduced to forty-eight-year-old David Dwight, who is going through a protracted mid-life crisis, as a friend of Sarah Dennet on page 65, underscoring that *Skyscraper* is not his story. In the novel, he does not orchestrate the rise of stocks; he simply enjoys the financial benefits of buying low before a merger. Moreover, there are no board members ruined by his deeds; instead, Shepherd gets fired from the bank for inadvertently revealing confidential information to Harding. Not a robber baron capitalist, Dwight is a celebrated, silver-tongued lawyer, whose upper-story office is inundated with precious objects that represent his upper-class pretensions and lust for commodities. Appearing less like a business office than a private dwelling, there are "paneled walls and built-in bookcases," "fine oriental carpet on the floor," and a "modernistic bar-celarette-humidor," which "presided with illegal charm over the working quarters of a man at law." Unlike Shepherd, who occupies ultimately the lofty reaches of enlightened architectural space, the radio tower, Dwight's workplace bespeaks pretension and decadence. His business suite is matched by an equally self-indulgent country estate and a Manhattan penthouse apartment. He comments to Harding as he sizes her up, "I like lovely things around me." In accord with his cinematic counterpart, he tries to seduce Harding by deception and subterfuge, but he is foiled by Dennet, who continues her professional life with dignity, albeit some regret. His unethical behavior encompasses the personal and professional; he is both a serial philanderer, as "harmless as a serpent," and a trader in inside stock information. He also actively attempts to undermine Shepherd and Harding's relationship. Thus, his view of the skyscraper as both sexual icon and a cage for women represents a projection of his own intentions:

> Every day you go to one, are swallowed up by it, every day you
> work there, never thinking of the life teeming in the building,
> beating against the walls . . . unaware people spend most of their
> waking hours under the impossibly high roof. A skyscraper is a
> little city . . . a phallic symbol.[99]

Ultimately Dwight sails for Europe, or the Old World, and later divorces his wife and marries a nineteen-year-old chorus girl, symbolically banished by his own unscrupulous behavior.

Dwight's departure and Harding and Shepherd's ascent in Baldwin's tale is consonant with the skyscraper's triumph as an image of ingenuity and progress rather than one of debased capitalist exploitation in the cinematic version. In the book, philanderers, cheats, and vamps are routed out, leaving those with dreams and aspirations to fortify the building. Shepherd's "great height and breadth" and visionary mind, which match the tall building's physical and metaphorical scale, and Harding's lofty professional ambitions now inhabit the premises. Recently married, they appreciate working in close proximity to one another—he in the tower, she a few floors below—especially in such trying economic times. Their companionate marriage and the skyscraper are seen ultimately as bulwarks against the debilitating effects of the Depression. The novel concludes with the tall building rendered as a monument to strength and human ingenuity: "Skyscraper. Roots embedded in earth, towers reaching to the far and azure empyrean. Symbol of man's need for stability, for endurance, for progress, for aspiration, *Skyscraper*."[100]

Baldwin's story "Wife versus Secretary" employs the office triangle theme (boss, wife, secretary) to explore the dilemmas that beset an attractive, highly competent businesswoman, an equally handsome boss who has come to depend upon her, and his striking wife of eight years. It recapitulates the numerous fictional delineations of the skyscraper as a charged heterosexual space due to the introduction of women into a previously homosocial environment. However, the prior tales of office romance between the boss and secretary are extended with the introduction of the wife and the manner in which the office events affect the domestic realm, thereby temporarily upsetting marital felicity. The serialized novel "Wife versus Secretary" recasts the secretary as a New Woman and suggests that she can admire her boss, even going so far as to develop a full-blown crush, but still perform her job with dignity and aplomb. It concludes with the suggestion that a woman may seek fulfillment in her job, preferring the fast-paced world of business and finance to romance and marriage. The boss's wife also finds a voice in Baldwin's fiction, given an opportunity to respond to the impact of office dynamics on her marriage, and coming to appreciate the invaluable service that a female assistant provides her husband, rather than simply responding jealously, the standard fare in films. The boss learns how to mediate his erotic feelings toward an attractive woman in his midst while still maintaining domestic harmony.

In contrast to *Skyscraper Souls* of 1932, the outward parameters of Baldwin's later story are not egregiously distorted in the film *Wife vs. Secretary* (1936), although her original intent and didactic message are compromised. The alteration of Baldwin's serious message is due to the intervention of producer Hunt Stromberg, who assumed an active role in the script's formulation, writing over twenty lengthy, prescriptive memos (most over six pages single-spaced) to the film's three scriptwriters, John Mahin, Norman Krasna, and Alice Duer Miller, and directing them to adjust aspects of Baldwin's story and character delineation.[101] The studio commissioned Baldwin to write an adaptation of her magazine serial, and she met with the producer on at least two occasions.[102] Stromberg corresponded with Baldwin after these sessions, instructing her on the particular slant he envisioned. When Baldwin did not conform to these dictates, Stromberg turned to the screenwriters to do his bidding. At the outset, he altered the tale from a drama to a urbane comedy in the tradition of Nick and Nora in the *Thin Man*.[103] He was also responsible for blaming the temporary rift in the Stanhope (Sanford in the story) marriage on gossiping upper-class women (only mildly suggested by Baldwin), on whom he manages to vent particular spleen. "They just can't believe anything but the worst and see their sly looks, mingled with expressions of sympathy for Linda, tell the vicious story." We must be "made to feel that it is a pity that these people can't be permitted to lead their own lives unhampered by the gossip which begins to spread insidiously and grows like a cancerous growth." These secretaries are "a damned sight more honest than the socialites and hypocrites who travel on a higher plane."[104] Sanford, the veritable good guy of the tale, is depicted as not "the type to let idle gossip of women kick him around."[105] The advertising campaign played up this angle: one of the catch lines read, "Wives and Secretaries—Their gossip will make or break a picture."[106] In a veritable replay of the Cinderella tale, Stromberg draws a distinction between these destructive biddies and the hardworking, attractive heroine Whitey, who, in accord with Baldwin's intent, is rendered as infinitely competent and honest, a woman of consummate integrity.

To his credit, Stromberg underlines the superior skills of a boss's right-hand executive secretary, who knows as much as there is to know about a major publishing firm. She is as competent as any man, but is at a "disadvantage" because of her looks, not the vamping secretary so prevalent in the formulaic skyscraper office films. The producer advised his screenwriters to exploit the following angle to the maximum:

> One of the chief feelings I think we must get over here is "women's place in business." I place this under the heading "showmanship." I would like the audience to really see a crack secretary at work—the one hundred one details that she has to do—but, more important, the responsibilities that she handles. It is quite customary to see stenographers working and the average secretary of a big league man like Sanford. These women sometimes carry as much responsibility as the man himself.[107]

One of the ways that Whitey's indispensability is enacted spatially is by situating her in the boardroom as Sanford's right-hand woman, a setting previously reserved for board members or rising young male executives. The script deals with this anomaly by having the discussion center more effectively around methods for promoting cosmetics in their advertising copy, a feminine concern necessitating the advice of a woman.

Stromberg is also the source of the redemption of Dave from a callow fellow who embezzles money, steals a car, and is banished to South America by Sanford to avoid imprisonment in Baldwin's version to an aspiring young man who counsels Whitey on the virtues of normative femininity, including home and children. By 12 April 1935 after reading Mahin's first script of two months earlier, the producer contemplates "altering Dave from a weak character to a strong one," adding that he would like to see her marry him.[108] By 4 May 1935, Stromberg had altered Dave from a thief to a "shoe clerk who dreams of someday encircling the globe with a chain of shoe stores. Dave, the one Jean finally marries in the end because she thinks it's only a question of time when he will be like 'her boss.'"[109] Whereas Baldwin's story was largely about the challenges faced by professional women, Stromberg shifts the emphasis to include both gender and class, replacing the original villain Dave with the villainous deeds of rich, gossiping women, and rendering this aspiring young man the film's moral conscience. When Whitey returns from the party at the Sanford residence, she finds the loyal Dave waiting in the car. He is understandably annoyed and he chastises righteously: "You see parties like tonight—and you see men like Sanford—millionaires. That spoils you, honey. . . . You'll get so you'll never want a home and kids and a husband until it's too late. . . . That's natural. What you're doing isn't."[110]

The story and film alike employ the skyscraper as the backdrop of quotidian business and a domestic locale in order to establish Sanford as a successful business titan. He commands a lofty business building that he owns and a penthouse apartment where he resides with his wife. The skyscraper office tower is described in the story as "active as a gentleman with a seven-day itch. It roared like a lion, and it hummed like a beehive. For this was the Sanford Building, which for two generations had housed Sanford publications [sic]." His residence is no less impressive: "Twenty stories above the world's most publicized Street, the Sanford dining room opened on a terrace not yet denuded of colorful bloom."[111]

The cinematic skyscraper penthouse apartment is employed as the site of a lavish anniversary party given by Mr. and Mrs. Stanhope in the film to celebrate eight years of marital felicity; it is stylishly rendered by art director Cedric Gibbons, who imbued the setting with classical elegance and the appropriate class-inflected accoutrements.[112] The penthouse is also employed to underline the Stanhopes' privileged life and the class aspirations of the secretary who is summoned to Stanhope's domestic space, thereby confounding the boundaries of public and private realms. Screenwriter Norman Krasna recommended deft cross-cutting from an underwear-clad Stanhope telephoning Whitey to a shot of her in slinky evening wear, which served as the embodiment of his unconscious intentions.[113] When she arrives at the gala affair, he whisks her up a grand staircase to a private room in the penthouse's second story, ostensibly to discuss business, a scene that is entirely absent from Baldwin's story, but laden with past associations of erotically charged, clandestine penthouse suites. In contrast to pre-Code variations, we are not permitted to view Stanhope and Whitey's business conference although we assume that they are on the up-and-up. But the implications are clear; the penthouse is embedded with traces of the illicit sexual encounter. A tracking shot of a string of leering men and suspicious women whose glances follow the couple at the party communicate the meeting's implications to the audience. Whitey has just been summoned from the crowded flat that she shares with her sibling and spouse, who argue continuously, to a party filled with wealthy luminaries of every persuasion, prompting her class envy. Her ascent of Stanhope's majestic stairway is also meant to imply the material possibilities of upward class mobility in exchange for sexual favors, although none actually occur.

The discovery of boss and secretary lodged in an office telephone booth by Stanhope's wife Linda and mother Mimi was put there by screenwriter Krasna. He is responsible for erotizing various scenes and their spatial analogues (bathhouse, automobile, skating rink), which serve to spice up the film without recourse to graphic detail. The telephone booth scene is meant to underline the meddlesomeness of leisured women, especially Mimi, whom Stromberg refers to as an "old meanie."[114] The necessity of phoning away from prying ears is ostensibly designed to keep an important business deal a secret, but anyone familiar with Harlow in *Red-Headed Woman* (1932) would have recognized the cinematic quotation. In the earlier film, Harlow plays an opportunistic clerical worker who is hell bent on wresting her boss from his upper-class wife, an ultimately successful feat that commences in a phone booth. Hence, when Stanhope and Whitey are revealed in the selfsame location, Stanhope's mother advises Linda to "get rid of that secretary at once."

The story blamed the Sanfords' temporary marital discord on the inappropriate actions of the husband/boss, who feels sympathy for his private secretary after she has been in an automobile accident. Rushing to her side at the hospital, he remains there for several hours, a gesture that is reported gleefully by the tabloids as "V. Sanford's Secretary Injured / Employer Leaves Dinner Guests and Rushes to Bedside."[115] This causes Linda and all concerned much embarrassment, which doesn't prevent Sanford from kissing Helen Walsh (Whitey in the film) when he returns for a second visit. Linda, who is also coincidentally visiting Walsh at the hospital, spots the incident from the corridor and leaves. When confronted about the episode later, Sanford claims that the kiss was only a sympathetic, platonic gesture, an explanation Linda is willing to accept. As the story progresses, it is Linda's liberality and reasonableness that prevail.

Baldwin's story pictured Sanford as a jealous, proprietary type, in contrast to his more reasonable wife. When he finds out that Walsh is lunching with an admirer, he offers thinly veiled advice that exposes his possessive nature: "Don't let the habit grow on you, Helen. It starts innocently enough. Lunch. Then it progresses to dinner, and after a while it's breakfast." While dining with his wife, he sees Helen and her date Dave Young at the same restaurant. Sanford is piqued. "I'd like to wring his neck!" he bursts out impulsively. To which Mrs. Sanford replies sagaciously, "Darling, you talk as if she were your unfaithful wife."[116]

Women are not only seen as irrepressible gossips in the film, but wives such as Linda Stanhope are so detached from the world of finance that they devolve into confusion at the slightest mention of pecuniary matters, which accentuates the rift between husband and wife, and wife and secretary. Mrs. Stanhope shows up at the office only twice, once on her way to lunch with her mother-in-law in tow and finally to salvage her marriage. The film promotes the idea that important business deals must be kept from women because of their naïveté and tendency to spread rumors. In contrast, Baldwin rendered Linda Sanford as intelligent and capable of understanding business even though her inquiries about Sanford's day at the office are often met with little or no reply. Her ignorance is due not to her inability to understand, but because "he doesn't tell her much," thereby shifting the blame to his incommunicable nature.[117]

The conclusion of Wife vs. Secretary reinforces Dave's pivotal role in the film. Whitey joins Stanhope in Havana, in order to clinch a deal because of crucial information she obtained inadvertently. Although he had promised to take his wife on a vacation, a business deal and an overzealous secretary interfere. Divorce thus seems imminent. Mrs. Stanhope telephones his hotel room at 2:00 a.m. after he forgets to call her, and Whitey answers, further provoking her already aroused suspicions. While it is true that boss and secretary have danced the night away to celebrate and are tempted to consummate their flirtation, they do not transgress any boundaries. Yet Linda disbelieves their innocence and decides to leave Stanhope, convinced that some untoward behavior has occurred. Just as she is about to embark on a cruise by herself, Linda is intercepted by Whitey who warns her that she will gladly accept her husband on the rebound. Mrs. Stanhope reconsiders and comes to trust her husband again, while Whitey leaves the building with Dave. Domestic felicity is restored, and a renewed commitment between Dave and Whitey ensues as they drive off together, leaving the skyscraper in the distance. The extreme long shot from above and the nocturnal lighting lend the scene a romantic finality, signaling their departure from the work-a-day world of the city. We are not certain when they will marry. Stromberg changed his mind yet again, preferring to let the audience make their own inferences, but Dave's didactic speech delivered earlier in the film leaves little doubt that Whitey is poised to heed the wisdom of his words.[118]

Baldwin believed instead that the solution to the marital discord lay in the friendship of wife and secretary, who had different but crucial roles to play in Van Sanford's life. Linda is not a sniveling wife bent on divorce in the story; instead, she strides confidently into Helen's office in order to work out their differences. "Are you in love with my husband?" she inquires forthrightly, to which Helen replies, "No. I don't know your husband. But I am in love with my boss." She leads Linda to an open doorway where she can see Sanford negotiating aggressively an impending deal, and Linda finally admits that she is wholly unfamiliar with this side of him. Helen reassures her that she is not after her husband, but simply wishes to bask in his glory. Both agree that they will hang on to their respective jobs, and they shake hands to cement the deal. The story ends with the Sanfords setting off on a long-awaited vacation, with tickets purchased with Helen's assistance. Linda invites Helen to see them off, but not before they all lunch together. The Sanfords embark on their journey, while the chauffeur asks Helen where she would like to go. She answers definitively, "I thought you knew. To the office, of course."[119] The story is about the cooperative spirit of women who initially distrust each other, whereas the film is about female gossip and competition, which threaten to undermine both marriage and business. The female bachelor of Baldwin's tale is replaced by Whitey who finally capitulates to the conservative ideological intent of the film, that marriage and class realignment are the only ways for women to attain happiness rather than through status-seeking and professionalism.

SECRETARIES FIGHT BACK

The production of "sexational" dramas such as *Skyscraper Souls* or the formulaic depictions of the office triangle theme that eroticized cinematic skyscraper space were often produced with female viewers in mind.[120] The *Film Daily* described *Wife vs. Secretary* in the following terms: "With Clark Gable, Jean Harlow, and Myrna Loy in a story, which should appeal to the millions of office and shop girls who picture themselves as the Harlows and the wives who imagine themselves to be the Loys, this picture should hit the box office in a big way."[121] These films adhere in part to the genre that has been labeled "women's film" in their inclusion of prominent female protagonists and their purposeful address to female viewers.[122] Not only did these films provide the requisite romantic angle believed to be preferable to women, but they sought to fashion an image of an urban working woman that would appeal to the so-called flapper trade.[123]

There has been some debate concerning the preponderance of a female viewing audience in film scholarship. Accepting the idea that large female audiences affected studio practices has led some film historians to conclude that the attendance figures, themselves problematic, suggest that women preferred salacious subject matter.[124] In contrast, film historians such as Kuhn, Doane, and Hansen have argued that there is a difference between the female spectator constructed by the studios and the empirical female movie attendee, and between the feminine subject position, both within the film and those addressed by the film, and the female audience as a numerical entity.[125] Recently, Melvyn Stokes has partially resolved the matter by providing preliminary, impressionistically gathered statistics from newspapers, the trade press, and industry surveys that claimed that approximately 51–83 percent of audience members were women in the 1920s and 1930s. Stokes concludes that the numbers collectively support the idea of the preponderance of female customers but, more important, convinced the studios that women audience members' putative tastes required serious consideration.[126] All argue that women audiences should not be viewed as a homogeneous entity but need to be studied with regard to their class affiliations, demographics, and age, among other factors, thereby avoiding the stereotyping and universalizing of female tastes so characteristic of the trade press and the studios, which assumed that women preferred romance, weepies, and seduction plots.[127] As Stokes claims, "Very few scholars have as yet examined what women movie goers really made of the films they attended or how they responded to the discourse of consumerism that accompanied such films."[128]

At least two groups of women found the skyscraper/office romance films deeply troubling, thereby reinserting female voices at the level of reception, which had been expurgated in the filmic adaptations of Baldwin's fiction. The authors of advice literature for working and professional women and secretaries and clerical employees alike adopted what cultural critic bel hooks terms an "oppositional gaze," dismissing current cinematic delineations of the office as hotbeds of romance as "chiefly mythical."[129] While a discussion of their responses does not possess the rigors of scientific audience research, which was largely absent from the industry at this time, it does provide a partial understanding of how several groups of women resisted the depictions of themselves

in cinema, thereby supporting the notion that women were more active spectators than has generally been assumed.

In at least two books offering advice to job-seeking women, the subject of sex
was deemed so important that separate chapters entitled "Sex in Business" and
"The Love Motif" were included to refute popular cultural depictions in favor
of sound information for female employees on how to comport themselves in
an appropriate manner.[130] A secretary named Gladys Torson complained in the
Saturday Evening Post: "The movies have led people to believe that all secretaries work for titans of finance, handsome romantic fellows, usually married but
never understood by their wives. . . . The picture presented is not true."[131] Another quipped, "This sort of ogling-with-a-national-circulation . . . contains . . .
the fatuous belief of nonworking perennial adolescents that women are kept in
offices for the same reason that women are kept in harems."[132] In the book *She
Strives to Conquer,* Maule commented specifically on two recent films:

> According to the movies and to the popular romantic novels
> about "skyscraper souls" and "office wives," the natural and
> appointed destiny of every business girl is to marry the boss—
> which is for the most part fiction pure and simple. Persons who
> ought to know better do, however, seem to think that every girl
> goes to business with the idea that she *will* marry the boss.[133]

The title of another article, "Romance versus the Boss," demonstrates that the
author, a secretary named Marjorie Holmes Mighell, had seen the film *Wife vs.
Secretary* and had decided to replace the premise of female competition for the
boss's attention, which had never been part of her own experience, with the
idea that bosses and romances were incongruous.[134]

Office Romeos and flirtatious male superiors who preyed upon their attractive female subordinates was the most widely contested aspect of cinematic depictions of skyscraper office space by businesswomen. Although some writers
acknowledged that offices might have sexual undercurrents in isolated cases,
the vast majority of female employees claimed that the existence of office dalliances couldn't be further from the truth. Mighell, who began her career as a
secretary at the age of fifteen, described six different bosses she had worked
for, including a conceited and corpulent big mouth, a Presbyterian elder with
a mania for orderliness, a temperamental young man, a disorganized gentleman
with a gargantuan appetite, a fresh-air fiend, and an avuncular cardiologist,
none of whom had ever made a pass at her. For her part, she found these men
unappealing on both a physical and an emotional level. In spite of the fact that
she was required to cater to their various idiosyncrasies, she was pleased to
keep her professional relations with them confined to the office. She asserted,
"It is my firm conviction that the average employer and the average female office

attendant are inordinately glad to see the last of each other at the close of the day, fiction and motion pictures to the contrary not withstanding."[135] Most secretaries and purveyors of professional advice concurred, often describing the boss as bald, pudgy, and undesirable, not someone a young secretary would be interested in.

The relationship of female clerical employees to boss's wives was also considered but with an emphasis not found in films, fiction, or tabloid headlines. Because the relationship between secretaries and spouses was rendered as a source of continuous travail, secretaries and wives were encouraged to be pro-

What a let-down! That first boss was plump, jowly, pudgy-fingered, insipidly mustached, losing his hair

Romance versus the boss: cartoon by Charles Dunn, from Nation's Business *25 (August 1937): 21.*

active, by reaching out to one another to avoid potential conflict. In her book *Manners in Business* (1936), MacGibbon observed that "the famous triangle, the man, the wife, and the secretary, would reach the front pages less often if home women and business women could only understand each other better." She recommended that they dispel preconceived notions and stereotypes: "When a wife calls at the office, she usually acts as if she thought the women working there were either servants or sirens, when actually they are neither." Similarly, the businesswoman is also mistaken about the boss's wife, whom she views as a women of leisure, a typecast no doubt gleaned from movies, "Pretty soft, to sit around doing nothing all day while her husband works to buy her pretty clothes and automobiles!"[136] An article written specifically for the wives of bosses advises them to be more considerate of their husbands' secretaries by refraining from unfounded jealousy; after all, these women are not "petticoat Machiavellis."[137] Assigning them extraneous, personal tasks, such as checking a grocery bill or exchanging Junior's underwear, is also frowned upon. "She is probably so busy that she doesn't want to double as The Other Woman—fiction to the contrary—any more than she wants to double as his governess, your errand girl, your nursery maid, or your willy-nilly guest."[138] By the same token, secretaries are encouraged to bridge the gap with wives by discussing common interests such as childrearing and recipes to defuse the idea that their primary goal is to vamp their husbands.

Imitating the glamorous presentations of a Jean Harlow, Loretta Young, or Maureen O'Sullivan was also frowned upon by those seeking to ensure female success in the office. Instead of the theatrical makeup worn by actresses, which was clearly in the minds of those offering advice, most manuals recommended a more subdued application of cosmetics so as to avoid looking tawdry. Loire Brophy included a chapter entitled "Dress Your Role" in her book *If Women Must Work* (1936), in which she cautioned readers not to "allow the faint and glamorous image of your favorite movie star queen to hover in that glass and suggest what you think about yourself." The author described a secretary who had the look all wrong. "She had on a dress which hit a new high in extreme style. . . . She was made up as if she were about to appear before the footlights. . . . She had so overdressed the part."[139] Others warned likewise: "The girls who are making such desperate efforts to acquire Garbo-esque eyebrows had much better save themselves the pain of plucking."[140] As an alternative, Brophy recommended "a conservative, natural daytime make-up," which excluded the "exotic and artificial type." A secretary who worked for a judge concurred: "Clothes—so important to that feminine vanity which we have to submerge in most other instances. We must be tailored and well groomed in good, *right* clothes that make us look our best . . . but toned down to the conservative background effect we must create."[141] Some were more specific, recommending dresses that were in dark or subdued colors, simple in line, and devoid of baubles, bows, and frills so as not to stop men in the elevator or cause a commotion among the other female employees.[142] While most concurred that bosses were interested in competence rather than beauty and sartorial appearance, given the choice of a well-dressed attractive woman or an ill-kept homely type, bosses would opt for the looker.

It is worth remarking how films conformed to current ideologies concerning secretarial labor and the "proper" way that romance should be handled in the office. What films did get right was that secretaries were expected to serve as boss's wives in every other area save sex, echoing the gendered expectations that characterized both wives and secretaries in 1930s America. Rae Chatfield Ayer, a married secretary, claimed, no doubt from her own experience, that "a good secretary plays much the same role in an office as a woman in the home." She facilitates matters, "smoothes down rough corners, acts as a thoughtful hostess to her husband's callers. In other words—she 'keeps' his office household in an efficient, pleasant manner."[143] A host of other secretaries and job experts joined the chorus, "A secretary's job is a strange job. It is closer to wifehood than any other job in the business world." In order to be proficient, "a secretary must be unendingly and unobtrusively cooperative, loyal, sympathetic, admiring. For eight hours a day she's her employer's background and 'builder-upper.'"[144]

If romance was to ensue in the business arena, professional writers advising women asserted that these should be between employees of similar rank and station, which echoed the prescriptive endings of the majority of skyscraper office films. This strategy was recommended for several reasons. First, by accepting or initiating a social invitation with an office superior, secretaries would inevitably be perceived as garnering favoritism among their peers, which would engender resentment and instability in the office environment, resulting in decreased productivity. Maule, who entitled one of her chapters "Stepping Out," was adamant on this point: "a girl may not make any social advances to an office superior—either male or female—either inside or outside the office," and if the boss did so, it was obligatory for his wife to be in attendance. The author continued with an additional caveat, flying in the face of cinematic renditions, "You may stay at the office and work alone with your chief late into the night; you might travel with him to Timbuctoo—as long as you are not seen dining with him in an evening dress or otherwise going out with him socially."[145]

The privations occasioned by the Great Depression may have also prompted advice givers to caution women against being covetous of material possessions outside their means and class stations. MacGibbon acknowledged that women understandably longed for the class privileges of the boss's wife because of her intimate knowledge of his tastes in the way of theater tickets and custom-made clothing, since she did so many of his private errands. Nevertheless, it was important to keep these desires in check, by realizing that thirty years ago he was probably considerably less well off.[146]

Depression-era films and instructional books advised women to seek ro-mance only with men of equal station instead of with superiors, if at all. Indeed a secretary could accept any social invitation that she wanted with a "young man of her own office rank." MacGibbon had a few trepidations concerning office romances; she was of the opinion that businesswomen should avoid them in favor of impersonal relationships with male coworkers, thereby obviating gossip and messy breakups. She conceded that sometimes love affairs were in-escapable; and if this were the case, they should be "between people who are of practically the same rank."[147] The filmic denouements of *Big Business Girl, Skyscraper Souls,* and *Wife vs. Secretary,* among others, coincided with these recommendations, perhaps because of their appeal to lower- and middle-class audiences experiencing the harsh economic realities of the Depression. Rich men and women were rendered chiefly as greedy villains in most films of the 1930s, hence fraternizing with them would occasion resentment by associa-tion. In order to guarantee the entertainment values of these films, the studios set up hypothetical temptations and vicarious enjoyments, so that the public could ultimately renounce status-seeking greed in favor of an adherence to class confederates and homespun values, much like the class-inflected instructions offered to female clerical staff in the skyscraper office.[148]

In Depression-era cinema, the skyscraper is frequently rendered as a nefari-ous emblem of the economic debacle, perpetrator of greed, economic exploita-tion, and sexual predation. Once a symbol of lofty aspiration and individual initiative, the tall office building is regarded as a product of wanton egotism and speculation after the stock market crash. In accord with its evil denizens, its grandeur was viewed as a dissembling facade to an inner world marked by entrapment and profligate sexuality. Actual megalopolitan skyscrapers (e.g., the Empire State Building) were often mined by the studios for their luxurious ac-coutrements, if not literally as in the film *Counsellor at Law* then figuratively. To these location films were added fictional adaptations by set designers such as Cedric Gibbons from a host of sources, both skyscraper and otherwise, to augment themes of debauchery. Cinematic tall buildings were atomized sub-jectively to highlight various sites of exploitation; hyperbolized penthouses, opulent suites, and bathhouses, among others, were embedded with the taint of illicit behavior. These multifaceted dens of iniquity were the settings of moral-ity tales that discouraged class rise while promoting an adherence to one's con-federates and a return to one's traditional gender position. Luxurious settings provided the requisite entertainment value before the ineluctable return to a life of homespun values and hard work.

These spaces acted on and were acted upon by the diverse class and gen-der types that were marshaled in the service of the films' prescriptive conclu-sions. Various gender categories from corrupt bosses to mid-level clerks, from fallen women to New Women are seen in relational terms to reinforce the ideal variants. Hence, while bosses may temporarily enjoy the privilege and lavish accommodations of penthouse suites, these spaces lead ultimately to their demise. On the other hand, middle-class Joes are seen as the only ones capable of toppling the proverbial apple cart or undermining the seemingly intractable power structure in favor of a redeemed patriarchal space controlled by the little people. Women are poised to renounce temptation and materiality and capitulate to the moral homilies voiced by their Joes; their implied return to the domestic sphere is a foregone conclusion.

One may ask why the studios were offering up this type of fare. It seems commonsensical that unemployed men or those suffering from the privations of the Depression did not wish to view the paeans of individual initiative given their own feelings of disempowerment. The studios did not desire to alienate their male audiences by pointing to their implied failure. In accord with contemporary New Deal murals that featured muscular men rebuilding the nation, the films sought to instill a feeling of hope in the future by promoting a class-based manly instrumentality. Yet the depiction of women in these films is more complicated. Because of the marriage bar instituted by private corporations and the firing of the female member of a married couple when both were in the employ of the federal government, women were the first economic casualties of the Depression. This echoes previous paternalistic corporate economic strategies in which women were paid less, rationalized by the false premise that they regarded their employment as a temporary way station. Although the New Woman is rendered as a competent professional in cinematic space, her attractiveness and sexuality are seen as detriments to her success, and her aspirations are viewed as unnatural. The fallen woman and the office drones who also share her environs underscore that the studios wished to characterize all manners of the female presence in skyscraper offices as somewhat abnormal.

The distorted depiction of female labor in cinematic space is underscored by two unorthodox strategies I have sought. By contrasting the original texts for these films written by Faith Baldwin to their cinematic adaptations, one realizes that some women did not concur with the latter depictions of female office labor; their voices had been hijacked by the studio apparatus and its retinue of cultural producers. Censorship had occurred in an egregious manner before the official censors ever saw the script, resulting in a skewed spatiality. Additionally, a class of women, namely pink-collar workers, viewed these films as gross distortions of their tasks, physical appearance, and office space, which was not to them a hotbed of illicit sexual activity. By giving voice to both Baldwin and actual secretaries, I have sought to create phantasmic films, or alternative cinematic spaces, in order to shed light on the manner in which skyscraper space was ideologically configured in Depression-era cinema.

THREE

Masculine Heroes, Modernism, and Political Ideology in *The Fountainhead* and *The Big Clock*

The director King Vidor and the novelist Ayn Rand collaborated to create *The Fountainhead* (1949), based on Rand's 1943 best-selling novel, a film in which modernist skyscraper architecture and a tough, austere masculinity mutually promoted the author's political ideology.[1] During the writing of the novel, Rand was an ardent supporter of the Republican Party. The author even took off seven months from her literary endeavors in 1940 to work on the Wendell Willkie campaign during his presidential bid to unseat Franklin Delano Roosevelt, viewing this particular election as a battle between the New Deal and the very survival of the capitalist system.[2] In the early years of the cold war and the making of the film, Rand was part of the extreme right wing of American politics. Rand, Vidor, and Gary Cooper, who played the hero Howard Roark, were members of the Motion Picture Alliance for the Preservation of American Ideals, an organization that invited the infamous House Un-American Activities Committee (HUAC) to Hollywood to help them rout out Communists from the film industry.

In 1948, the novel *The Big Clock* (1946) by Communist Party fellow traveler Kenneth Fearing, also a modernist poet and pulp-fiction writer, was adapted to the cinema.[3] The screen version by the popular mystery writer Jonathan Latimer was dissimilar to Fearing's novel but nevertheless preserved the latter's depiction of corporate America as a crushing mechanical bureaucracy.[4] Despite their political differences, Rand the conservative and Fearing the leftist employed skyscraper space as a hotly contested terrain in which a battle is waged for individual freedom against corrupt values, played out by vast media conglomerates bent on social control. Both films were also decidedly conservative in their construction of gender and sexual identity, resulting in the virile hero's reconquest of the skyscraper that symbolized "American territory" from the hands of effete, feminized men with foreign accents (aliens from within),

thereby restoring heterosexual masculinity and an individualist, entrepreneurial spirit that had suffered a setback during the Depression. For Rand, the
skyscraper was a heroic monument, an icon of individual genius and capitalist
progress, whereas Fearing and Latimer rendered it as a devouring behemoth
that subjected workers to prison-like regulation.

The gender identities of heroes Howard Roark (Gary Cooper) and George
Stroud (Ray Milland) are represented by visual and thematic images of male
power. Roark is an iconoclastic architect who creates skyscrapers for uncompromising patrons by drawing on his personal genius or "I," which Rand
signified by visual analogues such as drills and lofty modernist buildings, while
Stroud's tall, lean physique is matched by a superior intellect, which he employs to outsmart his adversaries. In accord with earlier films, the characters'
gendered bodies, personalities, and the manner in which they negotiate space
are linked to architectural styles, discreet skyscraper components (e.g., offices,
boardrooms, lobbies), and the mise-en-scène in order to buttress each film's political agenda.

Rand constructed part of her tale as a struggle between historical, traditional idioms (e.g., Beaux-Arts and Rococo) and a utilitarian modernism, while
Fearing's story was situated in a labyrinthine, entrapping modernist skyscraper.
Architectural modernism's appropriateness for symbolizing American values
was at issue in both *The Fountainhead* and *The Big Clock*. For Rand, it was a
sign of freedom against outworn idioms and the embodiment of reason and
efficiency, while Fearing viewed modernist architecture as a cold, impersonal
prison that spelled conformity masquerading as corporate independence. The
films' opposing stances concerning the legitimacy of the International Style in
America were indicative of the parallel debates being waged by the architectural profession. Joan Ockman has recently pointed out that the International
Style "as developed in the corporate and aesthetic framework of postwar
America explicitly embodied the values of *technocracy*—the ethos of rationalism, bureaucracy, and technoscientific progress on which both big business and
government were predicated."[5] Others such as Mumford and Wright viewed
the style as the epitome of a mechanical foreign importation that resulted in
an artificial, constricted existence. These differing views underscore how the
International Style skyscraper was cast as politicized territory that was poised
to epitomize American capitalist principles, a physical and ideological space in
the aftermath of World War II. A battle ensued in which gendered actors fought
for ideological hegemony, for "ideal" gender positions and sexual identities,
and "appropriate" architectural idioms to represent their aims. Despots, fifth
columnists, fascist infiltrators, scenes of destruction and death, attest to the
war's continued relevance for the delineation of the tall office building and its
role during the cold war.

Even though both Rand and Fearing utilized the seemingly benign, entertaining venues of pulp fiction and Hollywood melodrama to tell their tales, they also wished to disseminate propaganda to the mass audience. Writing to one of her conservative allies, Rand intoned, "I want . . . the ideas of this book to be spread all over the country. When you read it, you'll see what an indictment of the New Deal it is." To combat what she perceived as a leftist hegemony, she chose to circulate her capitalist credo, "as the Reds do . . . in the form of fiction."[6] Fearing likewise wished "to write about the people and events of this time and this place, through imaginary characters and transposed circumstances," characterizing *The Big Clock* as a story that took place on "the eve of the first coup staged by the Americaneers in and with a world of communication already moribund." Writing a few years after the film, he characterized the American mass media as a conspiratorial alliance between Pennsylvania and Madison Avenues, which resulted in the excesses of "The Investigation" launched by McCarthy and his cronies.[7] As he told his editor, "the novel is apt to be received merely as an action murder mystery. . . . This was the last thing in mind when I wrote the book."[8]

RAND'S ARCHITECTURAL SOURCES: AN INTRODUCTION

Rand's architectural research belies the pulp designation of her novel and screenplay. By her own admission, Rand knew little about architecture in general and the history of the skyscraper in particular when she began *The Fountainhead,* a deficiency that she sought to remedy with earnest and extended research.[9] With the help of a lengthy bibliography prepared for her by the New York Public Library staff and one obtained from the journal *Architect's World,* she commenced her study.[10] The first annotated bibliography prepared by the library, dated 18 March 1936, was divided into categories consisting of sources on the history of architecture, modernist architecture (especially the skyscraper), the architectural profession, and biographies of important architects, next to which she placed Xs for the fifteen books that she probably read.[11] Like her main character Howard Roark, she supplemented her academic pursuits with practical knowledge, which included a two-month internship in the office of New York architect Ely Jacques Kahn who is known for skyscrapers and housing projects alike. The position paid off. It provided her with information on the day-to-day operations of a major architectural firm and enabled her to visit construction sites. Her careful research and hands-on experience inspired professionals and the common person alike: the novel was a wartime best seller and continues to enjoy cult status. As architectural critic Edward Gunts has pointed out, "It is a testament to Ayn Rand's writing that many architects vividly remember what they were doing when they first read *The Fountainhead*."[12]

The bibliographies Rand used included pivotal modernist texts by practitioners such as Le Corbusier, Frank Lloyd Wright, and Louis Sullivan; architectural historians and critics such as Lewis Mumford, Sheldon Cheney, and Nikolaus Pevsner; and builders Alfred Bossom and the Starrett Brothers, among others.[13] She was not simply a passive reader; rather she made lengthy notes that reveal her interest in history, aesthetics, criticism, and the architectural profession, which she employed in the service of her gender-inflected character delineation, plot construction, and for the depiction of specific buildings. For example, she used her skyscraper research in general and her study of the Empire State Building in particular in the portrayal of the Wynand Building, the tallest in the world, which its newspaper baron refers to as "the greatest and the last."[14]

As important as her study of tall buildings was her research on public housing, which she employed for her critique of government-subsidized housing, the architectural nemesis of the novel that is destroyed by Roark. Her perspective reflected minority views on public housing articulated in the periodical *Architectural Forum* of 1938, which coincided with many of the attacks Rand employed in the novel and the screenplay. The periodical's inflammatory accusations that the poor were being awarded "good homes at the expense of the middle class" and that public housing was synonymous with socialism were arguments that resonated with her merit-based, individualist credo.[15] The architectural showdown between the preeminent Wynand Building and government-sponsored dwellings at the end of the novel, which Rand used to signify the battle between unfettered capitalism and New Deal policies, must be seen in light of debates that raged during the Depression concerning the efficacy of public housing.[16]

RAND'S EARLY FILM AND LITERARY CAREER

Rand's life and early career provide insight into her abiding love of skyscrapers and the values she believed they represented. She was born Alisa Rosenbaum in 1905 in St. Petersburg, Russia. As she recalled, her father was a deeply principled man whose "strongest issue was individualism" and reason.[17] The ravages of World War I on Russia, including mass military desertions, rampant inflation, and violence, left the country ripe for revolution. At first Rand supported the 1917 abdication of the czar in favor of the Kerensky regime, which she associated with democracy.[18] However, after the triumph of the Bolsheviks, her father's shop was nationalized and her family experienced a series of hardships and privations. The stinging humiliation of watching her father's possessions confiscated prompted her desire to emigrate. When Chicago relatives who had fled earlier wrote the family in 1925, Rand began a correspondence with them, resulting in her arrival to the United States a year later, at the age of twenty-one.

Rand began her career as a writer and a cinema enthusiast during her college days in the newly formed Soviet Union, where she studied performance and screenwriting at the prestigious State Institute for Cinematography in Leningrad. While still in Russia, she published film reviews and essays on American cinema.[19] She was especially taken by the cinematic views of urban America, often viewing movies several times just to get a glimpse of the New York skyline. After a few months in Chicago, she arrived in Manhattan in 1926, at the height of the skyscraper building boom, and resolved to write a novel that would "infect my readers with my love of New York."[20] She recalled one building, probably Cass Gilbert's Woolworth Tower (1911–13), then the tallest in the world, "ablaze like the finger of God," and "the greatest example of *free men*."[21]

Her love of metropolitan New York and its tall office buildings mirrored the American enthusiasm for modernity that characterized the decade.[22] A popular exhibition of 1925 was *The Titan City: New York* at the Wanamaker department store, which featured depictions of dramatically illuminated skyscrapers by the architectural renderer Hugh Ferriss. The Chicago Tribune Tower Competition (1923) produced an array of original skyscraper designs, which generated an enthusiastic public response when they were exhibited throughout the country. The decade also witnessed Paul Frankl's skyscraper furniture, John Alden Carpenter's ballet *Skyscrapers* (1928), and Margaret Bourke-White's sublime urban photographs of business and industry in *Fortune* magazine.

Rand moved to Hollywood late in 1926 and secured a job as a junior screenwriter for the director Cecil B. DeMille. One of her initial assignments, and a precursor to *The Fountainhead,* is her screenplay for Dudley Murphy's short story "The Skyscraper" (1927), which melded her love of cinema with a powerful expression of urban optimism.[23] Altering Murphy's original intent, Rand chose the heroism of the skyscraper as her primary focus. The main character, Howard Kane, is commissioned to build the tallest and most unusual skyscraper in the world for a newspaper owner. While engaged in the project, he falls in love with a burlesque dancer and ultimately saves the skyscraper from a disastrous fire. The story fuses illicit eroticism with masculine ingenuity and courage, themes Rand later expanded upon in *The Fountainhead*. Murphy's and Rand's final scene in "The Skyscraper" features a triumphant architect standing atop his monumental building, dramatizing his epic achievement, a scene that was employed in her later novel and Vidor's film.

THE FOUNTAINHEAD: NOVEL AND FILM

Rand began her first novel set in the United States in 1935, in the middle of the Depression, and completed it in 1943, at the height of World War II. Originally entitled *Second-Hand Lives,* it was rejected by twelve publishers before being accepted by Bobbs-Merrill.[24] Archie Ogden, an editor there, wrote in his review of the manuscript: "Some of the best parts . . . deal with architecture—for architecture is as much a character of the plot as Roark. She makes architecture seem vital, even to the layman. You get a feel of the buildings . . . without any technical knowledge on the part of the reader."[25]

The book established her reputation as a writer. Although it was either ignored or dismissed by most reviewers—responses Rand attributed to a partisan leftist press—its popularity spread by word of mouth, and it soon appeared on the *New York Times* best-seller list.[26] Warner Bros. bought the rights to the film in 1943, but because of the war did not begin production until 1948. The contract stipulated that Rand come to Hollywood and write a preliminary script; Warner Bros. liked what she produced and commissioned her to complete it. In return, Rand demanded that no part of the script be altered without her permission, an accomplishment in an industry where novelists often lost control of their original product's meaning. In contrast to Faith Baldwin's book *Skyscraper* (1931) and her story "Wife versus Secretary" (1935), Rand's intentions were strictly adhered to. She condensed the almost seven-hundred-page magnum opus, omitting extraneous detail and strengthening her thesis. Perhaps the most significant change from the original was Roark himself: in the book, he is an architect who undertakes a variety of commissions; in the film, he prefers skyscrapers to all other buildings.

The film pits the iconoclastic individualist Roark against a corrupt profession whose cronyism and bureaucratic practices spawned mediocre, historicist buildings. Roark's confrontation with architectural conservatism loosely mirrored the career of Frank Lloyd Wright, whose innovative architecture and heroic, uncompromising personality Rand admired. The battle is couched in elevated ideological and moral terms: a mediocre, stylistically retrogressive building is not merely aesthetically objectionable, but constitutes a moral affront to democratic institutions. Group decision-making (synonymous in her mind with collectivism) forced architects to produce retrograde architectural styles that were antithetical to modernism, which she averred. In accord with many early modernists like Sullivan and Wright, she considered originality essential to good design, although like Wright, she rejected the International Style as cold and rigid.

The modernist Roark is expelled from the architectural academy for his refusal to design conventional buildings with historical referents. Undeterred and idealistic, he locates and apprentices himself to the once-prominent pioneer skyscraper architect Henry Cameron (Henry Hull), now a cantankerous alcoholic, who has been broken down and marginalized by the profession. After Cameron's death, Roark sets out on his own, but his refusal to capitulate to the philistine tastes of juries and corporate boards reduces him to poverty. Instead, he chooses manual labor in a stone quarry—honest, manly work—and encounters the wealthy scion and frustrated dilettante Dominique Francon (Patricia

Neal). She also tries to bend him to her will but is herself ravished by his determination and independent spirit and falls in love with him instead. Although their relationship is marked by mutual competition, his indomitable will ultimately triumphs over her fatalistic attitude. Meanwhile, Roark earns the support of an enlightened businessman, Roger Enright (Ray Collins), who hires him to design a high-rise apartment building, the first of several commissions from independent, forward-looking patrons.

In an act of rebellion and defeatism, Francon marries newspaper magnate Gail Wynand (Raymond Massey; modeled after William Randolph Hearst) rather than Roark, whom she believes will be crushed, like Cameron, by the forces of mediocrity. Roark soon encounters his adversary, a powerful newspaper columnist who defines public standards of taste, the effete and nefarious Ellsworth Toohey (Robert Douglas). Like an insidious mole, he writes for Wynand's newspaper *The Banner,* in which he supports the revivalist architecture that Rand repudiated. Toohey begins a smear campaign to discredit Roark in the paper, at the same time that Wynand hires him to design his private residence. Eventually realizing that Toohey's vindictive editorials have all but destroyed Roark's reputation, Wynand tries to undo the damage but succumbs instead to a board of directors who encourage compromise during a newspaper strike instigated by Toohey. Although Toohey has successfully overtaken *The Banner,* Wynand's last act of courage is to commission Roark to build a skyscraper as a testament to his person and empire, while destroying his corrupt newspaper empire.

Throughout the story, the ideological battle between individualism and collectivism is played out between Roark and Toohey. A major housing project commission called Cortlandt Homes is awarded to Roark's former classmate, the once-successful architect Peter Keating (Kent Smith), a Toohey prodigy who is now down on his luck. Unable to complete the job, he enlists Roark to ghost-design the buildings with the latter's stipulation that no part of his original design be altered. Upon his return from a vacation with Wynand, Roark discovers that the impotent Keating has allowed a government committee to impose incongruent historical features onto his experimental modernist design. For Roark there is only one solution: to blow up Cortlandt Homes. He does this with the help of Francon, who has finally come over to his side. Roark is subsequently arrested for vandalism and is acquitted after a rousing courtroom speech in which he equates his actions with the issues at stake during the war: the fight for individualism and democracy against fascism and collectivism, themes that would resonate anew during the cold war. After the trial and Wynand's suicide, Roark completes the ultimate in skyscraper design, the Wynand Building, a monument to the newspaper baron and a celebration of private enterprise, his answer to federally subsidized housing projects.

THE MAKING AND RECEPTION OF THE FILM

Rand was gratified that the film was made by Warner Bros., a studio that she believed had been purged of Communists. She wrote somewhat anxiously to a friend, Isabel Paterson, "King Vidor . . . is said to be a conservative."[27] For his part, Vidor carefully read and annotated the novel, in order to remain faithful to Rand's prescriptive directorial intentions, rendering them virtual codirectors of the film. In one of his many notes made on his copy of the novel, he wrote, "Roark's arch [sic]—important as foundation for the story."[28] Rand also liked the choice of Gary Cooper for the lead role because of his conservatism.[29]

Much to Rand's chagrin, her ideological intentions were not appreciated by the majority of reviewers. Most characterized Roark not as an exemplar of democratic principles, but as an "egocentric architect whose monomania was 'Modernism,'" thereby identifying his quest as self-serving and his process as dictatorial.[30] Tom Criley went even further, lambasting the ideas in the film as "only a little less fascist than *Mein Kampf.*"[31] Critics were also disturbed by Roark's destruction of the housing project, which was viewed as a socially irresponsible act of vandalism of the most odious sort. In the years after World War II, a severe housing shortage had made public housing and slum clearance popular federal programs. Bosley Crowther of the *New York Times* inquired rhetorically, "Dismissing the first consideration that he has willfully destroyed property, we ask by what moral reasoning his act can be justified? Others have rights, including the right to protect themselves against cheats and dishonest people."[32] Rand answered Crowther and other detractors, crediting Warner Bros. for faithfully adapting her script. Rationalizing Roark's destructive act, she stated,

> Man has an inalienable right to his own convictions and his own work . . . neither forcing his ideas upon others nor submitting to force, violence or breach of contract . . . the only proper form of relationship between men is free exchange and voluntary choice.[33]

Critics leveled their most intense opprobrium at the film's architectural set designs, which they believed added to its lack of credibility, since one of its major themes concerned an architect-genius, and more generally the triumph of individual accomplishment over collective mediocrity. The architect George Nelson characterized several of the sets as technical impossibilities and blatant examples of plagiarism. He noted that Roark's Wright-inspired house had no fewer than three cantilevered overhangs and no evidence of structural support for its balcony. A factory that lacked visible windows was accused of having been "cribbed from the Chicago 1933 Fair."[34] Even though these criticisms were directed ostensibly at the film's set designers, they demonstrated that the film was at cross purposes with its intended message. They implied that its main protagonist was incapable of constructing technically sound, original buildings, which likened him to the secondhand practitioners and copyists of Rand's critique. Rand herself privately concurred. While she appreciated Vidor's efforts and the faithful translation of her script, she confided to a friend that she did not "like the sets at all."[35] Some of Carrere's designs were influenced by Wright's work while others were adaptations of International Style modernism, which Rand found cold and conformist in spirit.

WORKING-CLASS MASCULINITY, LEWIS HINE, AND THE CONSTRUCTION OF THE EMPIRE STATE BUILDING

Central to the book and the film is the equation of the skyscraper with male heterosexual virility, which was employed as a metaphor for health, freedom, and democracy. Since Rand began the novel *The Fountainhead* during the Depression and completed it during the war, Roark's masculinity must be viewed against a backdrop of male disenfranchisement and subsequent empowerment through military mobilization. Because masculinity in America was predicated on work and instrumentality, Depression-era unemployment occasioned pervasive feelings of male self-doubt. The businessman and the go-getter, often represented by Henry Ford, were special favorites of Rand. In a letter to Tom Girdler, a likeminded manufacturer and the founder of Republic Steel, she praised heroic inventors and entrepreneurs: "It is true that the real benefactors of mankind have been the creative, productive men. No humanitarian ever has or can equal the benefits men received from a Thomas Edison or a Henry Ford."[36]

There has always been a tension between the aspiring businessman and the worker as American masculine ideal types, between the heroic individual and the rugged team player. In the 1930s, the self-made man represented earlier by well-dressed Harold Lloyd was often replaced by the worker, a revival of the nineteenth-century "heroic artisan," who was promoted as an antidote to effete snobbery and the feminization of American culture.[37] In numerous New Deal murals commissioned by Roosevelt's Works Progress Administration, Herculean men performing cooperative manual tasks served as visual propaganda to instill feelings of hope in the face of rampant unemployment.[38] Roark encompasses both varieties of masculinity, combining the singular vision and creativity of the inventor/entrepreneur with the physical strength and virtue of the artisanal laborer.

Lewis Hine's book *Men at Work* (1932), a photographic chronicle of the Empire State Building's construction, offered some of the first Depression-era images to shift the visual emphasis away from disembodied machines to workers, serving as a prototype for Rand's and Vidor's depiction of Roark.[39] Unlike his earlier socially conscious photographs, which served as sharp indictments of corporate exploitation, in these images, Hine resolved to document the positive side of labor at a time, ironically, when the worker "was as underprivileged as the kid in the mill."[40] Thus, he dedicated his book to all the "men of courage, skill, daring and imagination." "Cities do not build themselves," he declared, "unless back of them all are the brains and toil of men."[41] The book is filled with close-up images of heroic men high atop lofty steel beams who were in full control of massive phallic tools, a new masculine sublime. The same type of virile laborers inspired the character of Limpy Bill in Lloyd's films, serving as a contrast to the contained office worker of Harold seeking release. Vidor's image of Gary Cooper's Roark driving his drill forcibly into seemingly impenetrable granite is a composite of Hine's derrick man and driller. Rand owned Hine's book *Men at Work,* which she lent to the film's art director Edward Carrere, pointing to the collaborative process of image-making and gender formulation in the film.[42] The melding of body and machine communicates male power and virility, which are themselves embodied in the phallic skyscraper. Roark's physical mastery of tools is the conceptual and political inverse of what Rand saw as Communism's use of men as tools—extensions of the state. His triumph over raw, inert rock (nature) and his singular command of machinery implies that determined individualism triumphs over fate and robotization.

Rand was fascinated with the lore of the Empire State Building, including

Howard Roark drills the granite in The Fountainhead.

Lewis Hine, Foundation Man, *from* Men at Work, *1932.*

Roark and the Empire State Building in The Fountainhead.

the extensive publicity surrounding all aspects of its planning and construction. After she moved to Hollywood, she wrote, "I have a huge office, a secretary and all the usual grandeur. . . . Only I do miss New York and the Empire State Building."[43] Her architectural research is replete with notes on all aspects of the building's construction. She read Alfred Bossom's *Building to the Skies: The Romance of the Skyscraper* (1934), which describes the singular structure's gargantuan cubic footage, steel tonnage, and height.[44] She supplemented this information with Paul Starrett's *Changing the Skyline* (1938), an account of the author's thirty-year career building skyscrapers.[45] One of the final chapters, suggestively entitled "The Climax," is devoted to the Empire State, his culminating achievement. In several scenes, Roark is compared to the Empire State Building's stature in Wynand's office. Echoing Starrett's dramatic finale, *The Fountainhead* ends with Roark's preeminent Wynand Building triumphing over a dwarfed Empire State Building.

ROARK'S BRAWN AND BRAIN: THE ARCHITECTURAL SOURCES

Roark's body is athletic and tall, echoing his functional skyscrapers. In an early draft of the novel, Rand describes Roark and his buildings in similar terms.

Francon "sees, alone, tall, erect, against the sky, Howard Roark on top of the building, his red hair flying in the wind."[46] The name Roark is itself richly layered with Randian symbolism: it is a synthesis of the words *roar* and *rock,* while the full name Howard Roark evokes the city appellation New York.[47]

Roark's erect and singular body is a visual analogue of both his virility and his ego, or "I." The superiority of reason over emotion and the equation of rationality with genius were among Rand's most revered principles, hallmarks of her ideal masculinity. In a speech to a group of architects, delivered after the completion of the novel, she asserted, "I choose architecture because a sense of structure is the essence of man's creative faculty, the base of every achievement . . . a sense of structure is impossible without a possession of reason— and reason is the attribute of the individual."[48] Roark is thus imbued with an unemotive and austere affect; he is a detached and analytical man who does not suffer fools gladly. Rand described him in a preliminary script as having "a strong, calm, implacable face. A man so completely sure of himself that he never resorts to a raised voice or a display of emotion."[49] Vidor directed Cooper's Roark as stern and laconic, only breaking character when he physically overpowers Patricia Neal's Francon.

Although Rand disliked the International Style, she turned to Le Corbusier's seminal text *Towards a New Architecture* (1927) for her concept of the superior man and new architect. Le Corbusier describes the heroic man as "intelligent, cold and calm," adjectives that perfectly suit Roark. He admires the honest workman and is suspicious of elitism. He devotes an entire chapter to the relationship of the architect and the engineer, from which Rand copied several pages that reinforced her notion of the engineer's practical superiority over the antiquated character of the conventional architect. Le Corbusier writes: "Our engineers are healthy and virile, active and useful, balanced and happy in their work. Our architects are disillusioned and unemployed, boastful and peevish." Employing class and gender-inflected innuendo, Le Corbusier believes that only engineers are producing real buildings, while architects are incapable because of their education in schools "where hothouse orchids are cultivated."[50]

Sheldon Cheney echoed Le Corbusier's masculinist rhetoric in *The New World Architecture* (1930), from which Rand also appropriated many ideas. Cheney asserted that the new architect must be a composite of architect and engineer, an active man who possessed both theoretical knowledge and practical experience.[51] Cheney named architects Louis Sullivan and Frank Lloyd Wright as exemplars, men who served as prototypes, respectively, for Roark's mentor, Cameron, and Roark himself. This original engineer-architect should possess a structural imagination suitable to rational problem-solving, prefiguring Rand's speech to the profession, while eschewing tradition that leads to passive adaptation. Rand was also adamant in her view that men should be active. She claimed: "From the beginning of history, two antagonists have stood face to face . . . the Active and the Passive. The Active Man is the producer, the creator, the originator, the individualist."[52] These beliefs coincided with the self-help literature that was available to men seeking successful careers.

Drawing on the view of the architect put forth by Le Corbusier and Cheney, Roark is both builder and architect, commencing his career in the engineering department of an architectural firm. In the novel and preliminary scripts, he climbs a steel scaffold to inspect a building and encounters workmen engaged in various tasks, gaining their respect by helping to solve technical problems.[53] On one occasion, he instructs a skeptical electrician how to wrap conduits around beams. When the worker refuses to heed his instructions out of pride, Roark seizes the torch and completes the practical and symbolically inseminating job. "Where did you learn to handle it like that, Red?" the man inquires, to which he replies, "I've been an electrician, a plumber, and a rivet catcher, and many other things."[54] As explained in chapter 1, men who worked on high-steel structures were hailed as fearless "cowboys of the skies," willing to take risks to conquer the uncharted upper domain. They represented the rugged manhood associated with western pioneers and the idea of Manifest Destiny.[55]

In *Skyscrapers and the Men Who Build Them* (1928), W. A. Starrett differentiated among the architect/designer, the engineer, and the builder but suggested that some men could combine these diverse tasks. Paraphrasing Starrett, Rand wrote, "Architects design buildings, engineers design steel skeletons, other engineers design heating, lighting etc. The builder or contractor takes care of accomplishing the actual building from these plans. . . . Lately some have combined all these functions."[56] Rand concurred. In her commentary on Starrett's book, she inquired, "Important thing for Roark—can he be his own contractor?"[57] Although she found this unfeasible for the novel and screenplay, she tried to imbue Roark with a builder's pragmatism, an engineer's rationality, and an architect's creativity.

Roark's intrepid spirit and logical mind prompt him to refuse to capitulate to an architectural panel that requests alterations of his skyscraper designs, aware that his repudiation will forestall future opportunities. The film pictures him as a singular towering presence in contrast to the undifferentiated board or yes-men who are seated at a horizontal table, a passive collective body, incapable of original thought. Rand's directorial instructions for this scene reinforce the magnitude of Roark's accomplishment and independence:

> FULL SHOT MODERN SKYSCRAPER. A magnificent building of sculpted simplicity. It stands alone, against what looks like an empty sky. THE CAMERA SHOOTS UPWARD, stressing the impression of immeasurable height and triumphant soaring. A man's hand comes into the shot and closes possessively over the top of the building. CAMERA PULLS BACK TO FULL FIGURE SHOT ROARK.

Roark and skyscraper model in The Fountainhead.

> He stands alone by a table, his hand on the building. We see now
> that the skyscraper is a miniature on the table.[58]

A later sequence at a stone quarry establishes him as a worker-architect—a
modern Renaissance man—while underscoring his lone-wolf status. His decision to work at a stone quarry after losing his architectural commission represents both his virtuous embrace of manual labor and his dogged refusal to leave
the building profession, even if it means a humiliating demotion.[59] Vidor employs a long shot of a row of heroic construction workers that are reminiscent
of Lewis Hine's Empire State Building laborers, which stressed male cooperative
labor, one of the hallmarks of Depression-era iconography. By appropriating
Hine's heroic Depression-era workers, Vidor underscored their instrumentality
in times of strife while emphasizing Roark's singularity. A contrasting close-up
of him operating a drill suggests that this virile individualist works alone.

Roark's nickname "Red" is a reference to his fiery hair (and the implied passion that accompanies it) and his radical spirit, which is curiously appropriated
by Rand to disseminate her conservative ideology. She describes him on the
skyscraper scaffold: "Roark's arm was steady, holding the hissing streak of flame

in leash, shuddering faintly with its violence. There was no strain. . . . And it seemed as if the blue tension eating slowly through the metal came not from the flame but from the hand holding it."[60] Throughout her work, we find such confused and ambivalent adaptations of leftist images of the heroic Common Man, such as those appropriated from Hine. Rand's fondness for this hearty figure is parallel to her taste for a type of modernism that is commonly associated with leftist political ideology. This attempt to make progressive models serve her conservative politics is a hallmark of Rand's work. She admired workers and yet detested the use of collectivism.

One of the keys to interpreting Rand's mixture of ideologies is sexuality and power. It is while thrusting his drill into the pure, obdurate granite that Roark first sees the heiress Dominique Francon, and she him. Her name alludes to her desire to dominate, her abstinence (like St. Dominic) from bodily sensuality, and her elite, Francophile roots. Rand's script directs her to gaze at him longingly from a high vantage point, meant to illustrate her superior class status. In a fantasy sequence, she lords over him with masculine attire from her superior perch, bent on bending him to her will. Later in the scene she imperiously slashes his face with a riding crop, introducing a Sadean iconography that combines eroticism and violence. Not surprisingly, the film's publicity campaign was built around the protagonists' erotic power struggle rather than the political or social issues they faced. Posters and trailers featured a dominant Roark in laborer's garb, either rapaciously embracing or towering over a subservient, fawning Francon, often in formal evening attire: working-class masculinity triumphs over corrupt, pretentious, upper-class femininity.[61] Vidor wished to underscore the gender and class tensions inherent in their relationship, noting in the margin of the novel concerning their first meeting, "Dominique admitted to an affair with a workman."[62] The camera cross-cuts from the drill-wielding Roark to the intrigued Francon in order to evoke her fantasy of sexual consummation by conquest.[63] His body conquers hers, just as his buildings conquer space and his creativity conquers the forces of mediocrity and collectivism.

SULLIVAN AND WRIGHT

Roark's austere body and spirit—analogue to his functional, unadorned buildings—rehearses the modernist architectural discourse of Louis Sullivan and Frank Lloyd Wright. The former was the model for the talented but defeated Henry Cameron, while the latter's indomitable spirit was the inspiration for Roark's.[64] Rand adopted the aesthetic philosophies of the two architects and their often vitriolic and xenophobic rhetorical style. Sullivan and Wright wrote in support of an indigenous American architecture that was free of European influences, which they defined as derivative and unoriginal.

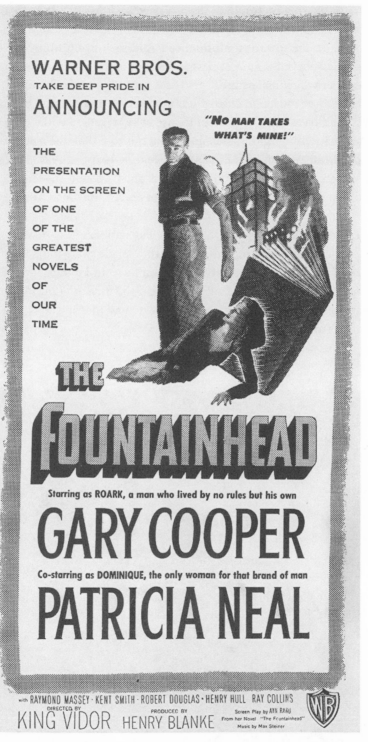

Roark standing over Dominique from The Fountainhead, *press book, Warner Bros., 1949.*

Sullivan's support of functionalism was echoed by Rand, even though his rhetoric was not always congruent with his use of historicist architectural ornamentation (e.g., the Byzantine-influenced Auditorium Building of 1886–89 in Chicago).[65] He believed that in every form "there is something or other which we do not see, yet which makes itself visible to us in that very form. . . . In a state of nature the form exists *because* of its function."[66] In a passage borrowed from Sullivan, Rand has Cameron gaze up in awe at skyscrapers while en route to the hospital in a speeding ambulance and launch into a diatribe against historical architectural borrowings as a didactic lesson for Roark. The image of the car's Red Cross logo superimposed on the image of the towering skyscraper identifies the building as a monument to functionalism and capitalism. Cameron inveighs:

> Howard, look at those buildings. . . . Skyscrapers, the greatest
> structural invention of man. . . . Yet they made them look like
> Greek temples . . . and Gothic cathedrals . . . and mongrels of
> every ancient style. . . . I told them that the form of a building
> must follow its function. Howard, every new idea in the world
> comes from the mind of one man.[67]

Towering skyscraper seen from Cameron's ambulance in The Fountainhead.

Sullivan employed a gendered and sexualized language to support his opinions concerning what he deemed appropriate architectural strategies and styles, a vocabulary that was appropriated by Rand. In his highly influential "Kindergarten Chats" (1901–02), later published in book form, he celebrated Henry Hobson Richardson's Marshall Field Store (1885–87) in Chicago as "a man that lives and breathes, that has red blood, a real man, a manly man, a virile force."[68] Contrastingly, his rejection of eclecticism reflected his desire to rid the American architectural body of effete Europeanisms that he associated with upper-class feminine fashion, illness, and degenerate masculinity. Borrowing his vocabulary from fin de siècle medical and psychiatric discourse, Sullivan diagnosed the unjustified use of ornament in buildings as "profoundly antisocial," "hysterical," and "neurasthenic." Hysteria and neurasthenia were considered feminine and cosmopolitan ailments, which Sullivan found particularly repulsive.[69] Architectural historian Mary McLeod has noted that European modernist architects "shunned the transient and commercial qualities of fashion, associating it with the superficiality of ornament," and rejected "women's fashion, as frivolous, unfunctional and wasteful," in favor of "nude" architecture.[70] Sullivan concurred. Referring to a typical college library, he complained, "It is precious. It is modish. . . . It is of the rubbings of hands of our leading man-milliner," thereby likening it to the supposedly transient world of feminine fashion (and implied homosexuality).[71] As art historian Sarah Burns has pointed out, the jargon of aesthetic pathology reached its apex in America with the conviction of the writer Oscar Wilde in 1895 on charges of sodomy. Healthy American art was frequently associated with normative gender characteristics and a robust ruralism, in opposition to the foreign, effeminate, and metropolitan, which were construed as diseased and perverse. "Man-milliner" was an appellation linked to male effeminacy and homosexuality, initially employed to smear political adversaries.[72]

In Sullivan's 1924 *Autobiography of an Idea,* which appeared in Rand's bibliography, Sullivan recommended a steady diet of exercise to rid the body of pathological femininity, a ritual he likened to building. Admiring the muscular instrumentality of construction workers and their steel structures, Sullivan added, "And what new words too—circulation, calisthenics, dietary, suspension bridges and others." He often waxed poetic about "naked mighty men, with the power to do splendid things with their bodies." Awed by a great suspension bridge, he exclaimed: "And to think it was made by men! How great men must be, how wonderful and powerful" that they could realize such a technological wonder.[73] This type of gendered Whitmanesque rhetoric and the conflation of the male body with seminal male creativity and a functionalist aesthetic were absorbed into the persona of Roark. Indeed, the title *The Fountainhead* may have been suggested by a passage from Sullivan's biography, in which he traced his own creativity to a childhood power "arising from the fountainhead of all tears," and who recalled his first boyhood act of building as the creation of a dam that began as a torrent of water. "Ego the I am," his signifier of identity, must have also appealed to Rand.[74]

If Sullivan's functionalist discourse formed the basis of Roark's physical appearance, Wright's biography and aesthetic philosophy defined the parameters of the hero's life mission. In 1937, Rand began a correspondence with Wright that continued intermittently until 1957. With typical enthusiasm, she asked to meet him in order to have "the inspiration of seeing before me a living miracle."[75] Informing him of her intention to write a novel about an architect, she added, somewhat disingenuously, "My hero is not you. I do not intend to follow in the novel, the events of your life and career. His life is not yours—I think."[76] After encountering Wright briefly at a professional dinner in 1938, she wrote to him again and sent him the first three chapters of her book. Wright was dismissive at first: "No man named 'Roark' with 'flaming red hair' could be a genius that could lick the contracting fraternity," he commented.[77]

Perhaps the theme that Rand most admired in Wright's *An Autobiography* was his abiding belief that the architectural calling was the struggle of genius against an uncomprehending and mediocre mob. Wright was never guilty of false modesty. Employing a histrionic, persecuted tone, he inveighed against "prejudice, provincial, quotidian," as his "implacable enemy. A genius? Well, that term damned him as it was intended to do."[78] His motto, "Truth against the World," figured repeatedly in his life story and clearly appealed to Rand, who made it Roark's reason for being.

As Rand was working on *The Fountainhead* in 1936, she blocked out *An Autobiography* in outline form and selected salient parts of Wright's life to incorporate in the novel. She did not duplicate events so much as adopt their tenor to buttress her theme of the heroic genius pitted against the masses. Thus Roark, like Wright, has red hair; studies with an iconoclastic, pioneering architect who dies defeated; is resented for his achievements and unique vision by fellow beginners; is subjected to frivolous lawsuits by wealthy patrons in collusion with unethical special interests; is ignored by his peers in the official architectural establishment; and is continually and unfairly harassed by a sensationalist and corrupt press.

According to Wright, the "herd instinct," or mob mentality, was encountered in any institutional forum, including the university, which churned out "mass products"; the American Institute of Architects, which supported antiquated idioms and promoted cronyism; and the federal government, which fostered a disenfranchised mentality and undermined initiative and autonomy with its relief programs and subsidies. Wright insisted, "Life itself demands of Modern Architecture that the house of a man who knows what home is should have his own home his own way if we have any man left after F.H.A. or A.I.A."

The architect's mission was to battle these deadening organizations because they were detrimental to the inventive spirit. Creativity could not be taught because it was "the salt and savior of the natural ego."[79] The first issue of his journal *Taliesin* (1940) included the following bold manifesto:

NO INSTITUTES

NO PETTY OFFICIALDOM

NO LANDLORD ------------------- NO TENANT

NO POLITICIANS ---------------- NO ACADEMICIANS[80]

Roark's ingenuity is also sui generis and completely independent. Echoing Wright in the film's courtroom speech, he praises men who are independent of officialdom: "The thinkers, the artists, the scientists, the inventors—stood alone against the men of their time. Every great thought was opposed. . . . Every great achievement has come from the independent work of some individual mind."[81]

Rand also adopted Wright's aesthetic philosophy, which derived from Sullivan's belief that a building is an organic entity with a single unifying principle. In a note on Roark's buildings, she asserted unequivocally:

> Among present-day architects, it is the style of Frank Lloyd Wright—and ONLY Frank Lloyd Wright—that must be taken as the model for Roark's buildings. Wright holds a unique position with the general public—even the people who cling to traditional architecture and hate modernism of the concrete-and-steel-pipe school, love and admire Wright's work.[82]

She made a valiant effort to hire Wright to design the sets for *The Fountainhead* with the help of Gerald Loeb, vice-president of E. F. Hutton and one of the architect's clients. Sometime in 1945, she had dinner with Wright, probably at Loeb's invitation. In a handwritten note to the film's producer, Henry Blanke, she boasted, "I got Frank Lloyd Wright for you, if Warner Brothers will let you. I've done my part and you a personal victory by persuading him . . . to do the buildings."[83] Rand reported that Wright's fee was $250,000 but that she believed she could bargain with him.

Wright was apparently quite interested in the job but imposed certain conditions. His main concern was the preservation of the integrity of his designs and Rand's story, not monetary remuneration. He insisted just like Roark that none of his buildings, drawings, or architectural miniatures be altered and that all be produced by his own apprentices at his architectural compound Taliesin. Rand reported their conversation to Blanke:

> He wants a guarantee that the final sets used in the actual produc-
> tion will not depart basically from the version he has sent. He will
> not object to changes in lines or details, but he insists that the
> basic story, its themes, its main events and climax must remain as
> they are in the book. (No, I didn't prompt him to insist on that.)[84]

He also wished to provide an educational opportunity for his Taliesin pupils
and offered to come to Hollywood, if necessary, to supervise the installation of
the sets.[85] Thrilled, Rand besieged Blanke, begging him to consider the prestige
the film would enjoy by including "the actual work of a genius," which would
ensure "a permanent classic in the history of art."[86]

Wright's initial interest in designing the sets was due to his revised opinion
of the novel. "Your grasp of the architectural ins and outs of a degenerate profession astonish me," he wrote to Rand in 1944. In a letter to Loeb, he referred
to *The Fountainhead* as "the best exposition of the principles of democracy
ever written in fiction form."[87] However, in his correspondence with Warner
Bros. he was more equivocal, expressing a fear that Rand's important concepts
would be compromised in favor of sensationalism. He wrote to Blanke that if the
novel were translated accurately, "it would go far to redeem not only the state
of Hollywood but the state of the Union," but not if it were merely "glamor-
ized hero worship or sex-coated pill."[88] Ultimately, however, he turned down
the offer to design the sets, confiding to Loeb, "I could not believe that there
was anything to work with and not for any sum of money would I lower my
standards."[89]

When the film was released, Wright hated it, criticizing it in a characteristi-
cally vituperative tone. He worked to divorce himself publicly from any association with the novel, film, and Rand. This response was probably due in part
to the widespread attacks on the film from the architectural profession, and
perhaps also the producer's refusal to pay his fees, which in the interim had by
his own admission increased to $400,000, or 10 percent of the film's budget. He
railed, "I did not see the movie. . . . I do not want to become identified with its
thesis . . . but I think she [Ayn Rand] bungled it. It's a treacherous slant on my
philosophy. She asked me to endorse the book but I declined."[90]

Wright's ire was prompted at least by the manner in which his architectural
style and tenets were bastardized by the set designers. Although the dialogue
echoed his views, the sets did not live up to his standards. Carrere and his associates had studied Wright's architecture and theory in earnest, consulting
An Autobiography, The Nature of Materials, and his published letters.[91] Even
so, the sets only superficially reflect his style. The Wynand residence has the
planar horizontality of Wright's Kaufmann House (1936) and a factory refers
to the Johnson Wax Building (1936–39), but many of the sets resemble generic
International Style buildings, which both Wright and Rand detested. As ar-

chitectural historian Dietrich Neumann has noted, Roark's high-rise Enright apartments are similar to the Dutch architect Bernard Bijvoet's entry to the 1923 Chicago Tribune Tower Competition, and an early skyscraper model echoes Wallace Harrison's United Nations Building (1947–50).[92]

THE POLITICS OF ARCHITECTURE AND THE REDEMPTION OF THE SKYSCRAPER

Rand used architecture itself as a protagonist in her fiction. When she began her novel, many Americans were out of work. Her figure of the virile and competent architect-builder was a means to rescue an instrumental, active masculinity. Curiously, this figure closely resembles the healthy construction workers portrayed so often in the government-sponsored murals that she so despised. The message of the Roosevelt administration was that America could literally build itself out of the Depression.[93] Just as she appropriated the leftist nickname "Red" for her conservative purposes, Rand co-opted popular New Deal mural imagery of men building and Lewis Hine's photographs of instrumental workers to buttress her own antithetical Republican political and economic agendas and to celebrate unfettered capitalism. For Rand, strong, seminal men such as Roark were not part of a collective or an anonymous working class as much as individuals whose bodies were often outward signifiers of inward geniuses.

Rand viewed building as "one of the most eloquent representatives of man's creative faculties."[94] During World War II, a staple of American propaganda was to delineate Nazis and fascists as barbarians who destroyed architectural monuments, hence civilization, while the Allies were depicted as its protectors.[95] Rand adapted this logic to denigrate collectivists. In 1943 she wrote that she had chosen architecture as the hero's profession because it served as an "eloquent symbol of man as a creator. . . . His antithesis, the collectivists, are destroyers."[96] She viewed architecture as most suited to the theme of the "individual against the collective."[97] The architect Roark is thus engaged in an ideological war to extirpate homegrown collectivism, which Rand equated with the Roosevelt administration.

Although he is awarded a variety of commissions, Roark is depicted in the film primarily as a designer of skyscrapers, who thrives in an urban milieu. Major visual tropes include panoramas of New York's tall buildings, romantic nocturnal views of scintillating skylines seen from atop penthouse roofs, and particular Manhattan monuments such as the Empire State Building. An aggregate of Manhattan skyscrapers, one of which metamorphoses into an image of the book *The Fountainhead* under the opening credits, announces one of the film's major themes: the skyscraper is literally the skeleton or backbone of the novel and the film. This singular building appears later in the film as the Enright House, the skyscraper high-rise Roark designs to redeem the housing project.

Skyscraper metamorphosing into the book in The Fountainhead.

As seen in the last chapter, when Rand began the novel in the mid-1930s, skyscrapers were frequently viewed as tombstones of capitalism rather than proud monuments of industry and commerce. Mumford blamed these behemoths for creating the dehumanizing environment for the "little people" who were forced to live or work amongst them. He complained:

> One need not dwell upon the ways in which these obdurate overwhelming masses take away from the little people who walk in their shadows any semblance of dignity as human beings; it is perhaps inevitable that one of the greatest achievements in a thoroughly dehumanized civilization should, no doubt, unconsciously achieve this very purpose. It is enough to point out that the virtues of skyscrapers are mainly virtues in technique. They have little to do with the human arts of seeing, feeling and living.[98]

The *New Republic* columnist Edmund Wilson proclaimed tall buildings "superfluous, ironically advertised as a triumph in the hour when the planless competitive society is bankrupt."[99] As discussed in chapter 2, films such as *Skyscraper Souls* (1932) and *Baby Face* (1933) depicted the tall building as a site of class and gender tension, where predation was a commonplace activity. Rand's celebration of skyscrapers in *The Fountainhead* novel and film was meant to restore it as a proud American icon and a linchpin for the virtues of unrestrained capitalism, which had been tarnished during the Depression.

In addition to their association with the virile male body in *The Fountainhead*, they were also depicted as a product of the human mind and a metaphorical analogue to individual aspiration. Seeming to pierce the heavens, they superseded ecclesiastical architecture and religious dogma. For the atheist Rand, they were the replacement for sacred structures. In the novel, Wynand praises the skyline and the men who created them in awe: "I would give the greatest sunset in the world for one sight of New York's skyline. Particularly when one can't see the details. Just the shapes. The shapes and the thought made visible. What other religion do we need?"[100]

Wynand's poetic soliloquy was meant to recapture the popular idea, articulated most commonly in the 1920s and seemingly lost during the Depression, that skyscrapers were designed to inspire awe and wonderment, a manifestation of the "technological sublime."[101] In particular, Alfred Bossom's laudatory pronouncements provided Rand with thematic, metaphorical, and visual elements for her depiction of tall buildings. He regarded skyscrapers as the epitome of American inventiveness, paragons of daring and self-confidence. Their sheer scale served as a visual trigger for lofty thoughts and aspirations. He wrote:

> It seems to me a good thing for the spirit of a people that they should be able to gaze upon very high buildings, erected by their own contemporaries. The habit of looking upward is a strengthening habit. It encourages self-confidence, it gives a soaring turn to one's thoughts and ambitions; it sets up a current of sympathy and emulation between one's hidden self and the towering object upon which the eyes are turned, it lends wings to the imagination, it acts as a call to energy and will-power. No people spend so much time looking upwards as the Americans.[102]

In her final script, Rand recommended that the director employ the upward gaze as a visual strategy, when Cameron and Roark gaze admiringly upward at the former's towering achievements.[103] The camera too gazes upward at the end of the film as Francon rises in an open construction elevator to the Wynand Building while looking up reverentially at the skyscraper and Roark at its crest.

Finally, for Rand, the skyscraper exemplified the material incarnation of American business acumen, a consummate symbol of capitalist achievement.

The proliferation of ever taller skyscrapers, which had characterized building since the beginning of the twentieth century, proclaimed corporate prosperity. These buildings were meant to serve as the physical manifestations of vigorous capitalist competition and self-advertisement.

THE DEFEAT OF PROBLEMATIC GENDER AND BAD ARCHITECTURE

Unhealthy capitalist competition is exemplified in the character of Gail Wynand, who is a composite of a robber-baron capitalist and a refined but manly gentleman. He is a self-made man, born in Hell's Kitchen, whose rags-to-riches saga is predicated on raw power and lack of ideals. His masculinity is not weak or feminized but is damaged by his adherence to upper-class values. Wynand's majestic office illustrates his pretensions and lust for power, reminiscent of sets in Fritz Lang's *Metropolis* (1927). It is situated on a skyscraper's upper tier and commands a 180-degree view of the Manhattan skyline. His visual command of the cityscape represents his desire and capacity to exert authority and control over his surroundings.[104] As Anthony Vidler has noted, Roark too commands "ineffable space," which likewise opens up panoramically around his buildings.[105] When we meet him, Wynand is seated at his desk like a monarch receiving subjects paying homage. Upon Roark's entry to his inner sanctum, Wynand rises and matches the architect's stature and commanding presence, but later Vidor situates him in front of a window through which we see two skyscrapers of a bygone era: Graham, Burnham and Co.'s Equitable Building (1913–15) and Ernest Flagg's Singer Building (1906–08). The tip of the Singer is cut off by the frame, suggesting impotence and the imminent demise of antiquated, class-inflected masculinity.[106]

In accord with Wynand, Francon's gender identity is in need of rehabilitation. She is divided, both passionate and repressed, but in possession of too many masculine traits to be considered fully female. Rand renders her as a masochist "like most women" and a defeatist, capable only of destructive acts, in contrast to Roark, who creates.[107] At the beginning of the film, she flings a beloved classical statue out the window because she is unwilling to allow beauty to exist amid mediocrity.[108] The camera is positioned from below and records the statue plummeting downward, in contrast to Roark's efforts, which soar. She is unable to respond sexually to men until she meets Roark, whose masculine creative agency ignites her ardor, thereby completing her. In the novel, she is described as twenty-four years old and a virgin, even calling herself frigid. Roark's active warmth versus Francon's coldness evidences Rand's adherence to Aristotelian notions of biology, which have here been superimposed on their gender identities.[109]

Francon's sexual dysfunction and gender confusion are rendered visually by her numerous costume changes, from masculine riding attire to black lacy

Gail Wynand in his office in The Fountainhead.

Dominique Francon flings a statue downward in The Fountainhead.

negligee. Rand reported that the inspiration for Francon's gender-conflicted character was autobiographical, representing a conflation of the author in a bad mood and her husband Frank, if he were a woman.[110] Although she is literally and socially above Roark when they first meet, he will eventually change the power dynamic. Francon's father owns the quarry where Roark is employed. Seeing him at work, she is unable to get his drill out of her mind and summons him inside her house, to her bedroom.[111]

If Roark signifies the public, exterior realm and the skyscraper, the dilettante Francon embodies and inhabits a feminized and upper-class domestic interior that, in Sullivan's terms, must be excised from the American architectural body and psyche. She writes a newspaper column in *The Banner* called "Your Home." Rand considered upper-class women and their taste for interior decoration the bane of America's residential architecture, in accord with most modernists who equated women's tastes with the transient world of fashion.[112] This masculine-feminine architectural antimony reflects a firmly entrenched "separate-sphere" ideology that had been codified in the Victorian era.[113]

Francon's vacation home is a beautiful mansion, redolent of decadence. Rand chose this context after seeing a group of men on a chain gang and, later, a beautiful old southern mansion. The contrast of house and stone-quarry workmen provides both novel and film with their sought-after class tension.[114] The chain gang is replaced in the film by a long shot of muscular workmen drilling into stubborn granite. Vidor and the art director Carrere interpret Francon's space as an opulent country estate owned by her father, dripping in preciosity and adornments, including a canopied bed, enormous French windows, and an ornate Rococo fireplace framed by voluptuous mermaids. Francon illustrates the economist Thorstein Veblen's assertion, in *The Theory of the Leisure Class* (1899), which served as an important precursor to modernist architectural discourse, that upper-class women, with their possessions and ostentatious clothing, act as signifiers of their father's and husband's wealth and status, representatives of the most egregious examples of conspicuous consumption.[115] In this respect, Francon resembles the upper-class wives of corporate bosses in Depression-era cinema.

Francon contrives to bring Roark to her by cracking the paving stones of her bedroom fireplace and summoning him to fix them. The glistening white-marble surface of the damaged and fireless hearth signifies her coldness, while its sensuous nude sculptures hint at her untapped passion. Roark, drawn into this confined, feminine, private space, guesses her stratagem. He responds to her challenge by driving a long, hard stake into the marble, shattering it, and sarcastically proclaiming it now truly broken. When he later sends someone else to reset the marble, thereby foiling her plan, Francon flies into a rage, releasing her repressed emotions. It is then that she rides after him on horseback and strikes him imperiously and violently with her riding crop, in an effort to

Francon breaks the fireplace in The Fountainhead.

reduce him to a subservient beast. Her masculine riding habit and domineering behavior express her gender confusion and frigidity and liken her to cinematic depictions of lesbian characters.[116] When stars such as Marlene Dietrich began wearing trousers in the 1930s, they were able to articulate a more transgressive femininity. These mannish costumes were often erotic, drawing attention to the bodies they clothed, and a provocation, an example of gender ambiguity.[117] Like many other such female film characters, Francon ultimately casts aside her masculine attire to claim her "true" heterosexuality and normative gender identity.

After the confrontation with the whip, Roark waits until nightfall and forcibly enters her bedroom in his dirty work clothes. A sinister phallic shadow above his head underscores his sadoerotic intentions. Adjacent to Francon is a sphinx-based lamp, recalling the tale of Oedipus, in which the indomitable male hero outflanks his female adversary, often depicted as a monstrous femme fatale. The scene that follows was rendered milder in the film than in the book in an effort to appease the censors. In the film, Roark overpowers Francon in an implied rape that is signified by the gaping tear in her black lingerie. Rand referred to Roark as the "Marquis de Sade of architecture."[118] Working-class masculinity

Francon looking down at Roark in The Fountainhead.

Roark vanquishes Francon in The Fountainhead.

subdues upper-class femininity, and the crude rock drill overcomes the effete riding crop. Despite her humiliation, or because of it, Francon falls in love with her assailant. Her masochism and submission manifest Rand's adherence to a Freudian theory, articulated in the 1940s by Helene Deutsch, that women are essentially passive and secretly desire to be raped.[119]

After winning over Francon, Roark's final adversary is Ellsworth Monkton Toohey, who is an odd amalgam of elitism, collectivism, and power-mongering. His is a marginalized masculinity; he is a sexual hybrid who possesses feminine attributes and class pretensions while trumpeting collectivist values. Like the architecture he supports, his facade is incongruent with his belief system, an incarnation of Sullivan's man-milliner, rife with disease and perversion. He also represents the conflation of homosexuality and foreign intrigue that was so much a part of conservative cold war discourse, anticipated by Rand in the 1930s when she began the novel. He is replete with symbolic and literal allusions: his name Ellsworth is the reverse of worthless; his middle name evokes sexlessness and the suspect piety of Christian hypocrisy; and Toohey rhymes with hooey, slang for nonsense. Rand describes him in the novel as lacking in male bodily attributes and dressed in upper-class feminine attire—a more radical cross-dresser than Francon. When Keating visits him at home, he

Ellsworth Toohey smoking in The Fountainhead.

finds Toohey in "a dressing gown . . . made of silk, bearing the trade mark pattern of Cody's face powder." Under this foppish, coded homosexual exterior, Toohey's puny body is a "walking testimonial to the spiritual pus filling his blood vessels."[120]

Vidor toned down Toohey's homosexual persona somewhat; he fashioned the appropriately supercilious Robert Douglas with pomaded hair and dressed him in antiquated suits with stiff collars. Like many foppish villains of the period, he often sports an elegant cigarette holder, which he caresses while "exhaling devilishly."[121] Classist aspirations undergird this effete figure, who panders to the wealthy in order to achieve his collectivist agenda. He is a dissembler and an infiltrator; his voice and shadow imply that he is manipulating events behind the scenes.

Toohey is architecturally promiscuous, a transient fashionist who praises Beaux-Arts buildings and housing projects alike. By the end of the film, his true colors emerge as a champion of public housing, while Roark remains steadfastly associated with skyscrapers. Rand identifies the one as dependent on government agencies and the product of cooperative aesthetics, and the other as the sole purview of individual agency and creative ingenuity.

THE HOUSING PROJECT VS. THE SKYSCRAPER

Rand's temporary employer, the architect Louis Kahn, had opined that the biggest technical problem in architecture was the design of low-rent housing projects. She herself contended that her selection of a housing project as a battleground for the Toohey/Roark showdown represented an awareness of its architectural and political significance.[122] She consulted at least two books on public housing, Coleman Woodbury's *Housing Officials' Yearbook 1937* and *Current Developments in Housing* of the same year. She disliked public housing because it provided government-sponsored jobs for the unemployed and subsidized shelter for the weak, rewarded people based on want rather than achievement, and was dehumanizing in design. Of government rent subsidies, Toohey remarks hypocritically, "You know, underdog milked to help someone underdoggier *[sic]*."[123] Explaining the novel to a fan, Rand scolded: "Private property is based on the idea of *rights,* not *needs.* A man holds his property because it is his—regardless of how many parasites claim that they need it more than he does. Anybody who makes a claim upon others on the basis of *need* is a parasite." "Roark," she continued, "has CONTEMPT for those whose aim in life was to help others. Didn't you understand that it was a housing project which he blew up to hell, where it belonged?"[124] She also objected to the monotony of the communal structures often rendered in an International Style–inspired idiom. Quality of life was severely compromised by "a huge block of buildings all alike, with a series of windows like those in a jail, where your feeling of an individually owned house (my home is my castle) is reduced to owning three dots of windows out of a myriad of identical beehive cells."[125]

The development of Rand's antipathy coincided with the formation in 1933 of the Housing Division of the Public Works Administration, headed by Roosevelt appointee Harold M. Ickes. It was a short-lived federal agency devoted to intervention in the housing market in the form of loan guarantees, low-interest loans, and government home ownership. Ickes's public statements must have enraged Rand, such as when he declared, "We may not depend upon private enterprise or limited dividend corporations to initiate low-cost housing and slum clearance."[126] Toohey voices Rand's worst nightmares in the novel when he boasts that business is finished and the future belongs to public housing and post offices, which will engulf the entire country and, ultimately, the world.

During the Depression there was little opposition to government subsidies even by those who advocated privatization. However, by 1940, organizations such as the National Real Estate Board had launched an aggressive lobbying effort and all-out public-relations campaign in the media to close down the Housing Division. Like Rand, they asserted that home ownership should be the reward of industry, thrift, and ambition, rather than a natural right. They branded public housing as socialist, maintaining that it struck at the heart of American individualism and the desire for "home sweet home." Newspaper slogans such as "you pay this man's rent," accompanied by illustrations of wealthy-looking people in front of public housing with television antennas, then a luxury, were intended to persuade people that Roosevelt's housing program was intrinsically unfair, as well as rife with inequity and corruption.[127]

The fictional Cortlandt Homes is a site of ideological combat. In a scene meant to recall trench warfare and to underscore that a battle was being waged not merely for buildings but for freedom itself, Francon serves as a lookout while Roark dynamites the construction site. Roark proclaims that the common good of the collective was the aim of every tyrant in history, which necessitates his radically violent action. The dynamiting of the project is thus an act of creative destruction, an imperative, if self-contradictory, civilizing gesture in the face of collective aggression.

After Roark's purifying destruction of the defiled building, Wynand commissions him to design his namesake skyscraper in a final effort to seek moral redemption for his nefarious past. The housing project is destroyed but eventually resurrected in a better form as the private Enright apartments and the Wynand Building. It is significant to note that the skyscraper is built in Hell's Kitchen, Wynand's birthplace and a notorious Manhattan slum, meant to underscore the newspaper tycoon's poor, corrupt origins. Rand also selected the slum as a site of redemption by a capitalist icon rather than the false promise of public housing, her answer to New Deal advocates who claimed that government housing would ameliorate urban blight.

Cortlandt Homes housing project in The Fountainhead.

The climactic final scene synthesizes Rand's views on gender and skyscraper architecture, which are employed in the service of her conservative political ideology. Roark marries Francon and completes the largest skyscraper in the world in a joint act of consummation and procreation. Francon visits the construction site and embarks on a soaring orgasmic journey upward in an open elevator, a space laden with traces of heterosexual eroticism from Depression-era cinema, to the Wynand's pinnacle. Rand describes Francon's skyward sensations:

> She stood, her hand lifted and closed upon a cable, her high
> heels poised firmly on the planks. The planks shuddered, a cur-
> rent of air pressed her skirt to her body and she saw the ground
> dropping slowly away from her. . . . She felt the height pressing
> against her eardrum. The sun filled her eyes. The air beat against
> her raised chin.[128]

This is in stark contrast to Depression-era films in which impoverished pluto-crats leaped to their deaths from lofty pinnacles. At the top, Francon finds the individualist Roark standing with legs straddling the skyscraper, which seems to emanate from his lower body. He is depicted as a working-class hero, an

Francon rising in the skyscraper elevator in The Fountainhead.

Roark at the summit in The Fountainhead.

Lewis Hine, Finishing Up the Job, *from* Men at Work, *1932.*

American cowboy of the skies, enacting a final upward version of Manifest Destiny. The pose of the triumphant Roark seems to derive from Hine's photograph *Finishing Up the Job,* in which construction workers stand at the highest point of the Empire State Building, "a quarter of a mile up in the clouds."[129] On her journey to the celestial realm, Francon passes government buildings, churches, banks, and the now-dwarfed Empire State itself. However, the Wynand Building's true summit is Roark's head, expressing Rand's belief that only man's intellect and creative spirit is transcendent, thereby fusing male aspiration with unrestrained capitalist achievement.

FEARING'S SKYSCRAPER IN *THE BIG CLOCK*

In contrast to Rand's paean to the skyscraper as a product of individual genius and striving, Fearing's tall office building is viewed as a collective beehive that breeds sameness, conformity, and engulfment at a "foreign" megalomaniac's hands, although it too is finally reclaimed by a single man. One of the means to understanding the film's gendered characters is to analyze the manner in which the novel was adapted and rewritten by screenwriter Jonathan Latimer. The film also bears the stamp of director John Farrow and art director Hans Dreier (with the assistance of Roland Anderson and Albert Nozaki), the product of collaboration between the various textual and visual producers.[130] It has previously been considered in relation to film noir narrative conventions or the lack thereof by R. Barton Palmer, with scant attention devoted to an analysis of its gendered protagonists or the complex issues involved in the film's politicized delineation of skyscraper space.[131] Despite the differences between Fearing's and Latimer's narrative points of view, character delineation, and political intent, however, the former's ideas bubble up from the recesses and margins of Latimer's adaptation, often acting as the film's political unconscious, and are necessary for an understanding of spatiality and how it is mediated by its various masculine, feminine, and sexual identities. For example, the skyscraper's position as a centralized "nerve center" of a vast media conglomerate is the original author's creation. The Janoth Building houses the eponymous clock of the film's title, or the machine within the machine, which grinds down its largely male inhabitants. Hypertrophied rationality is but a veil for its opposite, a vast repository of subterfuge, criminality, and deceit, visualized by long, darkened subterranean passageways that are controlled by effeminate men. Formerly thought of as a capitalist icon and a beacon of communication, the skyscraper is here omnipotent, the corporate equivalent of one-party power that disseminates propaganda and prefabricated truths that have been diluted for mass consumption.[132] Most of the action occurs in the tall office building not as a microcosm of urban life as in Depression-era films, but because it is an automated, bureaucratized organization in which workers are regulated, surveyed, and often crushed. Speaking through the novel's main protagonist George Stroud, Fearing described the skyscraper as "looming like an eternal stone deity among a forest of its fellows. It seemed to prefer human sacrifices of the flesh and spirit over any token of devotion."[133]

Fearing's clock is multivalent; it is an overarching *vanitas* symbol whose omnipresence eventually drains human life, a cold mechanical apparatus similar to a computer, a vast trap, and the arbiter of artificial, company time. Stroud describes his confinement in the large timepiece:

> One runs like a mouse up the old, slow pendulum of the big clock . . . strays inside through the intricate wheels and balances and springs of the inner mechanism, searching among the cobwebbed mazes of this machine with all its false exits and dangerous blind alleys. . . . Then the clock strikes one and it is time to go . . . to become again a prisoner making once more the same escape.[134]

The clock's jail-like nature is underlined by Latimer who situates Stroud in the two-story clock tower at the film's outset. Clock and skyscraper are conflated, which reflected a real fear among postwar commentators that office technology was wholly altering spatial practice in favor of gigantic new machines. Writing in the influential book *White Collar,* sociologist C. Wright Mills spoke of the radical increase in office machinery, which had jumped from a prewar allocation of $270 million to $1 billion in 1948. In addition to mechanical collators, ticket and money counters, and gadgets that could add, subtract, and multiply, the most startling was the "new electric calculators." These hugely expensive machines, and others like them, "required central control of offices previously scattered throughout the enterprise." As Mills pointed out, the machines were prompting a new mania for measurement of workers' tasks to increase production, which affected the physical layout of the office in favor of the "straight line flow of work," a more radical reemergence of scientific office management of the 1910s.[135]

The imprisoned hero Stroud begins his tale in retrospect, by recounting the events of the past thirty-six hours, thereby subverting logical, linear time.[136] Latimer's story is a battle between an enterprising individual and a corporation that would render the hero an Organization Man, a theme that would be more fully explored in literature and cinema in the 1950s. The camera surveys the clock at an acute angle from below, enforcing Stroud's lofty presence as he presides over its geometric innards, which resemble both a nocturnal skyline replete with lights and the core of a giant computer that seeks to transform workers into robots. The screenwriter and art director seemed to have plumbed the novel for this imagery, evoking Fearing's description of Stroud's encounter with a titan who "connected a number of adding machines to a single unit, and

View of the clock in The Big Clock.

this super-calculator was the biggest in the world."[137] Tripping the switch while still imprisoned, Stroud brings the clock to a temporary standstill, which presages his eventual conquest of the entire office building.

Fearing is also the originator of the emasculating character of corporate skyscraper space, which he refers to as "a gilded cage full of gelded birds," or castrated men who are well paid but lose their creative spirit.[138] Fearing even infers that Stroud's extramarital affair represents a healthy outlet for his repressed heterosexual libido that has been squelched by a corporate space presided over by effeminate men. The author implies further that the antihero Earl Janoth, a closeted homosexual, is less than a man, provoked to murder his part-time mistress when she accuses him of carrying on a secret relationship with his loyal assistant Steve Hagen. Although Latimer and director Farrow are unable to depict homosexuality overtly because of the Production Code, they infuse the effete Janoth (Charles Laughton), supercilious Hagen (George Macready), androgynous Pauline York (Delos in the novel; Rita Johnson), and glowering Bill Womack (Harry Morgan), Janoth's ersatz bodyguard and masseur, with coded homosexual referents.

Drawing on both Fearing's novel and Latimer's script, art director Hans Dreier and his assistants rendered the tall office building as a product of the

George Stroud in the clock in The Big Clock.

International Style, an architectural idiom that was christened in 1932 on the occasion of an exhibition at New York's Museum of Modern Art.[139] Characterized by ascetic functionalism, an antipathy to decoration, and clean white surfaces, among other characteristics, the style was celebrated by its proponents as an antidote to historicism. By 1948, after a hiatus in building occasioned by the Depression and World War II, architects, critics, and urban planners saw fit to reevaluate its efficacy for American practitioners in frequently partisan terms. The decision to employ the International Style in *The Big Clock* as the product of foreign-born bosses and effete, feminized men must be evaluated in the context of the often politicized rhetoric that accompanied discussions on it both before and after World War II by such prominent members of the architectural community as Frank Lloyd Wright, Lewis Mumford, and others.

FEARING'S LIFE AND POLITICS

Fearing's leftist political sympathies, manifested in an abiding distrust of corporate America and its organs of communication, is written into the very fabric of *The Big Clock*. In spite of his lionization as a pulp-fiction mystery writer, he is best known as a socially conscious poet who employed modernist experimental strategies to uncover the fragmentation and vacuity of contemporary life, beginning in the 1920s. As literary theorist Rita Barnard has noted, "his Whitmanesque enumerations often have the effect of a newsreel shown at double-speed: rapid fire montages juxtapose shots of a statesman at the microphone, the aviator stepping from his monoplane, of scabs arriving in guarded trucks."[140] Yet Fearing superseded the role of a mere seismograph of modernity's pulse and political temper, employing populist vernacular and imagery to expose its stultifying, numbing regime, an approach he would later employ in *The Big Clock*. His poetry is often dark and dystopian; its metropolitan landscape is replete with brazen, unfeeling businessmen, faceless bureaucrats, and suicides occasioned by loss of purpose and material failure.

In accord with Rand, Fearing chose pulp to effectuate change in the mass audience, and because it afforded him the freedom to explore politically and socially transgressive issues.[141] Indeed the format of the novel, which is almost postmodern in its narrative structure, relays the tale from several characters' vantage points, seizing the monolithic presentation of "truth" from the centralized media giant that Fearing is critiquing. A realization of Benjamin's injunctions in the well-known essay "The Author as Producer," the author's radicalism occurs at the levels of content, production, and structure.[142]

Fearing was born in 1902, spending most of his childhood in Oak Park, Illinois, a suburb in proximity to Chicago.[143] After graduating from the University of Wisconsin, where he served as editor of the college literary magazine, he moved to New York in 1924 to embark upon a literary career. Coming under the sway of modernism, he infused his poetry with the everyday speech and clipped jargon of American business and advertising as a purposeful stratagem. "Portrait of a Cog," written in the mid-thirties, traces the work-a-day world of a typical underling overcome by his own routine:

> You have forgotten the monthly conference. Your four
>   o'clock appointment waits in the ante-room. The
>   uptown bureau is on the wire again.
> Most of your correspondence is still unanswered, these bills
>   have not been paid, and one of your trusted agents has
>   suddenly resigned.
> And where are the morning reports? They must be filed at
>   once, at once.
>   . . .
> When they dig you up, in a thousand years, they will find you
>   in just this pose,
> One hand on the buzzer, the other reaching for the phone,
>   eyes fixed on the calendar, feet firmly on the office rug.[144]

The final stanza of "Portrait of a Cog," apportioning a man's life by tasks, machines, and quotidian numerics, is repeated in the poem "Dirge," in which the subject's existence is chronologized by a series of numbers, seemingly sequential and haphazard. He buys stock, gambles at the races, and plays golf, all of which record information on his life's symbolic scoreboard. "1-2-3 was the number he played but today the number came 3-2-1; Bought his carbide at 30 and it went to 29; had the favorite at Bowie but the track was slow——," representing his economic and emotional downturn. But one day, this gray tweed-suited businessman exceeded his metaphorical score by one too many, got fired, and suicided in one fell swoop. He was dubiously missed by the staff of the newspaper where he worked and by his fellow subway riders. However, corporate slogans, vernacular exclamations, and the mechanical din of everyday life continued, punctuating his demise with a repetition of mechanical "bongs."[145] The inexplicable suicide of a magazine writer, illustrating the presence of a similar corporate malaise, is repeated in the novel *The Big Clock,* an event that is recalled in passing by Stroud, who observes nonchalantly, "Down the hall, in Sydney's office, there was a window out of which an almost forgotten associate editor had long ago jumped."[146]

The novel also considers the manner in which human life is quantified as if it was a stock option or a financial investment. Stroud and his colleagues are researching the issue of Funded Individuals, meritorious persons whose lives serve as investments early on, with the expectation of a monetary return. Moreover, a painting entitled *The Temptation of Judas,* which was the original title of the novel, depicting two hands exchanging coins, is purchased by Stroud in both story and film, referring to the way the Organization Man is a traitor to self for mere material reward.

Fearing's critique of capitalism may be explained by his political affiliations, at the very least a fellow traveler and at most an associate of the Communist Party, if not an outright member. His poetry was both published and praised by the leftist press, including the *New Masses* and the *Menorah Journal.* Reviewers of his Depression-era verse almost universally referred to him as a party poet, although there is some question as to whether he actually joined. Even though he attended meetings of the John Reed Club, he found them excruciatingly boring, supposedly exclaiming to his colleague Philip Rahv after the latter lambasted Stalinism, "And you recruited me into the party?"[147] In spite of later efforts by his family members to disavow his connection, describing him instead as an independent humanist, it is almost certain that he had Marxist sympathies, although he resisted regimentation whether it emanated from Moscow or Washington.[148] Like many American leftists, he became disillusioned with the Soviet Union after the Moscow trials, and especially after the Russian invasion of Finland in 1939. He was equally disdainful of the strong-arm tactics of

McCarthy and his cronies. When he was summoned before HUAC, and asked the proverbial question concerning his suspected affiliation in the Communist Party, he brashly and irreverently replied, "Not yet!"[149]

Fearing's decision to attack corporate media interests in *The Big Clock* was not only motivated by his Marxist sympathies in the abstract, but by his own tenure at Henry Luce's *Time* magazine, for which he wrote book reviews in the late 1930s. Leading the life of an impecunious poet, he was forced to supplement his income with freelance and hack work, even writing for the sex pulps under a pseudonym for one and a half cents a word. The challenge for Fearing, which he explored in the novel, was the dilemma faced by writers to maintain their artistic integrity in the face of mounting pressure to conform. In accord with his creator, the character Stroud decides to harness the strategies of the mass media to beat it at its own game. Fearing also worked in the entertaining, pulp-fiction medium as a means to raise the consciousness of the general public and convert them to his political viewpoint.

Most of his novels explored the effects of major bureaucratic institutions on ordinary people. *The Hospital* (1939) is a fast-paced exploration of a large medical establishment's impact on the lives of its patients.[150] Told from the perspective of several characters, *Clark Gifford's Body* (1942) is the story of a modern-day John Brown (Gifford) who stages an attack on a radio station. Despite his capture and execution, the revolution he initiates is successful.[151] It prefigures *The Big Clock* in the expression of rage directed at a media giant that had hijacked accuracy in favor of partisan political agendas in the service of economic interests. As the author later stated, he had grown weary of the "absolute power exercised in, and through, the networks of communication, captive and menaced as they are."[152]

Fearing directed his frustration and anger at Time-Life Inc., often drawing on his personal experiences for his thinly veiled critique. He located the fictional Janoth Enterprises in the nine upper stories of a lofty thirty-two-story skyscraper, which resembled Luce's occupancy of the new thirty-six-story Time-Life Building's top seven stories in Rockefeller Center.[153] The use of a singular tower for all operations reiterates the theme of the centralized, monolithic distillation of reality by a legion of subservient employees in the service of a partisan media tycoon. The fictional "nerve center" was "fed" by twenty-one large cities at home and twenty-five abroad, resulting in an "empire of intelligence."[154]

Janoth's magazine syndicate was all encompassing, publishing "fiction and news, covering business and technical affairs."[155] Fearing's conflation of fiction and news is purposeful, referring to the slim line that differentiated the two and the company's decided lack of objectivity. Janoth published a collection of diverse magazines, many of which looked like those put out by Luce. The weekly publication of general interest *Newsday* resembled *Time,* although similar in title to *Newsweek,* while *Commerce,* a highly influential business weekly, bore a likeness to the monthly *Fortune.* Others included *Crimeways, Sportland, The Frozen Age, The Actuary, Frequency* (concerning radio and television), *Plastic Tomorrow, Homeways, Personalities, Fashion,* and *The Sexes.* More far-reaching in subject matter, Fearing sought to draw a symbolic parallel with Luce's self-conscious effort to engage in political "opinion engineering," while selling American products through his advertisers.[156]

Luce enterprise's support of a product-oriented, managed existence is signified spatially in the film by the elevator's journey aloft. It stops on various floors, each of which is occupied by a different magazine and an elaborate set design, advancing various consumer goods and concomitant ways of life, a literal and metaphorical display of upward mobility. This is coupled with the requisite flirting that is characteristic of such elevator antics, linking erotic pleasure with the acquisition of commodities. The elevator serves as the vertical counterpart of Benjamin's arcade with artful display windows that represent the material compartmentalization of American life and identity.

The elevator in The Big Clock.

When Fearing was writing the novel in 1944–45, Luce's magazines were enjoying an unprecedented readership. It was estimated that for every subscription at least four other people shared the magazine, further increasing the publishing magnate's tentacle-like reach. For example, *Time* had a weekly circulation of 1,160,000 and printed special editions for the classroom and for the Canadian, European, Asian, Mexican, and South American markets, among others. He also broadcast the Radio March of Time to an audience of eighteen million in the United States, while *Time*'s Views of the News was broadcast daily to millions. Early in 1944, he bought a 12½ percent share in NBC's Blue Network, which further hooked him up to over one hundred radio stations.[157] As historian James L. Baughman observed, after Luce had secured his readership in the United States in the late 1930s, he spent the remainder of his life trying to convert his audience. "For the American middle," Henry Luce, Republican and virulent anti-Communist, "assumed the role of propaganda minister."[158] He traveled the world and met with international leaders, importing his notion of an American Century, which he had formulated in 1941. Luce held an abiding belief that American capitalism and religious values should serve as the blueprint for the entire globe. The function of his vast media empire was to disseminate these ideals both nationally and internationally, much like the fictional Earl Janoth.

Luce's overarching political and economic agenda is central to an understanding of Latimer's appropriation of Fearing's source material. Both writers created an authoritarian media tycoon who could be construed either as a foreign fascist dictator or as the personification of a merciless, home-grown, right-wing fanatic. This conflation of external and internal threat became a prevalent theme in both American film noir and the HUAC investigations. Hollywood's effort to grapple with intense political scrutiny in a climate of fear and paranoia was often absorbed into the affective and thematic character of its cinematic productions.[159] Latimer's adaptation represents an amalgamation of Fearing's left-wing ideas and conservative prescriptions prompted by the current political environment, a pastiche representing the conflicted nature of the era itself.[160]

This is seen particularly in the persona of Janoth, whose identity seems to have been informed by one of the most notorious cold war personalities, Whittaker Chambers, and Luce himself. Luce's own foreign editor of *Time,* Chambers accused the prominent Roosevelt administration ambassador Alger Hiss of spying for the Soviets in 1948. Janoth's physiognomy and gender identity as fashioned by Fearing and Latimer bear the imprint of the fleshy, homosexual Chambers, who was known among *Time*'s staff in the 1940s as a dangerous ideologue who distorted the news, while the tycoon's overbearing, authoritarian manner resembles that of Luce. Chambers had been a Soviet courier who had supposedly quit the party after Stalin's purges and refashioned himself as an impassioned red baiter, a conflicted political character who provided fodder for the delineation of the dangers from both sides of the political spectrum. For leftists such as Fearing, and perhaps even Latimer, the double-edged nature of Janoth's character was a deft maneuver to outwit the cold war censors and ideologues who were intent on policing the text for ideological correctness.

Fearing did not have to wait until the official commencement of the HUAC activities in 1947 to recognize that a renewed persecuting force had been unleashed against Communists and fellow travelers in the United States. In *The Big Clock,* the author's depiction of a man wrongly investigated for a crime he did not commit, compelled to define himself against an onslaught of misinformation, had its roots in the investigative mania sweeping the country, beginning in 1938. The Dies Committee, which was heir to the Anti-Nazi League organized to fight fascism, soon shifted its attention to the Communist Party. That year, Dies placed an ad in the *Hollywood Reporter,* putting the film community on notice that he would give them an opportunity to defend themselves on charges "that they were participating in communistic activities."[161] In 1939, he set his sights on the Federal Theater Project, resulting in the cessation of their funding and the institution of a loyalty oath for all Works Progress Administration employees. The following year, Dies and company arrived in Hollywood with a list of so-called subversive screenwriters, informing them that they could clear themselves by voluntarily disclaiming their past Communist affiliations. Few complied. As Larry Ceplair and Steven Englund have pointed out, there were no fewer than thirty-nine anti-Communist bills introduced in Congress during this era.[162]

Fearing's response to the investigative zeal of Dies and men like him is recorded in the poem "A Tribute, and a Nightmare" (1941), a parody on the congressman's ersatz contribution to HUAC, referred to as the "Committee to Investigate Gloom," which promised to restore laughter to the world.[163] "Will the planet be Red with revolution (you hope) from the tropics to the poles?" Fearing inquired rhetorically. If this was at all plausible, "You will have to deal (you fear, and rightly) with Commissar Dies, Chairman of the Committee to Probe Versive Activity." Applying the title commissar to Dies prefigures the author's blurring of the boundaries between right- and left-wing authoritarian types in *The Big Clock*. The poet also betrays his apprehension that Dies's investigations will result in legal strictures detrimental not only to political freedom but to the creative process itself, hence his use of the neologism "versive." "A Tribute, and a Nightmare" ends by linking the dictatorial Dies to corporate profiteering, depicting him as a man who, like the fictional Janoth, harnesses the institutional apparatus to unethical ends.

In the later essay, "Reading, Writing, and the Rackets" (1956), Fearing explored further the stifling of creativity and the censorship of dissident ideas by the "communication cartels" such as Time-Life Inc., who hired writers to mold public opinion for their financial enrichment.[164] What the author termed "the Investigation" was but a ploy to promote certain values and suppress others for the sole purpose of attaining ideological hegemony and power. Couched in the language of good versus evil, the Investigation's mesmerizing show was designed for "total darkness, total silence and total secrecy," which resulted in the escapist, nonconflictual products of cowering writers.[165]

George Stroud in *The Big Clock* enacts this battle between conformity and artistic freedom, a character confined to the twin regimented domains of skyscraper and prefabricated suburb who seeks release in zany bars, dubbed museums, filled with heterogeneous collectibles from around the world. An aesthete of sorts, Stroud is also an art collector. He covets the paintings of bohemian Louise Patterson (Elsa Lanchester), who specializes in depictions of atomized body parts replete with cryptic meaning concerning the nature of mercenary human existence. An inveterate nonconformist and iconoclast, the unmarried Patterson, who in the novel has several illegitimate children by different men, becomes Stroud's accidental accomplice, refusing to identify him as the man who bought her painting, thus undermining Janoth's unlawful murder investigation.[166]

Patterson's excessive, histrionic personality is juxtaposed with the constricted, craven men employed by Janoth Enterprises, who are forced to write prepackaged copy from which all inventiveness has been extracted. Fearing explained that corporate prose, in accord with its physical space, is one of economy and distillation, the equivalent of the International Style in architecture—lean, pared down, functional. Reduced to terse phrases these "simplified bulletins," written using the "technique of subtraction" (sound bites in modern parlance), are constructed to dissuade readers from engaging in thoughtful analysis or interrogation.[167] In the novel, Stroud reports that he and his colleagues at *Crimeways* magazine decide that their audience will accept their written assessments and "in the end their crystallized judgments would be one with ours."[168] The result is a psychic prison that serves as an analogue to the material one created by the rationalized spaces of the skyscraper and suburb. In a sleight of hand, Fearing has Stroud utilize a surfeit of unintegrated "facts" in the investigation of himself in order to paralyze the corporation's depraved regime, knowing that no one will have the synthetic imagination to integrate the information to solve the conundrum. Stroud represents another example of Fearing's intention to employ the corporation's own means of production to undercut its stranglehold.

FROM NOVEL TO FILM

Fearing's novel *The Big Clock* is a complex pulp mystery novel, the story of which is told from the diverse vantage points of several primary characters, almost prefiguring the postmodernist use of split subjectivities. Its structure enforces the author's belief in the illusory, personal nature of reality and is a prescient challenge to an overarching metanarrative. Despite the tale's protean postmodernism, however, George Stroud is clearly its main protagonist with eleven of the nineteen chapters told from his perspective. His thoughts, adventures, and exploits are valorized, thereby echoing the singular masculinist perspective of many adventure and mystery novels and noir films. Latimer's script underscores Stroud's hero status, pitting him against, and ultimately outsmarting, media tycoon Earl Janoth with his instrumental intelligence.

Stroud is regimented at work and relegated to a bland suburb populated by rising executives, prompting him to feel psychically and physically hemmed in. At the outset of the novel, he meets Pauline Delos, a "tall icy blonde" who appears as the epitome of innocence but is to the "instincts" little more than "undiluted sex."[169] Two months after their initial encounter while his wife and daughter are vacationing, Stroud begins an affair with Delos, which leads ultimately to her murder by Janoth. When the media tycoon arrives unexpectedly to her apartment, he sees a stranger shrouded in darkness, stealthily descending the stairwell. After discovering a man's tie draped over a miniature sundial, which confirms his suspicions, he confronts Delos, which leads to the deadly altercation. In the novel the weapon is a glass decanter, while in the film the murderous sundial (introduced in the film's opening credits) serves as a heavy-handed symbol of Janoth's obsession with time.

Janoth's irrational rage is also prompted by Delos's accusation that he is not only having multiple affairs with female subordinates but that he is carrying on a long-term relationship with his assistant of twenty years, Steve Hagen. "Did I ever see you two together when you weren't camping," she inquires, continuing provocatively, "As if you weren't married to that guy, all your life. And as if I didn't know. Go on, you son of a bitch, try to act surprised."[170] In the film, covert references to Janoth as "pathetic," "disgusting," and "flabby, flabby" are employed to signify his homosexual persona.[171] Flying into an uncontrollable rage in the film, Janoth strikes her with an old-fashioned sundial, a symbol of his primeval rage and his obsession with controlling time. In need of emotional support and an alibi, he rushes to Hagen's apartment, thereby corroborating Delos's accusation in the novel of a clandestine homosexual relationship. Not only does Hagen provide the alibi, but he hurries to the scene of the crime to doctor the evidence. Fearing depicts Janoth as a weak, cowardly man who breaks down in tears, while the Machiavellian Hagen is more concerned with the corporation's survival and his own economic well-being. Like the protagonist in Wagner's opera *Siegfried* (1870), Hagen serves as the villain to King Gunther's fool.

Hagen assigns Stroud the task of finding a so-called mystery man seen leaving Gil's bar, who later buys a painting called *The Temptation of Judas* by Louise

Patterson at an antique shop. Stroud knows that Hagen is looking for him since he has frequented the above locations with Delos prior to the murder. Yet Janoth's conniving right-hand man does not mention the murder; rather he explains the search as linked to a colossal business and political conspiracy, which is in fact an allusion to the tycoon's own subterfuge. Stroud is instructed to marshal his entire staff at *Crimeways* magazine to help crack the case, clearly a misuse of the media's truth-telling mission for mendacious purposes. He thinks that he is about to lose his cover when a *Crimeways* employee locates various witnesses who can place him at the aforementioned locations. Artist Louise Patterson could blow his cover but decides to protect his anonymity simply because he values one of her paintings, a partial triumph of artistic creativity and nonconformity over corporate regimentation. He ultimately evades capture in the novel because the negative publicity surrounding the murder has forced Janoth to resign from the board. It ends with Stroud reading an enormous tabloid headline: "EARL JANOTH, OUSTED PUBLISHER, PLUNGES TO DEATH."[172]

Shortly after *The Big Clock*'s debut in the fall of 1946, Jonathan Latimer was at work on the first of several versions of the screenplay for Paramount Studios. The film was directed by John Farrow and released in April of 1948. Latimer, who was originally trained as a newspaper writer, soon became a popular mystery novelist in his own right.[173] He began authoring scripts for Columbia, Metro-Goldwyn-Mayer, United Artists, and Paramount in 1938. Due to his mystery-writing experience and his success at adapting Dashiell Hammett's *The Glass Key* (1942), he was commissioned to revise Fearing's novel. When questioned by an interviewer in 1980, Latimer identified *The Big Clock* as his most illustrious effort, quite a testament since he continued as a Paramount screenwriter until 1965.[174]

Latimer is responsible for a host of alterations to the original, including the transfer of the bulk of the action to a lofty International Style skyscraper, the battle for normative heterosexuality against effete homoerotic foreigners, and the creation of an overarching mechanical clock only hinted at by Fearing. R. Barton Palmer has unwittingly given credit to Latimer for his structuring of the film as a thriller, rather than an orthodox film noir, in which the law and patriarchal authority are restored, in an effort to demonstrate that the screenwriter's solutions were more conservative than the author's.[175] Yet it is apparent that Latimer deftly sifted through Fearing's novel, retaining much of the original's political underpinnings, often by playing on double entendre and the use of coded references. He preserved the author's trenchant attack on corporate domination by imbuing Janoth with a monomaniacal concern for efficiency and exactitude. Ironically, even though Fearing was the one who had been employed by Time-Life Inc., Latimer created a sinister antihero who possessed Luce's intimidating traits with the personality of a ruthless, Hitlerian foreign dictator. In spite of the Production Code and the HUAC investigations, Latimer

Hercules figure and maps of the world in The Big Clock.

maintained Fearing's leftist indictment, albeit in a more covert likeness, for anyone who cared to see it.

Latimer's critique of Luce begins thematically and spatially in the film's initial scene, with an introduction to the skyscraper lobby. Distinct from its former characterization as a democratic area given over to the mingling of diverse
classes, in *The Big Clock* it is a spectacular, engulfing space that is controlled
by an enormous timepiece, whose reach is limitless. Peering down into the vast
public space from the multistoried clock, Stroud records retrospectively the
events leading up to his imprisonment. From a high vantage point that echoes
Stroud's downward gaze, the camera surveys a group of tourists who are being
led through the lobby by a guide. They are small in proportion to the clock's
enormous circular drum, which dominates the central core, both mesmerized
and dwarfed by the machine's grandeur. The spectacle of the clock and the commodious lobby obfuscates the work-a-day world of office denizens in their austere, spatially constricted compartments and is meant as the material counterpart to Luce's sensationalist journalistic practices. Like the theatrical, circular
lobby in Raymond M. Hood's Daily News Building (1931), which includes a
twelve-foot spherical globe and "wall maps that included maps of the world,

the solar system, the United States, New York City," the Janoth Building is designed to announce that the publishing empire is all pervasive in its scope.[176]
Its tower-like presence in the skyscraper's heart also conjures up Bentham's
eighteenth-century panopticon tower as described by Foucault, which exerted
power and controlled behavior by human surveillance, here transformed into
an inanimate, seemingly autonomous mechanism.[177] Its omnipotence and control of lives outside its immediate purview is underscored by the guide who
informs the gawking spectators that it is

> the most accurate, most unique privately owned clock in the
> world. Behind a huge map of the world is a single huge master
> mechanism built at a cost of $600,000. It is set so you can tell time
> anywhere on earth—London, Chicago, Honolulu and so forth. It
> is also synchronized with those in secondary printing plants in
> Kansas City, San Francisco and forty-three foreign bureaus in the
> Janoth Organization.[178]

The purposeful use of terminology such as "master mechanism" and "synchronization" imbues the clock with a menacing, seemingly independent capacity
to dominate while pointing to its monolithic ability to extend its reach to all
corners of the globe, a description that must have held a particular negative
resonance for a postwar public recovering from the evils of fascism.

The skyscraper's clock and numerous maps may serve as a hyperbolized
depiction of Luce's design to export a U.S. version of capitalism and its concomitant institutions throughout the world. His "American Century" was but a
veiled attempt to establish American economic and ideological hegemony as the
paradigm for a new internationalism, distributing copies of his global vision in
the national mainstream media and beyond. While it was praised by some as an
idealistic method to export democracy in a world threatened by authoritarianism, others viewed it as a new form of cultural and economic imperialism. Luce
continued to promote his vision of a new world order after the war, calling for a
"United States of Europe," sponsored by Great Britain and the United States.[179]
Perhaps the mistrust was due to his abiding admiration for Mussolini and his
benign acceptance of Hitler right up to the latter's incursion into Poland.

Luce enterprises are invoked further by the purposeful placement in the
lobby's upper alcove of a sculpture depicting a muscular Atlas holding up an
armillary sphere of the world. The gargantuan strongman and his globe bear
a marked resemblance to Lee Lawrie's bronze *Atlas* (1936), situated at the entrance to Rockefeller Center's International Building.[180] This deliberate association was not lost on film reviewers; one described the skyscraper setting as
located "over in Radio City, in a building that must adjoin *Time-Life*" where
"Earl Janoth (Charles Laughton) is about ten times as big a publisher as Henry

Luce."[181] Architectural historian Carol Herselle Krinsky has noted that the Rockefeller Center's Atlas figure served to highlight the International Building and its numerous shops, which offered imported goods from Italy. But as Krinsky reported, the Italian connection went even further. It was widely rumored that the figure resembled none other than Benito Mussolini.[182] Thus, Paramount's art staff not only employed the sculpture to refer to Luce, but sought to equate the figure with the fascist designs of Earl Janoth, who sought world domination from his monolithic skyscraper outpost.

Skyscraper space in *The Big Clock* is both expansive and constricted; it forces confinement and conformity, but its seemingly vast reach extends beyond its physical boundaries. Fearing's description of Janoth's corpulent body, portrayed exquisitely by Charles Laughton, is meant to signify both excess and lack of limits, masquerading as parsimony. This dialectic relationship between surplus and economy is underscored by Latimer, who rendered the mogul as obsessed with waste, bent on firing an employee who left a light bulb on too long. At a board meeting presided over by Janoth and Hagen, which ostensibly concerns increasing subscription rates, the discussion devolves into a tirade against excess. The various magazine editors present who have expressions of "harassed tension that shows on their faces," according to the script, are each given one minute to present their best pitch on increasing sales. The overbearing Janoth demands extemporaneous ideas, intoning, "All this waste, sheer waste under the leadership of chuckleheads."[183]

Latimer's formulation of the scene is designed, in part, to draw a parallel between the dictatorial Janoth and Luce. The fictional tycoon's imperious manner and his belief in intimidation in the service of production seemed scripted from Luce's own personnel philosophy. According to numerous employees who worked for him over the years, Luce was notoriously rude, thought to be "part of his idea of efficiency, eliminating all time-wasting amenities," including business etiquette.[184] Like other publishing barons, he deemed his employees' bodies and souls to be his own during and after business hours. Janoth also tried to force Stroud to work instead of taking a planned vacation, something he had not done in seven years! At staff meetings and luncheons where the nervous tension was palpable, Luce fired unpredictable questions at his executives, under the assumption that the strain kept them on their toes. Without warning, he summoned the unknowing, frequently unprepared to his office, meetings that were variously nicknamed the terror, the rack, or the last judgment.

THE CONSTRUCTION OF GENDER AND SEXUAL IDENTITY

George Stroud begins his recollection of events when he arrives to work early one morning, a typical day by all accounts. He is seen striding confidently and aggressively past the group of stationary tourists observing the clock in the Janoth Building's lobby. A man in the group inquires, "What if the clock should stop?" to which Stroud replies, "Mr. Janoth would never permit that." The scene encapsulates the hero's masculinity seen also in the boardroom scene; he is instrumental, speaks out of turn, and is a nonconformist who is differentiated from the crowd, although he refers to himself as normal. Stroud's unsolicited rejoinder to the tourist's question also serves to prefigure later events; even though Janoth might object, Stroud has the wherewithal and power to stop the clock, breaking Janoth's lock grip on the building. A description of his office defines him further as an individualist and an iconoclast. Although his room is "ultramodern, as are most of the executive offices in the building," it is decorated with Louise Patterson's painting of a man and woman, which resembles a Renaissance portrait.[185] Iconographically, the work is meant to restore heteronormativity to the severe surroundings and their implied regimentation, while identifying him as an art lover.

Stroud's gender identity is informed by the growing fears among social critics concerning the loss of masculine autonomy in the ever-expanding corporation, which threatened to reduce him to a group man rather than an individual. In *The Lonely Crowd* (1950), David Riesman identified a new salaried class of

Stroud's modernist office in The Big Clock.

professionals who were in danger of becoming extensions of their jobs. "We did not assume that an individual would be the replica of his social role," Riesman lamented, but that there "might be great tension between an individual's search for fulfillment and the demands of the institutions in which he had a part."[186] William H. Whyte concurred in his book *The Organization Man* (1956), labeling the new middle-class office worker an "organization man" who was no longer a singular entity but an interchangeable unit in a "collective," given over to group decision-making and consensus. According to the author, this represented a "major shift in American ideology," from the autonomous go-getter to the conformist, deeply affecting notions of manhood.[187] The old slogan *ad astra per aspera* (The stars were far away, but he still aimed for them), which characterized manhood from the late nineteenth century until the 1920s, no longer seemed applicable, Riesman observed.[188] Rather than capitulating to this debilitating mindset, Whyte encouraged the corporate employee "to *fight* the Organization" from within by not relinquishing his individual courageousness and creativity.[189]

George Stroud is a man who is willing and able to heed Whyte's injunction, an idealized view of a lone individual against an all-consuming corporation. He is a man seemingly without a past, with no hint of his activities prior to and during World War II, yet his take-charge attitude and his supervision of an entire department recall the authority of a general in command of troops. Tall and authoritative, Stroud possesses a lean physique that ostensibly harmonizes with the austere corporate office. Latimer describes him in a preliminary script as a paragon of normative masculinity, dressed in a typical corporate uniform: "Appearance—Brown Hair and Eyes—5' 11"—175, Clothing—Gray Flannel Suit—Brown Shoes—Nassau Hat—Striped Necktie, Age—34."[190] Yet his suit is replete with pinstripes, the geometric regularity of which echoes Stroud's office furniture and opaque grid-like windows. The viewer initially fears that Stroud is in danger of engulfment, but his commanding stature and commanding persona are at odds with his sartorial appearance.

Director John Farrow constructs the aforementioned scene in which Janoth badgers his cowering employees to increase subscription rates as one overtaken by Stroud. Shot from below, a huge cruciform table bisects the frame, setting the bloated Janoth who stands at one end apart from an empty seat at the other. Bursting out from a private elevator to the left in tardy disregard of Janoth's obsession with punctuality, Stroud walks rapidly to his chair in contrast to the obsequious seated others. His demeanor, authoritative height and gait, and winning pitch show that he is a personality to be reckoned with. Janoth is duly impressed with his distinguished charge, but the battle lines are drawn between normative masculinity and its obsessive, nervous variant.

Stroud's virile heterosexuality has been undermined by Janoth, who refuses

Boardroom in The Big Clock.

to allow him either a vacation or a belated honeymoon, so he rebels by step-ping out with the boss's own mistress. In the film version, he merely engages in a night of carousing with York, signified by dissolve shots of neon signage advertising various nightspots to the accompaniment of upbeat music, but in the novel he seizes deliberately what he perceives as the boss's own. When he must leave York's apartment upon Janoth's unexpected arrival, he assumes a devil-may-care attitude concerning the possibility of being recognized. "And what if he had?" Stroud queries. "He didn't own the woman. He didn't own me either."[191]

The threat to normative masculinity is underscored in Latimer's delinea-tion of Stroud's family. Georgette Stroud (Maureen O'Sullivan) is a nurturing mother, the glue that binds the family that has been temporarily destabilized by Janoth's demands and George Stroud's carousing.[192] She is rendered in the domestic safety of a bucolic, implicitly restorative West Virginia cabin, which serves as an antidote to the debilitating, claustrophobic skyscraper in which Stroud is mentally and physically trapped. Fearing depicted Stroud with a daughter named Georgia, but the screenwriter saw fit to depict the overworked, absentee father with a young son in need of paternal attention. In fact, the only way that wife Georgette can get the boy to eat his oatmeal is by putting dad on the telephone, who gratifies the child by informing him that a gift is waiting under his pillow. The delighted child hauls out a strange weapon and exclaims, "Oh, boy! . . . An atomic disintegrator!" Latimer's inclusion of the phallic toy represents Stroud's efforts to shepherd his son into his appropriate gender role, which is reiterated by Georgette's expression of their dual abandonment: "We should have stayed in West Virginia. We'd be a family now. . . . Oh, George, the whole thing is wrong. Little George doesn't even know you. A boy needs his father. . . . Someone to teach him how to play football and make model airplanes."[193] The presence of the strange plaything also suggests that aliens are present and must be neutralized, a chore that Stroud will accomplish with his wits rather than weaponry.

Stroud's superior intellect is acknowledged by Janoth who recalls him from his long-awaited vacation, which he has defiantly seized and been fired as a consequence, to supervise the phony investigation of a man supposedly involved in a political wartime scandal, but which Stroud knows is really a ploy to frame him for York's murder. He has no choice but to return to the metropolitan office, again ripped from the familial bond to the enervating influence of metropolitan space. Well-informed on the intricacies of the entire corporate media structure, which has been put at his disposal, Stroud uses his mental acumen to defeat Janoth. He employs a plethora of cold, hard, unmediated facts to gum up the rigid bureaucracy, which itself endlessly churns out "artless messages."[194] Latimer also invests Stroud with the autonomy to write his own character in a Pirandello-like maneuver, as an antidote to Janoth's effort to define him, thus regaining his identity from the corporation's clutches. Stroud even overtakes Janoth's office and the intercom system that has been used to eavesdrop on employees.

The film's turning point occurs with Stroud's entrapment in the clock tower within a tower, when he hijacks the virtual nerve center of the mechanical edifice. He inadvertently or perhaps symbolically hits the lever that stops the clock, sending Janoth into a panic, no longer at the helm of his tightly regimented domain. Although Janoth tries to regain control of the building by sending his goon Bill Womack to check his prized timepiece, Stroud knocks him temporarily unconscious. Now is the time for the hero to begin his literal and figurative ascent to the thirty-second floor or the top of the building, to Hagen and Janoth's offices. In the meantime, Womack awakens and begins his pursuit of Stroud. One step ahead, Stroud employs the skyscraper's own mechanisms to conquer it: he jerry-rigs the elevator and traps Womack inside, stuck between floors. By keeping the door slightly ajar on the upper floor, the elevator is effectively frozen, rendering his adversary impotent, an intervention that will finish off Janoth.

Stroud's ersatz affair with York is employed to assert his heterosexual virility, which has been confined in an institutional and matrimonial sphere, and to alternately serve as a caveat to those that would stray from the sanctity of marriage. The film renders York as the stereotypical noir femme fatale, who is introduced to the unknowing Stroud when she eavesdrops on his conversation via Janoth's intercom. In accord with her sugar daddy, she has no compunction about blurring the boundaries between public and personal space. Impressed by Stroud's rebelliousness, she follows him to a bar where she arranges to accidentally run into him. Dressed in sinister black gloves and a hat with a netted veil, she cradles Stroud's hand in her black predatory ones; her costume and gesture accord with her spider-like plan to ensnare her victim.[195] The bar and boudoir are her spatial analogues, in contrast to the normative domestic sphere inhabited by Georgette Stroud. York and Stroud order drinks called "green stingers," calling to mind poisonous insects or snakes and evoking the biblical temptation and fall. He meets her again in the same bar and is so mesmerized by York that he misses an appointment with his wife at the train station, where they are about to embark on their holiday. The consummation of their marriage is thus impeded by transgressive sexuality on two fronts, homoerotic and extramarital.

Stroud and Pauline York at the bar in The Big Clock.

Fearing named the femme fatale Delos to associate her with things Greek, while in the film her name is York, evoking the sophistication of a metropolitan woman. Fearing had Janoth accuse Delos of sleeping with both men and women, confiding to Hagen, "She's a part-time Liz, Steve, did I ever tell you?" The novelist underscored her gender confusion by describing her garments, seen through Stroud's eyes, as "a rather austere gray and black ensemble that looked like a tailored suit but wasn't."[196] Thus the name Delos might have also been invented to sound like Lesbos, a reference to her sexual preference. In accord with Rand's delineation of Dominique Francon, transgressive women represent a threat to hegemonic notions of gender identity. In *The Fountainhead* such women were tamed while in the noir *The Big Clock,* they are extinguished. In spite of Fearing's leftist political propensities, his views regarding gender and sexual identity are surprisingly traditional and are echoed in Latimer's adaptation.

Earl Janoth is portrayed with polymorphous sexual predilections, although in the novel he seems to prefer men. The casting of Charles Laughton as Janoth gives credence to his portrayal of the closeted homosexual since the role echoed the actor's own double life, reinforcing the idea that the construction of gender and sexual identity in cinema is the result of a number of variables knowingly employed by filmmakers.[197] Although he was married to Elsa Lanchester, Laughton carried on clandestine liaisons with young men. His cinematic name Janoth reinforces his divided nature, resembling a Germanic version of the two-headed Roman god, while his first name, Earl, signifies his royalist, antidemocratic leanings. Is he an upstanding Englishman or an embedded fascist posing as one, the film queries. Even though he exacts a rigid adherence to rules among his employees, it is merely a facade to shield a primordial id, which is on the verge of exploding. Fearing discloses his murderous impulses early on; upon meeting guests at a party, Janoth thinks, "I could have strangled them one by one."[198] His irrationality is represented spatially by his exaggerated use of the clock, and by the skyscraper's transformation into a trap and a labyrinth.

Janoth's body and face are like pliable soft putty, the antithesis of ideal masculinity. In a preliminary script, Latimer invested him with effete European attire by providing him with "a hand-stretched silk suit, neat bowtie and English shoes."[199] His expensive and elegant tastes signify overconsumption, at odds with the privation he exacts from his employees, which characterizes him as a greedy hypocrite and a dissembler. In this regard, he is similar to Rand's delineation of Ellsworth Toohey. Charles Laughton played Janoth as a high-strung fussbudget, with rapid, nervous speech, anxious twitches, and limp hand gestures, meant to alert the knowing viewer to his sexual proclivities.

He establishes close bodily contact with several male characters in the film, including Stroud, Hagen, and Womack, often mixing cloying familiarity with menacing threat. Richard Dyer refers to the depiction of homosexual characters

Earl Janoth and Bill Womack in The Big Clock.

in film noir as "elitist, powerful, and cruel."[200] When Stroud informs him that he intends to take his holiday, Janoth puts his arm around him and replies, "You'll see this through or you will cease working for Janoth Publications. I'll have you blacklisted all over the country," fusing his sexuality with cold war retribution.

Janoth's homosexual persona is also found in the skyscraper bathhouse or gymnasium, which is also inhabited by Bill Womack, the tycoon's silent young bodyguard, who offers his boss various "physical" services. Womack and this scene are absent from the novel, underscoring Latimer's intent to highlight a homoerotic liaison. Bath house and gymnasium scenes had been employed to convey homoerotic desire in cinema since the Depression era as explained in chapter 2. Janoth's recumbent, partly nude body is massaged with oily unguent by Womack, one of whose arms is decorated with a prominent tattoo. The amorphous image is a composite of Janoth: it is a devil's face with horns, but when viewed upside down, it is a fleshy nude man. Both Womack and Janoth are seen in an extreme close-up shot to convey the couple's intimacy and the hothouse environment's stultifying claustrophobia. The dialogue implies that he may take his protégé on a trip where people are more tolerant of sexually diverse practices.

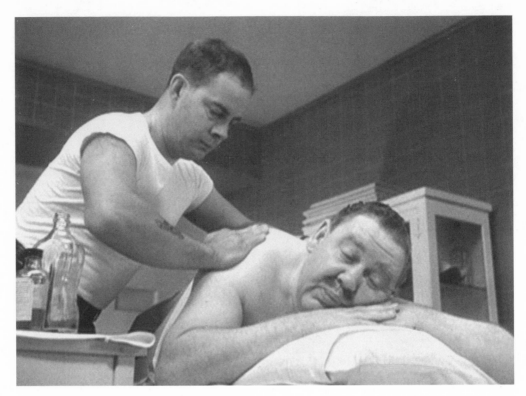

Bathhouse in The Big Clock.

Janoth complains, "Oh, I'm so tired and run down. I need a vacation. Should take an ocean voyage. Have you ever been abroad, Bill? It's stimulating . . . different people . . . different customs."

Bill Womack is himself a complex character who is entirely a creation of Latimer. Often designated by his dark suit, shirt, and light tie, he is a gangster type who acts as Janoth's protector and personal servant, part bodyguard and part houseboy. In spite of the fact that he packs a pistol, his small stature belies his ability to strong-arm anyone. Fearing's novel provides some clarification for Latimer's formulation and Farrow's direction, since he bears a striking resemblance to the author's physical description of Steve Hagen. Fearing writes that "Hagen was a hard, dark little man whose soul had been hit by lightning, which he liked. . . . I knew he was almost as loyal to Janoth as to himself."[201] Hence, Womack is a character split off from the original delineation of Hagen, reinforcing his function as an additional homosexual presence in Janoth's retinue. Latimer originally named him Womrath, which is a composite of woman and wrath, providing evidence of a feminized identity. Barely uttering a word and beset with a gloomy demeanor, he also fits the description of homosexual characters who, according to Richard Dyer, "are intensely physical beings who can not 'do anything' physical and hence vibrate with frustrated, twisted sexual energy."[202]

The primary homoerotic bond in the film is between Janoth and Hagen. The latter was played by George Macready who had previously starred as Ballin, the homosexual Nazi in *Gilda* (1946). Macready also possessed the requisite scar. His physical disfigurement conveys his association with abuse or sado-masochistic practices that were also associated with gay and lesbian characters in film. Hagen's sartorial presentation is in keeping with the stereotypically feminine and upper-class decadence. When Janoth flees to his private apartment after the murder, he finds Hagen dressed in a long satin robe and ascot, much like Ellsworth Toohey. He is surrounded by numerous extravagant objects, including a crystal pitcher, "antique furniture, many bookcases, a huge Victorian marble fireplace," and "Aubusson carpets," described as "the fussy dwelling of a well-to-do bachelor."[203] It is not uncommon for homosexual characters to be steeped in luxury not typical of the normal family home. As I have argued elsewhere, the overly decorated and the luxurious had been likened to depraved femininity, effeminate men, and illness in America since the late nineteenth century.[204]

Steve Hagen's apartment after the murder in The Big Clock.

Fearing's depiction of Hagen is more in keeping with Janoth's cold, unfeeling nature in the film; from Stroud's perspective, Steve's "mother was a bank vault, and his father an International Business Machine." In contrast, the author depicted Janoth as weak and voluble after the murder, in need of a man with criminal backbone, a task that Hagen relished. Their homoerotic liaison is underscored in the book by the melding of their identities, particularly their loose ego boundaries. While in Delos's apartment before the murder, Janoth regards his own attitude as cold and spent, musing, "It was a mood that Steve never had." For his part, Steve is concerned with protecting their joint interests, even if it means framing an innocent man. "I liked Earl more than I had ever liked any person on earth except my mother," he thinks.[205] Hagen's internal monologue underlines his dysfunctional character, the result of an unhealthy identification with a feminine role model.

Gender confusion is often rendered as pathological in film noir, associated with calculating dishonesty and overt criminality, principally during the later years of the cold war. As film historian Robert J. Corber has observed, homosexual identity was highly politicized during this period, associated with ominous plots and subversion.[206] The HUAC hearings were not limited solely to the identification and punishment of supposed Communist infiltrators, but were extended to include homosexuals, who were believed to be passing themselves off as straight. In 1950, two related political announcements were made: Senator Joseph McCarthy claimed that 205 Communists were secretly housed in the State Department while Deputy Undersecretary John Puerifoy declared that the government had dismissed ninety-one homosexuals from the same agency as security risks, the first of many purges, after several years of intensified harassment.[207] More homosexuals were expelled from government employment than were so-called Communists, revealing that the persecution of sexual difference was as overarching and oppressive as that of political dissidence; both were associated with foreign evil and "strange" practices. Indeed there was a slippage in cold war vocabulary concerning these two "alien" menaces, frequently establishing them as interchangeable. Psychiatrists and medical experts who testified before HUAC characterized gays and lesbians as safety threats because of their supposed susceptibility to blackmail by foreign agents. Their expulsion from governmental institutional space and suburban domestic space alike, because of their lack of adherence to the heterosexual nuclear family model, was viewed as the only way to rid the country of undesirables, which was seen as an additional bulwark against Soviet collectivism.[208]

The penultimate scene of The Big Clock is similar to The Fountainhead in its merging of dominant gender paradigms with political ideology. Echoing conservative cold war discourse, it enacts the ideological and spatial jettisoning or purge of homosexuals from American corporate skyscraper space. Stroud vanquishes the first of three homosexually coded characters before breaking free from his incarceration in the clock and proceeding to the skyscraper's upper stories. By the force of his intellect and with the help of his wife who appears at his side, they undermine Janoth's false alibi. Frank Krutnik has pointed to the "tough" investigative narrative of film noir as a device to consolidate so-called masculine law, thereby affirming the detective-hero as "potent, invulnerable, undivided, and also uncontaminated by both the machinating *femme fatale* and the corrupted male figures."[209] Here, the virile hero is dependent on his wife's resourcefulness and exclusive loyalty to solve the crime, thereby valorizing the heterosexual union and the sanctity of marriage, differentiating *The Big Clock* from most other examples of the genre. Georgette Stroud finds her husband's stained handkerchief that had formerly been in York's possession in Hagen's office, situating the two coconspirators in the femme fatale's apartment on the night of the murder. Stroud sets up a ruse to divide and conquer their alliance in the hope that they will betray one another, in keeping with cold war constructions of homosexuals. He summons them to Hagen's office, accusing Janoth's protégé of committing the murder. The heterosexual couple dominate one side of the desk, juxtaposed with the homosexual partners on the other side in the ultimate struggle for control of the building and ideological hegemony. To Hagen's astonishment, the opportunistic, double-dealing Janoth is willing to sacrifice him to save his own neck, prompting Hagen to identify or "out" his boss as the real culprit, echoing the stereotype of the easily compromised, disloyal homosexual. Realizing that the jig is up, Janoth shoots Hagen and bolts out of the office toward the elevator, which unbeknownst to him is caught between floors. He points his ineffectual pistol at Stroud before falling down the immense elevator shaft to his death, literally flushed from the architectural body. Echoing Rand, Latimer reasserts the primacy of heterosexual masculinity and matrimony at the expense of decadent homosexual infiltrators bent on using the power of the media to distort truth. Skyscraper territory in *The Big Clock* is thus liberated from the clutches of corrupt collectivists posing as enlightened entrepreneurs, reclaiming it as a heterosexual and individualist's domain.

As a final note, Joseph Breen, the Production Code chief, must be credited with helping to forge the film's ending, altering traditional cinematic skyscraper iconography and strengthening the punishment of the culprits. Fearing's novel did not include a triumphant Stroud; rather, Janoth's fall from grace was prompted by his dismissal from the board of directors, followed by his plummeting from the skyscraper's crest. In both Fearing's version and Latimer's preliminary scripts, Hagen lives on and Janoth commits suicide. The ending accords with Depression-era films in which corrupt plutocrats suicide because of financial ruin, loss of power, or the discovery of their malfeasance. However, Breen refused to allow the bad guys the privilege and autonomy to exact their own penalty. In a tersely worded letter, he stated unequivocally that before the story could be approved, it would be necessary "to eliminate the suicide of

The Strouds vs. Janoth and Hagen in The Big Clock.

Janoth plummets down the elevator shaft in The Big Clock.

Janoth" because "a suicide to escape justice can not be approved."[210] Latimer countered with an even more riveting conclusion, in keeping with Stroud's wholesale weakening of the skyscraper's mechanical apparatus, by consigning the coded homosexual Janoth to the metaphorical bowels of hell. Janoth's downward plummeting through an elevator shaft also serves as the reverse of the upward heterosexual erotics that characterized elevator scenes in Depression-era cinema. As Graham Thompson has suggested, the "elevator shaft manages to be both phallically and anally symbolic at the same time," strengthening the hypothesis that Latimer fashioned Janoth's death as a punishment for his "abnormal" sexual practices.[211]

THE GRID, THE LABYRINTH, AND THE INTERNATIONAL STYLE

A synoptic view of a city skyline at night, shot on location in New York, to the accompaniment of a moody jazz score by Victor Young, establishes the film's locale.[212] The camera lovingly pans the melting silhouettes of the city's lofty buildings, accented by tiny pinpoints of light. It is a romantic urbanscape borrowed from late eighteenth-century advocates of the picturesque, who considered individual skyscrapers unaesthetic, redeemed only by their collective irregularity,

Facade of the Janoth Building in The Big Clock.

landscape analogies, and distantly perceived, suggestive contours.[213] There is one building that stands out from the rest, a stark structure against "a cloudless April sky." Latimer's final script instructs: "THE CAMERA MOVES IN on this building, a clean-lined structure of white concrete and stainless steel," with only a cross section of its stories illuminated.[214] The culmination of the shot accords with the screenwriter's prescriptions, underscoring that the generic building comprises interchangeable mechanical parts that symbolize regimented labor and anonymity.[215] Art director Dreier and his assistants fashioned the skyscraper miniature in an International Style idiom, identifying the scene as a combination of buildings shot on location and creative artifice to underscore that style was employed for ideological significance.[216] Moody romanticism is thus revealed as a veneer to the city's harsh realities, which recalls a passage from Frank Lloyd Wright's *When Democracy Builds* (1945):

> Seen at night, heedless of real meaning, the monster aggregation has myriad haphazard beauties of silhouette and streams with reflected or refracted light. Undefined, the monster becomes rhythmical and appeals to what remains of our universal love of romance and beauty. . . . The skyscraper, in the dusk, is a shimmering verticality, a gossamer veil. . . . Then comes the light of day. . . . Sordid reiterations everywhere or space for rent! The overpowering sense of the cell. . . . Box on box beside boxes. Black shadows below with artificial lights burning all day long in little caverns and square cells. Prison cubicles![217]

Wright's renewed attack on both skyscrapers and the International Style during the war was echoed by many in the architectural community, most prominently Lewis Mumford, who was dismayed over what he viewed as hypertrophied functionalism at the expense of human values. Wright regarded the style as antithetical to American principles, particularly democracy and individualism. To its original practitioners and apologists, the International Style was the embodiment of reason and efficiency, representing an antidote to historicism and a slavish adherence to tradition. Wright's and Mumford's reactions to the International Style may serve as a conceptual framework for understanding its purposeful depiction as a form of sinister modernism in *The Big Clock*.

Latimer introduced the International Style into the script in an effort to superimpose the clock's mechanical properties onto the architectural space. Office workers are not simply regulated by abstract time, but by administered, spatial practice. Dreier, Anderson, and Nozaki embellished on the original idea in both the building's facade and its interior to augment the idea of a waste-free, regulated environment. Dreier believed firmly that architectural modernism should serve as the appropriate style for cinema's industrial and commercial building, advising: "For skyscrapers, broadcasting stations, steamships, factories, warehouses and other structures of an industrial and personal nature having few ties with the past, contemporary design and materials are indicated. The more functional the better."[218] Trained as an architect in Germany and well versed in the architecture of the Bauhaus, he also understood the implications of rendering the building in a foreign idiom, which coincided with Janoth's European background, imbuing the architecture with xenophobic overtones.[219]

International Style visual rhetoric is continued in the depiction of private office space, seen in the use of set design, lighting, indeed in the formulation of the entire mise-en-scène. In contrast to the long shots and deep-focus photography employed in the darkened corridors and public office spaces characteristic of most noir films, interior offices are shallow, cubical, unadorned rooms lacking in tactility, almost literal quotations of the International Style. Its advocates described it as a "utility–and–nothing–more," and recommended the restrained use of color, generally white.[220] High-key lighting is frequently employed to further flatten the space, while underlining its atonal, textureless geometric shapes. Another of the style's hallmarks is the insistence on seemingly weightless planes or curtain walls as opposed to massiveness and solidity. The interior cinematic space concurs, appearing scopic rather than haptic or illusionistic, sometimes rendering the actors weightless, perhaps to signify their dehumanization at Janoth's hands. When viewing *The Big Clock,* one is reminded of André Bazin's discussion of Orson Welles, in which the director's alteration of receding perspectives and low-angle shots, in this case extreme close-ups, function as "fully extended slingshots," adding to the contrast between the grid and the labyrinth.[221]

The exacting steel-frame construction of the International Style, often frankly exposed, is particularly exaggerated in Stroud's office, where the entire window, stretching from floor to ceiling, is likewise depicted as an enveloping metal grid. Dreier accentuated the hero's entrapment by rendering the glass as opaque rather than transparent, precluding the ocular possession of the city available to prestigious executives. International Style architects usually conceived of their buildings a priori, subsequently placing them in their intended locale. They were often accused of being too cerebral and forcing inhabitants to adapt to their buildings, much like Stroud in his confining space.

Many of the cinematic skyscraper's hermetically sealed public offices, which are shot in deep focus, seem too large, causing the actors to seem further dwarfed and compressed. One reviewer regarded Janoth as "incredible as the building he inhabits—one of those Hollywood skyscrapers in which almost every office is as big as the Municipal Loading House."[222] Except for a rare streamlined desk, the furniture is blocky and hard-edged, arranged in a balanced, asymmetrical fashion in accordance with International Style preferences. Stroud's investigation room is appointed with two rectilinear tables surmounted by pyramidal lamps that frame him in the foreground, while a single blackboard replete with bits of factual information dominate the background. Employees occupy the right middle-ground, marginalized in the frame by the overly rationalized office accoutrements, as if to suggest their inability to mediate their surroundings.

Perhaps the most sumptuous use of materials in the Janoth Building occurs in the hallways, which feature variegated marble paneling. A long shot of the austere yet richly decorated corridor features Stroud trying to evade discovery by those who might identify him. In spite of the enforced austerity recommended by International Style theoreticians such as Henry-Russell Hitchcock and Philip Johnson, the use of lavish materials was permissible if employed in a judicious, Spartan manner. For example, Ludwig Mies van der Rohe's Barcelona Pavilion (1929) was included in International Style's catalogue for the exhibition at the Museum of Modern Art, with an allowance for "aesthetic rather than functional considerations" because it was a pavilion at an exposition rather than a utilitarian building. "Rich materials such as travertine, various marbles, chrome steel," and multicolored plate glass were employed, as the curators ex-

Basement corridor in The Big Clock.

plained. An avid admirer of the Bauhaus, Dreier appears to be directly quoting Mies in this scene to underscore Janoth's materialism parading as austerity. An abstract expressionist–inspired sculpture on a table, composed of a tangled linear web, also signals the hallway's confounding identity.

To its original practitioners and apologists, the International Style was viewed as both contemporary and experimental, synonymous with modernity itself.[223] Perhaps aware of this judgment, Latimer and Dreier employed the International Style contrastingly to signify an irrational architectural language masquerading as its opposite. Dreier may have recommended the use of a German expressionist–influenced film vocabulary, including exaggerated long shots and radically oblique camera angles, especially in the skyscraper's subterranean realm, to conflate two antithetical, yet European-derived styles, strengthening the connotation of foreign evil. Thus, by the adept use of cinematography, the grid's flattened logic often metamorphoses into the confounding character of the labyrinth, a familiar film noir spatial trope. Stroud's negotiation of the skyscraper's dark subterranean passages, his entrapment in the clock, and his escape from York's high-rise apartment represent his containment in the maze. An article in Paramount's press book and the film's trailer describe the search for Stroud as one that "twists and turns through the vast labyrinth of a modern skyscraper."[224] The tall building's labyrinthine spaces may be viewed as analogues of its homosexually coded characters, who also dissemble, one of the "blind alleys" that threaten the consummation of Stroud's virile heterosexuality.[225]

The question that emerges is this: why was the International Style adopted as the stand-in for sinister foreign influences, homoerotic masculinity, and the dehumanizing regimentation of the corporation in 1948? This is a seemingly odd inquiry since after 1950 the style was largely embraced for commercial buildings and some public monuments by the architectural profession, including such prominent examples as Wallace Harrison's United Nations Building (1947–50), Skidmore, Owings, and Merrill's Lever House (1952), and Mies van der Rohe's Seagram's Building (1958).[226] However, in the years prior to and after World War II, the style came under renewed scrutiny. Was this perceived foreign import a viable reflection of American national values and topography?

An examination of the postwar complaints leveled at the International Style is best understood by a return to the views of Frank Lloyd Wright, perhaps its most consistently harsh critic. His searing attacks began immediately after its official christening as a coherent, worldwide movement in 1932. Ironically, Wright was invited the same year to show his work in the International Style exhibition at New York's Museum of Modern Art as a foil for the European works. Curators Henry-Russell Hitchcock and Philip Johnson categorized him somewhat dismissively as a precursor and a "romantic individualist," a position they were to revise after the war when Wright's reputation was under reevaluation. Many of Wright's assessments of the movement were revisited by the architectural profession at the height of the cold war in particular. The International Style was linked by some to fascist tendencies imported from abroad by aliens who were intent on undermining American democracy.

Wright asserted that in order for a truly organic architecture to emerge, a reflection of local physical and ideological conditions (institutions, people, and values), it must express a democratic and free life. This more authentic American architecture could not be realized by copying past styles or adopting foreign importations. In the nationalist-inspired "Of Thee I Sing" (1932), perhaps his most severe indictment of the International Style, Wright complained that architecture was not cold mathematics, science, or unoriginal conformity; rather, creative architecture was the result of architects' active dialogue with their surroundings. Echoing this viewpoint, he later cautioned, "Do not eliminate the individual in favor of the test tube or the mechanical laboratory." In gender-inflected prose that prefigured the film, he decried Spengler's notion that the western soul was dead, referring to his argument as impotent and sterile. He equated such barrenness with the "communistic," which was posing as an aesthetic, and the individual's unproductiveness in the name of discipline. Anticipating further the position in *The Big Clock,* he argued that "capitalistic centralization," which meant skyscraper cities built for profit, had embraced a "communistic exterior" or the monotonous, disciplined facade of the International Style.[227]

The same year, Wright accused International Style architects and their supporters of being propagandists, who did more to peddle their ideas than produce actual buildings. Employing xenophobic rhetoric, Wright charged the European "internationalists" of being little more than new eclectics, attempting to export their alien goods abroad. Their intentions were not merely benign, but reflected a desire to dominate the architectural opposition. Wright intoned:

> The predatory eclectic in the right eye. The predatory "internationalist" in the left eye. The one elects forms "ready-made" from the dead. The other elects a formula derived from an architecture living . . . and kills the architecture.

In view of the architect's appraisal, foreign infiltrators like Janoth and their mechanistic buildings seem almost a caricature. The architect's references to impotence may also help explain *The Big Clock*'s conflation of the style with the publisher's homosexual persona.[228]

Wright later elaborated on the overly mechanized nature of the International Style, what he thought of as its so-called antidemocratic properties. The architect was certainly no mechanophobe or Luddite; his pioneer essay "The Art and Craft of the Machine" (1901) argued that the machine was a beneficial tool provided that humans were in control of its processes.[229] According to

Wright, International Style proponents had turned this equation on its head, resulting in "the use of man by the machine."[230] He reserved his greatest opprobrium for International Style architects Le Corbusier and Walter Gropius, blaming them for taking his own ideas to their extreme, leading to sterility. The big clock within the skyscraper may be seen as the embodiment of Wright's view that the mechanization of architecture reduced humans to little more than automatons.[231]

The title of Wright's wartime essay, *When Democracy Builds* (1945), speaks to his determination to further politicize architectural discourse, taking renewed aim at centralized skyscraper cities. Gigantic, overwhelming, and wholly mechanized, America's urban centers created "mass men—a broker, vendor of gadgetry; a salesman dealing for profit in human frailties or a speculator in the ideas and opinions of others." Wholly divorced from nature, this money-oriented citizenry preferred mass entertainment and pollution to fresh air and native pastimes. They inhabited cubicles controlled by parasitic landlords in luxurious penthouses, wholly deprived of their manhood and autonomy. In order to be utterly free, Wright asserted, Americans had to reject this feudal thinking or "wagery" and seek communion with the land and their fellow citizens.[232] Wright envisioned a new decentralized or "Usonian" city (an American utopia) in which each family owned an acre of land connected to services via broad highway networks. A continuation of wanton centralization and overmechanization was tantamount to servitude, not the independent values upon which America was built. In Wright's estimation, the skyscraper as an architectural type and the International Style as an architectural idiom were the Scylla and Charybdis of antidemocratic values.

The opening postwar salvo against the International Style was initiated by Lewis Mumford upon his resumption of the weekly "Skyline" column in the *New Yorker* in 1947. After an almost four-year absence, Mumford saw it as an opportunity to take stock of American urban architecture, which had suffered an almost fifteen-year hiatus, and as a chance to mold future tastes.[233] Prior to that date, there was a single article by Hugh Morrison, entitled "After the International Style—What?" that appeared in the *Architectural Forum,* a Luce-owned periodical.[234] Morrison enumerated the style's ersatz weaknesses, including its lack of true functionalism, its unsuitability for American landscape conditions, the harshness of its forms, and its incongruence with American architectural traditions, many of which had already been put forth by Wright. Although Morrison acknowledged its contributions in the use of new materials and elements of design, he called for a synthesis of these features with existing architectural traditions. In anticipation of Mumford, Morrison predicted that this synthesis would result in the formulation of various regional modernisms.

As seen earlier in chapters 2 and 3, Mumford had been a relentless detractor of regimented skyscraper living since the 1920s and was, in accord with Wright, an advocate of more humane, decentralized cities. After the war, he continued his diatribes, dismissing Le Corbusier's famous dictum, "The house is a machine for living," as simply old hat. Labeling Le Corbusier, Mies, and Gropius as inflexible "mechanical rigorists" and stylistically *retardaire,* he rejected them and their successors as little more than academic copyists. Yet Mumford's complaints were not only leveled against what he believed to be the style's more formulaic aspects; he considered its limitations as more philosophical, privileging the machine over the art of living. By bastardizing Louis Sullivan's legacy in favor of more extreme functionalism, the internationalists had ignored the integration of people in their buildings. Mumford declared, "The rigorists placed the mechanical functions of a building above its human functions; they neglected the feelings, the sentiments, and the interests of the person who was to occupy it."[235] This perception accords with its depiction in *The Big Clock,* in which mechanical time and corporate profit determined human activity, an environment in which one was prevented from seeing one's family or even enjoying a holiday.

Instead of a foreign form of internationalism that valorized formalism and mechanics, Mumford encouraged American practitioners to reevaluate their indigenous traditions, thus promoting a form of architectural nationalism. Echoing Morrison, he identified a homegrown modernism that had emerged in the United States in the work of Bernard Maybeck and William Wurster in northern California. Dubbing it the "Bay Region Style," he observed that it was actually the product of diverse traditions, melding the Orient and the Occident, hence more genuinely universal than its European counterpart. He predicted that it would serve as a future paradigm rather than a monolithic formulaic prescription for the development of a plethora of universal architectural modernisms in America.[236]

Mumford's 1947 column sparked an immediate response in the architectural community, prompting the Museum of Modern Art to organize a symposium entitled "What is Happening to Modern Architecture" on 11 February 1948, at the very moment that Dreier and company were planning the sets for *The Big Clock.*[237] Mumford served as the moderator for the evening and introduced the first of several speakers, including the original exhibition organizers, Henry-Russell Hitchcock and the Museum of Modern Art's director Alfred H. Barr Jr. Other participants included Walter Gropius, Marcel Breuer, Ralph Walker, Peter Blake, Eero Saarinen, and George Nelson, among others. A multiplicity of viewpoints was offered, but there was general agreement that a style should never serve as a straightjacket. Clearly the implications of lockstepping to authoritarian decrees held very different connotations in 1948 than in 1932. In addition, there was a concerted effort, even among speakers holding different positions, to promote architectural pluralism and celebrate regional modernist solutions. Former advocates of the style such as Barr and Hitchcock now celebrated the work of Wright as one of the most seminal modernists, or "the Michelangelo of the twentieth century," in contrast to their appraisal sixteen years prior, thereby acknowledging the American contribution to modernism.[238] Yet, both insisted that his more recent work was influenced by the International Style or was perhaps itself a regional variation. Their rhetorical strategy was designed to demonstrate that the International Style was not rigid but elastic enough to encompass both Le Corbusier and Wright. The general need to counter Mumford's charges of architectural authoritarianism and antidemocratic tendencies in the political climate of the day is evidenced by Barr's rather curious assertion that the International Style was not fascist since Hitler and the National Socialists detested it.[239]

The German International Style architect and former Bauhaus director Walter Gropius, who emigrated to the United States and held a prestigious position at Chicago's International Institute of Technology, began by chastising Mumford for artificially pitting the machine against man, thus creating a false antimony. At the time when Le Corbusier's famous dictum was written, "emphasis was not so much on the machine itself as on the greater use of the machine in service for human life," he claimed. Moreover, the current call for regional variations of the International Style was nothing new but served as one of the modernists' original aims. Gropius concluded by calling for a new internationalism, based not on "chauvinistic national prejudices," a reference to the environment that spawned fascism in Europe, leading inexorably to further limitations, but on enlightened cooperation that would respect regional differences.[240]

Mumford ended the symposium by renewing his summons for a style based on special native circumstances, a dialogue between the universal and the local, such as that seen in the Bay Region. Echoing Gropius, he insisted that future building must be devoid of chauvinism, sectarian battles, and nationalism. He regarded architecture as the living symbol and physical embodiment of a "new civilization," a view prompted by the destructive philosophies and deeds of the last war, still a fresh wound in the national psyche. In order for future architecture to realize its mission, Mumford called for a synthesis of humanist and universal values, without sacrificing the needs of its inhabitants.[241]

The consensus and civility that characterized the symposium, its sense of the need for flexibility, respect for the individual, the absence of authoritarian restrictions, and the marriage of national and international traditions, while trumpeting American accomplishments, soon gave way in some quarters to warnings concerning the viability of the International Style, no doubt influenced by the overheated character of much cold war rhetoric. Perhaps the most vituperative account, entitled urgently "The Threat to the Next America," was authored by Elizabeth Gordon, editor of *House Beautiful* in 1953, who mercilessly attacked the style as a veritable conspiracy by a "self-chosen elite" who would "presume to tell us how to live." Even more insidious, Gordon argued, was that the "propaganda comes from these highly placed individuals" in our most respected institutions. Likening these experts to Hitlerian or Stalinist infiltrators, she continued, "For if we can be sold on accepting dictators in matters of taste and how our homes are to be ordered, our minds are certainly prepared to accept dictators in other departments of life." Repeating the cold war fear of a coordinated cadre of Communists insinuating themselves into the very fabric of American life, Gordon referred to International Style advocates as a "well-developed movement with social implications," representing "a social threat of regimentation and total control." She even went so far as to identify two prominent German practitioners in the United States, Gropius and Mies, implying that foreigners may indeed be the culprits of the aforementioned conspiracy. Gordon ended by imploring Americans to exercise their own opinions and tastes rather than passively trusting questionable experts. If average citizens would simply apply common sense, they would undoubtedly realize "that less is *not* more. It is simply less!" Reducing the option to a conflict between fascism and democracy or evil versus good, personified earlier by Janoth versus Stroud in *The Big Clock,* Gordon encouraged her readers to exercise their own "freedom of choice," the only road to "personal growth."[242]

The Big Clock's visual language was informed by the almost two-decade-long critiques of the International Style by its most prominent detractors, Wright and Mumford. The Janoth Building's mechanomorphic facade and radically stripped-down interior echoed the idea that the style was rigidly formal, the architectural counterpart of fascism, rendering workers little more than entrapped, impotent automatons. In accord with the eponymous clock, the building was a regulating machine, replete with elevators, telephones, and intrusive intercoms, analogues of the artificial conveniences of Wright's critique, which removed Americans from contact with the land and the pursuit of freedom. Like Wright, Latimer, Dreier, and Farrow meant for the style to signify principles that were antithetical to ideal notions of American democracy. Janoth and his building were viewed as foreign importations, which in 1948 were associated with German émigrés who held prominent positions in American universities. Passively accepting the style was here equated with corporate authoritarianism that would deprive Americans of their autonomy and even their strength, the converse of healthy, virile heterosexuality. Janoth's corpulent, effeminate body, dressed in imported finery, more akin to the subterranean labyrinth than the logical grid, was an illustration of the European-derived skyscraper's "true" nature, its facadism. The film suggests that the only hope for the liberation of the International Style skyscraper was through Stroud's initiative, the only one capable of stopping the clock and reclaiming corporate territory.

FOUR

Mid-century Corporate Renewal and Gender Realignment in *Executive Suite* and *Desk Set*

Following the recovery of politicized office terrains from the clutches of fascist-leaning or "foreign" Communist interlopers in such films as *The Big Clock* and *The Fountainhead,* which reflects the seemingly pervasive xenophobia and fear of "aliens" in the early cold war era, by the mid-fifties, skyscraper cinema refocuses attention to the home front. The internal dynamics of office buildings are explored, particularly interpersonal relationships and power struggles, and the breadwinner's attempt to reconcile professional identity with family life in both ideological and spatial terms. It is a time of transition, when corporations and their gendered employees are at a crossroads, encouraged to modernize and plan for the future, to rebuild, remodel, and rethink their way out of a wartime economy. An imbalanced "ideal" masculinity is staged in such diverse melodramas as *Executive Suite* (1954), *Woman's World* (1954), *The Man in the Gray Flannel Suit* (1956), and *Patterns* (1956), accompanied by a temporarily destabilized corporation in search of creative expression, leadership, and ethics in the face of an increasingly demanding work life.[1] Femininity is likewise reconfigured in the depiction of women; they are also challenged to serve as the new helpmate of the corporation, shadow employees of sorts, or ancillary office liaisons, who are also expected to supervise the new suburban dwelling, linking public and private space in an increasingly important manner. If the new executive is a more domesticated breadwinner, then his wife is a new corporate homemaker.

Wartime technological know-how prompted the wholesale restructuring of "real" interior skyscraper space through the introduction of technological innovations such as pressed plywood and fiberglass furniture, advanced office machinery, and computers, resulting in early conceptions and depictions of cyberspace. Office room increased exponentially by the end of the decade due to the economic prosperity that occasioned a postwar building boom. For example in New York from 1947 to 1954 alone, nearly eight million square feet of new office quarters were added, a number that rose to twenty-six million by 1959.[2] A concomitant ideological campaign accompanied these material modifications, calling for an enlightened and benevolent capitalism to assist in the integration of business employees in both the corporate and personal family, hoping to enact a rapprochement between management and labor, humans and technology. For the first time in American history, white-collar workers constituted more than half of the workforce; their numbers rose from forty to fifty-two percent from 1940 to 1958.[3] Their status was buttressed by conservative business policies that included the purposeful elevation of corporation-friendly managers and the active suppression of blue-collar and union workers, who were branded as subversive or even Communists. Hence, the white male executive in a new modern office was promoted both economically and ideologically in the decade after World War II as the newest, most popular professional.

The enlargement of corporate staffs, coupled with the proliferation of new mechanical office effects, in turn prompted novel solutions for postwar skyscraper interiors and the refurbishing of extant business structures. Responding to these changes, which were actualized by a new cadre of space planners, automation experts, and computer advocates, gender dynamics shifted anew among office employees. Although there has been much written on the metamorphosis of residential architecture in these years, including the new suburban Levittowns and the glut of newly designed domestic consumer objects for women, little attention has been devoted to how changes in material culture affected office buildings and the gender relationships within them, much less the cultural depictions of them.[4] In accord with sociologists such as David Riesman, William H. Whyte, and C. Wright Mills, among others, mid-century films often began with the contrived assumption that corporate space was a bureaucratic environment filled with bland Organization Men. This served as a ploy to counter the stereotype by recasting the environment through modernization, thereby fusing tradition and modernity, and corporate and individual values. Like their inhabitants, skyscrapers were rendered as temporarily problematic spaces in which ultimate gender reconciliation occurred with strong men at the helm, assisted by their wives, renewing the idea of individual initiative through familial cooperation, in concert with a munificent corporatism.[5] A new cast of heroes and heroines appeared in the decade's skyscraper films in response to these shifts in material culture and business philosophies, including the industrial engineer, efficiency expert, white-collar executive, and Mrs. Executive, who, in turn, were entrusted with the redemption of corporate skyscraper space.

EXECUTIVE SUITE (1954): CHARLES EAMES VS. THE ORGANIZATION MAN

Don Walling (William Holden) of *Executive Suite* is a composite of several ideal paradigms of professional masculinity—architect, industrial engineer, and executive—in a large furniture corporation. Modeled after the industrial designer and architect Charles Eames, he synthesizes a creative, hands-on approach to manufacturing with the intellectual acumen of a scientist, at once a heroic artisan and seminal inventor, while in possession of the necessary instrumental leadership ability to manage a corporation. Recognizing the novelty of Walling's character type, well-known sociologist David Riesman, author of *The Lonely Crowd* (1953), characterized him as a new kind of professional, "the executive as hero," the man who, "despite obstacles and consequences, seeks the prize of high management and wins it."[6] The film is also about corporate restructuring, leading ultimately to multiple solutions offered for the melding of humans and machines: an ethical business model, affordable quality products, new design principles, a humanistic working environment, and community-based leadership, among others. The impact of Eames is felt in the manner in which the cinematic skyscraper space is redeemed by good design, forged in domestic space and the laboratory, a fusion of seemingly antithetical realms by the designer and architect.

Metro-Goldwyn-Mayer bought the option to adapt the best-selling novel by Cameron Hawley to the screen and subsequently requested that the author write a treatment.[7] Producer John Houseman asked Ernest Lehman, a former *Wall Street Journal* reporter, to write the screenplay because of "his technical knowledge of business procedures," and Robert Wise to direct the cast.[8] So influential was the producer on all aspects of the film that Arthur Knight of the *Saturday Review* referred to it as "Mr. Houseman's 'Executive Suite.'"[9] Houseman had a political agenda; he viewed the project as an opportunity to explore the subject of big business and its power struggles in the context of the HUAC hearings.[10] Perhaps he sought to exploit the story as a morality tale aimed at the potentially ruinous effects of paternalistic authoritarianism and unquestioning conformity on institutions, whether corporate or governmental. Due to Houseman's clout, he was able to attract a stellar cast, which included William Holden, Frederic March, Shelley Winters, Barbara Stanwyck, June Allyson, Walter Pidgeon, Dean Jagger, and Nina Foch. He was also a personal friend of Charles Eames whose "expert advice" he sought in the formulation of Walling's character, technical details, and a philosophy of design that could be adopted by the corporation.[11]

The film traces a twenty-four-hour period in an atypical day at the Tredway Corporation, from the unexpected death of its president Avery Bullard (Raoul Freeman) to the ineluctable rise to power of the youthful visionary Don Walling,

who is poised to lead the company into the future.[12] One of the important subtexts of the film is the manner in which old-fashioned corporations and their
employees must modernize and retool to stay competitive in the postwar era.
The fifty-six—year-old, seemingly omnipotent but flawed Bullard suffers a fatal
heart attack at the foot of a Manhattan skyscraper, the victim of relentless overwork and a failed personal life. His death is meant to serve as a sobering caveat
to executives and corporate bigwigs that wholesale immersion in corporations
will result in their demise and that homegrown dictatorial leadership is doomed
to failure. Prior to his death, the emblematic result of his constant upward striving, he has imperiously called an unannounced evening meeting of the company's executives, evidence that the long arm of the firm may encroach upon
their private time. Significantly, the group gathers in the home office building's
upper boardroom in anxious anticipation of Bullard's arrival, surmising that the
meeting's agenda concerns the appointment of a new vice president. The last
one had also met an untimely death due to overwork. In spite of the executive's
lofty spatial position at the pinnacle, their ascendance is far from guaranteed,
undercut further by the dark Gothic-inspired decor that exudes antiquated values and doom.

When Bullard doesn't show, the group departs, unaware that the ensuing
crisis will occasion both a collective and personal challenge for each of them.
One by one, they must take stock of their lives and careers by examining their
relationship to their boss, fellow workers, and respective families. The executives are a diverse lot, including a cold technocrat, a spineless glad-hander, an
effete and corrupt manipulator, a bland yes-man, and a bitter soon-to-be re-
tiree, all inadequate to take the leader's place. Bullard's fall is thus employed as a
device to explore various deficient masculinities in the service of the ascension
of Walling's ideal sort. Gender is depicted in terms of personality characteristics, the nature of interpersonal relationships, physiognomy and dress, and by
recourse to architectural analogues and spatial practice. It is also registered into
the construction of the mise-en-scène, particularly in the use of high and low
camera angles.

The film's women are largely ancillary characters, except for Mary Bullard
(June Allyson), the decade's quintessential executive wife, and Julia Tredway
(Barbara Stanwyck), major corporate stockholder. The latter is the granddaughter
of the company's founder and the only female inhabitant of the boardroom,
allowed entry through lineage rather than personal initiative, a commentary
perhaps on the paucity of professional opportunities for women in postwar
America. Despite her seemingly high status, she is marked with the stain of
mental instability and illicit eroticism, which she rehearses throughout the film.
Her father had committed suicide and she was saved from a similar fate by
Bullard who, in the novel, becomes a paternal substitute and a lover. She is
likewise only brought to her senses by the rationality and persuasive passion

of Walling, who becomes a platonic partner, signaling his assumption of the leader's shoes.

When the men finally learn of Bullard's death, a power struggle ensues, provoked by Tredway's technocratic controller, and Organization Man, Loren Shaw (Fredric March). An insidious power-monger, he has already compromised Bullard and the values upon which the corporation was originally founded, in favor of large profits at the expense of quality products and satisfying working conditions. He has stripped Tredway's on-line employees of a sense of accomplishment, prompting a pervasive malaise and a loss of manly purpose, an attitude that has already begun to infect the executives. Threatening to seize control of the entire corporation by recourse to disingenuous toadying, behind-the-scenes manipulations, and even blackmail, he believes that he has enough votes to stage a coup. Yet his dishonesty and subterfuge is no match for the winning philosophy of Walling, who promises to revitalize and renew grandfather Tredway's original vision of product integrity, which is in line with the prevailing beliefs of Charles and Ray Eames. In a rousing boardroom speech at the conclusion, reminiscent of Roark's in *The Fountainhead,* Walling persuades each board member, including Julia Tredway, that he is the man for the job. His vision is matched spatially by his position at the head of the table and his lofty place at the top of the skyscraper tower.

The viewer first meets the Eames-like Walling in the factory's laboratory, surrounded by a team of acolytes, a testament to his scientific bent, his creative drive, and his commitment to teamwork through inspired leadership. Dressed in a lab coat rather than a gray flannel suit, he is less a stuffy executive than an inspired nonconformist, on the verge of inventing a new type of production process. High atop an industrial perch, the camera's low-angle viewpoint imbues him with additional stature and augurs his eventual rise in the company. At home, Walling is a middle-class family man with a loyal wife, an admiring young son, and a California-style ranch house, which he designed and built himself, designating him as part artisan and part engineer.

Walling's ideal, executive masculinity was based, in part, on the life of Charles Eames and, to a lesser extent, his wife Ray Eames. In keeping with the era's notions of the architect and designer, Ray's contribution to the Eames aesthetic was overlooked in the novel and film in favor of an image of a singular masculine creative genius. Aspects of Charles's biography, the Eameses' artistic philosophies, and their contributions to furniture design and technology permeate all aspects of the film. Producer Houseman, screenwriter Lehman, and art director Edward Carfagno worked collaboratively to fuse Walling with many aspects of Charles Eames's persona, from the delineation of the hero's studio to researching the technical details necessary for the production of pressed plywood and plastic furniture in the Tredway factory.[13] In accord with Eames, Lehman depicted Walling as both a designer and an architect, who plans ultimately to

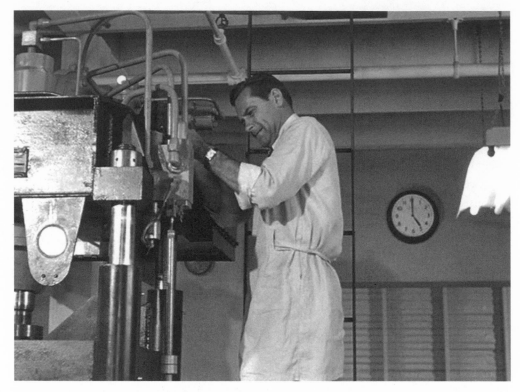

Don Walling on a perch in the factory in Executive Suite.

redeem the company's skyscraper, the Tredway Tower, by importing modernist ideas from his furniture, which fills the experimental studio of his private
residence. His goal is to return the company's product line, which had become
shoddy and old-fashioned under Shaw's influence, to its Craftsman roots of
sturdy workmanship by imbuing it with a contemporary modernist functionalism, informed by new materials, processes, and design elements.

Houseman's consultation of Eames may have been prompted by Hawley's
best-selling novel, on which the screenplay was closely adapted. A successful corporate executive turned writer, Hawley formulated a character who
resembled both Eames and himself. Hawley had joined the Armstrong Cork
Company in 1927, serving a distinguished twenty-four-year career in various executive capacities, including director of scientific research, before his
early retirement in 1951 to pursue a literary career. The novelist thus served
as a model for the creative executive, at odds with the conformist stereotype
of the insipid Organization Man offered by contemporary sociologists such as
Riesman, Whyte, and Mills. Armstrong began as a manufacturer of cork, but
he soon branched out to hardwood cabinets and vinyl flooring, ever sensitive
to the need to "diversify and innovate," which explains Hawley's admiration

of Eames.[14] At the very moment that the former was writing the novel, *Look* magazine christened Eames "the best-known United States designer of modern furniture."[15]

One of the ways that Hawley's Don Walling resembles Eames is in his training as both an industrial designer and an architect, someone who felt compelled to design his own home "totally unlike any house pictured in the clipping file."[16] The Eameses, too, designed their private residence, a 1500-square-foot, unabashedly modernist steel-framed structure, influenced by Bauhaus principles, filled with a curious array of eclectic objects. Both Eames and his fictional counterpart were, in Hawley's words, "artistic" types, who were successful in business or whose ideas dovetailed with corporate interests because of their abilities as designers and inventors.[17] Soon after Eames's arrival at the Cranbrook Academy in Detroit, a school devoted to designing for mass production, he was appointed a Professor of Design in the soon-to-be Department of Industrial Design while Walling was put in charge of Tredway's Design and Development Department. The latter had a mathematical and a "compartmentalized mind" combined with a concern for how the common man might use his objects.[18] Eames's oft-quoted credo that his job was "the simple one of getting the most of the best to the greatest number of people for the least" is equally applicable to Walling.[19]

Eames is well known for his many contributions to furniture design, including the invention of the bent plywood chair (1946) and the fiberglass-reinforced plastic chair (1950), among others.[20] His greatest feat was probably the manner in which he bonded synthetically produced seating materials to metal armatures, which obviated the need for upholstery, facilitating inexpensive mass production. The head of the design department at the Museum of Modern Art, Eliot Noyes, described Eames in 1946 as one who "exploited the possibilities of mass production methods for the manufacture of furniture . . . learning as he worked, *inventing* as he went along."[21] The lab-coated Walling is likewise characterized as an inventor and a tireless experimenter with new industrial processes and substances, who had even taken out "patents on a method of extruding plastic coating on steel tubing used for metal furniture."[22] Eames's alliance with corporations such as IBM and his belief in the benefits of mass production is echoed in Walling's manifesto to modernity, which resembles a statement by Buckminster Fuller that appeared in the Eames-edited journal *Arts & Architecture*: "We'll have a new line of low-priced furniture someday—a different kind of furniture—as different from anything we're making now as a modern automobile is different than an old Mills wagon."[23] Walling's mission to fuse the Arts and Crafts tradition of the company's founder with an inventive, technologically advanced modernism accords with the utopian philosophies of Eames and his corporate patrons.

Lehman continued Hawley's adaptation of the Eames persona. In one of his advanced preliminary scripts, all of which required approval from Houseman, the screenwriter described Walling in language similar to *Look*'s, as "one of the country's top industrial designers, a young man of courage and imagination."[24] Lehman provided evidence that he may have conducted his own research on Eames. An early ten-page treatment of the story has Mary Walling describing her husband in terms of the Eameses' creative credo. According to Mrs. Walling, Bullard had promised to put his protégé in charge of

> research, planning, development, designing—and furniture—
> furniture that would be revolutionary in design, function and
> price—unheard of beauty, radical design, new materials, new
> processes of manufacture—a whole new line of furniture that
> would be so cheap that everyone could afford it.[25]

Lehman went a step further, reporting that he "visited designer Charles Eames to get some accurate technical verbiage for several of the laboratory scenes," specifically those involving the correct machinery required in the production of Eames-inspired pressed plywood furniture.[26] After consulting with the designer, he changed the last part of his description of Walling's sidekick from, "He places the receiver down and looks up to where a man is perched precariously high up on the assembly line connecting a feed line," to "on the press securing a connection to an electrode."[27] Lehman's understanding of pressed plywood's cost effectiveness is further evidenced in a scene that was eliminated by director Wise. Turning to his subordinates, Walling encourages them to recycle excess wood fragments to produce molded furniture:

> We've got factory floors covered with scraps of wood . . . some-
> thing to be swept out and charted as waste material. The more we
> can use that waste—molded back into its original state, with the
> same tensile strength, the same beauty as natural wood.[28]

According to Lehman, the spatially and creatively elevated male inventor provides the necessary inseminating guidance to consummate the electrical process, while forging an aesthetics of economy.

It is likely that Metro-Goldwyn-Mayer's Oscar-winning art director Edward Carfagno accompanied Lehman on his sojourns to various furniture plants and the Herman Miller showroom, where the Eameses' furniture was displayed. In order to guarantee the accurate portrayal of "an experimental lab in a plastics factory," Carfagno revealed that he "toured Los Angeles and was shown different set-ups at local plants, including the latest types of vats and presses used in his recent arrival on the industrial scene."[29] He reported to the media that Houseman "insisted on his usual standard of excellence and authenticity" in the fabrication of all the set designs, especially the skyscraper and factory scenes.

Carfagno employed his knowledge in the service of Walling's residential workroom or studio, which is well-informed by all features of the Eames aesthetic and which Riesman identified, in his lengthy review of the film, as "an upper-middle-brow version of Charles Eames's studio."[30] It is the true site of Walling's creativity, the place where he invents and designs unencumbered by number crunchers and bureaucrats like Shaw. The private studio stands in marked contrast to the Tredway Tower's boardroom, which is steeped in historicism and antiquated ideas, symbolized by the lugubrious Gothic paneling, underscoring that Walling's modernist experiments in furniture will ultimately rehabilitate the skyscraper's executive suite. Lehman's description of the scene, annotated with the name "Eames" by director Wise, and the characterization "technical man here," lends further credence to the Eameses' imprimatur on the script, scenography, and directorial vision.[31] The screenwriter's lengthy prelude to the dialogue, which includes a deliberate chronicle of several Eames-inspired objects, is worth quoting at length:

> A hand—Don's hand—is seen working over a large sheet of graph paper on a series of designs. They are no more than mechanical sketches, really, yet there is beauty and excitement in their sweep. . . . AS CAMERA PULLS BACK INTO FULL SHOT, Don is seen standing before a large drafting board under a great blue light in the center of the bare room which because it is the workroom of a man of creative imagination, has acquired a beauty all its own. Handsome wood pieces, twisted and worked into strange yet aesthetically pleasing shapes, are seen standing on the floor, on a desk atop a book shelf. Here a plastic chair. There is a more radically-designed chair, still in a rough and incomplete stage of development. Big pieces of driftwood stand over the fireplace. A huge Japanese fish hangs from the ceiling. There are test models on the floor, a projection machine in a corner.[32]

Carfagno's sets did not conform exactly to Lehman's description, but the Eameses' imprint is clearly visible nevertheless. The fictional studio features several types of plastic and molded resin chairs, a modular storage unit, kites, a butterfly motif, a George Nelson light fixture, and a large number three that may be read as a backwards "E," which Eames borrowed from circus poster graphics, appearing in several of his films as a virtual numerical signature.[33]

One of the primary characteristics of Charles and Ray Eames's furniture was its adaptability to domestic and corporate space alike, a characteristic that Lehman and Carfagno acknowledged thematically and visually.[34] It was simple

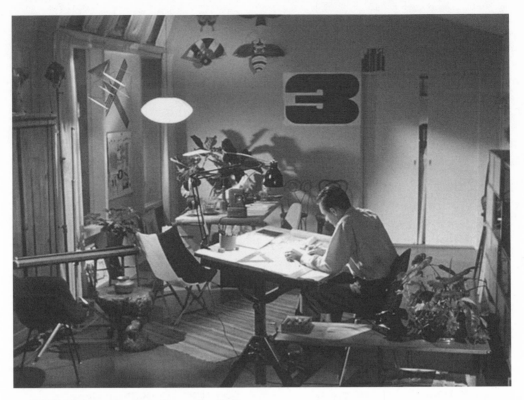

Walling's home studio in Executive Suite.

and organic and could soften an otherwise Spartan interior, as it did in the Eameses' own residence. The couple were also eclectics, filling their own otherwise industrial post-Bauhaus home with a variety of objects, including shells, Japanese kites, and folk and ethnic objects, effecting a reconciliation of the seemingly disparate—the mechanical and organic, high and low, minimal and excessive, serious and humorous, masculine and feminine. That being as it may, the collective Eames aesthetic is employed as a corrective and an antidote to the prevailing corporate malaise. The substandard products promoted by Shaw, and tacitly supported by Bullard, are thus tossed aside in favor of a more expansive, humanistic vision.

DON WALLING, IDEAL MASCULINITY, AND
THE RECLAMATION OF SKYSCRAPER SPACE

Avery Bullard's failed masculinity is introduced early in the film, inextricably linked to the skyscraper's lofty top and lowly bottom. It serves as an analogue for his elevated status as the Tredway Corporation's authoritarian and singular commander. Bullard is a postwar variation of the late nineteenth-century robber baron, who rules dictatorially and by decrees. The film begins with various images of New York's lofty skyscrapers. An aerial shot of New York's Wall Street, picturing congestion, traffic, and the scurrying of ant-like people, is accompanied by a voice-over, which points to Bullard's prominent position but augurs his demise. Speaking in the authoritative tones of a newscaster, the narrator characterizes skyscrapers as *vanitas* symbols:

> It is always up there close to the clouds. . . . On the topmost floors
> of the sky-reaching tower of big business . . . and because it is high
> in the sky, you may think that those who work there are somehow
> beyond the tensions and temptations of the lower floors. This is to
> say it isn't so.[35]

In accord with New York's office buildings, Bullard begins the film by walking tall, a man who strides confidently and imperiously through space. On the upper story, he embarks on a downward elevator journey to street level, symbolic of his imminent fate. Bullard's stature is enforced by the adept use of cinematography; the camera assumes a high vantage point in concert with him,

Skyscraper at the beginning of Executive Suite.

moving quickly as it tracks his commanding gait. But the viewer never actually sees Bullard; rather his importance is recorded in the people he encounters, whose eyes look up at him in awe, deference, and finally obeisance. At this moment, the camera's and his objectifying, controlling gaze are one and the same, a commentary on his omnipotence. At a Western Union office, he sends orders for a 6:00 p.m. meeting to pick a vice presidential successor back in Millburgh, Pennsylvania, but his lack of visibility renders him an already absent protagonist, which foreshadows his own replacement as company chief. No sooner has he summoned a taxi then he falls to the pavement, the victim of a fatal heart attack. The camera follows suit; a low-angle shot chronicles the gutter and the victim's fallen wallet, or lost fortune, which will soon be pilfered by an opportunist. The once grandiose Bullard is thus rendered an unknown body in the anonymous Manhattan metropolis. Wise's annotated script notes the importance of depicting high and low in spatial terms, designating the use of camera angles as key: "Important moment—whole character of the scene fade in symbolizes picture [sic]."[36] Thus, the film's prescriptions for mid-century masculinity are clear: authoritarian control, coupled with overwork, are ill-advised, and will ultimately lead to tragedy.

Avery Bullard falls to the ground in Executive Suite.

To his credit, Bullard's commanding character was once an asset to the company, which suffered a checkered past due to the profligate habits of the founder's son, the dilettante Orrin, who had compromised the proud Craftsman tradition of his father. In the novel, the decadent Orrin registered his vanity with the construction of the Tredway Tower, built as a "Gothic Christmas Cookie."[37] In a fit of mental instability, he jumped from the reaches of the "architectural monstrosity," but not before almost ransacking the company. In accord with Rand's philosophy and much modernist discourse, functionalism is associated with things virtuous while historical styles are linked to outworn values, feminization, decadence, and mental disease.[38] The mark of the profligate Orrin Tredway and the corporation's antiquated methods inhabit the film's skyscraper boardroom, the site of the final showdown (which in the novel occurs in the library of Julia Tredway's mansion), meant to underscore Bullard's continued feudal control and his ruthless, robber baron–style masculinity. Carfagno reported that Houseman instructed him to adhere closely to Hawley's description; hence "the penthouse atop a modern structure of steel and concrete, was strictly 18th century."[39]

Bullard saved the company with his designs, restoring integrity to the product and propelling the company to renewed success. He even rescued Orrin's daughter, the mentally unstable Julia, with whom he enjoys a paternal and romantic relationship. However, Bullard is led astray by his own vanity like the pride that killed Orrin, a point underscored in Walling's final boardroom speech. Bullard's arrogance was both his strength and his downfall; although it once benefited the company in a time of crisis, it was too all-consuming to allow other men their autonomy, his successor argues. Characterizing him as "the lonely man at the top of the tower," Walling asserts that "a great company has to be more than the pride of one man." Just as the architecture is rendered as outmoded, so, too, is the authoritarian corporate model.

In spite of Bullard's prior rehabilitation of the corporation, the damage he has wrought is registered in the deficient masculinities of his executives, rendered impotent, in part, by his domineering leadership. Their relative lack of power is registered architecturally in their identical nondescript offices that are located a floor below Bullard's commodious suite, and signify sameness and subservience. Their emblematic intent is underscored when Bullard's secretary Erica Martin (Nina Foch) descends the regal "medieval oak staircase" to announce Bullard's last command, the hastily scheduled meeting.[40] Shot from below, the scene emphasizes her downward movement to identical, warren-like offices, interconnected by a corridor, a reference to the dystopian modernism of both real and cinematic corporate spaces (e.g., King Vidor's 1928 film *The Crowd*). As she arrives at each opaque glass-paneled cubicle, a close-up shot creates a sense of claustrophobia. Only Walling is differentiated from the rest. In spite of the proximity of his office to theirs, he is not present; indeed he is rarely in.

Instead, his receives his summons in the ample space of his experimental factory, where he is loftily perched.

Bullard's wholesale control of the corporation is even rendered by architectural sound effects. Hawley depicted the skyscraper's loud carillon as only sounding to announce Bullard's presence in the company town of Millburgh, Pennsylvania, similar to summoning church bells and their implied omnipotence. Wise decided to extend this dramatic punctuation by including startling bell ringing at pivotal moments; it calls people to their senses, marks time, and accompanies Walling's assumption of power. There is no music or diegetic sound in *Executive Suite,* further embellishing the effects of the eerie, often ear-splitting carillon.

Each of the cubicle-bound executives has interpersonal and professional weaknesses that preclude his assumption of power, exploited by Bullard for his own end. Contemporary discussions of the executive personality by social critics such as Riesman, Whyte, and Mills, and in the advice literature concerned with businessmen, explored his strengths and foibles. Borrowing from such contemporary business discourses, *Executive Suite* fractures the male white-collar professional into a series of types, in order to create a template for inappropriate and appropriate masculinities, and finally an object lesson for professional male success in the corporate world. It also argues simultaneously for a restructured corporate model, the result of a new type of shared power, aided by the collective efforts of employees under inspired, forward-looking leadership.

Sixty-one-year-old Frederick Alderson (Walter Pidgeon), as his name implies (alderson not alderman), represents one version of masculinity in deficit, clearly unsuited to succeed his boss. Serving as Bullard's right-hand man for nearly thirty years, his subservience and old-fashioned manners preclude his ascent. Hawley's description of him was adapted by Lehman and employed as a strategy by Wise: "Fred Alderson was sitting behind his desk, his body squarely in his chair, his head held plumb-bob straight, not a white hair out of place on the high dome of his wax-pink face."[41] In short, he is a conformist. When we first meet him, the bespectacled, deferential character agrees immediately to Bullard's demand by proxy. His fastidiousness and pale complexion have long-held associations with wealth and a feminine preoccupation with appearance.

In mid-century terms, his other sin is to have a domineering wife, which executive advice peddlers schooled in the dangers of "momism," a fifties version of feminization, warned adamantly against. The writer Philip Wylie, who coined the term in his widely popular book *Generation of Vipers* (1942), accused mothers and then wives turned mothers of emasculating men. The mother and wife were to blame for forcing the husband to take "a stockroom job in the hairpin factory" while "trying to work up to the vice presidency" rather than pursuing a metaphorical survey of the Andes. He charged that America's women had literally "raped the men, not sexually, unfortunately, but morally," leaving them helpless neuters.[42] Fred Alderson conforms, in part, to Wylie's misogynistic characterization, being given over to tearful emotion, another sign of his weak feminine persona. He is given a pep talk by the acquisitive, power-hungry Mrs. Alderson (Virginia Brissac), who believes that her husband can finally assume his rightful place in the corporation. At a party of her well-heeled friends, she whisks him off to the domesticated bedroom, where she is clearly in charge, in order to bolster his courage in the face of Bullard's death:

> There's nothing you can do for him now. . . . You've got to think of yourself. . . . You've worked for it, Fred. Twenty-nine years of it. You've earned it. You have a *right*. So have *I*. . . . You gave your whole life . . . lived in his shadow.[43]

Sales executive Walter Dudley (Paul Douglas) is likewise emasculated by a domineering wife, who often exacts her control via the telephone, and later by Shaw who attempts to blackmail him. When Bullard's secretary arrives with his summons, Dudley is seen "pacing back and forth beside his desk with the phone at his ear," exasperated at the "QUERULOUS VOICE," but not man enough to disengage.[44] Instead of standing up to the harassment, he solves the problem by having an affair with his secretary Eva Bardeman (Shelley Winters). The once good-looking Dudley is a charmer and glad-hander rather than a leader, hence his ability to sell the company's products. His lack of gumption is highlighted spatially when Shaw intimidates him: the latter follows him to Eva's house or the site of their erotic liaison and barges in, making his way to the kitchen. Hiding in the domestic realm, Dudley occupies feminized space. Even Eva has more gumption than her craven boyfriend, terminating their relationship when he capitulates to Shaw's blackmail, insuring his lowly status in the executive pecking order.

The mercenary and effete, fiftyish George Caswell (Louis Calhern), cast as the crooked businessman Emmerich in the film *The Asphalt Jungle* (1950), also enjoys the company of younger women, more specifically a whining Marilyn Monroe look-alike.[45] To augment his taste in trophy women, he owns a luxurious penthouse suite, like the corrupt cinematic bosses of Depression-era skyscraper space, and dines at the elite Stork Club. His mercenary colors are revealed when he witnesses Bullard's fall from a skyscraper window above and sells 3,700 shares of Tredway stock short on the expectation that it will lose value. Like the anonymous pickpocket who empties Bullard's wallet, Caswell cares more about his own aggrandizement than the good of the corporation. His closest allies are the thick-accented Julius Stiegel (Edgar Stehli), who resembles the Jewish masculine stereotype seen in earlier films, and the corrupt Shaw.

One of the few happily married characters who inhabits the executive suite is, like Alderson, a senior board member who has seen better days. Jesse Grimm

Walter Dudley hiding in the kitchen in Executive Suite.

(Dean Jagger), the production manager, as his name suggests, is dissatisfied with the Tredway Corporation and longs to retire, a man more likely to retreat to his rural cabin to fish than to confront issues. When he is called to the board meeting by Erica Martin, he is absent from the premises, a spatial signifier of his escapism and alienation. Laconic and pipe-smoking, and thus infused with a stalwart and repressed masculine reserve, he resents "boy wonders" like Walling for his so-called newfangled ideas and scientific production strategies.[46] Like Bullard, he represents a bygone business era, a signifier of antimodernity that, coupled with his simmering demeanor, disqualifies him for the presidential position. He lacks the requisite humanity and the imaginative vision to usher the corporation into the future.

Walling's archnemesis, the double-dealing Loren Shaw, represents the film's Organization Man and efficiency expert, a caricature of the soulless conformist described by the social critics. Viewers encounter him initially through Miss Martin's eyes, listening to his own "metallic" voice through a dictaphone.[47] Is he man or robot? Controller Shaw is a number cruncher whose bottom line is company profits at the expense of quality products, reinforced by the sign

George Caswell in his penthouse in Executive Suite.

above his desk, which reads "Material Rejection." His dictaphone speech is de-signed to gain a leg up on Walling while promoting an inferior furniture line that will increase revenue. He drones:

> once again overrun the first estimate for experimental work, this
> time $23,254. In view of the consistent high profit curve achieved
> by our budget K-F Line, I should like at your earliest convenience,
> Mr. Bullard, to discuss with you the economic soundness of Mr.
> Walling's experimental program.

Lehman depicts the Organization Man, Shaw, as the antithesis of progress, in spite of his purported love of machines, efficiency, and planning. His resistance to improvements, unlike Grimm's and Alderson's, is not antiquated, so much as devoid of a human concern.

Shaw's fastidious hairdo, lean physique, and "well-ordered smile" reflect his choreographed, rigid personality. Lehman conceptualized him as very much the up-and-coming executive "of these FORTUNE magazine photos."[48] Yet his

Loren Shaw in his office in Executive Suite.

polished manners are contradicted by a compulsive hand gesture, a repeated reaching for his handkerchief to wipe his damp palms and upper lip. This high-strung fastidiousness defines his manhood as fussy and effeminate, thereby precluding his assumption of the symbolic throne despite all his behind-the-scenes manipulations. His herky-jerky motions also double as mechanical, enforcing his lack of fully human traits. Visible family ties or romantic liaisons are absent from his life, suggesting, in fifties terms, a gender and/or sexual dysfunction, rendering him an abnormal man. His first name, Loren, is a further testament to his gender ambivalence.

Julia Tredway is as close to an executive as any female character can get because of her lineage and substantial stock holdings, an equal power broker in the selection of Bullard's successor in the boardroom. The temperamental antithesis of Shaw, she is rendered as an irrational woman who is traumatized by her father's leap from the tower. Bullard's sudden death has rekindled her suicidal ideation; hence, in numerous scenes she stands staring tortuously out of skyscraper windows as if she is about to jump, a trait that Wise believed was "the key to Julia."[49] The film's spatial subtext of high and low, introduced with

Julia Tredway looking downward in Executive Suite.

Bullard's fall, is superimposed on Julia because she carries the family stain of mental instability and illicit eroticism. In spite of her volatility and grief, she is persuaded by Walling to participate in the vote, after threatening to "end all this," by the force of his personality and masculine reason, which brings her to her senses.[50] It is significant to note that Barbara Stanwyck had previously been permitted to enter the homosocial boardroom two decades earlier as the ruthless, mercenary Lily Powers in *Baby Face,* enforcing the idea that women in the cinematic boardroom serve as irrational, often unstable forces that must be tamed.

Lehman's delineation of Julia is markedly different than the one of Hawley's novel, one of the few characters to receive such a drastic overhaul, although both writers register a fear of autonomous women, continuing a trend inherited from Depression-era cinema. Although she suffered a traumatic past, Hawley's Julia has gone on to a happily married life to Dwight Prince, a circumspect, effeminate man who makes strawberry sauces to accompany dinner. Walling decides to visit her at the Tredway mansion, which serves as her upper-class spatial analogue, to convince her of his presidential viability. Expecting someone entirely different, Walling thinks, "It was plain that these old rumors about her sanity were only malicious gossip. She was a clever woman . . . damned clever," who possessed a "mind like a man's."[51]

Mary Walling is depicted in fifties terms as a woman with just the right balance of masculinity and femininity, a paragon of the newly emergent executive wife. Her job is to help facilitate his career, be his parental stand-in if required, and generally manage the domestic sphere. She is a devoted homemaker and mother, a chauffeur for her commuter husband, and a team player to her son's baseball aspirations, signifying her gender versatility. She even wears trousers on occasion, which a decade earlier would have signaled transgressive femininity but is here employed to identify the informality of the new suburban wife. Compared to her Depression-era counterpart, she is kept apprised of the firm's machinations, from Bullard's loss of direction to Shaw's manipulations. Her role in the film is to support his aspirations, always ready to dole out advice, even if unsolicited, because she always has his best interests at heart. In a preliminary treatment, Lehman made it clear that "it is a women's role to allow her husband to seek his fulfillment in the way he believes he must."[52] Wishing to preserve his creativity, which is in danger of being squelched, she urges him to

Mary Walling playing baseball with her son in Executive Suite.

leave the corporation if necessary in order to develop his full potential. "Be on your own," she advises. Pointing to his Eames-like domestic studio, she exhorts, "Design what *you* want . . . build what *you* want to build. . . . If it weren't for this room the past few months you couldn't have lived."[53]

Spatially she is a member of both private and public spheres, the personal and the professional, although her entrance to the latter is circumscribed by strict guidelines of decorum, discussed at length in the executive advice literature of the period. The key to her spatial location and dual gender identity is seen in the last scene. Mrs. Walling withholds information from her husband in an effort to prevent him from assuming the presidency, for fear it will extinguish his creative spark. Undergoing a change of heart, she rushes to the boardroom just in time to tell him. During Don's impassioned speech, she listens attentively and surreptitiously by the slightly ajar boardroom door. After he is done, he rushes out of the boardroom to symbolically consummate their relationship. Mary is allowed peripheral entrance to his professional world, to experience it vicariously, but is never able to fully inhabit it.

Unbeknownst to Walling, the real obstacle to his rise is the overarching, paternalistic presence of Bullard, for whom he has served as a surrogate son. After

The Wallings after the boardroom speech in Executive Suite.

the latter's death, Walling is prompted to question his authentic desires: is he a company man or a seminal designer? Or can he be both? Initially, he doesn't believe that he is in line to succeed the master, because of his inexperience and his deference to Alderson. Hawley and Lehman fashioned Walling as a new type of executive, pointing to their joint desire to create a youthful, slightly iconoclastic type of manhood to redeem the floundering corporation. As *Newsweek*'s film reviewer claimed,

> It took Hollywood a long time to recognize that the age of the "robber baron" is over, relegated to what James Truslow Adams once called the far off Jurassic period of American history. The modern businessman is apt to be young, aggressive, but used to working on a team—part of the new crop of managerial talent now running most of American industry.[54]

As we shall see in the next section, the fifties executive was more likely to be a fifty-year-old man from the Midwest who had risen up the corporate hierarchy slowly.

Walling's initial ambivalence about seeking the prize stems from his desire to preserve his own creative integrity. After Alderson encourages him to try, he resists, informing Mary of his decision by recourse to spatial metaphors: "*I'm* not going to die young at the top of the tower . . . worrying about bond issues . . . stockholder's meetings. . . . I'm a designer, not a politician. . . . *I think*."[55] Here Walling is rehearsing the current fear among executives that the corporation would wholly consume them, to the detriment of their health, family lives, and inventiveness. The top of the Tredway Tower has heretofore been inhabited by mental illness, authoritarianism, vanity, and a lack of healthy interpersonal relations.

Soon the hero has a double epiphany that prompts him to reconsider. Surveying his executive peers, he comes to the conclusion that he is the only man for the job, thereby becoming the spokesman for Hawley and Lehman's construction of hegemonic masculinity. He is at his son's all-American baseball game when he hears a plane. Glancing aloft in a gesture of enlightenment, which foreshadows his rise to the top, he decides to try to convince Dudley, who is returning on the selfsame airplane, of his viability. Rushing off to the airport where he meets Alderson, he informs the elder man that he has had a change of heart, which is predicated, in part, on the firm's current group of insufficient men. Aligning himself with manly workmen rather than bureaucrats like Shaw, he asserts forcefully:

> My picture's never been in *Fortune*! And I get my hands dirty once in awhile! I don't know the rules! I'm not *old* and *tired* or *weak* and afraid.[56]

Augmenting his declaration is the upward-tilted nose of a large phallic plane, which diagonally bisects the frame's middle ground, conjuring up the image of a war-time general while simultaneously suggesting upward mobility and industrial optimism. His head near the pilot's cockpit, Walling commands Alderson to convince Grimm of his presidential viability, to which the former replies in military fashion, "Is that an order?" Later he drives the wartime analogy home to his wife; he will not stand by and watch the firm fall "into the hands of a weakling like Dudley or an adding-machine like Shaw! Too many lives are involved! A whole town's at stake! Tredway's got to be kept alive!"

The location of the boardroom at the tower's crest serves as Walling's domain, no longer a symbol of Bullard's loneliness or Orrin and Julia's psychic maladjustment, but of his triumph. Hence the film comes full circle spatially: Walling arrives to dominate the skyscraper tower. In anticipation of his feat, Erica Martin has Bullard's throne-like chair placed against the wall in Walling's position. Director Wise's notes underscore the importance of the furniture maneuvering: "Start now real effect of the conference table. Bullard's chair and stained glass window.—Then action into the scene [sic]."[57]

Like numerous film heroes before him, Walling commences an impassioned speech that wins the blackmailed Dudley and the unstable Julia over to his side.

Walling and Alderson at the airport in Executive Suite.

His oration is not only convincing for its stirring persuasiveness, but for its articulation of a philosophy of corporate leadership that fuses creativity with team effort. By the force of his personality and vision, he provides each board member with an aspect of the corporation to believe in, and in doing so, a restoration of their self-respect. He claims that Bullard's literal and figurative death was caused by his need of no one; he was "the lonely man at the top of the tower." Isolationism and authoritarianism failed as models for governments and are destined to fall short in the new era, which stresses cooperation and interconnectedness. Countering Grimm, Walling does not reject pride out of hand, but only the type that sets leaders apart from their employees. In order for a corporation to be successful, "It has to be the pride of men working together."

With a nod to both production manager Grimm and salesman Dudley, whose jobs have become hollow, he vows to drop the inferior K-F furniture line that has made on-line employees and executives alike so despondent. In an important gesture, he picks up a faulty K-F chair and breaks it apart, signaling the death of the old era, in accord with Roark's creative destruction of the housing project, effecting the beginning of the symbolic redemption of the equally musty boardroom. At this juncture, he articulates the Eames-inspired commit-

Walling breaks a chair from the K-F furniture line in Executive Suite.

ment to produce a new, modern, low-priced line of furniture produced using the latest industrial processes and materials, thereby gratifying efficiency experts like Shaw without compromising quality. His position also satisfies Julia, who will be able to put her name on manufactured goods that she can be proud of. Thus Walling doesn't stop at the tower or the factory but links his creative vision to the needs of the postwar consumer. Eames argues that it is the designer's and, by implication, the architect's ethical responsibility to design products for the betterment of American citizenry after the hardships occasioned by the conflict.

The film makes a case for a rehabilitated version of artisanal masculinity, albeit with a modernist touch, which is both individual and team-oriented. In agreement with his son, Walling is the pitcher for the Tredway team, which wins in the end. A mid-range shot of the skyscraper's crest and the twelvefold tolling of the carillon announces that it is high noon when the sun, like Walling, has reached its apex. The hero manages to command concurrently skyscraper space and the corporate structure, while asserting a revised type of masculinity that is instrumental, cerebral, and given over to democratic values. It is only a matter of time before the experimental products of his domestic studio will replace the antiquated effects of the boardroom, effecting a synthesis between laboratory, factory, and skyscraper.

THE BELEAGUERED EXECUTIVE, MRS. EXECUTIVE, AND THE PURSUIT OF CREATIVE AGENCY

The main protagonist of mid-century skyscraper office films is the white-collar male executive on the rise, and his wife, supported by his peers, trying to define his place in both the professional and personal realms. Success is no longer measured simply by the proverbial ascent up the company ladder as in Harold Lloyd's earlier films but is gauged by his relationship to coworkers, bosses, subordinates, and family members. In addition, he is no longer a young man on the rise, but a thirty-something worker who has already established himself. He is Don Walling of *Executive Suite* (1954), Tom Rath (Gregory Peck) of *The Man in the Gray Flannel Suit* (1956), Fred Staples (Van Heflin) of *Patterns* (1956), the three executive hopefuls of *Woman's World* (1954), and to a lesser extent Richard Sumner (Spencer Tracy) of *Desk Set* (1957). These ersatz paragons of upper-middle-class prosperity and economic largesse are undergoing identity crises, one of the few instances in Hollywood cinema when the purported ideal model of masculinity is represented as so maladjusted or temporarily psychically wounded. The beleaguered executive is decidedly out of balance; he is rendered as a man in crisis who must effect the proper balance between dominance and submission in the workplace and a harmony between his professional life and his role as husband and father to his often neglected family. Although he is often the film's singular hero, his masculinity is in constant dialogue with, or seen in relation to, that of his executive peers, who are offered as object lessons in ill-advised or unproductive behavior, whether it be the obsequiousness of Walter Dudley of *Executive Suite* or the rigid control of Loren Shaw. Yet it is because of their inadequacies that a man like Walling is able to succeed.

Psychiatric problems, coronary disease, dyspepsia, and nervous twitches occasioned by overwork inhabit the 1950s executive suite and remind the hero that he must pay heed to his physical and mental health rather than lose himself in the "rat race," a popular and pejorative mid-century characterization of the quest for success. The company president or CEO is perhaps the most egregious example of maladjustment, lack, and inadequacy, despite his seemingly lofty position. Avery Bullard dies suddenly of a heart attack in *Executive Suite*; Ralph Hopkins (Fredric March) of *The Man in the Gray Flannel Suit* suffers from a multitude of physical and mental health issues, including a weak heart and an emotionally bankrupt relationship with his wife and daughter; and William Briggs (Ed Begley) of *Patterns* dies of a massive coronary due to overwork and harassment.

Mid-century literature on executives that was designed to help men achieve greater success and help them out of their malaise abounded. "Realize that you are a member of the newest profession," a self-help writer exhorted his readers.[58] In a book entitled *The Executive Life* (1956), devoted solely to understanding executives, the editors of *Fortune* also paid testament to his dominant presence in American popular culture:

> There is, of course, the old Hollywood stereotype of a high-salaried "Mr. Big" who barks his commands to timid subordinates. . . . This harsh caricature of the executive has been considerably softened in the language of advertising (e.g. "topcoats that give you the top-executive look") which caters to all those who want to think of themselves as executives. By this standard, a big income is no longer requisite to executive status; for example, any male willing to pay the extra fare of $3.30 can fly between New York and Chicago on "The Executive," United Air Lines special flight reserves as a "sacred haven for the tired businessman aloft."[59]

In order to make sense of his fictional counterpart, it is necessary to understand the political and economic factors that insured the executive's rise to prominence. T. J. Jackson Lears explains the 1950s obsession as the triumph of a Gramscian "hegemonic historical bloc." He argues that corporations had the economic wherewithal to dominate discourses involving business and masculinity, hence the valorization of their upper-middle-class white progeny while erasing other masculinities, classes, and races.[60] Historian Mike Davis traces the valorization of management, hence executives, to a concerted effort to suppress unions after 1946. After a crippling strike at General Electric in that year, the company hired personnel manager Lemuel Boulware to reassert management's authority, leading to the destruction of unions in the entire electrical industry. IBM followed suit with what Davis calls a "slick refinement of Ford-style authoritarianism," which led to "a refashioning of plant life along a white collar ethos" in its own union-free company.[61] At the pinnacle of Senator McCarthy's power, a Republican-controlled Congress put the legal stamp of approval on the corporate suppression of unions, which were repeatedly accused of Communist infiltration, with the passage of the Taft-Hartley Act (1952). In concert with Henry Ford's desire after 1914 to create a well-paid automobile worker able to consume his products, mid-century corporations with United States governmental support sought to shape company-loyal executive families as the prosperous consumers of its goods and services, promising them pensions, health benefits, and long-term employment.

The increase in white-collar labor in the decade after World War II was also the result of reduced financial opportunities occasioned by the Depression and the depletion of manpower during the war. When the country began to prosper anew, a swelling of the executive ranks followed to fill the gap in professional employment. The problem was anticipated as early as 1943 when the War Production Board in Washington asked the Harvard School of Business Administration to develop a special course for higher executives who might be needed for special assignments.[62] This led to the Advanced Management Program— one step in the education, hence professionalization of the Organization Man. Throughout the 1950s, there was much discussion concerning the proper way to instruct executives in view of the multiple tasks that were expected of them.

Cinematic depictions of executives are dependent on mid-century "constructions" by novelists and observers of popular culture, self-help writers, and sociologists, among others. Two of the aforementioned films, and perhaps the most popular business films of the decade, *Executive Suite* and *The Man in the Gray Flannel Suit,* were based on fictional accounts authored by businessmen turned novelists who had experienced firsthand the challenges of male professional identity within the corporate hierarchy.[63] Their observations were augmented by an enormous self-help literature authored by businessmen who felt compelled to weigh in on all aspects of the executive's experience. Perhaps the most prominent observers of corporate life, who received the most sustained coverage in the popular press, were the so-called social critics or sociologists who were strongly critical on the direction taken by corporate America, especially its treatment of professional men. David Riesman's *The Lonely Crowd,* William Whyte's *The Organization Man* (1956), C. Wright Mills's *White Collar* (1953), and Vance Packard's *The Status Seekers* (1960) described executives variously as outer-directed, commodity-hungry aspirants, whose creativity had been excised by bureaucratic corporations, replaced by group think and adaptation. In gendered language, they bemoaned the so-called disappearance of the stalwart corporate tycoons and individualists in favor of emasculated men who were more concerned with pension plans rather than trail blazing, a dystopian view of men deprived of agency.

The prevailing stereotype of the eviscerated executive particularly rankled businessmen, who viewed it as an absurd misrepresentation. Anticipating the views of contemporary historians by several decades, Crawford Greenewalt, a prestigious businessman himself, took aim at the prevailing caricature of the "bland leading the bland." In his book *Uncommon Men: The Individual in the Organization* (1959), he argued that executives were made up of all types of people, not "the morally weak or the culturally disenfranchised." He criticized the romantic longings of the social critics for the bold tycoons of yesteryear, declaring that their disappearance was chiefly mythical. "It is presented as though, by some process of eugenics, the bull terriers and bloodhounds of the past," have been "cross-bred to produce a race of socially-conscious poodles."[64]

In contrast to the social critics' diatribes on upper-level men in corporations, there was a virtual cottage industry devoted to executive development in various popular culture forums by executives themselves and those who would presume to insure their continued success. The literature on the executive and its relationship to the construction of professional mid-century masculinity has not been sufficiently studied. An examination of the prevailing conversations of business leaders, self-help writers, and self-proclaimed efficiency experts will lead to a more integrated perspective on the ideas surrounding the mid-century executive, including his character traits, physical status, family life, and mental health. This can lead to a greater understanding of the cinematic delineation of the executive and the ultimate restoration of the hegemonic model of masculinity, which the films prescribe. For example, Avery Bullard's heart attack derives from discussions on the sick, overworked executive among business leaders and popular commentators, who encouraged professional men to strike a balance between their work and home life or suffer the consequences. Even though it is too late for men like Bullard to realize their foibles, the next generation in the character of Walling is poised to provide the redemption. Likewise, the defeat of the technocratic Loren Shaw by the integrated business model offered by Walling is less comprehensible without an understanding of the social critics and their detractors, who instructed executives on leadership, motivation, and individual achievement.

The middle-aged white male executive breadwinner of the movies reflected, in part, his actual counterpart. No men of color or women, and few ethnic minorities, inhabit the cinematic boardroom, which matches the profile put forth by the editors of *Fortune* in their comprehensive *The Executive Life*:

> The typical big-company executive was born the son of a busi-
> nessman in the Middle West or East. He had four years of col-
> lege, during which he concentrated on business or science. After
> school, he went to work for one company before he joined his
> present company which hired him while he was still in his twen-
> ties, and which he now served for thirty years.[65]

Although *Fortune*'s composite was informed by sex, race, class, and demographics, they were less successful in their effort to define executive duties.
Hence, the authors sent out 1,100 questionnaires to executives to determine the
nature of their work and the responsibilities incurred. Out of these responses,
Fortune forged a picture of an autonomous individual who served as a liaison
for several functions, supervised subordinates and delegated responsibilities,
made decisions that affected finances and future policies, and generally represented the interests of the company, hardly the corporate minions described by
Whyte, Riesman, and Mills. George Kienzle concurred in the evocatively titled
Climbing the Executive Ladder (1950). Employing rhetoric more suitable to combat than the sober environs of the office building, Kienzle described an instrumental man always on the move, usually upward, who "thrills to the battle."[66]
The majority of business authors concurred with TWA president Ralph Damon's
characterization of the executive as a leader, who can "select, train, and lead
others" while still working as part of a team.[67] The cinematic technocrats and
lackeys like Shaw or the obsequious board members of *Patterns* are thus set up
as straw men who must ultimately be defeated, in concert with the model of
masculinity proffered by corporations.

Most agreed that the assumption of the prestigious title of executive, with
its concomitant responsibilities of leading, decision making, and policy formation, came with a hefty emotional and physical price tag. Corporate ethos dic-
tated long, hard hours, with little separation between a man's public and private life; indeed even social engagements were expected to take place between
likeminded individuals of the same corporate mentality or economic class, always alert to company interests. In addition to late-night meetings, many executives reported that they took their work home or read journal articles to
further their professional knowledge in their spare time. One author described
the typical young executive as an energetic and ambitious type who worked
approximately ten to twelve hours per day. *Fortune* agreed, adding, "On the
average he will work four nights out of five. One night he will be booked for
business entertaining—more, probably, if he's a president. Another night he
will probably spend at the office, or in a lengthy conference somewhere else."[68]
Added to this load was the often hour-long commute to and from the newly
mushrooming suburbs with their attendant traffic jams.

The overworked executive turned company president made his appearance in cinematic office space perhaps most forcibly in the person of Mr. Hopkins in *The Man in the Gray Flannel Suit,* setting an example for his protégé Tom Rath. The deceptively kindly character works from morning until late into the night, often scheduling meetings during mealtimes. Hopkins suffers a congeries of ailments, which his physician informs him are due to his trying, uncompromising schedule. Rath is invited to an early breakfast as well as an evening cocktail, designated as work meetings, at the married Hopkins's self-imposed bachelor apartment. Decorated in pink and red, the setting suggests that overwork is either synonymous with or will lead to gender dysfunction or hidden sexual proclivities.

The excessive workload led to the general perception that executives were a physically and mentally ailing breed in need of advice and rehabilitation. Some blamed the corporation's expectations, while others put the onus on the professional employee's own inability to set limits. In contrast to the vigorous executives who sustained sixty hours per week, his aging counterpart who was now overweight, bald, and sluggish experienced a decrease in his ability to sustain the pressure.[69] Kienzle observed soberly that continuing in this vein was detrimental to his longevity:

> Executives die young. Life ends for them in their forties or fifties. The hardier hang on for a few years longer. The fellow with the snowy crown, who reluctantly moves on at the age of ninety-seven, is quite likely a college professor, a retired farmer or a truck driver . . . a physician, a writer, a musician, or a painter.[70]

Ray Josephs concurred in *Streamlining Your Executive Workload* (1958), one of the numerous self-help books available to businessmen. Asking a rhetorical question to those that would continue to drive themselves, he presented a sobering caveat: "Are you working too hard? . . . Or has anyone you know suffered a heart attack or died when he and everyone else there thought there were a good many high potential years ahead?"[71]

Those that did not succumb to death reportedly suffered various health problems and were thought to be in imminent danger. Kienzle instructed his readers to pay heed to the executive's obituaries, which listed the causes of death as heart disease, high blood pressure, and a host of nervous disorders. Other typical executive ailments included stomach ulcers and mental and physical exhaustion. Perhaps to amuse themselves or embarrass their superiors, a New York advertising agency formed a Golden Ulcer Club.[72] In a chapter entitled "Ulcer Gulch," another writer claimed that ulcers had "even taken on a curious and perverse aura" among white-collar workers.[73] *Fortune* assumed the role of psychological diagnostician, pointing to the existence of several character types, including an "ulcer personality" and a "coronary personality."[74] A self-help expert even invented a new syndrome, which he dubbed "tenigue," a combination of fatigue and tension, resulting in a new form of debilitation, causing the executive victim to feel both enervated and agitated.[75]

Sid Burns (Fred MacMurray) of the film *Woman's World* (1954), one of three executives vying for the second-in-command position at a major automobile company, is depicted as a dyspeptic version of the "ulcer personality." Tense and driven, he is unable to moderate his work schedule, which is both compromising his health and leading to the failure of his marriage. Tom Rath's interviewer, Gordon Walker (Arthur O'Connell), in *The Man in the Gray Flannel Suit* is perhaps the most caricatured version of the debilitated, emasculated executive of the decade, who, unlike his name, is immobilized. From a bed-like recliner that resembles a hospital gurney, the supine Walker imperiously instructs Rath to write an autobiography as part of his job application. The passive posture serves as a preliminary warning to Rath that the corporation might exact a mighty price, a fact corroborated by boss Hopkins's numerous health issues.

Gordon Walker reclining in the office in The Man in the Gray Flannel Suit.

Psychological ailments were also reported to be the bane of executives in the skyscraper's modernized offices, prompting *Fortune*'s alarmingly titled chapter, "How Executives Crack Up," in its book-length treatment.[76] It is telling that Hopkins in *The Man in the Gray Flannel Suit* hires Rath to write a report on community mental health, perhaps as a way to take stock of his own psychological state. *Fortune*'s editors supposed that discussions of the businessman's mental health had become so prevalent that various professionals were vying for control of his psyche, including "psychiatrists, medical men, psychologists, management consultants, and members of Alcoholics Anonymous."[77]

A multiplicity of reasons was offered for the emergence of male mental instability, but management was often reluctant to assume responsibility for its part, characterizing those who suffered psychological problems or breakdowns as temperamentally predisposed, fertile ground for the appropriate trigger. Medical experts in collusion with corporations concurred, blaming male menopause or the male "climeractic" as one of the causes for the older executive's downward spiral.[78] Realizing that their biological clocks were ticking away, executives began to suffer feelings of anxiety, helplessness, emotional depression, and suicidal ideation. They felt less productive at work; their grown children were leaving home; and the only women attracted to them were middle-aged. This often led to their rebellion against the institutional stressors keeping them at bay, namely, their jobs and marriages. If they were unable to cope with their plights in a constructive manner, fiftyish executives often engaged in extramarital affairs or sought separations or divorce, claimed *Fortune*. This may explain Hawley's formulation of Walter Dudley of *Executive Suite,* who is harassed at home and has lost his purpose at work, leading him into the arms of the much younger Eva Bardeman.

Numerous remedies were offered both for the proactive executive who was beginning to feel the ill effects of stress and for the man trying to regain his equilibrium after experiencing a breakdown. Management and employees alike were encouraged to identify the problem early, thereby prompting the executive to seek treatment expeditiously. The American Management Association believed that corporations should require and incur the expense of physical examinations. A healthy, modern attitude toward psychology by management could also preempt increased stress and prevent breakdowns.[79] Organization consultants like Richardson, Bellows, Henry and Company began to appear, who provided a forum where executives and their staffs could come together in a "vertical round table," to express themselves on personalities and policies.[80]

Another indication of the prevailing awareness that executives were under undue stress was the proliferation of books, book chapters, and articles dedicated to relaxation. Perhaps the most popular was Dr. Edmund Jacobson's *You Must Relax,* which went through five editions from 1934 to 1957, with considerable attention devoted to the hectic pace of modern life and its particular effects on the businessman. Describing the typical professional man who hurries from task to task but gets little done because of his depleted energies, in accord with efficiency experts, Jacobson recommended effective planning of ample time for work, play, rest, exercise, and relaxation on and off the job.[81]

One method to relax was simply to take time away from work, to plan vacations into one's schedule. Perhaps a more effective way, according to Kienzle, who cited the experiences of numerous successful business people to support his claim, was the acquisition of hobbies or creative interests in order to become an integrated, better-rounded person, rather than a myopic Organization Man. Hobbies also provided the practitioner with an imaginative outlet and the requisite leisure to balance a life given over to the perpetual production demanded by the corporation. He reported that Edward Streeter, vice president of New York Fifth Avenue Bank, was the successful author of the popular *Father of the Bride*; Arthur B. Connor, an office management executive for Bell Laboratories, was an amateur artist and photographer; and John L. Lewis studied the writings of Shakespeare.[82] Leon Uris concurred in his self-help book, citing Winston Churchill whose methods of relaxation included "painting, bricklaying, and carpentry. Whether you resort to the Churchillian paint box or do it with bowling balls, you'll find that physical activity or a mind-easing hobby helps a great deal."[83] *Executive's Suite*'s Don Walling already has these dual characteristics— professional drive coupled with a creative spirit. His mission is to insure that the corporation does not lose sight of the importance of creativity in the work environment.

Achieving a balance between work and family, or one's professional and personal life, was offered as a crucial component of preserving mental health, which was seen as a seemingly elusive executive feat because of the long hours, commute, extended home work, and business-driven socializing. An executive in the *Fortune* study lamented the paucity of time that he devoted to his family, particularly his children: "I sort of look forward to the day when my kids are grown up. . . . Then I won't have to have such a guilty conscience about neglecting them."[84] A vituperative article that blamed paternal absenteeism on a domineering wife also held the emasculating demands of the job responsible for the executive's abandonment of his son.[85]

Cinematic heroes were constantly under the strain of mediating between these two realms, often to the detriment of their marriages and children. In *The Man in the Gray Flannel Suit,* Tom Rath's children watch violent cowboy programs on television, and his son even threatens to leave home, perhaps because of his father's long hours and benign neglect. Rath solves the dilemma by resigning as Hopkins's assistant for a job closer to his suburban home, even though it is less prestigious and will mean a cut in pay. Don Walling in *Executive Suite* is so busy and driven that he relinquishes the paternal responsibility of mentoring his son in baseball, abandoning the twelve-year-old to practice the game with his mother. At the film's conclusion, Julia Tredway tells Mrs. Walling that she will have to assume a secondary role to her husband's career, which she agrees to in order to preserve his genius.

Not only was the male executive called upon to juggle work and home equitably, but so was his spouse, hence the appearance of a new paradigm of fifties femininity, the executive wife or Mrs. Executive. In 1951, *Fortune* published a two-part article by sociologist William H. Whyte Jr. that claimed to be the first study made of the "ticklish subject."[86] Situated spatially in both the domestic and corporate realm, Mrs. Executive exploded the current breadwinner/homemaker dichotomy that seemed so much a part of prevailing gender ideology, hence Whyte's expression of discomfort.[87] The cinematic Mrs. Executive drives him to the train station *(Executive Suite, The Man in the Gray Flannel Suite)*, attends company functions *(Patterns, Woman's World),* and even waits outside the boardroom *(Executive Suite)*. While her husband is away at work, and in order for a married couple to achieve both professional success and marital bliss, the company spouse was advised to assume a more active role managing the household, to become a domestic executive. Tasks such as coordinating home repairs and managing family finances, tasks previously relegated to her husband, were now within her purview. The author of *The Man in the Gray Flannel Suit,* Sloan Wilson, paid homage to his wife for her self-abnegating spirit in helping him reach his goals while enumerating the expanded job of a professional's wife: "I'm grateful to Elise Pickhardt Wilson, my wife, for the help she gave me in writing this book. She mowed the lawn, took care of the children, and managed the family finances. . . . Many of the thoughts on which this book are based are hers."[88] Indeed Mrs. Wilson created the title for the novel, which became a popular description to signify male corporate conformity. The fictional Betsy Rath (Jennifer Jones) in the film even single-handedly sells the family home and hatches a scheme for subdividing the land on the Rath's newly inherited estate, accomplishments also based, in part, on the real Mrs. Wilson.

The executive wife's tasks were not solely limited to the home front; she was expected to assume an active role in her husband's career. Many corporations asserted that they were not simply hiring a man, but his wife and children, prompting company president Thomas Watson Sr. to speak of the existence of the "IBM Family."[89] Sensing that expectations concerning femininity were in a state of transition, *Newsweek* inquired rhetorically, while voicing the current anxiety concerning potential emasculation, "Should the executive suite have two pairs of pants—one for the husband and one for the wife?"[90]

Many corporations were interviewing not only prospective executives for employment, but their wives as well. According to a 1951 report in *Fortune,* half of all companies studied were screening wives as a regular practice, and qualified applicants were denied employment because of their spouses. The surveillance took both benign and insidious forms, from a tactful sizing up to a thorough, intrusive checkup of her popularity in the community, spending practices, independent monetary resources, and credit rating.[91] A company president declared wives with independent means suspect. The executive husband will invariably feel that "his wife wears the pants," hence feel impotent, and will be less likely to accept the corporation's authority.[92] This new phenomenon of "sizing up executives' wives" was one of the premises of the film *Woman's World,* in which all the wives ultimately prove inadequate. The man who ultimately gets the job is selected, in part, because of his decision to leave his pushy, overly acquisitive wife, choosing the corporation over marriage.

Several firms, such as George Fry and Associates and management consultant John L. Patton, were even hired to study the so-called "controversial issue" with business organizations in the Chicago area to determine its efficacy. According to Fry, educating the executive wife to be an integral part of her husband's job had become, in his opinion, an increasing and positive trend. Patton disagreed; he was of the idea that the long arm of the corporation had exceeded its reach. Nevertheless he decided to ask the wives themselves how they felt about the policy. To his surprise, fifty-five percent believed that they should be screened along with their husbands.[93]

Mrs. Executive's ideal personality traits were offered as a template for the aspiring executive and his employer. Some companies recommended that data on her should even be kept in his personnel file. For the husband, this meant that the selection of a companionable wife could further his career; for the corporation, a better wife could be used to advance its interests, a veritable executive by proxy. Experts generally agreed that executive wives should be attractive, well-adjusted, and most important, infinitely adaptable to the vagaries of high-end business life. The personality appraisal included the following questions:

> Does she complement him? Is she a helpmate or a millstone? A
> nagger? Understanding? Does she resent his traveling? Does she
> criticize him publicly? Is she loud? Is she a lady?[94]

Compromise and sacrifices were the keynotes, much like Mary Walling who recognizes that her identity will be subsumed, in part, by Don's. Aiming his advice at the husband, Kienzle asserted:

> She'll have to put up with such things as entertaining people
> who will help you rather than those she likes. . . . She'll have to
> see your money go into things you need for success rather than
> in things she wants. . . . She'll have to find as much happiness in
> your success as you do.[95]

In *Streamlining Your Executive Workload* (1958), Josephs enumerated ten wifely sacrifices that doubled as prescriptions for reducing his workload and stress level while increasing hers. These included "Had to keep dinner warm while he worked late at the office. . . . Suppressed that desire to scream at one more bulging briefcase of homework. . . . Cancelled her own appointments to suit his emergency schedule."[96] Executive wives were required to be so flexible that one self-help author instructed his male readers to marry a woman who likes to travel since on his way up the corporate ladder he may be required to move from one city to another.

Professional advice peddlers were also quick to prescribe the type of women to avoid, namely blunt and so-called domineering types, especially those who overstepped their boundaries in public situations—women like the objectionable stereotype of Edith Alderson in *Executive Suite* or Carol Talbot (Arlene Dahl) in *Woman's World,* who is even willing to sleep with the company president to insure her husband's promotion. Peggy Zimmerman, who worked for an executive recruiter, reported on a wife whose proprietary concerns for her husband's health and well-being supposedly cost him a job. When he accepted a cigar from the company president during an interview, she piped in, "Oh Charles, don't be silly. You know you'll have indigestion all night." These comments prompted the company president's own wife to wonder how such a pushy woman would fit into the garden club, which instigated the president to pass up the applicant. The head of St. Louis's Executive Service Inc., William Wiley, concurred, proclaiming a domineering wife "the kiss of death."[97]

Yet an affable, self-abnegating personality and an attractive appearance was not enough to make a consummate executive wife; she was expected to possess professional qualifications of her own that could be employed to assist her husband in his numerous tasks, further blurring the boundaries between public and private space, the skyscraper office and the suburbs. At one of Fry's management clinics, the topic was "How should the future Mrs. Executive be prepared through formal education?" The consensus was that "ideally she is a college graduate, and has some business experience" so as to guarantee what *Fortune* termed "growth insurance." Ironically, men were advised to wed someone superior, but not an intimidating type with a "Bryn Mawr accent."[98] Marrying up was necessary because often Mrs. Executive was expected to represent her husband and the corporation at clubs, churches, and community organizations, in essence, to serve as a walking public relations campaign. According to Lewis, one company had even graduated from wife selection to wife training by initiating a course called "How to Help Your Husband Get On," while others developed films, pamphlets, and brochures to get her excited about the business.[99]

In addition to her public relations function as the company's attractive and articulate spokesperson, her education was also seen as beneficial for the completion of her husband's work tasks, giving new meaning to the Depression-era appellation "office wife." Martin Revson, vice president of the Revlon Corporation, pictured her as an all-around factotum, a cross between a secretary and an executive herself, advising her: "If he has a lot of paperwork to do—learn to type. If you don't know how then give him a hand with the reports if he wants the help."[100] Employing essentializing rhetoric, many saw her supposedly inborn skills in interpersonal relations as assets in helping him decipher office politics. One wife expressed the sentiments of many when she said, "A wife must be . . . a sounding board. She must be ready to listen and even talk of business matters if her husband wants to talk," much like Mary Walling and Sara Grimm (Mary Adams) in *Executive Suite*. The wife of a man named Bob was a bit more directive in assisting her husband to reach his full potential. Well-versed in office politics because of his steady confidences, she advised him soundly to "quit acting like a scared baby and look at the facts," which prompted him to resign from his current position and obtain employment elsewhere for a higher salary. Thus, a wife's wisdom was seen as a necessary asset in helping her husband negotiate more expeditiously his way up the executive ladder.[101]

A college degree could also be useful to Mrs. Executive in assisting Mr. Executive with his speech-writing duties. Even the most circumspect of wives at Fry's Chicago business retreat, Mrs. James D. Robinson, who was averse to any sort of meddling, ever vigilant to the idea of not appearing too pushy, admitted that she helped her husband with speech writing, often telling him to edit his more long-winded explications. Like Mrs. Robinson, the fictional Mrs. Rath of *The Man in the Gray Flannel Suit,* who was probably based on the real Elise Wilson, served as both a sounding board and editor for her husband's speech, which he was ghost writing for Mr. Hopkins. Hence the educated executive wife may be viewed as the real ghost writer of many a mid-century corporate speech, veritable closet executives on the home front. *Newsweek* concluded its treatment on executive wives with one such accomplished "closet" executive who decided to renounce her behind-the-scenes activities. She was charming and brilliant and so skillful that her husband suggested that she secure her own job. "Now they're both happy even though she's making more money than he is."[102]

Autonomous executive wives turned executives or female executives were a rarity in mid-century America, even though the advice literature began to acknowledge their existence. The latter made their appearances in the film *The Best of Everything* (1959) as Amanda Farrow (Joan Crawford), a tyrannical, frustrated woman who fails at romantic relationships, and Caroline Bender (Hope Lange), an ivy league college graduate who aims for a management position because she has been jilted by her fiancé.[103] The ideal upper-echelon manager was still a seasoned middle-aged man, who was weary of the conformity expected by the corporation. Self-help business writers charged that social critics were selectively fashioning the executive as a bland bureaucrat, blaming "college professors" for proffering a "strange, false philosophy" concerning the corporation's view of creative agency.[104] In his book *Executive Performance and Leadership,* Carroll Shartle argued that although Americans gravitated toward greater uniformity, seemingly in concert with corporate values, at the same time they "respect individual initiative" and "rebel against control." In a section strategically entitled "The Individual and the Organization," he cited E. Wight Bakke, who regarded the corporation and the individual as mutually mediating forces, engaged in a tug of war, each effecting to stamp their values on the other, in a veritable "fusion process."[105]

Others were more cynical concerning the efficacy of corporate domination. *Fortune* recognized that executives were perennially trying to forge a healthy balance between adherence and autonomy but observed that younger executives were more apt to believe that "conforming is simply a phase—a kind of purgatory that one must suffer before he becomes progressively more independent."[106] The general consensus among business writers was that although the corporation may attempt to exact an unhealthy allegiance, the stalwart American executive, who was heir to the nineteenth-century upwardly mobile striver, continued to make his own mark, albeit with some modifications. These selfsame writers were more than willing to instruct the aspiring executive on how to avoid becoming "kindly poodles" or unoriginal technocrats by offering practical strategies and solutions.

Business writers touted leadership and creativity as the executive's most valuable assets in contradistinction to Riesman's false dichotomy of outer-directed or conforming vs. inner-directed or autonomous professional men. "We did not assume that an individual would be the replica of his social role, but rather that there might be greater tension between an individual's search from that which he felt alienated," Riesman lamented. In clearly nostalgic, gender-inflected prose, he claimed that it was better to be "an inner-directed cowboy than an outer directed advertising man."[107] After studying the responses of 1,100 executives, Whyte saw no evidence that the individual was being swallowed by the impersonal bureaucracy or in danger of losing his creative spark. Countering Riesman directly, he asserted that if there was anything that characterized executives it was "a keen sense of self—a desire to control one's environment rather than be controlled by it." Even in spite of the more sanguine, modulated facade of today's executive, there burned "an ego as powerful as drove any nineteenth-century buccaneer," he claimed in rhetoric as gendered as Riesman's.[108]

One of the keys to understanding Walling's triumph is to situate him within the context of business writers' prevailing definitions of the executive, defining him as an individual less in conflict with an impersonal corporation than a sound manager or leader by nature, who hoped to leave his imprint on several constituencies: subordinates, customers, shareholders, and the public. Hawley and Lehman appropriated Riesman and the social critics to set them up as foils in order to disprove their assertions, hence reaffirming corporate values of success. Shaw was employed as the stereotype of the bland Organization Man whose game plan is ultimately defeated. According to Chris Argyris and other business writers, a good leader was an ethical person who can maneuver himself in the hierarchy both vertically and horizontally, communicating worker's issues to upper management and vice versa, while maintaining a healthy camaraderie with his executive peers and superiors.[109] In the film *Executive Suite,* Don Walling is such a leader who brings together various teams, echoing his son's role in the baseball game. He commiserates with the on-line staffs who fear the loss of their sense of purpose and livelihood, carrying their message to the boardroom as he destroys a piece of inferior furniture. Speaking with drive and passion, he informs each member how he will enhance their job if he is elected leader. Most importantly, Walling has ingenuity, one of the crucial ingredients for executive success. Subject headings such as "Uncorking Ingenuity," "The Aggressive Mind," and "The Man in Action" speak to the prevailing expectation that executives required instrumental intelligence in order to succeed in business, traits that were imbued in Walling.[110]

DESK SET (1957): THE MARRIAGE OF SKYSCRAPER AND COMPUTER

The establishing shot of *Desk Set* continues where *Executive Suite* left off in its emphasis on the modernization of interior skyscraper space for human betterment, through the introduction of well-designed furniture and the inclusion of new technology, especially the computer. The seemingly omniscient camera zooms in from above, surveying several neatly arranged, modestly sized modular computers of varying shapes and sizes in sleek steely gray casings before resting on the logo of an IBM 403. A trick in lighting casts a subtle shadow over

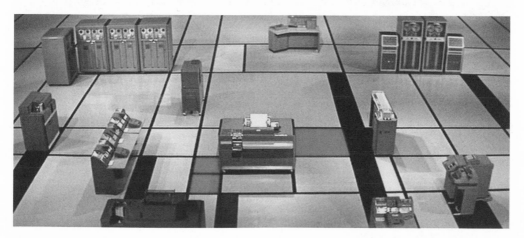

IBM showroom in Desk Set.

the machines, causing them to appear as attractive equipment or storage units rather than cold mechanical objects. Although devoid of human beings, the fictional space is a cheerful one, due to upbeat music and jazzy floor covering, offering an efficient, aesthetically pleasing utopia for prospective employees. Red, turquoise, light blue, and yellow rectangles comprise the asymmetrical grid that seems to continue limitlessly, resembling the nonobjective paintings of the Dutch artist Piet Mondrian, a modernist urban boogie-woogie for the new computer age in this fictional portrayal of IBM's New York showroom.[111] Shot in color and the new CinemaScope format pioneered by Twentieth Century–Fox, the state-of-the-art computer is matched by the excitement staged by the spectacle of the wider screen format, thereby simultaneously underscoring dual tropes of modernization.[112] The 403 machine prints out the film's credits, including Fox's special acknowledgement to IBM, who provided actual computers for the set designs and consultants for accuracy of detail.[113]

The machine's seemingly autonomous gesture printing the credits suggests new modular office computers may soon replace humans in the performance of routinized tasks. It also implies that the machines are now working in concert with one another, perhaps a way of pitching IBM's integrated electronic network, rather than one single computer, envisioning a future seamless mechanical stream of information in the skyscraper office. IBM's role as the film's advisor, promoter, and supplier of props, seen in its unprecedented sponsorship in theaters and its various company facilities, identifies *Desk Set* as the first film to actively endorse the computer's inclusion in the skyscraper office, serving as an early plea for the benefits of cyberspace.[114] The film also makes an initial appeal for novel, "improved" gender identities that were not only mediated by rela-

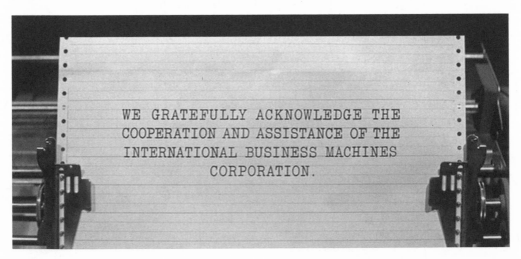

Acknowledgments to IBM in Desk Set.

tions with other humans, but a result of interfacing with the computer.[115] This multifaceted corporate strategy was advanced at a time when computers had recently become accepted outside of the defense establishment, and when fears still ran high that mechanical brains could deprive workers of their livelihood. Magazine article titles such as "Can a Mechanical Brain Replace You?" "Office Robots," and "Will Machines Replace the Human Brain?" caused anxiety in the public mind.[116] The technological optimism staged by the corporate partnership of Twentieth Century–Fox and IBM, designed to ward off this concern, is woven into the very fabric of the film's skyscraper location and delineation of space, which is also implicated in the plot and the delineation of characters.

Billed as a "big business" comedy, the story takes place in the upper offices of the fictional Federal Broadcasting Company (FBC), which is supposedly situated in Rockefeller Center's RCA Building (1931), linking computers, skyscrapers, and television in the inception of the new information age.[117] Norbert Wiener, the father of cybernetics, which melded the "control" of servomechanisms with the burgeoning field of communication, believed that the human mind could be extended via information, particularly in its dissemination or transport. Hence the computer's place in the film's fictional reference library was foreshadowed by Wiener when he wrote in 1950:

> The needs and complexities of modern life make greater demands
> on this process of information than ever before, and our press, our
> museums, our scientific laboratories, our universities, our librar-
> ies and textbooks, are obliged to meet the needs of this process or
> fail in their purpose. To live effectively is to live with adequate
> information.[118]

The association of computers and television in the distribution of information was augmented by the loftiness of skyscrapers, which served an important function as towers of communication. As the owners of the Empire State Building realized, a skyscraper's height made it eminently suitable for radio transmission, a capability soon extended to television. The National Broadcasting Company (NBC) leased the eastern half of the 85th floor in 1936 in order to begin distributing television programs to engineers and executives. By 1950, a 222-foot television antenna was added to the building, to prepare for the eight stations located therein.[119] The RCA Building, the exterior of which was used at the outset of *Desk Set*, also boasted twenty-six broadcasting studios with suitable lighting for television. A shot of the building's exterior strengthens the connection between skyscrapers, computers, and information. Subsequent to the inside view of well-functioning computers, the camera pans the building from entrance to skyward-reaching pinnacle to emphasize its modernity and height. The marriage of computer and skyscraper is echoed in the romantic consummation of reference librarian Bunny Watson (Katharine Hepburn) and efficiency expert Richard Sumner (Spencer Tracy).

The plot and delineation of characters reveal much about corporate expectations concerning gendered professionals and how they are required to inhabit and negotiate space. Richard Sumner is hired by FBC as an outside consultant ostensibly to complete a study on the feasibility of introducing a computer to the all-female reference department in order to increase efficiency. The rehabilitation of postwar corporate space, heir to the earlier masculinizing enterprise of scientific office management, which stressed efficiency through machines, measurement, and managerial surveillance, was reintroduced in the new postwar field of space administration, epitomized by the character of Sumner. Although he is sworn to secrecy, an obvious military-inspired cold war trope, the women discover through the office grapevine that Sumner is trying to foist a computer upon them that they believe will result in the loss of their livelihoods. Against a backdrop of Christmas cheer, some are concerned that the inscrutable Scrooge-like Sumner and his Electro Magnetic Memory and Research Arithmetical Calculator or EMMARAC (similar in name to Remington Rand's UNIVAC) will render their research work obsolete.[120] Others, like the brainy but unmarried librarian Bunny Watson, maintain that human intelligence is indispensable to the successful operation of her reference department. The film depicts the technocratic, absent-minded Sumner and the attractive spinster Watson as both in need of gender rehabilitation, which will be accomplished, in part, by the computer. After everyone in the corporation, including the president, gets an erroneous termination notice due to a computer glitch in payroll, Sumner explains that their incoming computer will ultimately prove beneficial. FBC's merger with the Atlantic Network will insure the bounty of employment into the limitless future, linking technology to growth, expansion, and corporate benevolence.

Desk Set attempts to neutralize the fear of computers by recourse to several strategies, most importantly to humanize the computer, borrowing terminology from cybernetics experts such as Norbert Wiener. IBM sought to capitalize on these human-machine analogies in its numerous ad campaigns and film commissions. They employed Charles and Ray Eames to make *The Information Machine or Creative Man and the Data Processor* in 1957, the same year as the release of *Desk Set*. The corporation borrowed further their rationale from automation experts such as John Diebold who viewed the computer as a helpmate rather than a threat to human agency. *Desk Set* goes a step further in humanizing the computer by assigning EMMARAC a gender identity, making it less a masculine-identified wartime machine and an adversarial opponent than an office partner, presaging women's role as the machine's primary tender in libraries.[121] It is feminized by the diminutive nickname Emmy, which sounds similar to the name Bunny, the name of one of the women in the already gendered en-clave of the all-female reference department.[122] As Richard remarks to Bunny, "you know that you and Emmarac have a lot in common. You're single-minded; you go right on relentlessly, trying to get the answer to whatever you want the answer to."[123] However the temperamental computer Emmy threatens to suffer a mental breakdown that is blamed on Sumner's nervous assistant, the man-nish Miss Warriner (Neva Patterson) who is called in to supervise the computer. Emmy is finally subdued by the more level-headed Bunny with the help of a hairpin, a further testament to the computer's girlish, unthreatening nature and her human-like personality.

DESK SET AND IBM: STRENGTHENING THE CORPORATE MESSAGE THROUGH PRODUCT PLACEMENT

Based on the successful play by William Marchant, which enjoyed an extended Broadway run, *Desk Set* was adapted to the screen by Phoebe and Henry Ephron, who removed much of the computer's equivocal character in the play in favor of an untarnished ending, crediting IBM with effecting a literal and fig-urative marriage between efficiency and humanism, seen in the rehabilitation of skyscraper space and corporate relations.[124] Preliminary scripts by the Ephrons locate the initial scenes in the Federal Business Machines (FBM) Building in midtown Manhattan, rather than IBM, indicating that the film did not begin as a specific propaganda ploy as much as a general plea for the acceptance of com-puters in corporate environments.[125] Bunny has been sent to the FBM showroom to learn about the computer's multifaceted capabilities, which the mechanical performers perfect with comedic zeal, meant to create a favorable impression for the viewer. There she meets the likes of Flash, who does mathematical cal-culations at lightning-fast speed, and the new programmable Rapid Robert the Rabbit who is even capable of learning from his mistakes. These friendly ap-pellations echo those in IBM's own publications, in which computers are given nicknames such as Bessie, Punch, Choosy, and Tabby.[126] Although these scenes were written out of the final version, Bunny reports to her charges early in the film that she has been to "IBM to see a demonstration of the new electronic brain."[127] Moreover, the computer's stunning performances and lighthearted character are preserved throughout, causing one reviewer to recognize the film's ideological content: "The Ephrons state clearly that the 'brain' isn't supposed to supplant humans—only to make their time freer for jobs Emmy can't do. This apologia pro/vita machine seems like a pitch for a bigger more loved I.B.M."[128]

In 1956, Twentieth Century–Fox and IBM entered into a mutual agreement to promote the film, while the latter simultaneously provided real computers in theater lobbies, which was part of a reciprocal tie-in strategy. For example, on the occasion of the film's run at the Fox Theater in San Jose, California, several tabulating and data-processing machines manufactured in the city's local plant were featured in the lobby display, expanding the idea of promotion to include extensive mechanical hardware.[129] In turn, Twentieth Century–Fox supplied trailers and lobby cards for the corporation's more than 350 offices and showrooms to guarantee that the corporate messages of unlimited opportunity and gender harmony were not lost on its own employees.[130] IBM also agreed to donate machines and six operations experts to Twentieth Century–Fox to assure the film's technical veracity and the machine's smooth performance. The company was, in effect, advertising its new computer products on Fox's new enlarged CinemaScope screen, especially its 701 model on which Emmy was based, the first time in IBM's history that it used motion picture promotion to sell its products and corporate message. The Ephrons, director Walter Lang, and two art directors even flew to New York to watch the computers in action at IBM's newly remodeled showroom at 590 Madison Avenue and to confer with company executives, locating the imprint of IBM on all aspects of production.[131] As a result of this visit that cemented the corporate partnership, the Ephrons were obliged to rewrite and enlarge the computer's role in the story, making it a "leading character," prompting Spencer Tracy to quip that Emmy had more backup men than he did.[132]

IBM's decision to use popular culture venues to sell its products was occasioned, in part, by the publicity enjoyed by its competitor Remington Rand, which had pioneered the UNIVAC (Universal Automatic Computer), a programmable, modular computer more suitable for commercial office space. By the early 1950s, both companies were trying to convince businesses that computers were no longer gargantuan, bellicose machines suitable only for wartime use but could be employed for both calculations as well as information processing. As the writers of *Fortune* noted presciently in 1952, "it appears that its [the computer's] first and heaviest impact . . . will be in the business-executive office."[133] Remington Rand upstaged IBM in 1952 when UNIVAC appeared with Walter Cronkite on CBS news and successfully predicted the results of the presidential election.[134] IBM also lagged behind Remington Rand in sales due to its president Thomas Watson Sr.'s inability to see beyond the computer's wartime applications.[135] The additional stress of a government antitrust suit launched against the company further weakened their image in the nascent area of computer placement in business.[136] Hence, IBM's new chief Thomas Watson Jr. began a public relations campaign, especially in the new television medium, positioning his products on quiz shows, news programs, and popular network variety venues. In March of 1955, for example, an IBM 701 was pitted against video broadcaster Jack Lescoulie in solving a complex multiplication problem on the popular morning "Today" show. When announcer Dave Garroway turned to Lescoulie to inquire if he would like to check his answer against the 701's, his weary reply indicated that he could not keep up with the computer.[137]

IBM's starring role in *Desk Set* made depicting the fictional machine in optimal terms all the more important as a ploy to ensure its actual acceptance in business space. This was seen in the studio's allocation of time and money, under the ever-watchful eye of IBM's consultants. An unprecedented number of set design staff and amount of resources were involved in fabricating EMMARAC, including the art, construction, property, mill, special effects, hardware, electrical effects, and electrical fixture departments, for a total cost of $150,000, far exceeding the cost of all the other sets combined. The result was a highly aestheticized machine measuring eleven feet high and fifteen wide, with a pulsating grid of colored lights created by special effects man Ray Kellogg, a virtual mosaic in motion, which matched the real mosaic in the office of FBC President Azae (Nicholas Joy).[138] As Reinhold Martin has recently pointed out, Thomas Watson Jr. had recently hired industrial designer Eliot Noyes to refashion both the company's Madison Avenue showroom and its computers. Noyes explained that in his design of the IBM 705 computers in 1954, he sought to display the computer's dynamic colored innards from behind its austere metallic casing.[139] Twentieth Century–Fox's art director Lyle Wheeler went a step further in beautifying the computer; instead of the militaristic, masculine gray suit, he dressed Emmy in stylish medium blue, which matched the color scheme in Azae's office, the company logo, and the garb of several librarians, a more feminized and fashionable version of corporate packaging. The color scheme parallels IBM's own blue system/360 released in 1956, which resulted in the appellation "Big Blue," but may also have been inspired by the new literature on office design, which encouraged the use of color to brighten the corporate environment for the pleasure of employees and customers alike.[140] The purposeful styling of Emmy was perhaps generated by IBM's own advertising campaign to picture its computers as responsible for the rehabilitation of skyscraper office space by making them efficient, well-organized, and visually pleasing, resembling tasteful Eames-inspired storage cabinets.

This strategy was echoed in the advertisements IBM presented in various trade journals and business magazines. By the mid-fifties, it pictured its own Madison Avenue showroom and service bureaus appointed with varied, attractive machines laid out in an orderly fashion, attended to by busy well-dressed male and female professionals.[141] In a 1953 ad encouraging the use of its service bureau, the entire office and its varied machinery arranged along a neat grid, and illuminated by crisp florescent light, implies that the lack of mess and clutter is a product of a well-organized, waste-free work process. The ad copy pledges that this efficiency will be passed on, with the assurance that buying power will be transformed into "cash profits for your company" at a modest cost. Men and women working together belies the gender-segregated spatial arrangements of most companies, promising a workplace free of tension, only hinted at in *Desk Set*'s finale.

Advertisement for an IBM service bureau; reprinted courtesy of IBM Corporate Archives.

IBM's design director Eliot Noyes was also responsible for hiring the Eameses for the first of several celebratory films completed for IBM on the liberating potential of the computer to solve a myriad of society's ills. *The Information Machine: Creative Man and the Data Processor* (1957) was commissioned by IBM for its pavilion at the 1958 Brussels World's Fair, which was dedicated to the overall theme of "nuclear energy working for peace."[142] It is useful to employ the film as a template for understanding the Hollywood-made *Desk Set,* since both bear the stamp of IBM's publicity apparatus in 1957.

Compared to *Desk Set,* which employed comedy, the Eameses relied on playful animation by Dolores Cannatta to present the computer as one of humans' most important allies. *The Information Machine* constructs a progressive, evolutionary tale that begins with primitive man's desire to come to grips with his environment, through speculation and prediction, often with dire consequences. Following a series of human trials and errors, the Eameses present the "visionary" invention of the wheel, followed later by the abacus, portraying the computer as the newest and most benevolent of a long list of tools in the human quest for mastery of the environment. Proponents of information technology are fond of tracing digital computers back to the abacus, and analog computers to Napier's rods and slide rules, or historically remote antecedents. However, computers have a much more recent, often repressed history. Modern analog computers date from the 1930s while digital computers that "can add and subtract discrete units of information fast enough to simulate complex logical processes, were a product of the war." Between 1949 and 1959, IBM and other major corporations still received about 59 percent of their revenue from the government. Even IBM's 701, on which Emmy was based, was developed with eighteen contracts insured by the Department of Defense.[143] However, in the Eames's visual tale, creators rather than destroyers are pictured as the enlightened few; artists and inventors possess the ability to explore, speculate, and predict the outcome of their actions.

After applauding human creative potential, the film sets up a parallel between human and computer processes, picturing the former as "building up stores of information in active memory banks," similar to *Desk Set*'s likening of Emmy to Bunny. A collection of comic book–like mental pictures from a caveman's head, accompanied by the mechanical sound of a cash register lever depositing coins in the till, conveys the human brain's ability to store information. If men are like machines, then how can a computer possibly render them automatons, the film proposes. According to the Eameses, free-thinking artists with the ability to propel society forward with their inventions are found in many fields, including architecture, mechanics, medicine, science, and politics, implying that resistance to the computer is a gesture against creativity and progress. In neither *Desk Set* nor *The Information Machine* is the computer ever a destructive agent; in these utopian tales, the computer is the offspring of all past tools used for society's betterment.

The nineteenth century is regarded as a century of chaos and complications, a time when man was plagued by his inability to speculate and overwhelmed by the development of industry, pictured by the twisted conduits of mass communication and energy delivery. A dystopian urban landscape is filled with belching smokestacks and tangled networks that multiply exponentially until blackened scribbles obliterate land and sky, the visual embodiment of chaos. The Eameses credit the computer with rescuing humans from this self-inflicted disorder: "Something has now emerged that might make even our most elegant theories workable. The recent acceleration has been fantastic. The electronic calculator has already become a tool upon which much of our daily activities depend." A Rube Goldberg-like machine composed of spinning wheels and gizmos replaces the darkened skies, leading to an orderly office filled with modular computers tended by happy programmers, akin to the fictional IBM showroom at the outset of *Desk Set*.

Interspersed in this cartoon-like story are working computer parts seemingly borrowed from the visual poetics of early modernist filmmakers such as

The dystopian city in Charles and Ray Eames, The Information Machine.

Man Ray, Fernand Léger, and Dziga Vertov. Punch cards, vacuum tubes, inner wiring, grid-like knobs of varying patterns and colors are displayed pulsating and bobbing, surpassing the complicated mental work previously done by humans. Hence the machine is not a threatening behemoth, but an interesting array of abstract patterns, an orderly aesthetics that "can bring a new dignity to mankind."

For the remainder of the ten-minute film, the computer's accomplishments and potentialities are explored, which the Eameses appear to believe lie in three major areas. First, the computer is a control mechanism with the capacity to insure the smooth operation of our public utilities and the management of our financial institutions (cost accounting, payroll, insurance billing, etc.). Second, as a function of design, it can be programmed with complex formulas by creative persons to perform multifaceted tasks. A man is shown working diligently to formulate the data to be fed into the computer, a creative artist at work, with the IBM logo "THINK" emblazoned over his desk. His lengthy and highly creative endeavor is meant to show that data processing removes the drudgery of work for the programmer and the public he serves. In accord with automation expert John Diebold, the Eameses suggest that white-collar jobs in particular

An office with computers in The Information Machine.

will become more creative in a world peopled by computers.[144] Last, as a simulation or model of life, from chemical plants to complete communities, the machine is a tool with the ability to predict the "probable effects of various courses of action," preempting the chaos of earlier periods. The machine's grid-like punch cards and dynamic innards are transposed onto the diagrammatic logic of artist Cannata's futuristic cities, which are analogues to the orderly office environment promised by Emmy.

The Information Machine concludes with several ethical imperatives, echoed by those in the cybernetics community such as Norbert Wiener, and with the recognition that the computer has both constructive and destructive use potential, as evidenced by its previous role in wartime. Charles and Ray Eames insist that the computer's direction must come from man, that "the task that is set and the data that is given must be his decision and his responsibility." If this injunction is followed, it may serve as a marvelous asset to human betterment. Concluding with the utopian language of endless possibilities, marked by an almost religious zeal, the Eameses claim: "But the real miracle is the promise that there will also be room for those smallest details that have been the basis for man's most rewarding wishes." A humble rose and a child-like heart are

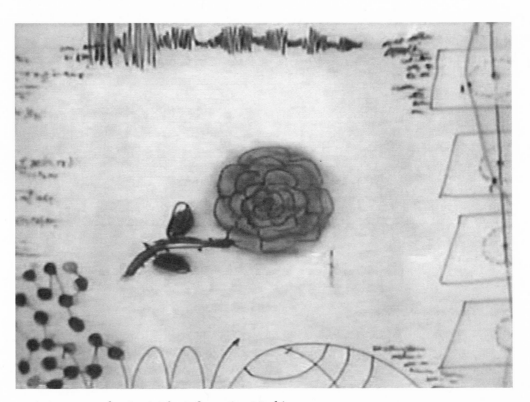

A computer valentine in The Information Machine.

offered up as these small details, veritable valentines to the computer's ability to liberate humans to enjoy greater leisure and pleasure.[145] As in *Desk Set,* the computer is depicted as a machine that is capable of affording people free time to pursue more enjoyable activities (e.g., aesthetic and emotive experience), a liberating agent that will enhance rather than detract from human life. The computer will not turn men into machines, as was the prevailing fear, but render humans more creative and sensitive beings at work and at home.

THE COMPUTER IS A LADY AND THE LADY IS A COMPUTER: GENDER AND SPATIALITY

The melding of the computer and various feminine identities furthered IBM and Twentieth Century–Fox's mutual desire to present the computer as a benevolent agent of change in a corporate office that is seemingly beset with endemic gender difficulties. Gender destabilization served as a ploy to allow the computer to serve as the mediator for characters to more fully realize their ideal selves, creating new subjectivities in concert with the machine. The computer's feminine identity is also implicated in the film's prescriptive plea for modernity and gender normality; only certain types of women can befriend the computer or anyone else for that matter, and others are just too old-fashioned or maladjusted to even try. Appointing the computer with the nickname Emmy had an additional feminizing and diminutizing effect, rendering it a compatible addition to the television station's all-female, gender-segregated reference department. The stylish, efficient computer that is able to store large amounts of data is also poised to rehabilitate the film's overtly feminized space, which is depicted as disorganized, homey, and less than optimally efficient.

Discussions concerning the interface of humans and computers, or what Paul Edwards has termed "cyborg discourse," in which computers were invested with linguistic and interactive abilities, often of an intimate nature, among other characteristics, was a prominent feature of the postwar era.[146] One of the most famous mid-century illustrations of this equation was the so-called Turing Test of 1950, in which the British mathematician Alan M. Turing posed the question, "Can a Machine Think?" At the outset of the experiment, gender is implicated with the so-called "imitation game," which included three people: "a man (A), a woman (B), and an interrogator who may be male or female." The "object of the game for the interrogator was to determine which of the two is the man and which is the woman." Gender-inflected questions such as "Will X please tell me the length of his or her hair?" were inserted to facilitate discovery, but subjects were encouraged to foil the questioner. The next step was to substitute a machine for either the male or female subject to ascertain whether the interrogator could decide the difference between the machine and the human, which replaced the original question, "Can machines think?"[147] An upshot of the test was perhaps to ascertain whether men and women think differently, an issue not pursued by Turing. Although designed ultimately to decide whether a computer possessed "intelligence," the test also set up a competition between men and women and between human and machine subjects that was explored in *Desk Set*. Indeed when Richard is administering an intelligence test to Bunny, he queries, "What is the first thing you notice about a person?" to which she replies, "Whether they are male or female?"[148]

The human-like character of computers was a theme fully explored by mathematician Norbert Wiener in his influential books *Cybernetics* (1948) and *The Human Use of Human Beings* (1950).[149] Drawing from over a decade of research, Wiener and his cybernetics' colleagues from fields as diverse as neurobiology, psychology, and anthropology claimed that "automatic machines and electronic computers—and living nervous systems, too—could all be studied from a unified viewpoint," through the lens of communication.[150] In the introduction to his second book he asserted that society could only be "understood through a study of messages, and the communication facilities which belong to it."[151] Infinitesimal cells, plants, animals, people, simple and complex machines, indeed all societies are unified by their use of control or self-regulation, accomplished by the process of feedback, Wiener and his colleagues believed. These communications are not simply isolated and discreet but exist along a constantly moving organic chain of circular causality that keeps both humans and machines effectively functioning. Both animate and inanimate entities may encounter glitches or negative feedback in their communication processes, but even these can prove beneficial in helping them self-correct. In addition to their analogous procedures, Weiner argued that computers and people were also physically similar; both had sensory apparatuses and storage and memory units. *Desk Set* employs the organic metaphor borrowed from the cybernetics group in representing skyscraper space as a vast, continuous chain of communications and miscommunications, from something as simple as Bunny's feeding of a plant to the invisible telephone network that keeps the women abreast of covert company policies.

Even though Wiener recognized that self-regulating, programmed machines could communicate with one another, thereby obviating the need for people, he became an ethical voice for the computer's use in human betterment. In response to the destructive manner in which computers had been used during World War II, and fearing their potential for hastening total Armageddon, Wiener refused to accept monies from the government or from corporations that were bound to federal funding, believing that the scientist had become "an arbiter of life and death."[152] Instead, he reached out to organized labor and to management organizations that could promote the use of computers to their best human advantage. Wiener was particularly sensitive to the effects of automation on manual labor, pledging to United Auto Worker president Walter

Reuther that he in no way wanted his expertise to contribute to "selling labor down the river."[153] Yet he also warned the Society for the Advancement of Management, to which he provided the keynote lecture in 1950, that the "second industrial revolution" occasioned by the computer could have dire consequences for "white collar labor, too." He challenged both the government and managers to assume the role of statesmen to protect those that would lose their jobs and those that "we never do employ again."[154] This could be accomplished by a respect for human agency in directing mechanical processes, emphasizing that "living systems were open . . . because the 'steersman,' the self correcting mechanism, was human in social systems and thus moved not by formal logic but by skill, experience, and purpose." According to Wiener, fascism and centralized control were more of a menace to the "inhuman use of human beings" than machines:

> Whether we entrust our decisions to machines of metal or to machines of flesh and blood which are bureaus and vast laboratories and armies and corporations, we shall never receive the right answers to our questions unless we ask the right questions.[155]

Nevertheless the human terminology used to describe the computer exacerbated the apprehension that humans were becoming obsolescent, especially since the word "computer" was previously employed to describe a worker who performed mathematical tasks with the help of calculating equipment, which prompted IBM to resist the term. Even IBM's own publication was christened with the neurological title *Think*. Since these associations were already part of common parlance, IBM and Fox sought to imbue the computer with benevolent characteristics and, in accord with Wiener, depict its human tenders as potentially problematic.

The creators of *Desk Set* explore the issue of human to machine interface, arguing in concert with Wiener that the computer's success is dependent on those who employ it for beneficial or nefarious ends. The film depicts FBC's President Azae under the advice of Richard Sumner as an enlightened manager, sensitive to labor issues and human betterment, at least in the firm's reference department (there are mass firings in payroll). The responsibility for the computer's success is placed more squarely on the shoulders of the corporation's employees, who are required to be in possession of "appropriate" gender identities to insure the smooth operation of business. The level-headed Bunny must cooperate with the computer rather than Emmy's nervous "mother," the mannish Miss Warriner. Space is ultimately rehabilitated by the inclusion of an efficient computer that requires human guidance and the expulsion of the dysfunctional Warriner, who finally suffers an emotional meltdown, paving the way for Bunny and Richard's romantic coupling.

Bunny Watson is an attractive and extremely bright librarian who is in charge of the FBC's all-female reference department but beset with a problematic gender identity. A college graduate, she has also completed a library course at Columbia University and might have gone on for a PhD but for a lack of funds. Her loyalty to her job and her boyfriend Mike Cutler (Gig Young) is both a strength and a weakness; she has been at the company for eleven years without a promotion while waiting for Mike to marry her for the last seven. She is so committed to Mike and the company that she even does his work, allowing him to take the credit. Straddling two types of femininity, the New Woman and a variation of the frustrated executive wife, who made her appearance in the 1950s, Bunny is both a modern professional woman and an advocate of old-fashioned values.

Bunny's traditional morals are viewed as an impediment to her success, a resistance to modernization, and an obstacle to gender normativity. She is neither married nor an optimum professional, a woman with neither a husband nor a computer. This is reflected in the specter of spinsterhood that haunts Marchant's play and the film, pictured in the latter by a zany old woman who has remained at the office for thirty-six years. Although she was formerly the model for the svelte youthful female of the company logo, the spinster's continued presence is meant to serve as an antidote to progress. Women who don't marry or stay current end up as crazy office fixtures, the film warns. Bunny's coworker Peg Costello (Joan Blondell) even quips that the two of them might eventually live together and keep cats, a covert reference to a potential lesbian relationship, but an idea that is quickly dismissed. The reference department's "frustrations" reflect the prevailing ambivalence concerning women's proper purview: while 35 percent of women worked outside the home, they were simultaneously expected to eventually marry and occupy the domestic sphere.[156]

Bunny's modern librarian is also rendered as a sometimes superior, more human version of the computer Emmy. She declares to her female charges, "No machine can do our job. There are too many cross references. I'll match my memory with that of any machine any day." A scene featuring Bunny and Richard on the skyscraper's wintery rooftop is meant to underscore her mental superiority. Even Richard has to admit to Bunny that the computer cannot fully evaluate, a task of which only humans are capable. Spatially, the scene underscores the loftiness of her intelligence and her ocular command of the city. While eating a bag lunch outdoors, in order to ensure the cost-efficient use of time, Richard administers a personality questionnaire designed to measure how much the "human mind" can "retain, reprogram, and rearrange." In reality, these tests were often given to persons a company believed had the most potential to operate a computer—those with high intelligence, the ability to think logically and reason abstractly.[157] Bunny masters the test with flying colors, much to Richard's bemusement. Her mental acumen, which rivals the computer's, may

Richard Sumner and Bunny Watson on the FBC Building roof in Desk Set.

be a parody of the Turing Test, illustrated by the way she presents her own re-search findings concerning Richard, spitting out the facts as fast and accurately as an electronic brain might.

> You were born in Columbus, Ohio, on May 22nd, which makes you
> a Gemini; you're a graduate of M.I.T. with a PhD in Science. . . .
> You're one of the leading exponents of the electronic brain in the
> country—and the inventor and patent holder of an electronic
> brain machine called EMMARAC!

Bunny's skyscraper reference library is the spatial analogue of her prob-lematic gender identity and her resistance to modernization. It is a nurturing, homey environment in which the women cooperate and protect one another, reinforced by numerous close-up shots of its stage-like space, which highlight its intimacy and its claustrophobic character. Even though Bunny is a supervi-sor, a large picture window separates her small office from the others, resem-bling those of the Levittown tract houses sold to postwar middle-class families. Within the confines of the office-kitchen, she even feeds a large philodendron plant, which loops its way around the whole room, a sign that she has domesti-cated and personalized the corporate milieu.

The layout of furniture in the reference department's communal office is haphazardly arranged, and there are piles of dusty books spilling out from each desk. Telephones are persistently ringing with endless reference requests, and the women talk over one another, creating a distracting cacophony. Work is interspersed with dress order requests, relationship advice, and the exchange of borrowed money, situating private activities in the public realm and under-scoring their compromised effectiveness. Still, the women get the job done,

Watson's office and the research department in Desk Set.

often staying late at the office to accomplish their tasks. The film argues for the betterment of this disorganized feminine environment through the masculinizing enterprise of spatial administration and computerization, while still retaining its feminine, personalized character. Richard tries to superimpose his efficiency model, but in the end the computer's organizing regime must learn to coexist with Bunny's philodendron plant, resulting in a successful, integrated machine-organic interface.

Bunny's office is also part of a larger feminized space that encompasses several departments in the building, linked via the telephone. The dissemination of information in this manner links all the female employees, whether librarian or secretary, in one vast, often invisible network or office grapevine, similar to the continuous organic communication loop described by Wiener. Design historian Ellen Lupton has pointed out that telephones have been traditionally regarded and thus designed as gendered objects, especially in the 1950s. They have been associated with female labor since the early twentieth century, in part because of women's so-called ability to diffuse potential tension because of their pleasant nonthreatening demeanors, especially among male businessmen. This belief was so common that Bell Telephone dubbed its female operator "The Voice with a Smile" in one of its ads, picturing the attractive worker tied to her headset.[158] Although the women in *Desk Set* comprise the largely lower-paid receptionist and secretarial staff, they employ their telephones as sources of power and control. The office grapevine undermines President Azae and Richard's desire to keep the computer a secret until the latter's report on its feasibility is completed. When Richard mistakenly arrives one day early to see Azae, he recoups by making his way down to the reference department unannounced. A split screen pictures Azae's secretary Cathy (Merry Anders)

Cathy and Peg Costello on the telephone in Desk Set.

talking to Peg, Bunny's assistant, on the phone, warning her that someone is on his way down. "I don't know exactly who he is—some kind of a nut, I think, or somebody very important—probably both. Look when he leaves your place; find out where he's going?" This prepares the reference staff to be on guard and cover for each other, which they do famously.

The computer's putative femininity, hence its humanity, is reiterated in many ways. Emmy is a romantic and office competitor, a machine with feelings and mood swings, a performer with a costume and a set of gurgling "lines," and ultimately an office helpmate to Bunny and her staff. The gendering of computers originated at IBM, where various computers were invested with masculine or feminine identities; thus the male "Sorter" is a "gifted" geographer "who knows all sorts of countries and cities," attesting to his far-reaching grasp of the public sphere, while the "Hen," who duplicates material and "hatches them in her quiet way," is depicted as a female reproductive body.[159] Marchant's play adopted IBM's gendering strategy, where Emmy is described as "9 feet tall, but of course, rather broad around the hips."[160] In the film *Desk Set,* prior to Bunny's introduction to Emmy, she views her as a competitor for Richard's romantic affections. When her feelings toward the opportunist Mike Cutler change in favor of Richard, she accuses the inventor of having never married because there is another female in his life. "Emily Emmarac—monster machine. You're in love with her." Indeed in Great Britain, the film was released as *His Other Woman,* pointing to Emmy's coupling with Richard in this revised version of the office triangle theme.[161]

The Ephrons sought to further render the feminized computer agreeable by imbuing her with moods, sexuality, and performative characteristics. Richard tells Bunny that Emmy is "very sensitive. When she's frustrated, the entire magnetic circuit can be thrown off," to which Bunny replies, "Something like that is happening to me." In addition to Emmy's blue costume, the Ephrons' initial desire to introduce activated computers in the film's opening scene was meant to give them "a kind of showmanship." Even though we don't meet Emmy until later, the staff begins to conjecture about her abilities. Peg asks if she can sing, which foreshadows the conclusion. After EMMARAC is "fed" like a baby by a towel-wielding Miss Warriner, she makes a characteristic sound "rather like what a really good mezzo soprano would make of Helen Kane's old 'Boop-boop-adoop' number if she were of a mind to sing it inarticulately," which tells the staff that she will be a sexy and entertaining coworker.[162] The Ephrons may have derived this idea from IBM's own publicity strategy: in the storefront window of its Madison Avenue showroom, passersby could stop and watch its giant performing 701 complete with "thousands of neon lights that flashed on and off, and switches which buzzed away . . . continuously."[163]

Both the level-headed Bunny and the sensitive but playful Emmy are contrasted with the technocratic and humorless Miss Warriner (warrior and whiner), who is more of a cyborg than the computer herself. The Ephrons describe her as manly and robotic, "with ice water in her veins," similar in spirit to Rottwang's robot Maria in Fritz Lang's film *Metropolis* (1927).[164] Like the elderly spinster who haunts *Desk Set,* Miss Warriner serves as a caveat to professional women who would chose a job over marriage, a more hyperbolized version of the Depression-era female office drone. A dysfunctional feminine addition to the office, her expulsion from it is necessary to its smooth operation and the well-being of Bunny and Emmy alike.

At the company Christmas party, Bunny's festive red costume is contrasted with that of Warriner, who is appointed in a stiff, steely blue suit, more forbidding in color than Emmy's and decidedly more masculine. Indeed when a group

Miss Warriner and the media in Desk Set.

of reporters come to take stock of the computer, Warriner is situated with the men, while the female reference librarians look on dejectedly. She is part spinster and part robot, double signifiers of asexuality and gender dysfunction. To assuage fears that computers would reduce humans to robots, apologists like Diebold claimed that the resemblance of machines and humans is too "superficial to warrant the conclusion that these machines *think* or are in any essential way *human*."[165] Warriner's first gesture is to rearrange the furniture to her liking and post warning signs all over the office—"NO SMOKING," "KEEP DOOR CLOSED," "DO NOT TOUCH"—asserting her authority and increasing the tension. After everyone in the office gets an erroneous pink slip, caused ironically by the calculating computer in payroll, Bunny and company stop working, forcing Warriner to "man" the office herself. Not only can she not spell, resulting in her feeding the computer false information (a plea for the expertise of librarians), but she becomes so unhinged that she detaches the computer's delicate red lever, which causes a temporary meltdown.[166] The red lever may be seen as a mechanical, eroticized bodily part that needs tender loving care, and a specter of nuclear annihilation, which, in the wrong hands, could lead to disastrous results, as Wiener had warned. As a result of Warriner's inability to manage Emmy or get along with anyone else, she leaves in a paranoid huff, claiming that one and all in the department are against her. IBM and Fox's message is clear: computers like humans are fallible and can make mistakes, particularly when guided by hysterical women who overstep their boundaries. The robotic, gender-dysfunctional Miss Warriner is ejected from the newly reorganized feminized space, paving the way for Bunny and Emmy to become friends.

Richard's gender identity, like Bunny's, is in need of corrective measures. Slightly off kilter and lacking in human skills and a feminine touch, he must be normalized, the film argues, through romance and marriage. As a methods engineer, Richard Sumner's mission in life is to rid the world of waste and inefficiency or, in his own ironic words, "to improve the work-man-hour relationship" in the all-female reference library. His name conjures up a general who delights in all things numerical. He tries to accomplish his goals with recourse to two strategies reminiscent of those employed by early twentieth-century scientific office managers as explained in chapter 1: to plan the office layout of furniture and office machinery, and to survey the employees and their work habits for maximum productivity. One scene in *Desk Set* has him calculating the office dimensions with a tape measure to ascertain the top location for the inevitable new computer. To increase the comedy of the film, he appears when the women are otherwise engaged or even celebrating, leading him to comment, "Nothing much gets done here."

In contrast to the Richard of Marchant's play, who is an exaggerated fussbudget, the Ephrons' scientist-cum-methods engineer is a frumpy version of the businessman in the gray flannel suit, much like the absent-minded Wiener

Sumner crawling on the floor in Desk Set.

himself. His calls to efficiency are undermined by his perennial inability to manage time. Either too early or hopelessly late, he loses the very tape measure with which he hopes to whip the office into mathematical shape. When the staff discovers him crawling on the floor with the selfsame yardstick, his infantile posture undermines his authority to discipline the office. Even his two different-colored socks discovered by Bunny are a charming touch, signaling that he too requires supervision.[167] The Ephrons rendered Richard and Bunny with more nuanced, yet unintegrated gender identities, which served as a convincing vehicle for the Tracy-Hepburn team known for their bantering and cinematic challenges to normative notions of masculinity and femininity. In both *Woman of the Year* (1942) and *Adam's Rib* (1949), Hepburn plays a professional woman, whose career causes problems with her husband (Tracy), necessitating both to make compromises.[168] At the end of *Desk Set,* Richard needs the brainy but nurturing Bunny to complete him, while she requires his modernizing regime, seen in the spatial overhaul of her office and the introduction of the computer, to render her work more effective and inspired.

The film ends with all potential tensions resolved, while the corporate benevolence of FBC, with the assistance of IBM, is underscored. In accord with the marriage of management and labor, Bunny and Richard's relationship is consummated with the help of human to computer feedback and vice versa, creating new gender normativity that is mediated by the machine. Richard employs Emmy in a gambit to pop the question, the answer of which he has already programmed in. The computer's performative and upbeat human character is seen further in her gurgling emissions, syncopated sounds, and flashing lights, which echo Bunny and Richard's passion. A benevolent cyborg, Emmy is no longer perceived as a threat but is a productive, albeit finicky female officemate and matchmaker and an agent of endless jobs and creative opportunity. Bunny

Watson and Sumner's consummation in Desk Set.

finally gets a well-deserved promotion as the inefficient Mike Cutler is transferred out. All this occurs against a backdrop of holiday cheer; the computer is
the office's new Christmas gift, rendering the skyscraper more efficient, well-
designed, and agreeable.

GENDER, SPATIAL ADMINISTRATION, AND THE REHABILITATION OF SKYSCRAPER SPACE VIA AUTOMATION

An understanding of Richard's technocratic masculinity is tied up with discourses concerning professional identity and the reorganization of interior skyscraper space, particularly with regard to the introduction of automation. His
job category of efficiency expert or methods engineer was developed in the
early twentieth century by Frederick Winslow Taylor and others to insure that
factory machines and humans working therein operated efficiently to maximize
production and profit. These ideas were extended to the corporate office by
William Henry Leffingwell's scientific office management and Frank and Lillian
Gilbreth's motion studies. The profession enjoyed a resurgence, albeit in a novel
form, in the 1950s as a reaction to various ideological and material developments. Although the profession suffered a setback during the 1930s due to the
complaints of labor unions that feared the dehumanization of their constituencies, the wartime success of efficiency and the postwar suppression of unions
jointly affected the corporate sphere's appearance. With the postwar skyscraper
building boom, which created a substantial increase in the square footage of
new offices, efficiency experts were called in to organize the new space. There
was also a mounting pressure to modernize older business interiors in response
to the erection of novel skyscrapers and the development of new synthetic
materials and workplace technologies, particularly the computer, which held

the promise of a more automated, factory-like office. In his book *Tomorrow Is Already Here* (1954), Austrian émigré Robert Jungk reported disparagingly of the reinvigorated profession, which he claimed was "highly unpopular among American workers":

> The man leaning against the wall opposite the long row of elevator doors in the new Standard Oil Building, is not noticed by the hundreds of people passing in and out. . . . How superior he is to every individual, every secretary and every boss who steps through the doors of this skyscraper today Mr. White Collar alone knows. For he is here to make a survey, a study of the behavior of the genus *Man*. . . . One firm after another engages "methods analyst," "systems engineers," or scientific managers to rationalize its offices.[169]

"Space Planning Called New Art" appeared in the *New York Times* in 1954, attesting to the manner in which efficiency analysis and methods engineering had metamorphosed in the postwar period.[170] The article included an explanation by Walter Jacobs, president of Michael Saphier Associates Inc., one of the first companies of this type, which encompassed engineering, architecture, office functions and work flow, and interior decoration and design. Six years later, office planner Kenneth Ripnen included an entire chapter on the "space administrator" in his book *Office Building and Office Layout Planning,* calling for a wholly new conception of "space for the organization man."[171]

Although he is described as a "methods engineer," Richard's modernized version of the job more closely approximates the work of the space administrator.[172] Prevailing discussions, which circulated among management organizations, industrial designers, interior decorators, space administrators, automation consultants, and architects, among others, provide further clarity for understanding his rehabilitation of office interiors. In spite of his lovable forgetfulness and fumbling, he conforms to a kind of masculine professionalism—rational, technocratic, and preemptory—suggesting that his disciplined automating of skyscraper space will insure greater productivity in the name of profit. Ripnen's assertion that the space planner's role should be carried out by "a qualified man with enough backing to make his decisions authoritative" points to the hierarchical nature of his enterprise with regard to workers and their access to power.[173] Richard comes to the FBC at the president's behest, much to the chagrin of the female reference staff, who are never consulted and who fear that his spatial discipline will result in their unemployment. In accord with new space administrators, however, Richard also professes to care about worker creativity and job satisfaction, while IBM's styling of Emmy accords with current humanistic discourses concerning the beneficial effects of an aesthetically pleasing work environment for employees and as an advertisement for prospective customers.

The rehabilitation of actual office interior space in the 1950s was occasioned by a confluence of economic forces and material changes in architecture and technology. Instead of the height mania that characterized the early years of skyscrapers, new office buildings, such as Skidmore, Owings, and Merrill's Lever House (1952), were decidedly smaller, and hence more cost effective and efficient, leading Robert Jungk to dub these new structures "baby skyscrapers."[174] Moreover, the rise in owner-occupied buildings instead of speculative ventures, and the rehabilitation of older offices in response, increased the need for interior office designers and planners.[175] While the architect was still an important figure, the new skyscraper heroes of the decade were the spatial planner, furniture designer, and industrial designer.[176] As early as 1945, before the building boom had commenced, Rockefeller Center architects L. Andrew Reinhard and Henry Hofmeister announced that the focus had shifted to the office interior:

> The modern office is brightened and enlivened by dozens of
> new materials, both structural and decorative; by new forms
> and curves; by modern lighting and air conditioning and acous-
> tic treatment and office machinery and conveniences of many
> kinds . . . it has improved the efficiency of the office.[177]

The introduction of air conditioning and florescent lighting to the skyscraper further altered the spatial configuration of interior space, enabling the computer's arrival and the necessity for space planners.[178] Workers were no longer required to sit close to windows for illumination and comfort. Office space changed from a compartmentalized, rigid model in favor of an open, mutable plan that also meant more design flexibility on an ongoing basis. The new expanded spatiality is underscored in *Desk Set* by recourse to the advantages of CinemaScope, in which characters were often spread out along an expanded horizontal axis to keep the viewer's eye moving over the entire frame, unlike the constricted office interior of noir films. After the arrival of the computer to FBC, the space is finally cleared with ample room between characters and office machinery and effects.

Computers also required certain temperature and humidity control to remain functional, as evidenced by the numerous warnings emblazoned on the finicky computer Emmy in *Desk Set,* so these changes in interior space were compulsory. The machines also necessitated special electrical outlets for increased outage and reinforced, double flooring, often arranged in a logical grid, to accommodate their heavy weight. Demanding technological and structural requirements had a dual outcome, affecting both the space administrator's job and the office's interior layout and aesthetics. By 1961, architects Harrison and Abramowitz incorporated a chapter entitled "Planning Office Buildings for Automation" in their book on office buildings, which included the various technological requirements for the computer's successful introduction to skyscraper space.

The expense of early computers was a challenge to spatial administrators, requiring them to make the office more cost-efficient. The rapid development of office machines and computers after the war was also responsible, in part, for the discourse on the need for office flexibility, whereby its interior configuration could change at a moment's notice. Modular furniture such as George Nelson's Executive Office Group (1947) and Florence Knoll's integrated office furniture suites may be viewed as necessary, aesthetically pleasing expedients to office environments given over to brisk changes in technology.[179] Space administrators and their corporate employers argued that only those firms that could readily alter their office spaces, thereby keeping pace with rapid modernization, would remain profitable just like the FBC in *Desk Set*. Maurice Mogulescu, the owner of Design for Business Inc. (formed in 1946), one of the first postwar firms devoted to the efficient and well-designed office, underscored this issue when he claimed that new office interiors required planning and engineering, which integrated "problems of efficiency, economy and aesthetics."[180] In his later book *Profit through Design* (1970), he discussed the entire office from boardrooms to lunchrooms in view of its contribution to the economic health of the corporation, or how space itself produced revenue.

Material changes in the office were accompanied by a corporate campaign to guarantee the computer's inclusion in skyscraper office space, hence the creation of cyberspace. Technological optimism among businessmen, corporations, and their apologists paved the way for the manner in which computers altered skyscraper space in both architectural and human terms. By 1955, at the same moment that Marchant was writing the play *Desk Set,* an extensive, highly ideological literature was available for business managers, executives, and controllers by members of their own professions who promoted the inclusion of automation, the computer, and the introduction of integrated electronic data-processing systems to the factory and office building alike. For example, in October of that year, a subcommittee of the 84th Congress listened to three days of testimony from an automation expert, an economist, representatives of various industries (metalworking, automobile electronics, transportation), and union representatives on the subject of "Automation and Technological Change," which resulted in an over six-hundred-page printed report.[181] *Harvard Business Review* and the American Management Association were among a host of professional organizations and journals also responsible for publishing consistently throughout the decade on various aspects of the subject.[182] One of the most prominent congressional witnesses was John Diebold, an editor of *Fortune* and owner of Diebold and Associates Inc., the largest consulting firm of its kind, whose job was to help businesses adopt computers in their factories and offices.[183] A synopsis of Diebold's highly influential book *Automation* (1952) was placed in the record, challenging congressmen and businessmen alike to think in flexible terms or "rethink" to make way for the inevitability of the computer.[184]

Embedded in this vast literature were several articles, book chapters, and symposium proceedings that dealt specifically with the feasibility of the computer's inclusion in the business office, which accords with Richard's assignment in *Desk Set* and serves as one of its primary thematic concerns. Articles and book chapters sporting such titles as "Electronics in the Modern Office" and Diebold's "The Office of the Future," a synopsis of his lengthy book chapter "Automatic Handling of Information," and the congressional committee's section, "Automation in Data Processing and the Office," attested to a keen interest in promoting the computer in offices in general and skyscrapers in particular.[185] Many of these writings began with dispelling so-called fallacies and prevailing fears about automation and computers, laying the groundwork for their a priori conclusion that if computers were adopted, well-oiled machine operations and business procedures would ensue. As Diebold testified before Congress:

> We have heard automation characterized variously as a potential threat to the national economy; as a key to increased leisure opportunities; as a mystical pseudoscience of robots and giant brains; and as a press agent's description of automatic operation, from the kitchen toaster to subway turnstile. If you follow the progress of Dagwood, you may notice that as of this morning Dagwood is faced with possible replacement by an automatic machine.[186]

Several arguments designed to overcome these misconceptions that were offered by the business community have significant bearing on *Desk Set* and its construction of gender and spatiality. Perhaps the most common falls under the rubric of cost-efficiency, which implicates employees, machines, indeed, the entire layout and configuration of the office environment. It also involves the spatial environment temporally because efficiency was also measured in terms of the time required to complete various tasks. There was general agreement that bureaucracy had grown to unmanageable proportions due to greater productivity and consumption. In order to successfully administer this huge output of paper, costly clerical workers were hired and subsequently blamed for draining companies of their profits. Ralph W. Fairbanks wrote alarmingly in "Electronics in the Modern Office" (1952) that the office was operating much less efficiently than the factory. While production costs had gone down due to better planning and automation, "office costs" were "all out of proportion in ratio to plant costs," resulting in a "losing battle being waged in the war against rising clerical costs."[187] Harry L. Wylie concurred, characterizing clerical wages as the "greatest single office expense" in *Office Management Handbook* (1958), although he blamed the increase on salary adjustments negotiated by the unions. Wylie believed that in order to combat the problem, it was incumbent on management to compensate by either larger income or improved procedures, of which automation was a possible solution.[188]

Neither these writers nor the authors of *Desk Set* acknowledged that clerical staffs threatened with obliteration consisted mostly of women, one of the film's many repressions concerning the effects of automation and computerization. Although people are likened to computers throughout the film, the human cost of introducing them is glossed over and never fully resolved. Passing reference is made to layoffs in the payroll department due to the introduction of a digital computer, but Bunny's reference staff seems more concerned with losing their own jobs. One of the librarians goes to the union but once she and the others realize that they will be retained rather than replaced, the plight of other workers is quickly forgotten in concert with IBM's antiunion policy. Perhaps the introduction of a computer to an all-female reference staff in the film was a ploy to dispel fears among all women that their jobs would be eliminated, thereby asserting corporate benevolence.

Rising clerical costs and the concomitant bureaucratic disarray was envisioned in spatial and temporal terms as a complicated labyrinth, the unraveling of which could be achieved by recourse to mechanization. Skyscrapers were needed, in part, in the early years of the twentieth century as centralized repositories for the vast quantities of paperwork produced by insurance companies, banks, and other bureaucracies. With the change from an economy largely given over to the production and distribution of goods to one that emphasized administrative and executive operations, the proliferation of paper and information had increased exponentially, necessitating a more cost-efficient manner of storing and analyzing the vast amount of data.[189] Advocates promised that computers could now accumulate this information on cards or magnetic tapes, which would reduce clutter, liberate space, and create a seamless flow. Diebold dramatized the compartmentalization of information that occasioned the liberation of space that was afforded by the computer: "By the use of magnetic tapes, the storage space for the policy information of a large insurance company can be reduced from ten or fifteen floors of files to 350 or 400 spools of magnetic tape which, with control gear, would occupy one medium-sized room."[190] Robert Fisher observed in *The Boom in Office Building* (1966) that a reduction in paper storage, coupled with the invention of smaller computers, resulted in a more cost-efficient management of skyscraper space:

> Expanding office work forces and increased per-capita use of floor space in office buildings have put a premium on efficient office management. Hence consulting firms, educational courses, and management of office personnel and records, have proliferated during the postwar period. So have sales of compact office furniture, equipment and machines designed to take up as little floor space as possible.[191]

Returning to the opening scene in *Desk Set,* the mastering shot from above that pictures the steely computers along a depopulated grid may be seen as an allegorized version of the corporation's managerial gaze, which subjected workers and machines alike to a predetermined belief in rationalization and profit, an updated version of Fordist efficiency. The frame's seemingly limitless expansion is enhanced by the horizontal axis and larger screen format of Cinema-Scope. The film's depiction of space anticipates Fredric Jameson's discussion of information technology's representational solution to the world's "cognitive mapping," employed here to sing the praises of a paternalistic managerial revolution and renewed surveillance. The "object-world" of *Desk Set* is a product of joint corporate (Fox and IBM) wishes to dominate space and workers alike while prescribing a putative improved vision of "being-in-the-world" for viewers.[192]

The messiness of Bunny's desk, the haphazard arrangement of furniture, and the disorganized manner of conducting business was tantamount to wasting corporate resources. In the medium-range shot of the office also discussed above, furniture and objects are placed along a diagonal axis and threaten to collide with things on the room's left side. Seen in the middle ground, Bunny stands adjacent to a glass doorway that frames more clutter, overtaken by all that is in her shrinking domain, which is blamed, in part, for the office's general lack of speed and efficiency. In one of the film's last scenes, Bunny's response time is measured against the computer's ability to do the same task. The seemingly benign question put to the machine—"How much damage is done annually to American forests by the spruce bud worm?"—may have doubled as a reference to the shortage of trees, hence paper, buttressing the case for conservation of space and resources. It takes Bunny three weeks to figure out the exact figure while the computer requires only a few minutes, reinforcing the sense of human inefficiency. Fairbanks and others argued that the best way out of the morass was to adopt the rationalized, assembly-line flow of the automated factory model in the office, insuring the rapid, efficacious completion of tasks.[193] Commentators such as Wylie offered pictorials of various machines connected up to one another in an uninterrupted stream of productivity devoid of human intervention. Dubbed integrated electronic data-processing systems, they linked various business machines to one another, and in the future, planners promised to meld factory machines to those in the office for a more efficacious flow of information.[194]

Another ploy to convince businesses to adopt computers was that in the long run they would lead to human betterment. One of the advantages envisioned by both the single computer and the assembly line–like electronic data-processing system was the obliteration of boring, uncreative tasks, which simultaneously explained away the reduction of the expendable female clerical staff. In accord with Wiener, Diebold, and the Eameses, office managers and executives employed liberatory rhetoric, claiming that workers would be free to perform more creative jobs that would provide more time for leisure, which meant that white-collar positions would increase at the expense of blue- and pink-collar jobs.[195] Indeed in *Desk Set,* Bunny gets a promotion and is told that her department will expand with the computer's arrival, that the computer is there to help. As Diebold claimed, instead of massive unemployment and robotized Organization Men, automation "may bring us back to the human and psychological values of the self-respecting craftsmen whose alleged demise the professional mourners decry by wailing and bawling 'debasement,'" thereby "enabling us to do more and different things and satisfy human wants in new and better ways."[196]

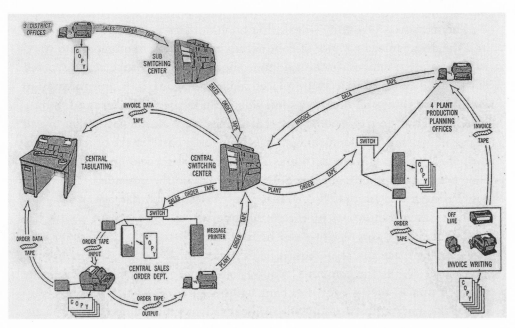

Flow chart of integrated order-invoice processing system. From Wylie, Office Management Handbook. *Copyright 1958; reprinted with permission of John Wiley and Sons, Inc.*

Most management analysts agreed that a more highly skilled staff would be required to operate the computer, including programmers, procedure analysts, coders, and machine operators, but many believed that this work pool could be drawn from the retraining of current employees. Roddy Osborn, who oversaw the installation of a UNIVAC at General Electric, recommended selecting and administering psychological tests to college graduates and MBAs from inside the corporation as a cost-saving measure, rather than hiring outside experts.[197] High intelligence and the ability to think logically and reason abstractly were a few of the desirable characteristics for a successful outcome.[198] Richard's administration of an intelligence test to Bunny on the skyscraper's rooftop, which she passed with flying colors, was designed to ascertain whether she would be a suitable candidate for computer training.

Desk Set's Bunny reflected management's belief that computers would benefit educated or white-collar employees, leading to her promotion. The computer in the film also underscores the utopian conclusion of harmony and reconciliation between the sexes. But the formulation of Bunny also represented the computer's own problematic gendered history. When computers were developed within the largely male-dominated military establishment, women were originally allowed limited access to them, their tasks often circumscribed by their sex.[199] As early as 1935, IBM's Thomas Watson Sr. established a token training program in response to a challenge from the Institute of Women's Relations. He decided to begin by training twenty-five women from colleges such as Bryn Mawr, Cornell, Smith, and Wellesley in order to teach customers' employees how to operate their newly purchased IBM equipment. In contrast to IBM men who were trained in sales, women were asked to assume the traditionally female role of teachers within the corporation.[200] Indeed women were an integral part of the development of Mauchly and Eckert's wartime ENIAC computer at Moore's School of Electrical Engineering in Philadelphia, where they worked as "computers" on desktop calculators, a job considered too repetitive for men. Adele Goldstine was among the pioneers in programming for ENIAC, which paved the way for several women being trained as programmers, although they were not given the same ratings as their male counterparts despite their identical education and experience.[201] Hence, when Bunny programs or feeds the library's contents to Emmy, keys in questions, and modifies her inquiries in response to the computer's replies, she is engaged in a majority of its operations, a multitude of professional tasks that women were rarely afforded.

Managers and human relations experts writing on women and computers in the fifties, in spite of IBM's advertisements to the contrary, envisioned the office's gendered workspace undergoing a major transformation, but often not to women's advantage. When John Diebold testified before Congress in 1955, he posed but failed to answer the question, "Does automation increase or decrease the range of jobs for which women are qualified?"[202] In spite of managers' recognition that employees had to be retrained, there was little discussion on how traditionally gender-specific jobs would be recast. Human relations specialist Robert Dubin predicted that the introduction of the computer would result in increased gender tensions, entitling a subsection of his automation chapter "Males vs. Females." He believed that the necessary retraining effort would be exclusionary:

> With increasing automation in the office, and the high skills required for automation specialists, it is probable that the monopoly of office jobs now held by women will be broken. More and more male specialists will come into the office to program and maintain automated equipment.

Dubin included a photograph of an all-male workforce dominating a newly automated office, with the caption, "Office automation showing a view of various types of data processing machines using punch cards. The absence of females is notable among this office staff." In a prescriptive tone that was consonant with fifties ideology concerning women's appropriate sphere, he conjectured further that women might just retreat to the home as their only real alternative to working for wages.[203] When exploring the gendered spatiality of Desk Set, it is necessary to contrast its IBM-inspired corporate message against female workers' actual access to the putative creativity afforded by the computer in the 1950s.

Ironically, although technological optimists often maintained traditional gender distinctions in the office, they argued that resistance to the computer was synonymous with a retrogressive stance. This echoes the way modernity was contrasted with the old-fashioned in Desk Set, which is superimposed on the gendered protagonists, who reflect these respective positions. For example, Bunny's old-fashioned professional and personal identity, echoed most prominently in the aging spinster who haunts the film, results in inefficient, outdated procedures that are a detriment to business productivity. Likewise, computer apologists used modernizing rhetoric to convince their colleagues that automation was progressive and, above all, profitable. Since the computer itself enabled businesses to plan ahead or forecast, as advocates argued, not having one was economically disadvantageous. In the aforementioned article, "Electronics in the Modern Office," Fairbanks asserted a position, echoed by many, that ignoring the computer represented a danger, condemning companies to unhealthy, risky economic positions. He concluded with a sobering caveat: "On the surface the stakes seem to be high, but the potential is much higher. Stop and think about the old adage about business firms, if they try to stand still . . . they are actually moving backwards."[204]

Office automation showing a view of various types of data processing machines using punched cards
The absence of females is notable among this office staff.

Males vs. females. From Dubin, World of Work *(1958).*

Cinematic skyscraper space and its gendered protagonist begin in a state of destabilization, in need of modernization in the mid-century era. Filled with antiquated furniture, inefficient work methods, and outworn industrial processes, it requires the creative spark of visionaries sporting new technological solutions in order to remain competitive, while providing workers with a more rewarding experience in the corporation. In response to social critics who identified bland Organization Men, skyscraper films responded by creating new heroes and heroines—the enlightened executive and Mrs. Executive, the spatial planner, and the industrial designer—while staging men like *Executive Suite*'s Shaw and women like *Desk Set*'s Warriner as foils, ultimately defeated by a renewed corporation given over to both individualism and teamwork. Other characters were marshaled to signify old-fashioned values or obstacles to modernity, which like old furniture require an overhaul, including aging, craven men, spineless glad-handers, spinsters, and overly technocratic masculine women. In contrast to the films of the immediate postwar period, these call for a new strategy of teamwork, including the balance of work and family life, seen as a joint effort by Mr. and Mrs. Executive, and the integration of inspired leadership within a renewed corporate structure wholly controlled by a managerial elite of which they were a part. Mid-century skyscraper cinematic space is offered in such films as *Executive Suite* and *Desk Set* as representative of a more enlightened corporate capitalism, a well-oiled machine, with modern fiberglass furniture, fluorescent lighting, and automation that supposedly created a more humanistic environment for employees.

Recent Skyscraper Films

The technological optimism staged by Twentieth Century–Fox and IBM in *Desk Set,* seen in their celebration of skyscraper modernization in the new age of computers and television, was replaced in succeeding decades with a grim depiction of its crushing effects on the individual spirit, commencing with *The Apartment* (1960). Critiques on corporate greed reached a virulent new pitch in subsequent decades in such films as *Network* (1976) and *Wall Street* (1987), outdistancing even those of Depression-era cinema. They present a dehumanizing "screen" culture of flattened television monitors, and later computer displays, that mesmerize, desensitize, and threaten to robotize office inhabitants.

While continuing to indict corrupt business practices, skyscraper space also became more perilous in one of the greatest cinematic disasters of the century, *The Towering Inferno* (1974), anticipating several homages to the World Trade Center tragedy in a case of life imitating art. According to cultural theorist Slavoj Žižek, after the downing of the Twin Towers, American citizens were introduced to the "desert of the real," which had already been "corrupted by Hollywood." The shots of "collapsing towers could not but remind us of the most breathtaking scenes in the catastrophic big productions." Žižek asserts further that the media had already been "bombarding" the American public with virtual threats before the actual events.[1] This assault or spectacularization of disaster began in 1970s cinema with blockbuster movies that implicated "giant" skyscrapers as suitable targets for fear mongering. Over a decade prior to September 11, 2001, the cinematic skyscraper was often cast as an American hostage, meant to be restored as a renewed beacon of democratic values under threat from foreigners and terrorists. It became an increasingly politicized terrain poised to be reinstated as a national territory in *Die Hard* (1988), *Skyscraper* (1996), and *Independence Day* (1996). Many of these films relied on wounded blue-collar masculinity as a source of this redemption, while often marginalizing female employees as exchangeable commodities or feminist caricatures, responsible for the destabilization of normative American values.[2]

Billy Wilder's *The Apartment* (1960) begins its critique of modernized bureaucracies with the depiction of C. C. "Bud" Baxter (Jack Lemmon), a lowly functionary who is employed in a large insurance company.[3] In a tacit quid pro quo agreement, Bud is pressured to loan his apartment to his superiors for their extramarital dalliances with promises that he will be promoted to an executive ("You're on your way up, Buddy-boy"), a Faustian bargain that strips him of his manhood and self-respect. We first meet the "nebbish" in his skyscraper environment, punching numbers into a desk computer while monotonously spewing out a plethora of statistics that highlight the company's magnitude, while underscoring his own small stature, an analogue to the office machinery to which he is attached:

> We are one of the top five companies in the country—last year we wrote nine-point-three billion dollars worth of policies. Our home office has 31,259 employees—which is more than the entire population of Natchez, Mississippi, or Gallup, New Mexico.

The film establishes location with a one-dimensional view of an apartment facade. The camera shifts to an aerial shot of Manhattan before panning the equally leveled grid-like exterior of Consolidated Life's skyscraper, the name of which is, no doubt, a metaphor for Bud's own containment. Once inside, a low-angle, seemingly limitless long shot of neatly arranged desks with identical desk computers and a grid of harsh florescent lighting underscores that Bud is just one identical cog in this vast corporate machine. Indeed his repetitive head nodding in sync with the musical score's mechanical sound effects threatens to turn him into an automaton. The oppressive spatial environment, coupled with his own "sell out," denotes his wholesale emasculation at the hands of the corporation. Jeff Sheldrake (Fred MacMurray), the firm's chief executive, renders him a putative feminine presence, part bordello madam and part secretary for his sexual liaisons.

Profiteering companies also intrude upon Bud's threadbare apartment via the television set. Leading him on with false promises of the film *Grand Hotel,* an allusion to what has become of his apartment, the network interrupts his program with intrusive advertisements. At the end of the film, in a Chaplinesque gesture, he and Fran Kubelik (Shirley MacLaine), an elevator operator who is also trapped in a machine, a charged, sexualized space in which she is continually harassed by the company's executives, take leave in order to preserve their integrity and, in the case of Bud, his masculinity.

A novel type of cinematic rhetoric emerges in Sidney Lumet's *Network,* based on Paddy Chayefsky's black comedy, to underscore the deleterious effects of a sensationalized media culture on the nation's sense of external and internal spatiality.[4] Most of the drama takes place in the lofty headquarters of a television station in midtown Manhattan, a skyscraper behemoth among many. After rapidly cutting from one skyscraper exterior to another (CBS, NBC, etc.) to establish location the camera fixes on the glassy modernist facade of Emery Roth and Sons' MGM Building (1965), which serves as the fictional location of UBS-TV (United Broadcasting Systems).[5] Seen below from a radically acute angle, the geometrically divided curtain wall creates the illusion of weightlessness; once inside, the scene culminates in the control room, which features an analogous bank of television monitors. Of the film's many subtexts, it underscores the manner in which news has been hijacked in favor of ersatz truth. A series of repetitive veneers or screens serves as a method of public pacification, behind which roils incipient rage and rebellion, which the network exploits for ratings, hence revenue.

The story begins with the firing of veteran news anchorman Howard Beale (Peter Finch) because his audience ratings have declined; instead of issuing statistics like Bud of *The Apartment,* he becomes one, a corporate casualty. An anonymous narrator reports matter-of-factly at the film's outset:

> in 1969 . . . he fell to a 22 share, and, by 1972, he was down to a 15 share. In 1973, his wife died, and he was left a childless widower with an 8 rating and a 12 share. He became morose and isolated, began to drink heavily, and, on September 22, 1975, he was fired.

In Beale's final salutation, he promises to kill himself on the air, before being summarily yanked off. Other media venues pick up the story and his ratings soar anew, prompting predatory young programming executive Diana Christensen (Faye Dunaway) to exploit the mentally unstable Beale by continuing his show. Deciding on stardom not suicide, Beale becomes the prophet for a generation of the passive, disenfranchised, and "sullen." As Christensen explains, the American people have "been clobbered on all sides by Vietnam, Watergate, the inflation, the depression. They've turned off, shot up, and they've fucked themselves limp. And nothing helps."

Beale exhorts his audience to open their windows and scream, "I'm mad as hell and I'm not going to take this anymore." A mid-range shot from above of a twenty-three-story Manhattan apartment building, the domestic equivalent of the confining skyscraper office, shows a diverse population bursting from their cubicle-like dwellings in response to Beale's injunction, implicating architecture as one of the causes of their passivity and pent-up rage.[6] A pelting rainstorm complete with thunder and flashes of lightning suggests that the anger generated by their regimented existences is of cosmic proportions, as they articulate Beale's "group think" slogan.

UBS-TV's skyscraper interiors are large characterless spaces that are rendered in cool gray-blues, filled with long and narrow, seemingly endless glass-paneled corridors; the camera rapidly tracks the workers as they shuttle from one office to another, creating palpable tension. Camerawork and the use of transparent doors and windows serve to signify that individuals are lost in this "network," which is no longer the possession of a singular individual or company, but an anonymous, shady conglomerate (C.C. of A. or the Communications Corporation of America) about to be swallowed up by a larger Arab consortium.[7]

In order to make one's mark in this new corporate environment, it is necessary to be ruthless, calculating, and devoid of ethics. Hence, the old guard is replaced by two novel gender paradigms, young power-hungry executives: the aforementioned Diana Christensen and executive senior vice president of UBS, Frank Hackett (Robert Duvall). The latter is a hypertrophied version of the Organization Man, described as a "marketing-merchandising management machine, precision-tooled for corporate success." Unlike his mid-century predecessor, he is foul-mouthed and authoritarian, a true hatchet man, as his name implies. A C.C. of A. henchman, he answers only to stockholders, ready to axe any portion of the news division for its inability to turn a profit. In one scene, when Hackett, too, fears falling out of favor with the company president, he refers to himself as "a man without a corporation" rather than a country.

Diana Christensen is the film's Organization Woman who possesses an admittedly "masculine temperament" and a Machiavellian outlook. She is an unflattering caricature of a feminist, her dialogue often laced with homophobic rhetoric. When her subordinates fail to read a concept analysis for television shows that she has prepared, she begins demurely—"I don't want to play butch boss"—and then threatens to "sack the fucking lot" of them if it happens again. She is the only woman in the organization big enough to inhabit an executive-sized office, "looking out on the canyons of glass and stone skyscrapers on Sixth Avenue."

When we first meet Christensen, she is dressed in fiery orange, which references her as a livid seductress, in sharp contrast to her bland surroundings. "I want angry shows," she demands, including ones with crimes, riots, and kidnappings. At the end of the film, she even hatches the idea to have Beale assassinated on the air because his ratings have begun to decline. Tall and lean, and often dressed in pants, she is able to go toe to toe with the men in the organization. In order to achieve her ends, she augments her efforts with sexual conquests, as she does with Max Schumacher (William Holden), the head of the news division. She informs Max before she beds him, "I'm going to take over your network news show and I figured I might as well start tonight." Yet, her passionate exterior is but a veneer; the only way that she can achieve sexual satisfaction is by watching her ratings soar on television, drunk on the potential of total control.

In previous films such as *The Fountainhead* and *The Big Clock,* the sky-scraper is restored as a beacon of communication, an upright architecture that is equated with the dissemination of democratic principles. *Network* proposes that such time-honored notions are illusory anachronisms, no longer relevant in a world dominated by omnipresent international corporations. C.C. of A. president Arthur Jensen (Ned Beatty) delivers this message to Beale in almost messianic terms after the newscaster has prompted the little people to articulate their rage against the invisible power structure. In the long darkened and sumptuously decorated boardroom to which Beale has been summoned, Jensen inveighs:

> You are an old man who thinks in terms of nations and peoples. There are no nations! There are no people! . . . There is only one holistic system of systems, one vast and immense, inter-woven, interacting, multi-variate, multi-national dominion of dollars, petro-dollars, electro-dollars, multi-dollars. . . . There is no America. There is no democracy. There is only IBM and ITT and AT and T.[8]

Director and screenwriter Oliver Stone ups the ante in *Wall Street* (1987), a trenchant attack on a seemingly all-consuming, predatory corporate universe, which was shot on location in the offices of Salomon Brothers and the streets of lower New York. Gordon Gekko (Michael Douglas), the film's anti-hero, a corporate raider forged in the image of Ivan Boesky, among others, echoes *Network*'s cynicism concerning the existence of real freedom during the deregulated Reagan-Bush era.[9] The film is reminiscent of Depression-era sky-scraper films that pit the upper-class boss against an average office employee, who ultimately serves a redemptive function. When Gekko's protégé Bud Fox (Charlie Sheen) challenges him to reconsider liquidating Blue Star Airlines, where Fox's working-class father has labored for twenty-four years, the entrepreneur delivers a speech on gamesmanship and money's abstract properties. Echoing Jensen in *Network,* he claims that money

> isn't lost or made, it's simply transferred from one perception to another. . . . Capitalism at its finest. . . . You're not naive enough to think we're living in a democracy are you, Buddy? It's the free market.

In Stone's dog-eat-dog world, true liberty is the ability to outwit one's competitors with impunity, hence win the contest, and achieve ultimate authority.

In accord with Frank Hackett of *Network,* Gekko is a hypertrophied example of corporate masculinity gone awry, who employs Sun Tzu's philosophy in *The Art of War* to triumph over his adversaries. In frighteningly bellicose language, he instructs an underling to "Dilute the sonofabitch. . . . I want every orifice in his body flowing red." The results of his spoils are registered in his larger-than-life office, which is appointed with an enormous grid-patterned, gilded doorway, echoing his numerical concerns, a prestigious contemporary painting collection, reflecting the speculative art world of the 1980s, and a majestic view of the East River. A masseur is even on hand to ease his tensions, evoking the earlier homosocial nature of corporate space. Reaffirming Ayn Rand's philosophies in *The Fountainhead,* he tells Bud that capitalist values and skyscrapers are inextricably linked and later asserts that greed marks "the upward surge of mankind." Looking skyward from his chauffeur-driven limousine, he boasts:

> . . . see that building? I bought into it ten years ago. It was my first real estate deal. I sold it a couple of years later and made an $800,000 profit. It was better than sex. At that time, I thought that was all the money in the world. . . . Now it's a day's pay.

In contrast to Gekko's lofty possessions and palatial office, the film opens with a hellish view of a freeway underpass filled with the homeless before converging with commuters onto the downtown streets of the nation's financial capital, highlighting spatially the economic disparities of the era. Beginning with a panorama of Manhattan's skyline seen from a moving car, the scene shifts to a lurching subway where one is vicariously subjected, along with Bud, to the jostling crowds, enhanced by the use of a claustrophobic, low-angle shot. Passengers are disgorged from its mechanical innards, and once on the street, the camera assumes the vantage point of a pedestrian gazing up at and dwarfed by four mammoth skyscrapers. Seen from a worm's eye perspective, the office buildings resemble shards that slice the sky while threatening to impale the reduced urban worker, who is situated at the center of the target. This dystopian vision is reinforced in the script, which describes them as "towering landmark structures" that "nearly blot out the dreary gray flannel sky." The scene is accompanied by Frank Sinatra's seemingly incongruous rendition of "Fly Me to the Moon" (1964), which speaks to Bud's desire and wish fulfillment. It is no wonder that he seeks release from this spatially imprisoning urban world and his own apartment that looks out from barred windows onto an alley.

Once inside the brokerage house, a handheld camera proceeds at a rapid clip as it tracks Bud Fox amidst a congeries of telephones, blocky desktop computers that threaten to envelope him, and continually moving digital stock quotes that capture the manic pace that the company demands. A similar technique is employed in *Working Girl* (1988), in which Tess McGill (Melanie Griffith) is seemingly swallowed up by a welter of desks and office accoutrements.[10] As

Stone admitted at the time, "We did enormous amounts of moving camera in this film because we are making [sic] a movie about sharks, about feeding frenzies, so we wanted the camera to become a predator."[11]

The film is also about Bud Fox's quest for manhood in this overheated environment driven by acquisition and performance, which includes homosocial investment houses, bars, and steam rooms, where women are exchanged as commodities. Squeezed by economic and spatial privation despite his $50,000-a-year salary and cognizant of his potential to become a corporate casualty, Bud is presented with three paradigms of paternal authority from which he must chose: multimillion-dollar Wall Street trader Gordon Gekko; investment house supervisor Lou Mannheim (Hal Holbrook), a bulwark of stability and corporate ethics (a character based in part on Stone's father); and Carl Fox (Martin Sheen), Bud's own father, a Blue Star Airlines machinist and union representative, the site of the film's defiant, yet injured masculinity.[12] Mesmerized by Gekko's mythic reputation for acquiring wealth, he attempts to gain entrance to the financial pirate's domain, which he does eventually by a combination of persistence and subterfuge. As in *Working Girl,* it takes either dissimulation or overtly illegal actions to rise from the obstacle-ridden, class- and gender-constrained 1980s cinematic office, which breeds anonymity. However, in his effort to curry Gekko's favor, he forges an inadvertent Faustian bargain (much like the other Bud of *The Apartment*) by divulging confidential information concerning Blue Star Airlines, which Gekko employs to pressure Bud to engage in more overtly unlawful activities.

The film represents Stone's own personal experiences: his father was a vice president at Shearson Lehman for over five decades but died in debt, while the character of Bud Fox was, in part, prompted by a friend who lived the high life and lost it all.[13] However, *Wall Street* is also a critique of Reagan-Bush America, a deregulated environment that saw the creation of junk bonds, a new breed of Wall Street barons, and corporate raiding. Reagan was responsible for breaking the backs of organized labor, beginning with his destruction of the Air Traffic Controllers union, a task he learned in the 1950s at General Electric under the mentorship of personnel manager Lemuel Boulware who was hired to reassert management control.

Stone sets the values of Gekko in opposition to those of Carl Fox who believes that a man's true value lies in the things he makes rather than a parasitic quest for money. After Bud has been apprehended for his crimes by the SEC, Carl encourages his son to engage in real "manly" work, thereby offering him his salvation:

> It's gonna be rough on you but maybe in some screwed up way,
> that's the best thing that can happen to you . . . stop trading for
> the quick buck and go produce something with your life, create,
> don't live off the buying and selling of others.

Hence in a period of actual disempowered manual and white-collar labor, *Wall Street* serves as a nostalgic and somewhat ineffectual plea for a lost artisanal masculinity to counter the values of new mediated marketplace men. Bent on acquisition, the latter inhabit a disorienting, mechanized bureaucracy of cellular spaces replete with rapidly moving computerized screens, spewing forth an endless relay of information. Stone counters his own dystopian vision by creating the character of Lou Mannheim, the ethical white-collar voice of reason in the tradition of Don Walling in *Executive Suite,* a film he admired, but who is ill-equipped to ward off the new generation of corporate raiders and the accelerated spaces they inhabit. Stone also has Bud orchestrate Gekko's arrest and the takeover of Blue Star by a more benevolent international financier, Sir Lawrence Wildman (Terence Stamp). However, blue-collar union men are little more than pawns in this high-stakes game, undermining the valorization of working-class values that Stone sought to uphold.[14]

The elevation of working-class masculinity also occurs in *The Towering Inferno* (1974) and *Steel* (1979), films in which the skyscraper is the main character; the former is concerned with its destruction while the latter explores its construction.[15] Both identify tall buildings as the site of corporate-caused accidents and/or disasters, employing the sensationalist ethos *Network* sought to critique, and offer blue-collar camaraderie and heroism as the only means to insure safety for these structures and their inhabitants. *The Towering Inferno* is the more important of the two, not only because of its box office appeal—it generated an incredible $200 million in the first year, locating it as an early blockbuster as audacious as its fictional skyscraper—but because of the way it presciently linked tall buildings with catastrophic events.[16]

The film was indirectly inspired by the debates accompanying the construction and safety of Yamasaki's World Trade Center (1970–73) and foreshadows its demise. It was based on two novels, Richard Martin Stern's *The Tower* (1973) and Frank Robinson and Thomas Scortia's *The Glass Inferno* (1974), both of which blame mercenary builders for the calamities that occur in their hazardous skyscrapers.[17] Indeed, many hold engineer John Skilling partly responsible for the World Trade Center's ultimate collapse in 2001, due to his decision to omit load-bearing columns on every floor (a feature of traditional skyscrapers) and reduce the usual amount of structural steel by forty percent.[18] Lack of adequate fireproofing was also implicated in the building's downfall. Fires had also plagued the World Trade Center since its inception. According to urban studies specialist Leonard Ruchelman, by 1971, there had been more than thirty fires, and in January of 1973 "the sight of belching smoke from the South Tower caused some momentary alarm in the neighborhood."[19] In Stern's tale, New York's fictional World Tower Building is 125 stories, fifteen more than the World Trade Center, topped by a radio and television spire. Situated near the "twin masses of the nearby Trade Center," the building appears "slim, almost delicate," perhaps a reference to its vulnerability.[20]

Screenwriter Stirling Silliphant likewise faults the accident in the film's 1,800 foot, 138-story fictional glass tower, "the tallest building in the world," on avarice and upper-crust hubris.[21] Modernism and limitless height are here haunted by the double specters of purposefully shoddy workmanship and image-making rather than safety. Instead of constructing a skyscraper for its business and residential inhabitants, builder James Duncan (William Holden) raises the building as a status symbol for San Francisco's greedy politicians while ensuring future monies for his pet urban-renewal projects. The futuristic glass tower has an external elevator that adds to its distinctiveness and promotional appeal for the city's tourists, evoking the actual glass elevators of San Francisco's Westin St. Francis Hotel on Union Square.[22] Highlighting the hazard, the conflagration occurs even before the building's completion, on its inauguration day, a star-studded spectacle of politicians and glitterati, many of whom perish on the upper reaches of the 134th-floor promenade room. Almost biblical in proportion, the disaster renders the building a punishing tomb rather than their landmark. To augment the drama and the magnitude of the calamity, the monumental skyscraper is surveyed from numerous angles with the use of jump-cut shots, employing at least five cameras. A nocturnal spectacle of belching smoke, fire, and exploding glass creates an urban sublime reminiscent of images of Babel's destruction, meant to evoke terror, awe, and caution.

Duncan's greed is only superseded by that of his ne'er-do-well son-in-law, Roger Simmons (Richard Chamberlain), a now familiar stereotype of marginal masculinity, an effete, homosexually inflected character who resides in a Pacific Heights mansion, wears ruffled shirts, and suffers marital problems. His sin is even more egregious: skimping on proper wiring and other safety features and accepting kickbacks for his own financial enrichment, which leads ultimately to the major fire that reduces the mammoth structure to a hellish inferno. Architect Doug Roberts (Paul Newman) later reports to Duncan that "The duct holes weren't fire-stopped! Corridors without fire doors and the sprinklers won't work." After the female dignitaries and revelers alike have been lowered to safety in a breeches buoy or giant cage, the craven, opportunistic Simmons tries to save his own skin but plummets to his death instead, a penalty for his class pretensions, feminized gender identity, and mercenary practices.

The effete Simmons and negligent Duncan are juxtaposed with the film's two heroes, stalwart men who labor with their hands. We are initially introduced to Doug Roberts, an architect in the tradition of *The Fountainhead*'s Howard Roark, as he surveys the urban panorama from a helicopter, a testament to his power and commanding gaze. His manly appeal and virile, heterosexual persona are soon reinforced by his love interest Susan Franklin (Faye Dunaway) who nibbles his lip, causing him to protest, "Well, I'm not a cheeseburger, you know." Later Roberts confronts Simmons at his plush abode, prompting the latter to tell his wife, "They say he used to wrestle grizzly bears in Montana," highlighting their disparate masculinities and spatial analogues. The promotional materials liken Roberts to Frank Lloyd Wright, reporting that the fictional architect sought to "break away to build communities more compatible to the contours of nature far away from the concrete canyons of metropolitania [sic]."[23] His only sin was to be absent during the construction of his magnum opus, which allowed the unsavory Simmons unchecked license. However, the skyscraper's perilous interior ensures his recovery, where he makes dramatic Tarzan-like rescues by braving collapsing stories, swinging from detached pipes, and withstanding flood-like torrents.

The film's other hero is uniformed Fire Chief Michael O'Hallorhan (Steve McQueen), a paragon of blue-collar competence and readiness, who directs the rescue of those trapped with military precision and the assistance of both Roberts and the United States Navy, an interesting compensatory ending in the years after the Vietnam War, hence restoring a wounded masculinity.[24] The conclusion of the film places O'Hallorhan as the putative architectural expert and voice of moral authority, while ironically pointing to the multiple vulnerabilities of such a grandiose building, originally meant to serve as an image of strength:

> ROBERTS: Maybe they just ought to leave it the way it is. Kind of a shrine to all the bullshit in the world.
> O'HALLORHAN: You know, we were lucky tonight. Body count's less than two hundred. One of these days, they'll kill 10,000 in one of these firetraps. And I'll keep eating smoke and bringing out bodies . . . until somebody asks us . . . how to build them.
> DUNCAN: Okay. I'm asking.
> O'HALLORHAN: You know where to reach me. So long, architect.

Prior to the first bombing of the World Trade Center in 1993, spy thrillers, action films, and science fiction films cast the skyscraper as American territory under terrorist attack by foreigners and "aliens" from outer space. As BBC investigative reporter Steven Bradshaw noted in 2002, with the breakdown of the Soviet Union, terrorists replaced Communists as the new enemies of choice.[25] The first film to feature the tall building as the site of such international intrigue was *Die Hard* (1988), followed by *Skyscraper* (1996), and *Independence Day* (1996). In this new era of external threats, there was an effort to restore the cinematic skyscraper as an icon of American democratic values, often wrestled from the aliens by strong men in uniforms.

Die Hard depicts the skyscraper and its inhabitants as the victims of a motley ring of international and homegrown terrorists led by the sinister German national Hans Gruber (Alan Rickman).[26] The postmodern skyscraper headquarters of the American branch of the Nakatomi Corporation, an international conglomerate located in Los Angeles's Century City, is the site of their hostage-taking gambit.[27] However, they never plan to release their prisoners; after stealing the money, they intend to blow up the entire building in order to destroy the evidence. In contrast to other cinematic skyscraper depictions, the ostentatious "foreign" Japanese corporation's American headquarters are rendered as a magnet for such intrigue, resulting in the murder of its senior vice president of sales, Joseph Takagi (James Shigeta). The dual threat of Japanese capital, which characterized the 1980s, and German criminality reference America's World War II enemies, here recast as a new "axis of evil." However, these terrorists are not ideologues; rather they seek the 640 million non-traceable bonds hidden in the company vault, whose code they must break. Terrorist Gruber claims that he has selected the firm for its greedy practices worldwide, which are evident in its expensive art collection and upscale decor, solidifying the critique of multinational corporations.

The villains gain access by using the building's sophisticated computer technology and surveillance system against it, another swipe at overly mechanized corporate space.[28] The hostage-taking occurs during an evening Christmas party, to enhance the illuminated spectacle of fire, explosions, and the shattering of crystalline glass and to underscore the terrorists' lack of religious values. Yet, the upscale Gruber, who boasts of his classical education, and his ragtag bunch are no match for the film's hero, New York street cop John McClane (Bruce Willis), referred to as Mr. Cowboy, who "thinks he's John Wayne . . . Rambo . . . Marshal Dillon," but who prefers Roy Rogers. Just like Doug Roberts in *The Towering Inferno,* McClane outwits the terrorists' high-tech smarts by conquering the building's structure as his territory; he scales the elevator shaft and crawls through air ducts and passageways with bare feet while picking off the terrorists one by one, hence underscoring the film's individualist masculine credo. In contrast to the incompetent LAPD and FBI, a Reagan-era critique of governmental bureaucracies, McClane single-handedly thwarts the bad guys with the support of on-duty Sergeant Al Powell (Reginald Veljohnson) who is situated outside the building. Only after McClane's reconquest of the skyscraper—he saves the hostages and causes Gruber to plummet to his death—is he able to reconcile with his estranged wife. African American Powell is also capable of shooting his gun after a thirteen-year hiatus; thus each man assists in the restoration of the other's temporarily deficient masculinity while accentuating racial harmony.

While not predominantly a skyscraper film, *Independence Day* (1996) likewise features several American skyscrapers under threat by aliens. It concerns the restoration of American territorial and ideological hegemony, opening with the United States moon landing before the camera cuts to the Iwo Jima monument, both darkened by a looming shadow. The film explores the United States under siege by extraterrestrials bent on the wholesale destruction of the earth's civilizations in order to harness its natural resources. One may view this fear of space invaders as reminiscent of mid-century science fiction films that reflected the cold war–era dread of real foreigners and the potential of Armageddon. Pei Cobb Freed and Partners' United States Bank Tower (1987–89) in Los Angeles, the tallest skyscraper in California, serves as the first architectural victim of an enormous black enemy space craft, which hovers over its helicopter port before blowing it to smithereens.[29] The illuminated nocturnal skyscraper glows like a jewel before it explodes into flames, underscoring its spectacular function. Other space vehicles are simultaneously situated above the U.S. Capitol and the Empire State Building, which also suffer the same fate, conflating skyscrapers with the landmarks of American political life and the democratic principles they are meant to signify. Masculine agency is again called upon to stop the menace and restore liberty. Through a combination of smarts and drive, while trumpeting the values of interracial, interethnic, and international solidarity, brainy Jewish cable company employee David Levinson (Jeff Goldblum) and African American Army Captain Steven Hiller (Will Smith) save the country and, by implication, the world. Underscoring the film's propaganda message, the President Thomas J. Whitmore (Bill Pullman) of the United States declares, "From this day on, the fourth day of July will no longer be remembered as an American holiday but as the day that all of mankind declared we will not go quietly into the night."[30]

The president's speech in *Independence Day* may have served as the refrain of Oliver Stone's *World Trade Center* (2006), a film about the survival of the human spirit rather than the spectacle of the world's largest skyscraper disaster.[31] In accord with previous cinematic depictions of catastrophic events but devoid of sensationalism, Stone renders the heroic stories of two Port Authority policemen, an homage to blue-collar agency. The screenplay by Andrea Berloff records the "real life" experiences of Sergeant John McLoughlin (Nicolas Cage) and Patrolman Will Jimeno (Michael Peña) who rush to the scene to assist in the rescue effort, but who are buried beneath the rubble after the South Tower's collapse. It also pays homage to Dave Karnes (Michael Shannon), a lone marine who, after receiving an omen from God, heads to Ground Zero and is ultimately responsible for saving the two men. In addition, it traces the emotional journeys of both men's wives, children, and extended families as they try to cope with the unknown fate of their loved ones.

Countering conventional expectations, the terrorist perpetrators are absent from this tale, thereby depoliticizing the film. The World Trade Center's office employees, among other victims and survivors, are likewise omitted. Even the lofty Twin Towers are seen only briefly just as the North Tower is hit; hence this so-called skyscraper film, even though it is based on actual events, the downing of the United States' tallest buildings, is a subjective portrayal, a private journey rather than a public spectacle. Stone shows individuals in different parts of the world responding to the horror of the event. Yet, the film still adheres to several ideological formulas derived from previous skyscraper films; it pays homage to the heroic efforts of blue-collar men and their loyal domestic wives, while underscoring the importance of family. As film critic Philip French noted, it is a "tribute to cops, firefighters, soldiers and other workers" done "in the manner of a Second World War propaganda entertainment."[32] A consummation occurs at the hospital where the wives finally reunite with their husbands after the successful rescue effort. The joyful, pregnant Allison Jimeno (Maggie Gyllenhaal) banters with her husband concerning the selection of their prospective daughter's name, a scene that serves to enforce the matrimonial bond and provide life-affirming hope for the future.

Visually, the film works in antimonies. While the skyscraper retains its material presence, its prior loftiness and orderly steel structure is reduced to twisted skeletal remains and horizontally dispersed, chaotic rubble. After the World Trade Center's South Tower implodes, Stone shifts the emphasis to the buildings' inverted mirrors, an underground netherworld of "toxic smoke, twisted metal, and concrete that continually" shifts "under their weight."[33] Space is both constricted and expansive; while the men's bodies are pinned into immobility by weighty concrete, their minds are disembodied, even boundless in scope. Stone and photography director Seamus McGarvey underscore this dialectical tension with the use of extreme close-up shots, focusing on McLoughlin's and Jimeno's blood- and dirt-encrusted faces as they articulate their incorporeal, limitless thoughts. Radical contrasts in dark and light are also strategically utilized to reinforce meaning while re-creating their tortuous ordeal; in the abyss, the screen is almost devoid of light, a black hole in which one can only see shadowy faces: glowing eyes are intended as a visualization of the human soul. Unlike this charred underworld, high intensity illumination is employed above ground to render their family's tribulations.

Thus, this study ends in an unorthodox way with the cinematic skyscraper as an absent presence. Jimeno exclaims incredulously after he is raised from his underground tomb to street level: "Where did the buildings go?" To which a rescuer replies, "They're gone." Yet, in spite of the buildings' material demise, the cinematic site is embedded with the World Trade Center's prior identity, with much of its gendered physical and ideological foundation still intact. In this seemingly empty space that is redolent with significance, equally laden structures are poised to be built, and appropriated strategically for the screen.

Acknowledgments

This book has often required extended sojourns into several areas of inquiry (from skyscraper-climbing escapades to the impact of computers on office space) and necessitated the advice of experts in a myriad of fields. I corresponded with scores of scholars too numerous to mention who generously offered advice. For their willingness to answer more sustained questions, provide materials and practical advice, read drafts or portions thereof, and make suggestions, I am indebted to Diane Borden, Zeynep Çelik, Sabine Haenni, Alan Marcus, Lary May, Dietrich Neumann, Elaine O'Brien, and Katherine Solomonson. Special appreciation is extended to Ed Dimendberg, who helped shepherd this project to completion. His encyclopedic knowledge coupled with his willingness to read various versions of the manuscript improved its quality. I am also thankful to Mark Shiel, who anonymously reviewed my manuscript for the University of Minnesota Press and subsequently agreed to divulge his identity. His knowledge of film history and theory, combined with his sage recommendations on a host of issues, prompted me to define more clearly the political underpinnings of my arguments.

My colleagues at the University of the Pacific provided an intellectually stimulating environment in which to conduct interdisciplinary research. During my tenure as the coordinator of the gender studies program from 1993 to 2001, I had the pleasure to discuss my ideas with Diane Borden, Caroline Cox, Cynthia Dobbs, and Gerald Hewitt. During this time I was part of a critical theory reading group with Borden and Hewitt, which enabled me to extend my notions of space beyond the boundaries offered by prevailing architectural and cinematic discourses.

This project could not have been completed without the assistance of numerous librarians and archival collections, echoing Katharine Hepburn's quip in *Desk Set*: "No machine can do our job. There are too many cross references." Jeff Britting of the Ayn Rand Archives helped me initiate this study by granting me full access to a previously guarded treasure trove of materials at a time when they were still being catalogued. The erudition of Ned Comstock at the University of Southern California's Cinema and Television Library is unsurpassed; in my lengthy discussions with him, he often came up with creative ideas for plumbing the collection's archival sources. The Margaret Herrick Library of Cinematography's Barbara Hall and Faye Thompson encouraged me to read scripts and mine scrapbooks, which turned up unexpected materials. Paul Lasewicz and Dawn Stanford of the IBM Corporate Archives in Somers, New York, and Lauren Buisson at the University of California's Young Library Department of Special Collections engaged me in discussions about their respective collections, which prompted me to dig further. The library staffs of the New York Public Library for the Performing Arts, the Library of Congress, the Henry Lee Library at the University of Utah, and the University of Wisconsin were generous with their time and advice. Special thanks are extended to the library staff at the University of the Pacific, notably Gail Stovall, Robin Imhof, and Monica Schutzman, who helped me track down rare and esoteric materials, often persuading other libraries to lend otherwise noncirculating materials.

This book could not have been completed without the generous financial support of the Graham Foundation during my sabbatical in 2004. Their generous aid was augmented by several Scholarly Activities Grants from the University of the Pacific from 2002 to 2005. Deans Robert Benedetti and Gary Miller both provided me with supplemental funding for aspects of the project not covered by traditional funding. The university was kind enough to provide financial support so I could present my preliminary findings at conferences devoted to cinema and the city sponsored by University College Dublin in 1999 and the University of Manchester in 2005. I had the opportunity to present my findings at other conferences as well, including those of the American Studies Association, the Society of Architectural Historians Association, the Society of Cinema and Media Studies, and the Popular Culture Association. The intellectual exchange with panelists and audience members provided sound advice and strategies for further inquiries.

At the University of Minnesota Press, director Doug Armato provided the necessary advice and encouragement to undertake this project. Both he and Pieter Martin were also helpful in answering a myriad of questions along the way. I am deeply indebted to Deborah A. Oosterhouse, who read the manuscript with care and consideration. Not only did she provide editorial suggestions, but she often looked up my source materials, thereby amplifying the text. Appreciation is also extended to Denise Carlson, who did an exceptionally good job indexing this book

The support of friends and family was crucial to the successful completion of this book. I am grateful to my sister, April Schleier, who offered love and support while I was in New York City doing research, as well as for many hours via telephone. This project owes the most to my husband, Dr. Glenn Lapp, who watched all the films under discussion multiple times, listened to my ideas, often challenged me to think further, offered cogent insights, read many drafts, and even helped with the photography. There are no words to express his many years of untiring devotion and love.

Finally, I thank my research assistants over the years, who worked tirelessly during the writing of this book: Ann-Marie Cook, Brianna Toth, Sarah Mansfield, Lauren Gallow, and Harrison Inefuku were often presented with a topic or a problem and returned with a gold mine.

Notes

—————

Unless otherwise noted, all illustrations in this book from films are frame enlargements.

INTRODUCTION

1. See Paul Goldberger's *Up from Zero: Politics, Architecture, and the Rebuilding of New York* (New York: Random House, 2005), 56, for a discussion of all aspects of the commission to rebuild, the architects and constituencies involved, and the skyscraper's multivalent symbolism, including memorial, witness, healer, renewer, and democratic icon, among others. Goldberger himself subscribes to the idea that the skyscraper is a purveyor of American cultural values. He believes that "the skyscraper is the ultimate American building type, the most important contribution of American architecture and American technology to world building, and where better to conceive of the next generation of American skyscrapers than in America's greatest city, on the site of which American culture has been so ruthlessly attacked?"

2. See my *The Skyscraper in American Art, 1890–1931* (Ann Arbor: UMI Research Press, 1986). See also the revised paperback edition (New York: DaCapo, 1990).

3. General works on gender, architecture, and space include Griselda Pollock, "Modernity and the Spaces of Femininity," in *Vision and Difference: Femininity, Feminism and the Histories of Art* (London: Routledge, 1988), 50–90; Daphne Spain, *Gendered Spaces* (Chapel Hill: University of North Carolina Press, 1990); Elizabeth Wilson, *The Sphinx in the City: Urban Life, the Control of Disorder and Women* (Berkeley and Los Angeles: University of California Press, 1992); Beatrice Colomina, ed., *Sexuality and Space* (New York: Princeton Architectural Press, 1992); Jane Brettle and Sally Rice, eds., *Public Bodies—Private States: New Views on Photography, Representation and Gender* (Manchester: University of Manchester Press, 1994); Diana Agrest, Patricia Conway, and Leslie Kanes Weisman, eds., *The Sex of Architecture* (New York: Abrams, 1996); Jane Rendell, Barbara Penner, and Iain Borden, eds., *Gender, Space, Architecture* (London: Routledge, 2000). For sources specifically on gender and skyscraper space, see Margery Davies, *A Woman's Place Is at the Typewriter: Office Work and Office Workers, 1870–1930* (Philadelphia: Temple University Press, 1982); Lisa Fine, *The Souls of the Skyscraper: Female Clerical Workers in Chicago, 1870–1930* (Philadelphia: Temple University Press, 1990); Sharon Strom, *Beyond the Typewriter: Gender, Class, and the Origins of Modern American Office Work, 1900–1930* (Urbana: University of Illinois Press, 1992); Angel Kwolek-Folland, *Engendering Business: Men and Women in the Corporate Office, 1870–1930* (Baltimore: Johns Hopkins University Press, 1994).

4. See my "Ayn Rand and King Vidor's Film *The Fountainhead*: Architectural Modernism, the Gendered Body, and Political Ideology," *Journal of the Society of Architectural Historians* 61 (March 2002): 310–30.

5. Donald Albrecht, *Designing Dreams: Modern Architecture in the Movies* (New York: Harper and Row, 1986).

6. Dietrich Neumann, ed., *Film Architecture: Set Designs from Metropolis to Blade Runner* (New York: Prestel, 1996).

7. David Clarke, ed., *The Cinematic City* (London: Routledge, 1997).

8. Mark Shiel and Tony Fitzmaurice, eds., *Cinema and the City: Film and Urban Societies in a Global Context* (Oxford: Blackwell, 2001). See both Shiel's and Fitzmaurice's stimulating introductory essays. See also their *Screening the City* (London: Verso, 2003). Shiel's more specialized *Italian Neorealism: Rebuilding the Cinematic City* (London: Wallflower, 2006) also considers the way postwar Italian cinema engaged in a dialogue with the actual city, including reconstruction, modernization, migration, and other urban issues.

9. James Donald, *Imagining the City* (London: Athlone, 1999); Maria Balshaw and Liam Kennedy, *Urban Space and Representation* (London: Pluto, 2000); Mark Lamster, ed., *Architecture and Film* (New York: Princeton Architectural Press, 2000); Katherine Shonfield, *Walls Have Feelings: Architecture, Film and the City* (London: Routledge, 2000); James Sanders, *Celluloid Skyline: New York and the Movies* (New York: Knopf, 2001); Giuliana Bruno, *Atlas of Emotion: Journeys in Art, Architecture and Film* (London: Verso, 2002); Neza Al Sayyad, *Cinematic Urbanism: A History of the Modern from Reel to Real* (London: Routledge, 2006); Alan Marcus and Dietrich Neumann, eds., *Visualizing the City* (London: Routledge, 2007). See also the DVD *Picturing a Metropolis: New York City Unveiled* (New York: Anthology Film Archives; Frankfurt am Main: Deutsches Filmmuseum, 2005).

10. Sarah Bradford Landau and Carl Condit, *The Rise of the New York Skyscraper, 1865–1913* (New Haven: Yale University Press, 1996).

11. Rick Altman, "A Semantic/Syntactic Approach to Film Genre," *Cinema Journal* 23 (Spring 1984): 6–18.

12. Walter Benjamin, *The Arcades Project*, trans. Howard Eiland and Kevin McLaughlin (Cambridge, Mass.: Belnap Press of Harvard University, 1999).

13. Henri Lefebvre, *The Production of Space* (1974), trans. Donald Nicholoson-Smith (Oxford: Blackwell, 1999), especially 38–40. My turn to Lefebvre was inspired by Edward Soja, who referred to him as "the incunabulum of postmodern critical human geography, the primary source for the assault against historicism and the reassertion of space in critical social theory." See *Postmodern Geographies: The Reassertion of Space in Critical Social Theory* (London: Verso, 1989), 41. See also Elizabeth Grosz, "Bodies-Cities," in Colomina, *Sexuality and Space,* 241–54, who extends Lefebvre's analysis of the way humans and spaces are mutually mediating.

14. Judith Butler, *Gender Trouble: Feminism and the Subversion of Identity* (London: Routledge, 1990). See also Butler's "Gender Is Burning: Questions of Appropriation and Subversion," in *Bodies That Matter: On the Discursive Limits of "Sex"* (London: Routledge, 1993), 121–40. Here Butler discusses Jennie Livingston's film *Paris Is Burning* (1990; DVD, Off White Productions, 2005), taking issue with bel hooks's treatment of

the film as a misogynistic and ethnocentric depiction of drag, arguing that not all the appropriations are taken from white, heterosexual culture.

15. Judith Lorber, *The Paradoxes of Gender* (New Haven: Yale University Press, 1994).

16. Robert Connell, *Masculinities* (Berkeley and Los Angeles: University of California Press, 1995).

17. Davies, *A Woman's Place Is at the Typewriter*; Fine, *Souls of the Skyscraper*; Strom, *Beyond the Typewriter*; Kwolek-Folland, *Engendering Business*.

18. Kwolek-Folland, *Engendering Business*; Wilson, *Sphinx in the City*.

19. John Kasson, *Houdini, Tarzan, and the Perfect Man* (New York: Hill and Wang, 2001).

20. "Bull Market Architecture," *New Republic* 68 (8 July 1931): 192; Lewis Mumford, "Botched Cities," *American Mercury* 3 (October 1929): 143–50; Mumford, "Is the Skyscraper Tolerable?" *Architecture* 55 (February 1927): 67–69; Mumford, "The Intolerable City," *Harper's Monthly* 152 (February 1926): 289–93.

21. Antonio Gramsci, *Prison Notebooks,* ed. with an intro. by Joseph A. Buttigies (New York: Columbia University Press, 1992).

22. Geoffrey Nowell-Smith, "Cities: Real and Imagined," in Shiel and Fitzmaurice, *Cinema and the City,* 100.

1. FROM STUMBLING BLOCKS TO STEPPING STONES

1. *Safety Last!,* directed by Fred C. Newmeyer and Sam Taylor (Hal Roach Studios, 1923; DVD, New Line Home Entertainment, 2005). The story was by Hal Roach, Sam Taylor, and Tim Whelan.

2. Lloyd named the character in *High and Dizzy,* directed by Hal Roach (Rolin Films, 1920; DVD, New Line Home Video, 2005), Dr. Harold Hall. In the later *Feet First* (1930), the star was called Harold Horne. Although the actor was referred to as "The Boy" in his other films, most reviewers referred to him as Harold.

3. This theme was taken up in other silent films, such as *Skyscraper,* directed by Howard Higgin (DeMille Pictures, 1928; VHS, Grapevine Video, n.d.), in which a construction worker loses his ambulatory ability, a thinly disguised reference to his manhood, due to an occupational hazard. He regains both limb and virility when he confronts his injury, which initially refuses to heal because of cowardice. His ability to walk and the renewed admiration of a burlesque dancer occur at the crest of the steel skeleton of an emergent skyscraper. Paul Sloane's *The Shock Punch* (Paramount Pictures, 1925) features a college boy who must also prove his mettle, not by completing his education, but by ascending a skyscraper scaffold. In the aforementioned films, the conquest of the tall building is equated with the realization of male heterosexual identity and the consummation of a romance. For a discussion of *The Shock Punch,* see Sanders, *Celluloid Skyline,* 39–41. The film was adapted from a play by John Monk Saunders.

4. Intertitle from *The Skyscrapers of New York* (American Mutoscope and Biograph, 1906) (original copyright *Skyscrapers*). The story takes place amidst all types of skyscraper buildings, and includes many elements of the "thrill" pictures popularized by Lloyd. During the fight between Dago Pete and the suited foreman, the latter falls and dangles from a beam, prefiguring Harold's near brushes with death. He is finally saved

by his workers. The film may be seen on the Library of Congress American Memory Web site, http://memory.loc.gov/ammem/index.html.

5. James C. Young, "Titanic Forces Rear a New Skyline," *New York Times,* 15 November 1925, sec. 4.

6. Kasson, *Houdini, Tarzan and the Perfect Man.*

7. Charles E. Fay, "Mountain Climbing as an Organized Sport," *The Outlook* 71 (7 June 1902): 384. In gender-inflected prose, Fay spoke also of its "alluring invitation to conquest." See also George Abraham, "Mountain Climbing as a Sport," *The World's Work* 16 (June 1908): 10323–36.

8. The most valuable sources on Lloyd include "Harold Lloyd in *Safety Last!*" (synopsis of the film), n.d., Harold Lloyd Papers, Margaret Herrick Library of Cinematography, Beverly Hills, California (hereafter MHLC); James Agee, *James Agee on Film* (New York: Mcdowell Obliensky, 1941); Arthur B. Friedman, "Interview with Harold Lloyd," *Film Quarterly* 15 (Summer 1962): 7–15; Nelson E. Garringer, "Harold Lloyd: Made a Fortune by Combining Comedy and Thrills," *Films in Review* 13 (August–September 1962): 407–20; "Harold Lloyd: The Funny Side of Life," *Films and Filming* (January 1964): 19–21; William Cahn, *Harold Lloyd's World of Comedy* (New York: Duell, Sloan and Pearce, 1964); Donald W. McCaffrey, *4 Great Comedians: Chaplin, Lloyd, Keaton, Langdon* (New York: A. S. Barnes, 1968); Harold Lloyd, "The Serious Business of Being Funny (excerpt from a talk given at the University of Michigan)," *Film Comment* 5 (Fall 1969): 46–57; Stuart Kaminsky, "Harold Lloyd: A Reassessment of His Film Comedy," *The Silent Picture,* Autumn 1972, 21–29; Gerald Mast, *The Comic Mind: Comedy and the Movies,* 2nd ed. (Chicago: University of Chicago Press, 1973); Frank Manchel, *Yesterday's Clowns: The Rise of Film Comedy* (New York: Frank Watts, 1973); Walter Kerr, *The Silent Clowns* (New York: Knopf, 1975); Adam Reilly, *Harold Lloyd: The King of Daredevil Comedy,* with a foreword by Gene Stavis (New York: Macmillan, 1977); Tom Dardis, *Harold Lloyd: The Man on the Clock* (New York: Viking, 1983); Annette D'Agostino, *Harold Lloyd: A Bio-Bibliography* (West Point, Conn.: Greenwood, 1994); Jeffrey Vance and Suzanne Lloyd, *Harold Lloyd: The Master Comedian,* intro. by Kevin Brownlow (New York: Harry Abrams, 2002); Annette D'Agostino Lloyd, *The Harold Lloyd Encyclopedia* (Jefferson, N.C.: McFarland, 2004); Noel Carroll, *Comedy Incarnate: Buster Keaton, Physical Humor, and Bodily Coping* (Oxford: Blackwell, 2007).

9. "Life, Liberty, Happiness and Harold Lloyd"; "Harold Lloyd's Next Skyscraper Romance," in NEVER WEAKEN, press book, 1921, p. 12, New York Public Library for the Performing Arts (hereafter NYPLPA). *Never Weaken,* directed by Fred Newmeyer (Associated Exhibitors, 1921; DVD, New Line Home Entertainment, 2005). The story was by Hal Roach and Sam Taylor. As early as 1920, Pathé Exchange was considering exploiting this successful genre of skyscraper scaling for Lloyd. "One of the exploitation values the offering has, along with its wealth of new 'gag' are some thrills that would be the making of a serial picture." See *"High and Dizzy* Sets New Record for Lloyd," *Pathé Messenger,* 1920, Harold Lloyd scrapbook #1 (hereafter HLS #1), MHLC.

10. "Safety Last," *Brooklyn Motion Picture Magazine,* 14 February 1923, *Safety Last* scrapbook #1, MHLC.

11. "Safety-First Stuff in 'Safety Last,'" *Literary Digest* 78 (14 July 1923): 43.

12. *Feet First,* directed by Clyde Bruckman (Paramount Pictures, 1930; DVD, New

Line Home Video, 2005), was Lloyd's last film to explore the theme of skyscrapers and upward mobility as a badge of normative masculinity in a sustained manner. In contrast to his earlier efforts, the hapless Harold is carried aloft accidentally, and he aims to reach the ground rather than the top of the building. In spite of its recourse to sound, the film recapitulates many of the themes and comedic devices seen in his silent skyscraper comedies. Biographer Adam Reilly categorized Harold as "an anachronistic character with the wrong set of values for 1930." *Harold Lloyd,* 115.

13. *Look Out Below,* directed by Hal Roach (Rolin Films), was released in March 1919 by Pathé Exchange. Unfortunately, it does not survive in its entirety.

14. "Comments—Pathé Exchange, Inc.," *Moving Picture World,* 15 March 1919, 1532.

15. In *Harold Lloyd: A Bio-Bibliography,* 124, D'Agostino speaks of the film's portrayal of emotions.

16. Frank Norris, *The Pit: A Story of Chicago* (New York: Curtis, 1902; repr., New York: Grove, 1956), 62.

17. Fine, *Souls of the Skyscraper,* 70–75. See also my "The Skyscraper, Gender, and Mental Life: Sophie Treadwell's Play *Machinal* of 1928," in *The American Skyscraper: Cultural Histories,* ed. Roberta Moudry (New York: Cambridge University Press, 2005), 234–54.

18. "High and Dizzy – A Synopsis," in HIGH AND DIZZY: *A Sparkling Comedy Cocktail with Thrills,* press book, 1919, p. 1. See also "High and Dizzy," *Moving Picture World,* 24 July 1920, 2.

19. "Thrilling Brody *[sic],*" in HIGH AND DIZZY, press book, p. 1, NYPLPA.

20. "Make Exploitation Extra Whizzy When You're Showing 'High and Dizzy,'" HIGH AND DIZZY, press book, p. 1, NYPLPA.

21. "Harold Lloyd's Next Skyscraper Romance," NEVER WEAKEN, press book, p. 12, NYPLPA.

22. For a further discussion of the use of what T. J. Jackson Lears referred to as "carnavelesque" tactics to sell products, see his *Fables of Abundance: A Cultural History of Advertising in America* (New York: Basic Books, 1994), especially 46–56.

23. For reviewers' responses to the film, which some regarded as novel skyscraper stunts, see C. S. Sewell, "Never Weaken," *Moving Picture World,* 21 October 1921, 4; Laurence Reid, "Never Weaken," *Motion Picture News* 29 (October 1921): 2.

24. Reid, "Never Weaken," 2.

25. "He Hits the Heart," NEVER WEAKEN, press book, p. 12, NYPLPA. In *Never Weaken,* Lloyd and company built the framework on the roof of the Ville de Paris department store in Los Angeles. The same store's interior was employed in *Safety Last!* See Harold Lloyd, *An American Comedy,* written in collaboration with Wesley W. Stout (New York: Longmans, Green, 1928; repr., New York: Dover, 1971), 85.

26. George M. Beard, *American Nervousness: Its Causes and Consequences* (New York: Putnam, 1881). The literature on feminization and neurasthenia is exhaustive. For a comprehensive discussion of neurasthenia and urbanism, see my "The Skyscraper, Gender, and Mental Life." For an excellent discussion of male fears of feminization, see Michael Kimmel, "Consuming Manhood: The Feminization of American Culture and the Recreation of the Male Body, 1832–1920," in *The Male Body,* ed. Laurence Goldstein (Ann Arbor: University of Michigan Press, 1994), 12–41; Kimmel, *Manhood in America:*

A Cultural History (New York: Free Press, 1996); Joyce Henry Robinson, "'Hi Honey, I'm Home': Weary (Neurasthenic) Businessman and the Formulation of a Serenely Modern Aesthetic," in *Not at Home: The Suppression of the Domestic in Modern Art and Architecture*, ed. Christopher Reed (London: Thames and Hudson, 1996), 98–112.

27. Interview with Harold Lloyd in McCaffrey, *4 Great Comedians*, 68.

28. Mark Garrett Cooper, "Love, Danger, and the Professional Ideology of Hollywood Cinema," *Cultural Critique* 39 (Spring 1998): 86.

29. Lynne Kirby, in *Parallel Tracks: The Railroad and Silent Cinema* (Durham: Duke University Press, 1997), 101–8, links railroads to heterosexual coupling. The goal is to unite the couple who have been separated. While the train in Lloyd's film serves as the initial agent of separation, Lloyd must complete a vertical rather than a horizontal journey, through his own physical prowess, to realize his heterosexual identity and the reunification with his sweetheart.

30. As Sam Stoloff argues, Lloyd's, Chaplin's, and Keaton's small bodies were meant, in part, to signify frailty but, at the same time, their slenderness was more "efficient" and easily incorporated into the machinery of civilization. See "The Normalizing of Stars: Roscoe 'Fatty' Arbuckle and Hollywood Consolidation," in *American Silent Film: Discovering Marginalized Voices*, ed. Gregg P. Bachman and Thomas J. Slate (Carbondale: Southern Illinois University Press, 2002), 158–59.

31. Susan Porter Benson, *Counter Cultures: Saleswomen, Managers, and Customers in American Department Stores, 1890–1940* (Urbana: University of Illinois Press, 1988), 23.

32. Ibid., 94. According to Benson, industry literature depicted the "woman customer as a spoiled overgrown child who would not be denied her whims . . . to have her own way."

33. See Kristen Ross's excellent introduction in Émile Zola's *The Ladies Paradise* (*Au bonheur des dames*, 1882), trans. Henry Vizetelly (Berkeley and Los Angeles: University of California Press, 1992), iv–xxiii. The serialized novel was first translated into English in 1883, and again in 1886 by Vizetelly. Zola's fictional department store was a composite of the Le Bon Marché (1851) and the Louvre (1855). All of the quotations from Zola's novel were taken from Ross's introduction. Appreciation is extended to Ed Dimendberg for bringing this novel to my attention.

34. Richard Dyer, *White* (London: Routledge, 1997), 13.

35. J. Mitchell Palmer, 1919, quoted in Lears, *Fables of Abundance*, 169.

36. In *High and Dizzy*, the delirious doctor looks in a mirror and sees a black porter's face reflected back at him, and for a panicky moment thinks he has changed color. The use of African American characters and exotic "others" who are the butt of racist and ethnically demeaning gags is employed in this early film to buttress Harold's white middle-class masculinity.

37. Donald Bogle, *Toms, Coons, Mulattoes, Mammies and Bucks* (New York: Viking, 1973), 3–9.

38. Daniel Leab, *From Sambo to Superspade: The Black Experience in Motion Pictures* (Boston: Houghton Mifflin, 1975), 44. According to Gerald R. Butler Jr., *Black Manhood on the Silent Screen* (Lawrence: University of Kansas Press, 2002), by 1910 films already established that black men were less manly because they were depicted as constantly fearful.

39. Jacqueline Najuma Stewart, "What Happened in the Transition? Reading Race, Gender, and Labor between the Shots," in *American Cinema's Transitional Era: Audiences, Institutions, Practices,* ed. Charlie Keil and Shellie Stamp (Berkeley and Los Angeles: University of California Press, 2004), 107–8. See also Stewart, *Migrating to the Movies: Cinema and Black Urban Modernity* (Berkeley and Los Angeles: University of California Press, 2005), 58–60, 84–85, for discussions of so-called baby switching scenes, which Stewart claims represent white anxieties about miscegenation.

40. Miriam Hansen, *Babel and Babylon: Spectatorship in American Silent Film* (Cambridge, Mass.: Harvard University Press, 1991), 71–76. Hansen's work prompted me to think about how Jewish audience members might have responded to the stereotypes in Lloyd's films, in view of producers' desires to homogenize the audience through uniform modes of address.

41. Tamar Garb, "Introduction: Modernity, Identity, Textuality," in *The Jew in the Text: Modernity and the Construction of Identity,* ed. Linda Nochlin and Tamar Garb (London: Thames and Hudson, 1995), 68.

42. Sander Gilman, *The Jew's Body* (London: Routledge, 1991), 99, 173.

43. Lester D. Friedman, *Hollywood's Image of the Jew* (New York: Frederick Ungar, 1982), 23. As Patricia Erens points out in *The Jew in American Film* (Bloomington: Indiana University Press, 1984), 12, 43, Jews were "admired and hated for their business acumen." Medieval Jews were unable to own land or enter certain trades, so they became proficient as moneylenders, who were considered un-Christian, and merchants. Their success in these arenas was a source of pride but also prompted resentment and fear among their Gentile neighbors, who often assigned them with "magical powers." In medieval morality plays, Jews were depicted as Avarita (avarice), one of the seven deadly sins. See also Garb, "Introduction: Modernity, Identity, Textuality," 21, for a discussion of other stock images of the Jew in Christian folklore, including the usurer, the horned devil, the seducer, the drinker of Christian blood, and the parasite.

44. Two of the most popular literary depictions of the Jew in the silent film era occurred in adaptations of Shakespeare's *Merchant of Venice* (1909 and 1912) and Dickens's *Oliver Twist,* which enjoyed six variations from 1909 to 1923. See Friedman, *Hollywood's Image of the Jew,* 16. Shakespeare's *Merchant of Venice* contained the character Shylock, perhaps the most famous villainous Jewish moneylender in literature.

45. Ibid., 18.

46. "Lloyd Gets Idea in a Flash for a New Comedy," *Safety Last!,* press book, 1923, p. 17, NYPLPA.

47. See the following by Tom Gunning: "The Cinema of Attractions: Early Film, Its Spectator and the *Avant-Garde,*" *Wide Angle* 8 (1986): 63–70; "An Aesthetic of Astonishment: Early Film and the (In)credulous Spectator," *Art & Text* 34 (Spring 1989): 31–45; "'Now You See It, Now You Don't': The Temporality of the Cinema of Attractions," *The Velvet Light Trap,* no. 32 (1993): 3–12. In the last essay, Gunning differentiates between the functions of narrative and attractions, claiming that narrative poses an enigma, which demands a solution, while attractions are exhibitionistic, confronting and shocking the audience. Ben Singer believes that there is no clearly defined rift between the cinema of attractions and cinema's early efforts at storytelling; see *Modernity and Melodrama: Early Sensational Cinema and Its Contexts* (New York: Columbia

University Press, 2001), 14. In accord with Gunning, I believe that it is not plausible that early cinema viewers believed in the shocking illusions, but were accustomed to cinematic rhetoric, while vicariously "feeling" the sensations of the cinematic protagonists. "Unhinged" spectators were often created by the studio's publicity apparatus to enhance the thrill potential. See my section on "Intrepid Men and Nervous Women" in this chapter.

48. Lloyd, *An American Comedy,* 85.

49. "Two Sensational 'Climbers' without Social Ambitions," *Literary Digest* 57 (20 April 1918): 60–61.

50. "'Human Spider' Plays in Lloyd's New Film," *Billings Montana Gazette,* 5 April 1923, *Safety Last!* scrapbook #1, MHLC.

51. Harvey Green, *Fit for America: Health, Fitness, Sport and American Society* (Baltimore: Johns Hopkins University Press, 1986), 236; Sarah Watts, *Rough Rider in the White House: Theodore Roosevelt and the Politics of Desire* (Chicago: University of Chicago Press, 2003).

52. Ernest Poole, "Cowboys of the Skies," *Everybody's Magazine* 19 (November 1908): 641–83. Poole is responsible for coining the appellation "cowboys of the skies." According to Watts, *Rough Rider in the White House,* 123–91, the cowboy soldier emerged in the 1870s as a new type of male personality, who appealed to eastern readers as a more masculine type. Poole may have borrowed this terminology to describe the fearlessness of construction workers who intrepidly braved skyward space.

53. "Two Sensational 'Climbers' without Social Ambitions," 60.

54. *New York Times* articles: "'Human Fly' Aids W.S.S. Campaign," 18 June 1918; "'Human Fly' Climbs for K of C," 10 August 1918; "'Human Fly' Falls to Death; Loses Grip while Climbing Baltimore Hotel for Charity," 24 April 1921; "'Human Fly' Falls 10 Stories to Death; Harry F. Young Scaling Martinique Hotel for a Movie Film, Misses His Grip," 6 March 1923; "City Forbids 'Human Flies' to Climb Skyscraper Walls," 11 April 1923; "Boy Tries to Be 'Human Fly,' Falls and Fractures a Leg," 26 March 1923; "'Human Fly' Quits Act," 5 January 1924; "'Human Fly' Loses to a Climbing Cop," 14 November 1925; "European Buildings Lure 'Human Fly,' Johnny Meyer Going to Tackle Steepest Walls and Steeples in Interest of World Fame," 13 August 1926; "'Human Fly' Thwarted," 8 January 1927; "'Human Fly' Stunt Kills," 19 March 1928; "'Human Fly' Falls as Big Crowd Gasps," 6 September 1928.

55. James Huneker, *Steeplejack,* vol. 1 (New York: Charles Scribner's Sons, 1920), 3.

56. Mabel Wheeler, "This Girl Steeplejack Fears Nothing but June Bugs," *American Magazine* 97 (February 1927): 68.

57. Horace Breese Powell, "Sitting on the Top of the World," *Illustrated World* 38 (December 1922): 525.

58. "European Buildings Lure 'Human Fly.'"

59. Merle Crowell, "Adventures of a Steeplejack," *American Magazine* 93 (March 1922): 30.

60. Powell, "Sitting on the Top of the World," 525.

61. "European Buildings Lure 'Human Fly.'"

62. "Two Sensational 'Climbers' without Social Ambitions," 60.

63. Crowell, "Adventures of a Steeplejack," 32.

64. Ibid.

65. Ibid., 33.

66. Bruce Bliven, "The Human Fly Is Dead," *New Republic* 34 (21 March 1923): 95.

67. "'Human Spider' Plays in Lloyd's New Film," HLS #1, MHLC.

68. See note 54 above.

69. "City Forbids 'Human Flies' to Climb Skyscraper Walls."

70. Powell, "Sitting on the Top of the World," 526.

71. "How to Wreck Your Records with Harold Lloyd in 'Safety Last' (Stunt No. 5— 'Human Fly' Mystery Man Climbing Department Store Building)" *Safety Last!,* press book, p. 3, NYPLPA.

72. Bliven, "The Human Fly Is Dead," 95.

73. Cahn, *Harold Lloyd's World of Comedy,* 126–27; Dardis, *Harold Lloyd,* 127–28.

74. See note 71 above.

75. See Mark Aldrich, *Safety First: Technology, Labor, and Business in the Building of American Work Safety, 1870–1939* (Baltimore: Johns Hopkins University Press, 1997).

76. "Stunt 1—Safety First and Traffic Tie-Up," in *Safety Last!,* press book, p. 3, NYPLPA.

77. "Men Who Dare, Adopt 'Safety Last' as Motto," *Safety Last!,* press book, p. 15, NYPLPA.

78. Kaminsky, "Harold Lloyd," 27.

79. Annette Michelson, "Dr. Crase and Mr. Clair," *October* 11 (Winter 1979): 30–53. Michelson refers to the Eiffel Tower as Paris's "icon of modernity." She provides a useful model for analyzing modernity as a "thematic cluster," including the city, crowd, and capital. She suggests that René Clair's *Paris qui dort* (1927; VHS, Nostalgia Video, n.d.) may have been inspired by the films of Max Sennett. It may be possible that Lloyd's skyscraper film *Safety Last!,* which explores the theme of accelerated motion and the subversion of rationalized time, was a source for Clair.

80. Kaminsky, "Harold Lloyd," 23.

81. Charlie Keil, "From Here to Modernity: Style, Historiography, and Transitional Cinema," in Keil and Stamp, *American Cinema's Transitional Era,* 51–65. In my analysis of Lloyd, and since many of his films are not in the so-called transitional era, I am not simply developing a causal relation between modernity and Lloyd's films, hence falling prey to what Keil calls the "modernity thesis." Since Lloyd himself constructed these films, he is the one staging modernity in the service of subversion and triumph.

82. Ben Singer, "Modernity, Hyperstimulus, and the Rise of Popular Sensationalism," in *Cinema and the Invention of Modern Life,* ed. Leo Charney and Vanessa Schwartz (Berkeley and Los Angeles: University of California Press, 1995), 72. See Singer, *Modernity and Melodrama* and my "The Skyscraper, Gender, and Mental Life," which considers the manner in which modernity affects gendered subjects. Kirby's excellent *Parallel Tracks* has also been helpful for a treatment of how modernity affected gendered subjects differently in America during the silent era.

83. Charles Baudelaire, *The Painter of Modern Life,* trans. Jonathan Mayne (London: Phaidon, 1964).

84. Georg Simmel, "The Metropolis and Mental Life" (1903), trans. Edward Shils, in *On Individuality and Social Forms,* ed. Donald Levine (Chicago: University of Chicago

Press, 1971), 324–39; Siegfried Kracauer to Ernst Bloch, 27 May 1926, in Bloch, *Briefe, 1903–1975,* ed. Karola Bloch et al. (Frankfurt: Suhkamp, 1985).

85. In "Genre, Narrative, and the Hollywood Comedian," in *Classical Hollywood Comedy,* ed. Kristine Brunovska Karnick and Henry Jenkins (New York: Routledge, 1995), 19, Frank Krutnik includes a brief discussion of the differences between Chaplin's tramp and Lloyd's "glasses" figure, who seeks social integration. Krutnik also recognizes that Lloyd employs the skyscraper as an image of upward mobility. In agreement with Krutnik, I believe that "the gags arise from the narrative rather than competing with it." As I argue in this chapter, the gags are often staged as comedic obstacles that the character must overcome in order to realize his fully integrated masculinity.

86. Siegfried Kracauer, "Cult of Distraction: On Berlin's Picture Palaces" (1926), reprinted in *New German Critique* 40 (Winter 1987): 91–95. Instead of the movie theaters of Berlin, Lloyd creates distracting entertainment for the masses in the street, thereby releasing them from labor. Kracauer eschews the organic unity of the distracting, anachronistic theater, arguing for a cinema that exposes the disintegration of modern life, so that the masses might recognize it for their own benefit.

87. Siegfried Kracauer, "Artisches und Amerikanisches," *Frankfurter Zeitung,* 29 January 1926, quoted in Miriam Hansen, "America, Paris, the Alps: Kracauer and Benjamin on Cinema and Modernity," in Charney and Schwartz, *Cinema and the Invention of Modern Life,* 373. See also Miriam Hansen, "'With Skin and Hair': Kracauer's Theory of Film, *Marseilles* 1940," *Critical Inquiry* 19 (Spring 1993), 460–61.

88. Mikhail Bakhtin, *Rabelais and His World* (1965), trans. H. Iswolsky (Bloomington: Indiana University Press, 1984); reprinted in Pam Morris, ed., *The Bakhtin Reader* (London: Edward Arnold, 1994), 195–206.

89. Gilles Deleuze, "The Law of the Small Form and Burlesque," in *Cinema 1: The Movement-Image,* trans. Hugh Tomlinson and Barbara Habberjam (Minneapolis: University of Minnesota Press, 1986), 170. Deleuze accords much more credit to Chaplin, arguing that Lloyd creates through visual analogy alone while Chaplin creates a "laughter-emotion circuit" in which the slight distance and the great distance between the two actions do not diminish each other. I would argue that Lloyd, too, is capable of creating this emotional circuit, especially in the death-defying climbing scene of *Safety Last!,* in which comedy and tragedy, success and possible failure are underscored. Deleuze also discusses the machine antics of Buster Keaton, who he claims creates the almost Dadaist or "anarchistic-machine," making them his allies by recourse to the small gesture or use of materials (e.g., a single piece of wood in *The General,* directed by Clyde Bruckman and Buster Keaton [1927; DVD, King Video, 2001]); see 169–77. See also Kristine Brunovska Karnick and Henry Jenkins, "Comedy and the Social World," in Karnick and Jenkins, *Classical Hollywood Comedy,* 265–81, for a lengthier discussion of Bakhtin's view of the "liberating" character of comedy and the opposing view offered by Umberto Eco, who views this type of folk culture as regressive.

90. Cecelia Tichi, *Shifting Gears* (Chapel Hill: University of North Carolina Press, 1987), 231.

91. Mark Sullivan, *Our Times, 1900–1925,* 4 vols. (1926–32; repr., New York: Scribner's, 1977), 3:296–97, quoted in Tichi, *Shifting Gears,* 232.

92. Frederick Lewis Allen, *Only Yesterday* (New York: Harper and Bros., 1931; repr., New York: Bantam, 1959), 120.

93. Benson, *Counter Cultures,* 104–5.

94. For a good discussion of the function of the rube, see Kirby, *Parallel Tracks,* 136–40. Kirby claims that the use of the rube provides the spectator with an elevated subject position, often signifying the "upward mobility" of the spectator. See Hansen, *Babel and Babylon,* 38.

95. Kimmel, *Manhood in America,* 83.

96. For a discussion of William Henry Leffingwell and scientific office management, especially its effects on the gendered work environment, see Davies, *A Woman's Place Is at the Typewriter*; Strom, *Beyond the Typewriter*; Kwolek-Folland, *Engendering Business*.

97. Charles A. Beard and Mary R. Beard, *The Rise of American Civilization,* vol. 2 (New York: Macmillan, 1927), 728.

98. Henry Ford, *My Life and Work* (New York: Doubleday, 1923), 68.

99. Mumford, "The Intolerable City," 283–93. For a further discussion of Mumford's over decade-long diatribe against the skyscraper and urban living, see my *Skyscraper in American Art,* 93–97. See the entire chapter, "The Urban Cauldron," 93–110, for an extended discussion of other critics of urban life, the machine, and the skyscraper in the United States, including urban planners, artists, playwrights, etc.

100. Nels Anderson and Edward Lindeman, *Urban Sociology* (New York: Alfred A. Knopf, 1928), 212, 218, 230, 234; Maurice Davie, *Problems of City Life* (New York: John Wiley and Sons, 1932).

101. Siegfried Kracauer, "The Mass Ornament" (1927), quoted in Janet Ward, *Weimar Surfaces: Urban Visual Culture in 1920s Germany* (Berkeley and Los Angeles: University of California Press, 2001), 150. My treatment of Kracauer's criticisms of cinematic architecture is indebted to Ward.

102. Lewis Mumford, *Technics and Civilization* (New York: Harcourt Brace, 1934), 14.

103. Simmel, "Metropolis and Mental Life," 328.

104. Soja, *Postmodern Geographies,* 191.

105. Carey McWilliams, *Southern California: An Island on the Land* (Santa Barbara: Peregrine Smith, 1973). For a further discussion of population and development patterns, see Robert M. Fogelson, *The Fragmented Metropolis: Los Angeles, 1850–1930* (Cambridge, Mass.: Harvard University Press, 1967); Reyner Banham, *Los Angeles: The Architecture of Four Ecologies* (New York: Harper & Row, 1971); and W. W. Robinson, "The Southern California Land Boom of the Twenties," in *A Southern California Historical Anthology,* ed. Doyce B. Nunis Jr. (Los Angeles: Historical Society of Southern California, 1984), 329–36. Robinson claims that between 1920 and 1924 at least one hundred thousand people a year poured into Los Angeles alone, which is at odds with McWilliams's estimates. See also Kevin Star, *Material Dreams: Southern California through the 1920s* (New York: Oxford University Press, 1990).

106. See D'Agostino Lloyd, "Safety Last!" in *Harold Lloyd Encyclopedia,* 306–14. D'Agostino Lloyd claims that the skyscraper sequences were filmed on at least four separate buildings. In addition, she cites the Hal Roach Papers, Cinema and Television

Library, University of Southern California for the information on the publicity stills. The addresses for the buildings employed for stills are as follows: Los Angeles Investment Company was located at 1016 South Broadway off Tenth Street; the twelve-story Western Costume Building was located at 908 South Broadway off Ninth Street (the site of the famed clock sequence); Merchant's National Bank Building, another twelve-story structure, was at the northeast corner of Sixth and Spring Streets; the Washington Building at 311½ South Spring Street off Third Avenue was the site of the upper portion of the climb sequence.

107. Sam Hall Kaplan, *LA Lost & Found: An Architectural History of Los Angeles* (New York: Crown, 1987), 75.

108. Simmel, "Metropolis and Mental Life," 324–29.

109. Architectural historian Meir Wigoder has recently noted that skyscrapers created a new lofty space in the early twentieth century that transformed the viewer's perception of himself. He posits the emergence of a new spectator who sought a creative outlet for the expression of his or her singular identity and vision, one that was characterized by aesthetic cultivation and detachment. This could be achieved by occupying the numerous roof gardens and observation towers of metropolitan office buildings. See Meir Wigoder, "The 'Solar Eye of Vision': Emergence of the Skyscraper Viewer in the Discourse on Heights in New York City, 1890–1920," *Journal of the Society of Architectural Historians* 61 (June 2002): 152–69. Anthony Vidler, "Bodies in Space/Subjects in the City: Psychopathologies of Modern Urbanism," *Differences* 5 (1993): 31–51. Vidler asserts on 37, "It is obvious that modernist space, and its late twentieth-century extensions, are for the most part constructed by and for men."

110. A similar characterization of the crowd may be seen in King Vidor's *The Crowd* (1928; VHS, Warner Home Video, 1998) in which Johnny Sims is almost overrun by a mob on the eve of his daughter's death. He pleads with them to stop their incessant noise, to which a police officer responds, "The crowd laughs with one, but cries with one for only a day." See Lynne Kirby, "Gender and Advertising in American Silent Cinema: From Early Cinema to the Crowd," *Discourse* 13 (1991): 3–20. Kirby sees the crowd in the Vidor film as a representation of a crisis in paternal authority, in which the father is traded for the corporation and its advertising apparatus. She views the ending in redemptive terms as an opportunity to reclaim his dignity as a father, husband, and individual. Kirby believes that Sims's relationship to the crowd is a feminized one, in accord with the position constructed for the female consumer. Lloyd's relationship to the crowd is more ambivalent, both a part of and separate from it, representing his effort to assert his individuality in a corporate environment. See also Kirby's discussion of Le Bon in *Parallel Tracks*, 152–56.

111. Gustav Le Bon, *The Crowd: A Study of the Popular Mind* (1895), introduction by Robert Merton (New York: Viking Press, 1960), xxxiii, 29. See also Susanna Barrows, *Distorting Mirrors: Visions of the Crowd in Late Nineteenth-Century France* (New Haven: Yale University Press, 1987). According to Barrows, Le Bon's thinking influenced the work of Sigmund Freud, Gordon Allport, Georges Lefebvre, and George Rudo.

112. Le Bon, *The Crowd,* 50, 68. For a further discussion on the crowd's potential destructiveness, see Elias Canetti, *Crowds and Power,* trans. Carol Stewart (New York: Viking, 1963), 19–20.

113. See Singer, "Modernity, Hyperstimulus, and the Rise of Popular Sensationalism," 88–90. Singer asserts that as the urban environment grew more and more intense, so did the sensations of commercial amusement, with its emphasis on spectacle, sensationalism, and astonishment.

114. Roland Marchand, *Advertising the American Dream* (Berkeley and Los Angeles: University of California Press, 1985), 59.

115. According to D'Agostino Lloyd, "Safety Last!" 309, the fictional Bolton Building was based on a sketch of the Los Angeles Investment Building on 1016 South Broadway off Tenth Street.

116. William R. Taylor, *In Pursuit of Gotham: Culture and Commerce in New York* (New York: Oxford University Press, 1992), 46; Katherine Solomonson, "Design for Advertising," chapter 4 in *The Chicago Tribune Tower Competition: Skyscraper Design and Cultural Change in the 1920s* (Cambridge: Cambridge University Press, 2001), 99–107.

117. Schleier, *Skyscraper in American Art*, 53–55, 83.

118. Solomonson, *Chicago Tribune Tower Competition*, 103.

119. Wanda Corn, *The Great American Thing: Modern Art and National Identity, 1915–1935* (Berkeley and Los Angeles: University of California Press, 1999), 20. See also T. J. Jackson Lears, "From Salvation to Self-Realization: Advertising and the Therapeutic Roots of Consumer Culture, 1880–1930," in *The Culture of Consumption: Critical Essays in American History, 1880–1980,* ed. Richard Wightman Fox and T. J. Jackson Lears (New York: Pantheon, 1983), 18, for a discussion of the visual strategies developed by advertisers

120. Edgar Saltus, "New York from the Flatiron," *Munsey's Magazine* 33 (July 1905): 382–83.

121. Kirk Varnedoe, "The Artifice of Candor: Impressionism and Photography Reconsidered," *Art in America* 68 (January 1980): 66–78. A similar discussion is put forth in Carsten Strathausen's "Uncanny Spaces: The City in Ruttmann and Vertov," in *Screening the City,* ed. Mark Shiel and Tony Fitzmaurice (London: Verso, 2003), 15–40. Strathausen discusses Bentham's Panopticon, Le Corbusier's architecture, and Foucault's modern surveillance systems that create a seemingly omniscient viewer. He cites Paris's Eiffel Tower and Place de l'Etoile as providing urban denizens with viewpoints from above. While Strathausen stresses the rational grid seen from these urban perspectives as an organizing principle that creates anonymity and regimentation, I am concerned with the manner in which these viewpoints reduce urban inhabitants to infinitesimal proportions.

122. Michel de Certeau, "Walking in the City," in *The Practice of Everyday Life,* trans. Steven Rendall (Berkeley and Los Angeles: University of California Press, 1984), 92.

123. Richard de Cordova, "The Emergence of the Star System in America," *Wide Angle* 6 (1984): 4–13; Richard Dyer, *Heavenly Bodies* (New York: St. Martin's Press, 1986); Gaylin Studlar, *This Mad Masquerade: Stardom and Masculinity in the Jazz Age* (New York: Columbia University Press, 1996).

124. Martin Berger, *Man Made: Thomas Eakins and the Construction of Gilded Age Manhood* (Berkeley and Los Angeles: University of California Press, 2001), 6.

125. Harold Lloyd, "The Autobiography of Harold Lloyd," *Photoplay* 25 (May 1924): 32.

126. D'Agostino, *Harold Lloyd: A Bio-Bibliography,* 14.

127. Dorothy Donnell, "This Is the Story of Harold the Hustler," *Motion Picture Magazine* 34 (September 1927): 18–19.

128. Horatio Alger, *Struggling Upward* (New York: Hurst, 1909; repr., New York: Arno, 1974). Brownlow, in Vance and Lloyd, *Harold Lloyd: The Master Comedian,* 53–54, claims that the real Lloyd was not above reproach; he had conflicts with his somewhat acquisitive, prying mother and engaged in extramarital affairs.

129. Horatio Alger, *Making His Way* (New York: Hurst, 1897; repr., New York: Arno, 1974), 53, 67.

130. Lloyd, *An American Comedy,* 15.

131. "*High and Dizzy* Sets New Record for Lloyd," HLS #1, MHLC.

132. "A Lloyd Cocktail," in *High and Dizzy* press book, p. 1, NYPLPA.

133. Harry Evans, "*Feet First,*" *Life Magazine* 95 (28 November 1930): 20.

134. Kaminsky, "Harold Lloyd," 23; D'Agostino, *Harold Lloyd: A Bio-Bibliography,* 12.

135. Calvin Colton, ed., *The Works of Henry Clay,* vol. 5 (New York: A. S. Barnes and Burr, 1857), 464, quoted in John G. Cawelti, *Apostles of the Self-Made Man* (Chicago: University of Chicago Press, 1965), 43–44.

136. Kimmel, *Manhood in America,* 23. For a further discussion of the self-made man, see E. Anthony Rotundo, *American Manhood: Transformations in Masculinity from the Revolution to the Modern Era* (New York: Basic Books, 1992), 18–25.

137. Calvin Colton, *Junius Tracts,* no. 7 (New York, 1844), 15. quoted in Kimmel, *Manhood in America,* 26.

138. Cawelti, *Apostles of the Self-Made Man,* 172.

139. Orison Swett Marden, *Success* (Boston: W. A. Wilde, 1897), frontispiece. Marden published the periodical *Success* (1897–1911) but failed to attract a large readership. He found a new backer in Frederick Lowry, a Chicago manufacturer, who underwrote *New Success.*

140. Orison Swett Marden, *Rising in the World, or Architects of Fate* (New York: Thomas Y. Crowell, 1895). The subtitle for this book is significant. It is described on the frontispiece as a book "designed to inspire youth to character-building, self-culture and noble achievement." See also *Success; The Secret of Achievement* (New York: Thomas Y. Crowell, 1898); *The Young Man Entering Business* (New York: Thomas Y. Crowell, 1903); *He Can Who Thinks He Can* (New York: Thomas Y. Crowell, 1908); *How to Get What You Want* (New York: Thomas Y. Crowell, 1917).

141. Marden, *He Can Who Thinks He Can,* 72.

142. See Tom Pendergast, *Creating the Modern Man: American Magazines and Consumer Culture, 1900–1950* (Columbia: University of Missouri Press, 2000), 113–19, 145–54, for a discussion of similar ideas in *Collier's* and *American Magazine.*

143. Reinhard Bendix, *Work and Authority in Industry* (New York: John Wiley & Sons, 1956), 254–67. Bendix provides a useful summary of the important writers of the New Thought Movement, including Helen Wilmans, Elizabeth Towne, Frank C. Haddock, and others. He refers to Marden as one of the most important, endorsed by President McKinley and the industrialist Charles M. Schwab.

144. "Lloyd Uses Coue [sic] Theory Filming 'Thrill' Comedy," *Safety Last!,* press book, p. 18, NYPLPA.

145. Lloyd, *An American Comedy,* 86.

146. Émile Coué, "Better and Better," in *Self Mastery through Autosuggestion,* trans. by C. Harry Brooks (London, 1922; repr., London: Unwin, 1956).

147. Marden, *Secret of Achievement,* 134.

148. Carroll claims in his book *Comedy Incarnate,* 142, that Harold in *The Freshman,* directed by Fred C. Newmeyer and Sam Taylor (Pathé Exchange, 1925; DVD, New Line Home Video, 2005), has only luck but no skills, demonstrating the "white-collar ethic of ambition with its notion of selling oneself as a key to success." I would suggest that Harold's success is a combination of strenuous physical exertion combined with innovative ideas, not simply through "appearances."

149. Marden, *He Can Who Thinks He Can,* 61–62.

150. Ibid., 72.

151. Marden, *Secret of Achievement.*

152. Ibid., 142.

153. Marden, *Success,* 142.

154. Bruce Laurie, *Artisans into Workers: Labor in Nineteenth-Century America* (New York: Hill and Wang, 1989), 16; quoted in Kimmel, *Manhood in America,* 82.

155. Lears, *Fables of Abundance,* 138.

156. Studlar, *This Mad Masquerade,* 13.

157. Paula S. Fass, *The Damned and the Beautiful: American Youth in the 1920s* (New York: Oxford University Press, 1977), 126. Fass reported that college attendance increased threefold in the years 1900–1930.

158. Stuart Ewen, *Captains of Consciousness: Advertising and the Social Roots of Consumer Culture* (New York: McGraw Hill, 1976), 146.

159. See Fass, *The Damned and the Beautiful,* 128; and Gilman M. Ostrander, *American Civilization in the First Machine Age, 1890–1940* (New York: Harper Torchbooks, 1970), 237–73.

160. Lloyd, *An American Comedy,* 59.

161. Ibid., 61. Lloyd claimed that when he "came to choose a pair of glasses, the vogue of the horn rims was new and it was youth, who was principally adopting them. The novelty was a picture asset and the suggestion of youth fitted perfectly with the character I had in mind."

162. This quotation appeared in Richard Corson, *Fashion in Eyeglasses* (Chester Springs, Penn.: Dufour, 1967), 206. See also Clara Hemphill, "A Quest for Better Vision: Spectacles over the Centuries," *New York Times,* 8 August 2000, sec. F; Alberta Kelley, *Lenses, Spectacles, Eyeglasses and Contacts: The Story of Vision Aids* (New York: Thomas Nelson, 1978).

163. Byron Y. Newman O.D., "Harold Lloyd: The Man Who Popularized Eyeglasses in America," *Journal of the American Optometric Association* 66 (May 1995): 310.

164. Samuele Mazza, *Spectacles,* trans. Joe McClinton (San Francisco: Chronicle Books, 1996), 5.

165. In the documentary film *Harold Lloyd: The Third Genius* (VHS, HBO Video, 1989), Roach claimed that it was his idea for Harold to adopt the glasses character. In the film, Lloyd disagreed, saying it was his own idea and that Roach didn't want him to change.

166. Kevin Brownlow has recently identified it as *When Paris Green Saw Red* (1918) in Vance and Lloyd, *Harold Lloyd: Master Comedian,* 26–27.

167. Lloyd, *An American Comedy,* 59.

168. Garringer, "Harold Lloyd: Made a Fortune," 407.

169. "Harold Lloyd: The Funny Side of Life," 19.

170. Marchand, *Advertising the American Dream,* 199.

171. Orison Swett Marden, "The Influence of Appearance," *New Success* 4 (January 1920): 25.

172. Anne Hollander, *Sex and Suits* (New York: Alfred A. Knopf, 1994), 79–84.

173. "Men Who Dare, Adopt 'Safety Last' as Motto," 15.

174. James W. Dean, "What's Doing at the Movies," *Poughkeepsie Star,* 20 March 1923, *Safety Last!,* scrapbook #1, MHLC.

175. "Interesting Inside Facts Filming a Thrill Picture," *Safety Last!,* press book, 18, NYPLPA.

176. Lloyd, *An American Comedy,* 86.

177. "Interesting Inside Facts Filming a Thrill Picture," 18.

178. Ibid.

179. "Lloyd Uses Coue Theory Filming 'Thrill' Comedy," 18.

180. Fass, *The Damned and the Beautiful,* 232, 442. For a discussion of the Coué craze and its relationship to applied psychology, see Richard Weiss, *The American Myth of Success from Horatio Alger to Norman Vincent Peale* (New York: Basic Books, 1969), 218–23. See also Coué, *Self Mastery through Autosuggestion.*

181. "Lloyd Uses Coue Theory Filming 'Thrill' Comedy," 18.

182. Coué, *Self Mastery through Autosuggestion,* 11.

183. Ibid., 15, 34.

184. "Coué Reestimated in the Light of His Visit," *Current Opinion* 73 (April 1923): 69–71. See also Dr. Harvey W. Wiley, "The Philosophy of Coué," *Good Housekeeping* 76 (May 1923): 84, 185–88; "Growing Better with Monsieur Coué," *Current Opinion* 74 (November 1923): 586–87.

185. "How to Wreck Your Records with Harold Lloyd in 'Safety Last' (Stunts 4 and 6—Ideas for Inside and Outside Your Lobby)," *Safety Last!,* press book, 3, NYPLPA.

186. "A Jazz Jester," *New York Times,* 2 April 1923, sec. 22. See also the following reviews of *Safety Last!: Variety,* 5 April 1923, 36; "Laughs Galore and Thrills of a Hair-Raising Nature in Lloyd's Latest," *Film Daily,* 8 April 1923; "Saves Your Picture Time and Money—*Photoplay*'s Selection of the Six Best Performances of the Month," *Photoplay* 24 (June 1923): 65. In the *Variety* review, it was reported that "children just screamed above the laughter of the entire capacity audience."

187. "Laughs Galore and Thrills of a Hair-Raising Nature in Lloyd's Latest."

188. "Hair-able Hair-raising Scenes in Lloyd's Sensational Comedy," *Safety Last!,* press book, NYPLPA.

189. "Mildred Favors American Fashions," *Safety Last!,* press book, NYPLPA.

190. S. Gillick to Harold Lloyd, 13 February 1923, HLS #11, MHLC.

191. Mary Mac, "The Screen," *Milwaukee Journal,* 6 March 1923, *Safety Last!,* scrapbook #1, MHLC.

192. Hilda Lippertz to Harold Lloyd, 26 October 1923, HLS #1, MHLC.

193. "Safety-First Stuff in 'Safety Last,'" 43–44; Adela Rogers St. John, "How Lloyd Made 'Safety Last,'" *Photoplay* 24 (July 1923): 33, 117.

194. Rogers St. John, "How Lloyd Made 'Safety Last,'" 117.

2. ICONS OF EXPLOITATION

1. Gene Markey and Kathryn Scola, "Baby Face," story outline, 21 November 1932 (42 pages), UA Series 1.2, box 23, folder 5, p. 9, Wisconsin Center for Film and Theater Research, University of Wisconsin, Madison, and the State Historical Society of Wisconsin, Madison (hereafter WCFTR). The African American characters were precluded from entering cinematic office space except as part of the maintenance staff. In Gene Markey and Kathryn Scola, "Baby Face" screenplay, 17 December 1932 (139 pages), UA series 1.2, box 23, folder 7, p. 33, Baby Face tells Chico to wait outside. See notes 78 and 79 for information on African American female office workers.

2. Lefebvre, *Production of Space,* 98.

3. Henry Blake Fuller, *The Cliff-Dwellers* (New York: Harper and Brothers, 1893).

4. Raymond M. Hood, "A City under a Single Roof," *Nation's Business* 18 (November 1929): 19–20. See also Joseph McGoldrick (letter to the editor), "Must We Soon Travel Vertically from Home to Office?" *American City* 42 (May 1930): 130; Arthur Dewing, "The City of the Future," *American North Review* 231 (January 1931): 75–80; Robert A. M. Stern, Gregory Gilmartin, and Thomas Mellins, *New York 1930: Architecture and Urbanism Between the Two World Wars* (New York: Rizzoli, 1987).

5. Gordon D. MacDonald, *Office Building Construction Manhattan, 1901–1953* (New York: Real Estate Board of New York, 1953), 1.

6. For a thorough discussion of the formation of the Motion Picture Producers and Distributors of America in 1921, under the leadership of Will Hays, a Hoover protégé, which asked for voluntary adherence to standards of "decency," the passing of the Production Code in 1930 under the consultation of Martin G. Quigley (publisher of *Motion Picture Herald* and devout Catholic), which again called for the studios' chosen compliance to certain General Principles, and the final enforcement of the Code in 1934, under pressure from the Catholic Church, see Frank Miller, *Censored Hollywood: Sex, Sin and Violence on Screen* (Atlanta: Turner, 1994). Miller attributes the Code's final success to the collaboration between Quigley and Joseph Breen, a zealot who became Hays's assistant. Punishment consisted of a fine and the refusal of a seal of approval, which, if denied, could prevent a member from releasing, distributing, or exhibiting a film. See also Lea Jacobs, *The Wages of Sin: Censorship and the Fallen Woman Film, 1928–1942* (Madison: University of Wisconsin Press, 1991); Gregory Black, *Hollywood Censored: Morality Codes, Catholics and the Movies* (Cambridge: Cambridge University Press, 1994); Francis G. Couvares, ed., *Movie Censorship and American Culture* (Washington, D.C.: Smithsonian Press, 1996); Mark A. Vieira, *Sin in Soft Focus* (New York: Harry N. Abrams, 1999); Thomas Doherty, *Pre-Code Hollywood: Sex, Immorality, and Insurrection in American Cinema, 1930–1934* (New York: Columbia University Press, 2001); Leonard J. Leff and Jerold L. Simmons, *The Dame in the Kimono: Hollywood, Censorship and the Production Code* (Lexington: University of Kentucky Press, 2001).

7. *Skyscraper Souls,* directed by Edgar Selwyn (Metro-Goldwin-Mayer, 1932; VHS,

MGM/UA Home Video, 1998). It was based loosely on Faith Baldwin's novel *Skyscraper* (Cleveland: World Publishing, 1931). Baldwin's story was serialized in *Hearst's International Cosmopolitan Magazine* from June to October 1931. It was adapted to the screen by C. Gardner Sullivan. Two scholars have discussed the film in brief terms, without recourse to archival sources and without considering the film's relationship to the novel. See Sanders, *Celluloid Skyline*; Sarah Berry, *Screen Styles: Fashion and Femininity in 1930s Hollywood* (Minneapolis: University of Minnesota Press, 2000).

8. *Big Business Girl*, directed by William A. Seiter (First National Pictures and Vitaphone, controlled by Warner Bros., 1931; VHS, MGM/UA Home Video, n.d.). The film was based on a short story by Patricia Reilly and H. N. Swanson, which appeared in *College Humor* 80–82 (August–October 1930): 15–21, 94–101; 57–60, 84–96; 60–64, 84–94.

9. Jane Addams, *A New Conscience and an Ancient Evil* (New York: Macmillan, 1912), 213, quoted in Fine, *Souls of the Skyscraper,* 58. See also Davies, *A Woman's Place Is at the Typewriter*; Strom, *Beyond the Typewriter*; Kwolek-Folland, *Engendering Business*.

10. Fine, *Souls of Skyscrapers,* especially 65–75.

11. Faith Baldwin, *The Office Wife* (Philadelphia: Babston, 1929), ix.

12. According to Stern, Gilmartin, and Mellins in *New York 1930,* 603, the builders of the unrealized Larkin Tower inaugurated the race for height in 1926 by proposing to build a skyscraper five hundred feet taller than Gilbert's Woolworth Building (1911–13), which is 792 feet. This set the standard for the fever pitch reached in the late 1920s and early 1930s with the simultaneous erection of Severance and Matsui's Bank of Manhattan (1930), Van Alen's Chrysler Building (1930), and Shreve, Lamb, and Harmon's Empire State Building (1931).

13. According to Stern, Gilmartin, and Mellins, *New York 1930,* 595, rectilinear slab-like towers, such as H. Douglas Ives's Fred French Building (1927), Irwin S. Chanin's Chanin Building (1929), and Raymond M. Hood's McGraw Hill Building (1931) were an efficient stylistic solution to the high cost of mid-Manhattan real estate and the ever more constricted sites.

14. "Edgar Selwyn's 'Skyscraper Souls' One of the Year's Great Films," *Skyscraper Souls,* press book, 1932, p. 1, NYPLPA.

15. "Catch Lines," *Skyscraper Souls,* press book, p. 1, NYPLPA.

16. Richard Watts Jr., "Skyscraper Souls," *New York Tribune,* 5 August 1932; Al Sherman, "Skyscraper Souls," *New York Telegraph,* 6 August 1932. Other reviews of the film (titled "Skyscraper Souls" unless otherwise noted) include Edward Cushing, *Brooklyn Eagle,* 14 August 1932; Thornton Delehanty, *New York Post,* 5 August 1932; Regina Crowe, "'Skyscraper Souls' Pulses with Staccato Rhythm of Metropolis," *New York American,* 4 August 1932; Rose Pelswick, "All-Star Cast, Expert Direction Make Absorbing Film of Faith Baldwin Novel," *New York Journal-American,* 5 August 1932; *Variety,* 9 August 1932. The aforementioned reviews are located in the *Skyscraper Souls* clipping file, MHLC. See also other reviews in the *Motion Picture Herald,* 16 July 1932; Mordaunt Hall, "A Banker's Ambition," *New York Times,* 5 August 1932, sec. 11; Richard Dana Skinner, *Commonweal* 16 (14 August 1932), 411.

17. Pelswick, "All-Star Cast, Expert Direction Make Absorbing Film of Faith Baldwin Novel."

18. Edith Fitzgerald, *Skyscraper Souls,* preliminary script, 17 August 1931, p. 6, Metro-Goldwyn-Mayer Archives, MHLC.

19. "Edgar Selwyn's 'Skyscraper Souls' One of Year's Great Films," *Skyscraper Souls,* press book, p. 2, NYPLPA.

20. John Lynch, *Skyscraper Souls,* preliminary script, 1 August 1931 (109 pages), p. 1, MHLC.

21. Doreen Massey put forth the view of the mutability of identities suggested by the kinetic character of film. See Doreen Massey and Karen Luny, "Making Connections," *Screen* 40 (Autumn 1999): 172.

22. John Tauranac, *The Empire State Building: The Making of a Landmark* (New York: St. Martin's Griffin, 1995), 167.

23. Kim Dovey, *Framing Places: Mediating Power in Built Form* (London: Routledge, 1998), 114–15. William Lamb, "The Empire State Building—XII. The Ground Floor Lobbies and Shops," *Architectural Forum* 54 (July 1931): 42. Lamb noted that the ground floor of an office building had additional functions: it must provide an imposing entrance to the offices above and it "must produce many times the revenue of any other floor of the building," since it often occupied more than one story.

24. "Build It Up with General Promotion," *Skyscraper Souls,* press book, p. 3, NYPLPA.

25. Siegfried Kracauer, "The Hotel Lobby" (1922), excerpt from *The Mass Ornament,* trans. Thomas Levin (Cambridge, Mass.: Harvard University Press, 1995) in *Rethinking Architecture,* ed. Neil Leach (London: Routledge, 1997), 53–59. See also Anthony Vidler, "Agoraphobia: Spatial Estrangement in Georg Simmel and Siegfried Kracauer," *New German Critique* 54 (Fall 1991): 31–45.

26. Benjamin, *Arcades Project,* 31–61.

27. *Empire State: A History* (New York: Empire State Corporation, 1931), 38.

28. *The Apartment,* directed by Billy Wilder (Mirisch, 1960); screenplay by Billy Wilder and I. A. L. Diamond; reproduced on http://www.dailyscript.com/scripts/apartment.html.

29. "Catch Lines," *Skyscraper Souls,* press book, p. 2, NYPLPA.

30. Film scholars such as Sarah Berry view these elevator scenes in which Tom accosts Lynn as part of a pattern of sexual harassment suffered by cinematic working women. See Berry, *Screen Styles,* 164. See also Mary Beth Haralovich, "The Proletarian Woman's Film of the 1930s: Contending with Censorship and Entertainment," *Screen* 31 (Summer 1990): 172–89. Haralovich discusses the shop girls' state of undress in cinematic fashion houses, subjecting them to sexual harassment by the boss.

31. Lynch, preliminary script, 1 August 1931, p. 5, MHLC.

32. Marchand, *Advertising the American Dream,* 239; David E. Nye, *American Technological Sublime* (Cambridge, Mass.: MIT Press, 1994), 96–97. See chapter 1, notes 109 and 114, for authors that deal with issues of ocular possession occasioned by lofty viewpoints.

33. For an excellent discussion of the rise of penthouses in New York in general and the buildings of Emery Roth in particular, see Steven Ruttenbaum, *Mansions in the Clouds: The Skyscraper Palazzi of Emery Roth,* foreword by Paul Goldberger (New York: Balsam, 1986).

34. For general discussions of cinematic penthouses, see Albrecht, *Designing Dreams,* and Howard Mandelbaum and Eric Myers, *Screen Deco* (New York: St. Martin's Press, 1985). Both Albrecht and Mandelbaum and Myers link the cinematic moderne to corruption.

35. Baldwin, *Skyscraper,* 89.

36. *Baby Face,* directed by Alfred E. Green (Warner Bros., 1933; VHS, MGM/UA Home Entertainment, 1995); the story was by Darryl F. Zanuck, with a screenplay by Gene Markey and Kathryn Scola. See note 1 above.

37. *Under Eighteen,* directed by Archie Mayo (Warner Bros., 1932; VHS, n.d.); the story was by Frank Mitchell Dazey, Agnes Christine Johnston, and Charles Kenyon.

38. Gaston Bachelard, *The Poetics of Space,* trans. Maria Jolas (Boston: Beacon, 1969), 18–23.

39. Michel Foucault, "Of Other Spaces," trans. Jay Miskowiec, *Diacritics* 16 (Spring 1986): 22–27. The original title in French was "Des Espaces Autres"; it was published in *Architecture-Mouvement-Continuité* in October 1984 and was the result of a lecture given by Foucault in March 1967.

40. Elmer Harris, *Skyscraper Souls,* shooting script, 3 May 1932 (145 pages), p. 81, MHLC.

41. Jonathan Weinberg uses the term "coded ambiguity" to describe the depiction of sexual identity in the paintings of the homosexual artist Charles Demuth. He asks whether it is possible to represent homosexuality without showing men having sex. He suggests that sexual conduct can be covertly represented and understood by those in the know. See *Speaking for Vice: Homosexuality in the Art of Charles Demuth, Marsden Hartley, and the First American Avant-garde* (New Haven: Yale University Press, 1993), 24–29.

42. Eve Kosofsky Sedgwick, *Between Men: English Literature and Male Homosocial Desire* (New York: Columbia University Press, 1984), 1–20.

43. See "Code to Govern the Making of Talking, Synchronized and Silent Motion Pictures." Formulated by The Association of Motion Picture Producers, Inc., and The Motion Picture Producers and Distributors of America, Inc., Section IX. Locations, quoted in Leff and Simmons, *Dame in the Kimono,* 300.

44. George Chauncey, *Gay New York: Gender, Urban Culture, and the Making of the Gay Male World, 1890–1940* (New York: Basic Books, 1994), 208–25; Marilyn Brown, "The Harem Dehistoricized: Ingres' *Turkish Bath,*" *Arts* 61 (June 1987): 58–68; Edward Said, *Orientalism* (New York: Random House, 1973), 190.

45. For a discussion of the role of bathhouses in American gay life from 1910 to 1940, see Weinberg, *Speaking for Vice,* 111–15.

46. Rem Koolhaas, *Delirious New York* (New York: Oxford University Press, 1978), 152.

47. "Downtown Athletic Club, New York City," *Architecture and Building* 63 (January 1931): 6; "The Downtown Athletic Club," *Architectural Forum* 54 (February 1931): 151–61. Koolhaas recognized that the seventeenth-floor roof garden's dance floor was a possible site of heterosexual romance and that the underlying building's intent was the celebration of bachelorhood, yet he did not acknowledge the potential for homoerotic encounters.

48. Haralovich, "Proletarian Woman's Film of the 1930s," 162–89.

49. Charles Eckert, "The Carole Lombard in Macy's Window," *Quarterly Review of Film Studies* 3 (Winter 1978): 1–22; Jane Gaines, "From Elephants to Lux Soap: The Programming and 'Flow' of Early Motion Picture Exploitation," *The Velvet Light Trap* 25 (Spring 1990): 29–43.

50. Harris, shooting script, 3 May 1932, p. 95, MHLC.

51. *Counsellor at Law,* directed by William Wyler (Universal Studios, 1933; VHS, Kino Video, 2002).

52. Lary May, *The Big Tomorrow: Hollywood and the Politics of the American Way* (Berkeley and Los Angeles: University of California Press, 2000), 274. Thomas Doherty makes a similar point in *Pre-Code Hollywood* in a section entitled "Professional Malfeasance," 58.

53. See chapter 1 for a discussion of Lloyd's manly go-getters, and Gaylin Studlar's excellent chapter on Douglas Fairbanks in *This Mad Masquerade* for another discussion of the assertive, often boyish achiever.

54. Mick LaSalle, *Dangerous Men: Pre-Code Hollywood and the Birth of the Modern Man* (New York: St. Martin's Press, 2002), 149.

55. *Wife vs. Secretary,* directed by Clarence Brown (Metro-Goldwyn-Mayer, 1936; VHS, MGM/UA Home Video, 1997); the screenwriters included Norman Krasna, John Lee Mahin, and Alice Duer Miller. It was based on a story of the same title by Faith Baldwin. See "Wife versus Secretary," *Hearst's International Cosmopolitan* 98 (May 1935): 20–21, 182–204.

56. Berry, *Screen Styles,* 164. See also Marjorie Rosen, *Popcorn Venus: Women, Movies and the American Dream* (New York: Coward McCann and Geoghegan, 1973), 101–8, 144–46. Rosen blames the 1920s depiction of the working woman whose professional ambitions were thwarted on the hypocrisy of the Hollywood magnates, who saw women as little more than ornaments. By the 1930s, she notes that despite the laying off of 20 percent of the female working force, one out of six women still were the sole wage earners of their families. The 1930s films accomplished the "paradoxical feat of showing vigorous working gals whose independence was a ruse, a passage to traditional marriage and social success," according to Rosen.

57. *Wife vs. Secretary* was referred to as the "greatest box-office triangle in film history." See "Catchlines," *Wife versus Secretary,* press book, 1936, p. 6, NYPLPA.

58. Frank Nugent, "Wife vs. Secretary," *New York Times,* 29 February 1936.

59. Photograph accompanying article "The Story of 'Wife versus Secretary,'" in *Wife vs. Secretary,* press book, pp. 7, 9, NYPLPA.

60. For discussions of the diverse nature of the concept "New Woman," see Lois Banner, *American Beauty* (New York: Alfred A. Knopf, 1983); Nancy Woloch, *Women and the American Experience* (New York: Alfred A. Knopf, 1984); Ellen Wiley Todd, *The "New Woman" Revised: Painting and Gender Politics on Fourteenth Street* (Berkeley and Los Angeles: University of California Press, 1993).

61. Sumiko Higashi, "The New Woman and Consumer Culture: Cecil B. DeMille's Sex Comedies," in *A Feminist Reader in Early Cinema,* ed. Jennifer Bean and Diane Fisher (Durham: Duke University Press, 2002), 298–332.

62. *Big Business Girl* press book, pp. 5–7, Warner Bros. Archives (hereafter WBA),

Cinema and Television Library, University of Southern California, Los Angeles (hereafter CTL-USC).

63. Thorstein Veblen, *The Theory of the Leisure Class* (New York: A. M. Kelly, 1899). Ella Dwight (Hedda Hopper) in *Skyscraper Souls* enjoys a marriage of convenience with her mercenary husband, visiting him only to wheedle money out of him for her profligate tastes. At the end of the film, she inherits the building, which she plans to sell.

64. Jacobs, *Wages of Sin,* 11.

65. Lea Jacobs, "Glamour and Golddiggers," in *Wages of Sin,* 66–81; Richard Maltby, "'Baby Face' or How Joe Breen Made Barbara Stanwyck Atone for Causing the Wall Street Crash," *Screen* 27 (March–April 1986): 22–45. Kathy Peiss posits the existence of a flamboyant working-class version of the New Woman in silent cinema. See *Cheap Amusements: Working Women and Leisure in Turn-of-the-Century New York* (Philadelphia: Temple University Press, 1986).

66. Markey and Scola, "Baby Face," story outline, p. 7, WCFTR.

67. Maltby, "'Baby Face' or How Joe Breen Made Barbara Stanwyck Atone," 43.

68. "'Baby Face' Exciting with Barbara Stanwyck, Swell," *Baby Face* press book, p. 3, NYPLPA.

69. Markey and Scola, screenplay, p. 26, WCFTR.

70. James Wingate to J. L. Warner, 19 May 1933, letter with recommended script revisions and eliminations (4 pages), Production Code Files, MHLC.

71. Markey and Scola, screenplay, p. 107, WCFTR.

72. Ibid., 26.

73. James Wingate to J. L. Warner, 26 April 1933, Production Code Files, MHLC.

74. "Shy, Barbara Stanwyck Oft Called Woman of Mystery," *Baby Face,* press book, p. 4, NYPLPA.

75. Ray Tevis and Brenda Tevis, *The Image of the Librarian in Cinema, 1917–1999* (Jefferson, N.C.: McFarland, 2005), 17.

76. Markey and Scola, screenplay, p. 38, WCFTR.

77. Frances Maule, *She Strives to Conquer* (New York: Funk and Wagnall's, 1934), 167–68.

78. As Fine points out in *Souls of the Skyscraper,* 33 and 173–75, female clerical workers were white, native-born women. By 1930, African American women made up only 1 percent of the clerical labor force.

79. Deborah King, "Multiple Jeopardy, Multiple Consciousness: The Context of a Black Feminist Ideology," in *Words of Fire: An Anthology of African-American Feminist Thought,* ed. Beverly Guy-Shefftall (New York: New Press, 1995), 146–55.

80. Thomas Doherty, "Women Love Dirt," in the chapter "Vice Rewarded," in *Pre-Code Hollywood*. Doherty points out that he is appropriating this phrase from a Depression-era article in *Variety*.

81. See Doherty, *Pre-Code Hollywood*; Jacobs, *Wages of Sin*; Haralovich, "Proletarian Woman's Film of the 1930s"; Leff and Simmons, *Dame in the Kimono*.

82. Maltby, "'Baby Face' or How Joe Breen Made Barbara Stanwyck Atone," 22–45.

83. Richard Maltby claims, "The production company's interest was satisfied if the source material was adapted to the conventions of its movie genre and the expectations of the audience." See "'To Prevent the Prevalent Type of Book': Censorship and

Adaptation in Hollywood, 1924–1934," in Couvares, *Movie Censorship and American Culture,* 101.

84. Baldwin's work was highly coveted by the movie industry. She wrote at least eleven novels that Paige Cooper categorized as "business and modern love" stories, in *Faith Baldwin and the American Family* (New York: Farrar & Rinehart, 1938), 4. Film adaptations of her work included *Office Wife* (1930), *Skyscraper Souls* (1932), and *Wife vs. Secretary* (1936).

85. Laura Hapke, "American Pulp Fiction of the Depression," in Baldwin, *Skyscraper,* 251.

86. Cooper, *Faith Baldwin and the American Family,* 4.

87. "Skyscraper Souls," *Motion Picture Herald,* 16 July 1932, 51.

88. Skinner, "Skyscraper Souls," 411.

89. *The Office Wife,* directed by Lloyd Bacon (Warner Bros., 1930; VHS courtesy of Thomas Doherty); the screenplay was by Charles Kenyon.

90. Suffragists were frequently depicted as mannish women, often categorized by their detractors as inverts and lesbians. Disparaging caricatures appeared in the British magazine *Punch* and the American *Vanity Fair* in the 1920s. See Laura L. Behling, *The Masculine Woman in America, 1890–1935* (Urbana: University of Chicago Press, 2001). According to David M. Lugowski, "At her most overt, the lesbian was clad in a mannishly tailored suit (often tuxedo), her hair slicked back or cut in a short bob. She sometimes sported a monocle and cigarette holder (or cigar!) and invariably possessed a deep alto voice and a haughty, aggressive attitude toward men, work or any business at hand." See "Queering the (New) Deal: Lesbian and Gay Representation and the Depression-Era Cultural Politics of Hollywood's Production Code," *Cinema Journal* 38 (Winter 1999): 4.

91. Baldwin, *Skyscraper,* 1.

92. "Director Calls Newspaper Film's Greatest Rival," *Skyscraper Souls,* press book, p. 2, NYPLPA.

93. John Lynch, 1 August 1931; Edith Fitzgerald, 17 August 1931; Edith Fitzgerald, 1 September 1931; 11 September 1931; Edith Fitzgerald, 19 September 1931; Gilbert Emery, 12 October 1931; Beth Brown, 28 October 1931; Harvey Gates, 7 December 1931; 21 December 1931; Edgar Allen Woolf, 14 December 1931; Edith Fitzgerald, 3 partial scripts: 21 January 1932, 1 February 1932, 7 March 1932; Elmer Harris, shooting script, 3 May 1932; dialogue cutting, 14 July 1932: Metro-Goldwyn-Mayer Archives, MHLC. The scripts include versions by both male and female writers, which became a commonplace practice at Paramount and other studios. For example, Ben Schulberg at Paramount believed that collaboration would accentuate the woman's perspective, which was viewed as opaque to male writers. See Lizzie Francke, *Script Girls: Screenwriters in Hollywood* (London: British Film Institute, 1994).

94. Baldwin, *Skyscraper,* 12, 62–63, 166.

95. "Skyscraper," *Books: A Weekly Review of Contemporary Life,* 1 November 1931, 16.

96. Baldwin, *Skyscraper,* 54, 231.

97. Ibid., 166.

98. Ibid., 14–16, 187.

99. Ibid., 85, 88–89, 92, 145.

100. Ibid., 309, 319.

101. The following memos were authored by Hunt Stromberg and sent to the various screenwriters. All are located in the MGM collection (hereafter MGM), box 229, files 1–5, CTL-USC. 25 October 1934; 27 December 1934; 28 December 1934; 10 January 1935 (this seven-page memo was sent to Faith Baldwin); 12 April 1935; 26 April 1935 (five pages, entitled "Revised Slant on Wife vs. Secretary"); 26 April 1935 (sixteen pages, entitled "Conference Notes on Wife vs. Secretary"); 30 April 1935 (fourteen pages); 2 May 1935; 4 May 1935; 7 May 1935; 8 May 1935; 15 May 1935; 10 July 1935; 11 July 1935; 16 August 1935; 24 August 1935; 27 August 1935; 5 November 1935 (entitled "Casting"); Ray Long's "Summary of Talks on 'Wife vs. Secretary' by Faith Baldwin," 18 October 1934. In the MGM Script Collection, MHLC, there are six scripts: John Lee Mahin, 21 February 1935, box 3710, file 782; Mahin, 27 April 1935, box 3710, file 783; Mahin, 28 June 1935, box 3710, file 784; Alice Duer Miller, 11 July 1935, box 3710, file 785; Norman Krasna, 15 July 1935, box 3710, file 786; Krasna, Mahin, and Miller, 12–22 November 1935, box 3711, file 788. There is one partial script with changes, box 3711, file 788. One can trace the changes in the scripts as a result of Stromberg's directives.

102. Faith Baldwin, "Wife vs. Secretary" (1935), box 3710, file 779, MGM Script Collection, MHLC. A memo by Ray Long, dated 19 October 1934, entitled "Suggestions for Situations in 'Wife vs. Secretary,'" in which Long writes, "The intensely interesting material Miss Baldwin referred to yesterday about the married woman in the office and her loss of efficiency after her marriage," speaks to Baldwin's early input. Box 3710, file 779, MGM Script Collection, MHLC. Stromberg's 10 January memo cited above is a corrected version of "Letter to Faith Baldwin," dated 9 January 1935. These two memos suggest that Baldwin's treatment was written between mid-January and mid-February 1935, since John Lee Mahin's first script is dated 21 February 1935 and refers to his consultation of her magazine serial and a short novel. See MGM Script Collection, box 3710, file 782, p. 1.

103. Long, "Summary of Talks," 18 October 1934, p. 1, MGM, CTL-USC. Long also discusses the casting of Dick Powell in the role of Sanford. By 28 June 1935, Mahin referred to Robert Taylor in the role; MGM Script Collection, MHLC. In a memo entitled "Casting," Stromberg expressed trepidation about the suitability of Gable for the lead male role. He described him as a man who possessed "brawn and muscle" and "sex appeal" but not "keen wit and intellect," which the role required. "I'm not sure whether Gable can accomplish this," he mused. This memo is dated 5 November 1935, MGM, CTL-USC.

104. Stromberg, "Conference Notes on Wife vs. Secretary," 26 April 1935, pp. 5, 11–12, MGM, CTL-USC. There is also a homely character in Baldwin's story, who has a crush on Van. In Stromberg's hands, Mary Conners is transmuted into another calculating gossip who has been passed over for a promotion in favor of Whitey and seeks revenge. She lies to Mrs. Sanford about the boss-secretary relationship. She is ultimately written out of the final film.

105. Stromberg, 24 August 1935, p. 2, MGM, CTL-USC.

106. "Catch Lines," *Wife vs. Secretary,* press book, p. 6, NYPLPA.

107. Stromberg, "Conference Notes on Wife vs. Secretary," 26 April 1935, p. 2, MGM, CTL-USC.

108. Stromberg, 12 April 1935, p. 7, MGM, CTL-USC.

109. Stromberg, 4 May 1935, p. 7. MGM, CTL-USC.

110. Krasna, Mahin, and Miller, *Wife vs. Secretary,* 12–22 November 1935, p. 49, MGM Script Collection, MHLC.

111. Baldwin, "Wife vs. Secretary," 181–82.

112. Jerome Lachenbruch, "Interior Decoration for the Movies: Studies from the Work of Cedric Gibbons and Albert White," *Art and Decoration* 14 (January 1921): 204–5; Michael Webb, "Cedric Gibbons and the MGM Style," *Architectural Digest* 47 (April 1990): 100–104, 108, 112.

113. Krasna, *Wife vs. Secretary,* preliminary script, 15 July 1935, p. 33C, MGM Script Collection, MHLC.

114. Stromberg, 16 August 1935, p. 3, MGM, CTL-USC.

115. Baldwin, "Wife versus Secretary," 194.

116. Ibid., 187–88.

117. Ibid., 185.

118. Stromberg, 27 August 1935, p. 6, MGM, CTL-USC.

119. Baldwin, "Wife versus Secretary," 204.

120. Skinner, "Skyscraper Souls," 411.

121. "Wife vs. Secretary," *Film Daily,* 19 February 1936, MHLC.

122. For discussions of so-called women's film, see Andrea S. Walsh, *Women's Film and Female Experience, 1940–1950* (New York: Praeger, 1984); Mary Ann Doane, *The Desire to Desire: The Women's Film of the 1940s: Theories of Representation and Difference* (Bloomington: Indiana University Press, 1987); Christine Gledhill, ed., *Home Is Where the Heart Is: Studies in Melodrama and the Woman's Film* (London: British Film Institute, 1987); Janet Todd, ed., *Women and Film* (New York: Holmes & Meier, 1988); E. Ann Kaplan, *Women and Film: Both Sides of the Camera* (London: Routledge, 1990); Jeanine Basinger, *A Woman's View: How Hollywood Spoke to Women, 1930–1960* (Hanover: Wesleyan University Press, 1993).

123. Maltby, "'Baby Face' or How Joe Breen Made Barbara Stanwyck Atone," 23.

124. See note 80 above.

125. Hansen, *Babel and Babylon*; Annette Kuhn, "Women's Genres: Melodrama, Soap Opera and Theory," *Screen* 25 (January–February 1984): 18–28; Doane, *The Desire to Desire.*

126. Melvyn Stokes, "Female Audiences of the 1920s and Early 1930s," in *Identifying Hollywood's Audiences: Cultural Identity in the Movies,* ed. Melvyn Stokes and Richard Maltby (London: British Film Institute, 1999), 42–44. Thanks to Lea Jacobs for recommending this work.

127. Lea Jacobs, "The Seduction Plot: Comic and Dramatic Variants," *Film History* 13 (2001): 424–42.

128. Stokes, "Female Audiences of the 1920s and Early 1930s," 51.

129. See bel hooks, "The Oppositional Gaze: Black Female Spectators," in *Black Looks: Race and Representation* (London: Turnaround, 1992), 115–31. Although hooks

discusses the so-called black female gaze, her analysis can be equally applied to anyone adopting an oppositional stance, although one must be cautious not to use the term in a totalizing manner. Rae Chatfield Ayer and Fred De Armond, "Are Men Better Secretaries?" *Rotarian* 57 (November 1940): 32. Ayer, who answered the question in the negative, made the observation about the cinematic representations of women.

130. Elizabeth Gregg MacGibbon, *Manners in Business* (New York: Macmillan, 1936), 116–27; Maule, *She Strives to Conquer,* 155–68. Maule also included a chapter entitled "Stepping Out."

131. Gladys Torson, "How to Be a Hero to Your Secretary," *Saturday Evening Post* 211 (7 January 1939): 20.

132. Marjorie Holmes Mighell, "Romance versus the Boss," *Nation's Business* 25 (August 1937): 21, 110, 112. See also "A Secretary Looks at Her Boss," *Saturday Evening Post* 209 (8 August 1936): 16.

133. Maule, *She Strives to Conquer,* 159.

134. Mighell, "Romance versus the Boss," 21.

135. Ibid., 112.

136. MacGibbon, *Manners in Business,* 125.

137. Jean E. Douglas, "Honor's Secretary," *Independent Woman* 18 (July 1939): 205.

138. Lois Whitcomb, "A Tract for Bosses' Wives," *Rotarian* 53 (August 1938): 26.

139. Loire Brophy, *If Women Must Work* (New York: D. Appleton-Century, 1936), 29–30.

140. Maule, *She Strives to Conquer,* 90.

141. Brophy, *If Women Must Work,* 32. See also Natalie Baner, "What Every Young Secretary Should Know," *Scholastic* 32 (12 March 1938): 6.

142. MacGibbon, *Manners in Business,* 31–32. Perhaps the author was thinking of *Baby Face* when she offered these caveats. See also Ruth Wanger, *What Girls Can Do* (New York: Henry Holt, 1926), 10–28.

143. Ayer and De Armond, "Are Men Better Secretaries?" 32.

144. Whitcomb, "A Tract for Bosses' Wives," 26; MacGibbon, *Manners in Business,* 124.

145. Maule, *She Strives to Conquer,* 174.

146. MacGibbon, *Manners in Business,* 123.

147. Maule, *She Strives to Conquer,* 172; MacGibbon, *Manners in Business,* 122.

148. James Hay offers a similar argument for the Grand Hotel films of 1930s Italian cinema, which are often sites of modernization and the *bel mondo* while registering the tensions between upper-crust and traditional values. See his *Popular Film Culture in Fascist Italy* (Bloomington: Indiana University Press, 1987), especially the chapter "The Myth of the Grand Hotel," 37–63.

3. MASCULINE HEROES, MODERNISM, AND POLITICAL IDEOLOGY

1. Ayn Rand, *The Fountainhead* (New York: Bobbs-Merrill, 1943; reprint with afterword by Leonard Peikoff, New York: Signet, 1993). Several versions of the screenplay (1944–48) are housed, with other materials concerning the film adaptation of *The Fountainhead,* in WBA, CTL-USC. I have mainly used the final version of the screen-

play, which is dated 20 June 1948. According to Jeffrey Meyers in *Gary Cooper: American Hero* (New York: William Morrow, 1998), the film was shot from 12 July to 8 October 1948. It was released in July 1949 by Warner Bros. For earlier discussions of the novel and the film, see Charles Higham and Joel Greenberg, *The Celluloid Muse: Hollywood Directors Speak* (London: Angus & Robertson, 1969); Kevin McGann, "Ayn Rand in the Stockyard of the Spirit," in *The Modern Novel and the Movies,* ed. Gerald Peary and Roger Shatzkin (New York: Ungar, 1978), 325–35; Barbara Branden, *The Passion of Ayn Rand* (New York: Doubleday, 1987); Andrew Saint, *The Image of the Architect* (New Haven: Yale University Press, 1983); Donald Albrecht, *Designing Dreams: Modern Architecture in the Movies* (New York: Harper and Row, 1986); Patricia Neal, *As I Am: An Autobiography* (New York: Simon & Schuster, 1988); Raymond Durgnat and Scott Simon, *King Vidor: American* (Berkeley and Los Angeles: University of California Press, 1988); Julian Petley, "The Architect as *Übermensch,"* in *Picture This: Media Representations of Visual Arts and Artists,* ed. Philip Hayward (London: University of Luton Press, 1988), 115–25; John A. Walker, *Art and Artists on Screen* (Manchester: Palgrave Macmillan, 1993); Meyers, *Gary Cooper*; Charles Affron and Mirella Jona Affron, *Sets in Motion: Art Direction and Film Narrative* (New Brunswick, N.J.: Rutgers University Press, 1995); Sanders, *Celluloid Skyline*. See also Ayn Rand, *The Illustrated Fountainhead,* with drawings by Frank Goodwin (New York: King Features, 1945; repr., Marina del Rey, Calif.: Ayn Rand Institute, 1998).

2. Branden, *Passion of Ayn Rand,* 160–61. It is interesting to note that in the 1932 election, Rand voted for Roosevelt over Hoover, believing that he was the more libertarian of the two candidates. Soon she viewed him as a collectivist of the worst order who was leading the country down the road to Communism.

3. Kenneth Fearing, *The Big Clock* (New York: Harcourt, Brace, 1946; repr., New York: Mystery Book Club, 1987). The film rights were purchased in the fall of 1946 from Fearing for $25,000. It was filmed from 24 February to 14 April 1947, with adjustments made until August of 1947. It was released on 9 April 1948. See Paramount Production Material, *The Big Clock,* files 1 and 2, MHLC. There is a discrepancy concerning how much Fearing was paid for the film rights. According to Robert M. Ryley, ed., in *Kenneth Fearing: Complete Poems* (Orono, Maine: National Poetry Foundation, 1994), Fearing earned about $60,000, about $10,000 in royalties and $50,000 from the sale of the film rights. For discussions of the novel and film, see Elizabeth Ward, "The Big Clock," in *Film Noir: An Encyclopedic Reference to the American Style,* ed. Alain Silver and Elizabeth Ward (Woodstock, N.Y.: Overlook, 1979), 25–28; Patricia Santora, "The Poetry and Prose of Kenneth Flexner Fearing" (PhD diss., University of Maryland, 1982); Robert Ryley, "More than a Thriller: *The Big Clock,"* *The Armchair Detective* 16 (Winter 1983): 354–59; J. P. Telotte, "*The Big Clock* of Film Noir," *Film Criticism* 14 (Winter 1989–90): 1–11; T. Jeff Evans, "Narratology in Kenneth Fearing's *Big Clock,"* *Journal of Narrative Technique* 23 (Fall 1993): 188–200; Rita Barnard, *The Great Depression and the Culture of Abundance: Kenneth Fearing, Nathaniel West, and the Mass Culture of the 1930s* (New York: Cambridge University Press, 1994); R. Barton Palmer, "*Film Noir* and the Genre Continuum: Process, Product, and *The Big Clock,"* in *Perspectives on Film Noir,* ed. Palmer (New York: G. K. Hall, 1996), 141–53; Alain Silver and James Ursini, eds., "John Farrow: Anonymous Noir," in Silver and Ursini, *Film Noir Reader* (New York: Limelight Editions, 1996), 145–60; Nicholas Christopher, *Somewhere in the Night:*

Film Noir and the American City (New York: Free Press, 1997); Edward Dimendberg, *Film Noir and the Spaces of Modernity* (Cambridge, Mass.: Harvard University Press, 2004). R. Barton Palmer is the only one of the aforementioned scholars who analyzes Fearing's story· in relation to the cinematic adaptation, and none compare Latimer's various scripts to Fearing's source material.

4. Jonathan Latimer completed five scripts dated 4 November 1946, 27 December 1946, 17 February 1947 (with inserts dated 20 February, 21 February, 27 February, 4 March, 5 March, 9 March, 12 March, 13 March, 31 March), 12 March 1947, and a release dialogue script dated 27 August 1947. *The Big Clock,* Paramount Script Collection (hereafter PSC), MHLC.

5. Joan Ockman, "Mirror Images: Technology, Consumption, and the Representation of Gender in American Architecture since World War II," in Agrest, Conway, and Weisman, *Sex of Architecture,* 191.

6. Ayn Rand to DeWitt Emery, 17 May 1943, quoted in Michael Berliner, ed., *Letters of Ayn Rand* (New York: Plume, 1995), 72. See also Melissa Hardie, "Fluff and Granite: Rereading Ayn Rand's Feminist Aesthetics," in *Feminist Interpretations of Ayn Rand,* ed. Mimi R. Gladstein and Chris Matthew Sciabarra (Philadelphia: Pennsylvania State University Press, 1999), 363–89.

7. Kenneth Fearing, "Reading, Writing, and the Rackets," in *New and Selected Poems* (Bloomington: Indiana University Press, 1956), xx, xxiii.

8. Kenneth Fearing to Lambert Davis, n.d., quoted in Santora, "Poetry and Prose of Kenneth Flexner Fearing," 136.

9. Ayn Rand, "To the Readers of *The Fountainhead,*" pamphlet, c. 1943 (8 pages), box 20, file 8, Ayn Rand Archives, Marina del Rey, California (hereafter ARA). This pamphlet served as a publicity vehicle to respond to the fan mail received by her publisher, Bobbs-Merrill.

10. The first annotated bibliography, dated 18 March 1936 and written on New York Public Library stationery, was "prepared by Jennie M. Flexner, Readers' advisor for Miss Rand, 66 Park Avenue." Box AYE, file B, ARA.

11. The New York Public Library bibliography included Le Corbusier, *Towards a New Architecture,* trans. Frederick Etchells (New York: Payson & Clarke, 1927); Frank Lloyd Wright, *An Autobiography* (New York: Horizon, 1932); Sheldon Cheney, *The New World Architecture* (London: Longmans, Green, 1930); Alfred Bossom, *Building to the Skies: The Romance of the Skyscraper* (London: The Studio, 1934); W. A. Starrett, *Skyscrapers and the Men Who Build Them* (New York: Scribners, 1928). The *Architect's World* bibliography included Louis Sullivan, *The Autobiography of an Idea* (New York: Press of the American Institute of Architects, 1924); Nikolaus Pevsner, *Pioneers of the Modern Movement from William Morris to Walter Gropius* (London: Faber & Faber, 1936); and Walter Behrendt, *Modern Building* (New York: McGraw Hill, 1937). She also borrowed from Arthur Tappan North, *Raymond Hood* (New York: McGraw Hill, 1931), for the delineation of some of her villains, characters who represent eclecticism and a collaborative spirit, both of which she equated with a lack of creativity. She also mined David Gray's *Thomas Hastings* (Boston: Houghton Mifflin, 1933) for her depiction of Keating and Toohey. It appeared in the initial bibliography.

12. Edward Gunts, "*The Fountainhead* at 50," *Architecture* 82 (May 1993): 36.

13. David Harriman, ed., *The Journals of Ayn Rand* (New York: Plume, 1997), 117.

Harriman included only about half of Rand's lengthy notes. In some cases, he silently omits portions of the notes that are included. Some omissions are more egregious than others. Rand took notes on Wright's *Autobiography,* of which Harriman reproduced only part on 118–22 of *The Journals.* Box 52-66B, ARA, contains the original document. A passage quoted by Harriman—"He gets a commission because the client saw in his house 'the countenance of principle.' Lack of general response to his work after a period of intensive labor, day and night"—should have this text before the word "lack": "Suggestion of a German aesthetic professional to go to Germany because America was not ready. Wright decided to stay, had future in America. Offer of book publication of his work." Her entire architectural commentary, including her annotated copies of architectural texts, is now available for study at ARA. The film's previously unexamined production notes and sketches are also available for study. The former are located in the WBA, while the latter are housed in the Harold B. Lee Library at Brigham Young University, Provo, Utah.

14. Rand, *The Fountainhead,* 592.

15. The *Architect's World* bibliography included a list of worthwhile periodicals, among them *Architectural Record, Architectural Forum, American Architect,* and *Journal of the American Institute of Architects.* It is unclear if she consulted all of these. However, she may have consulted "Public Housing," *Architectural Forum* 68 (May 1938): 345–55, since she employs many arguments concerning public housing presented in the article.

16. Coleman Woodbury, ed., *Housing Officials' Yearbook 1937* (Washington, D.C.: National Association of Housing, 1937) and *Current Developments in Housing* (Philadelphia: American Academy of Political Science, 1937) appeared in this bibliography.

17. Branden, *Passion of Ayn Rand,* 4.

18. For a further discussion of Rand's politics, see Chris Matthew Sciabarra, *Ayn Rand: The Russian Radical* (Philadelphia: Pennsylvania State University Press, 1995).

19. There is much research to be done on Rand's Russian cinema work, as well as that done after she emigrated to the United States. The ARA houses her early commentary on cinema. See Ayn Rand, *Russian Writings on Hollywood,* ed. Michael Berliner (Marina del Rey, Calif.: Ayn Rand Institute, 1999).

20. Claudia Roth Pierpont, "Twilight of the Goddess," *New Yorker* 71 (24 July 1995): 70–81; Ayn Rand to Euren Thomas, 18 October 1943, quoted in Berliner, *Letters of Ayn Rand,* 97.

21. Rand in Douglas Gilbert, "Skyscrapers 'Like Finger of God' Inspired Ayn Rand to Write," *New York Telegram,* clipping, 7 June 1943, box 23, file 11, ARA. Cheney also called the Woolworth "the finger of God," in *New World Architecture,* 119, which Rand knew well.

22. For a discussion of the skyscraper enthusiasm that characterized the 1920s, see my *Skyscraper in American Art.*

23. Rand's notes for the screenplay may be found in Harriman, *Journals of Ayn Rand,* 6–16. The film *Skyscraper* was completed in 1928, starring William Boyd and Alan Hale, but Rand's screenplay, for unknown reasons, was not used.

24. On 4 December 1935, Rand began the first of three notebooks developing the theme and characters of "Second-Hand Lives." The working title came from her definition of those who capitulated to the herd or betrayed their egos as possessing

"second-hand lives." See Harriman, *Journals of Ayn Rand,* 77. Wright employed the term "second-hand" when discussing passive adaptations of historical styles in his *Modern Architecture* (Princeton, N.J.: Princeton University Press, 1931), 9.

25. Archie Ogden, "Original Report on Ayn Rand's 'Second Hand Lives,'" c. 1943, box 93, file 1, p. 1, ARA.

26. Ayn Rand to Tom Girdler, 12 July 1943, in Berliner, *Letters of Ayn Rand,* 85.

27. Ayn Rand to Isabel Paterson, 28 February 1948, in Berliner, *Letters of Ayn Rand,* 197.

28. Vidor's annotated copy of the novel is located in the King Vidor Papers (hereafter KVP), CTL-USC. See *The Fountainhead,* 18, KVP.

29. Rand and Cooper later testified as friendly witnesses before HUAC.

30. "Architecture and Love in Mix-up," *Cue,* 19 July 1949, 22. The acting was also disparaged as "stagy and neurotic" and filled with a "vast succession of turgid scenes." See "Editor's Notes," *Senior Scholastic* 55 (26 October 1949); Bosley Crowther, *"The Fountainhead,"* *New York Times,* 9 July 1949.

31. Ted Criley, *"The Fountainhead,"* *Journal of the American Institute of Architects* 12 (July 1949): 27. Other reviews include John McCarten, "Down with Beaux-Arts," *New Yorker* 25 (18 July 1949): 41; Philip T. Hartung, "Lust for Lust," *Commonweal* 50 (29 July 1949): 390; *"The Fountainhead,"* *Newsweek* 34 (25 July 1949): 76; *"The Fountainhead,"* *Time* 54 (11 July 1949): 95.

32. Crowther, *"The Fountainhead."*

33. "Ayn Rand Responds to Criticism of Her Film," *New York Times,* 24 July 1949, sec. 2.

34. George Nelson, "Mr. Roark Goes to Hollywood," *Interiors* 45 (April 1949): 106–11; Aline Mosby, "Real Architects Flunk Colleague Gary Cooper," *Louisville Courier-Journal,* 28 July 1949, sec. 2.

35. Ayn Rand to Gerald Loeb, 11 September 1948, box 33-LO, ARA.

36. Rand to Girdler, 12 July 1943, quoted in Berliner, *Letters of Ayn Rand,* 82.

37. See Rotundo, *American Manhood,* and Kimmel, "Consuming Manhood," for a discussion of the various paradigms of masculinity in turn-of-the-century America, including genteel patriarch, marketplace man, and heroic artisan. See Kimmel, *Manhood in America,* for a further elaboration of these points.

38. For a discussion of New Deal images that merge political and gender propaganda, see Barbara Melosh, *Engendering Culture: Manhood and Womanhood in New Deal Public Art and Theater* (Washington, D.C.: Smithsonian Institution Press, 1991); Karal Ann Marling, *Wall-to-Wall America: A Cultural Study of Post Office Murals* (Minneapolis: University of Minnesota Press, 1982).

39. Lewis Hine, *Men at Work: Photographic Studies of Modern Man and Machines* (New York: Macmillan, 1932).

40. Elizabeth McCausland, "Portrait of a Photographer." *Survey Graphic,* October 1938, 504.

41. Hine, *Men at Work.*

42. Production notes, 26 January 1945, box 1, file 7, Fountainhead Material, WBA, CTL-USC. A note of 7 October 1948 mentions several books belonging to Rand, including *Men at Work* and Wright's *In the Nature of Materials,* box 23, file 54, ARA.

43. Ayn Rand to Walter Hurley, 30 November 1945, quoted in Berliner, *Letters of Ayn Rand,* 107.

44. Bossom, *Building to the Skies,* 135–37.

45. Paul Starrett, *Changing the Skyline* (New York: Whittlesey House, 1938), especially chapter 21, "The Climax," 284–308. Rand's notes on the book are in box 52-66B, file D, p. 126, ARA.

46. Summary of the last part of "Second-Hand Lives," 4 April 1938, box 5-66C, file D, p. 14, ARA.

47. See Meyers, *Gary Cooper,* 216. Meyers also likens Roark to *roar* and *rock* and identifies the name as Gaelic in origin. Rand used other hard items to describe Roark. For example, he had a "steel will, hardness and cruelty." See Harriman, *Journals of Ayn Rand,* 219.

48. "Ayn Rand, Speech to Architects," c. 1943, quoted in *The Objectivist Forum,* December 1985, 10–14, courtesy of ARA.

49. Preliminary script, 1945, Fountainhead Material, WBA, CTL-USC.

50. Le Corbusier, *Towards a New Architecture,* 14–16. The book was in Rand's bibliography; see Notes, 12 July 1937, box 52-66B, file C, ARA. A portion of her notes on Le Corbusier appear in Harriman's *Journals of Ayn Rand,* 134–35. Anthony Vidler has drawn a parallel between Roark and Le Corbusier, suggesting that both tried to conquer nature through modernist rationalism and create space by the use of, among other things, transparent glass. The connection between Roark and Le Corbusier is not entirely persuasive, since Rand disliked the International Style and did not admire the film's set designs. See Vidler, "Framing Infinity: Le Corbusier, Ayn Rand, and the Idea of 'Ineffable' Space," in *Warped Space: Art, Architecture and Anxiety in Modern Culture* (Cambridge, Mass.: MIT Press, 2000), 51–63.

51. Cheney, *New World Architecture,* 15, 85, and 92.

52. Ayn Rand, "The Only Path to Tomorrow," Committee for Constitutional Government, 1945, condensed from the essay "The Moral Basis of Individualism," 1945, box 1, file 6, p. 2, ARA.

53. See still photograph 707–67, Fountainhead Material, WBA, CTL-USC.

54. Rand, *The Fountainhead,* 92.

55. For a discussion of the figure of the courageous, risk-taking construction worker, see Poole, "Cowboys of the Skies," 641–53.

56. Rand, 6 July 1937, box 2-66B, file B, ARA. Starrett wrote: "Architects design buildings and draw plans in interpretation of the requirements of the owner. Engineers design the steel skeletons and foundations in accordance with the requirements of the design. Other engineers design heating, lighting, plumbing, ventilation in accordance with those same architectural requirements. Builders devise ways and means for payment of it all. Some men or organizations are combinations of two or more of the separate functions." Starrett, *Skyscrapers and the Men Who Build Them,* 76.

57. Rand, 6 July 1937. In a note dated 9 July 1938, she answered herself, "No!" box 2-66B, file B, ARA.

58. Rand, *The Fountainhead,* final script, 20 June 1948, The Fountainhead special box, file 1904, p. 13, Fountainhead Material, WBA, CTL-USC.

59. Starrett called stone "man's greatest and ever-lasting building material" and

"the most durable to start the base of a skyscraper." *Skyscrapers and the Men Who Build Them,* 190.

60. Rand, *The Fountainhead,* 92. The final script and the film originally included Roark's friendship with a working-class electrician named Mike Donagan, but this character was removed.

61. Still photograph 707–681, Fountainhead Material, WBA, CTL-USC. Lobby cards sent to movie theaters showed these images and had captions such as, "No man takes what's mine!" and "How much temptation did you think a man could stand?" See *The Fountainhead,* press book, 1949, 24 pages, courtesy ARA.

62. King Vidor, annotations on Rand's *The Fountainhead,* 266, KVC, CTL-USC.

63. According to Neal in *As I Am,* 97, "She looks at him wanting him. He looks up at her and then casts his weight into the drill, penetrating the rock. The sexual implications are obvious. . . . In those days, explicit sex was not permitted by the Hays Office, so Hollywood found another way to show that something sexual was going on."

64. Much of the scholarship on *The Fountainhead* concerns Rand's use of Frank Lloyd Wright as a springboard for her depiction of Roark and art director Edward Carrere's creation of architectural set designs that emulate Wright's style. The production notes, the early version of the screenplay, and Rand and Vidor's comments corroborate this adaptation. For the former, see Saint, *Image of the Architect,* and Branden, *Passion of Ayn Rand.* On Carrere, see Neumann, *Film Architecture.* For a minority opinion concerning Roark's dissimilarity to Wright, consult Meryle Secrest, *Frank Lloyd Wright* (New York: Random House, 1992).

65. According to Zeynep Celik, Sullivan borrowed extensively from Islamic ornamentation, especially in his and Dankmar Adler's Transportation Building (1893) at the World's Columbian Exposition in Chicago. For example, he employed a hierarchical treatment of surface elaboration from planar to complex ornament, which is common to Islamic architecture. Celik points out that Sullivan's search for ornamental motifs from the Orient displayed his dissatisfaction with classical sources. He sought a more egalitarian approach to ornamentation, which he believed must be an organic part of the design of a building, rather than simply affixed to the surface. See Çelik, *Displaying the Orient* (Berkeley and Los Angeles: University of California Press, 1992), 171–75.

66. Louis Sullivan, *Kindergarten Chats and Other Writings* (New York: Peter Smith, 1940), 46. *Kindergarten Chats* was originally published in serial form in the *Interstate Architect and Builder's News* between 16 February 1901 and 8 February 1902. It was first published in book form in 1918.

67. Rand, *The Fountainhead,* final script, 20 June 1948, p. 6, Fountainhead Material, WBA, CTL-USC.

68. Sullivan, *Kindergarten Chats,* 29.

69. Ibid., 64, 75–79, 129.

70. Mary McLeod, "Undressing Architecture: Fashion, Gender and Modernity," in *Architecture in Fashion,* ed. Deborah Fausch, Paulette Singley, and Rodolphe El-Khoury (New York: Chronicle, 1994), 39, 46. See also Mark Wigley, *White Walls, Designer Dresses: The Fashioning of Modern Architecture* (Cambridge, Mass.: MIT Press, 1995). For a discussion of architectural discourse and its borrowings from psychiatry, see my "Lewis Mumford's Gendered and Classed Modernism," *Architectural Theory Review* 3 (November 1998): 1–16.

71. Sullivan, *Kindergarten Chats*, 91.

72. Sarah Burns, *Inventing the Modern Artist* (New Haven: Yale University Press, 1996), 79–158.

73. Sullivan, *Autobiography of an Idea*, 31, 82.

74. Ibid., 79, 65, 271.

75. Ayn Rand to Frank Lloyd Wright, 12 December 1937, quoted in Berliner, *Letters of Ayn Rand*, 109.

76. Ibid.

77. Frank Lloyd Wright to Ayn Rand, 18 November 1938, quoted in Berliner, *Letters of Ayn Rand*, 111.

78. Wright, *Autobiography*, 7, 36.

79. Wright, *Modern Architecture*, 85; Wright, *Autobiography*, 371.

80. Frank Lloyd Wright in *Taliesin* 1 (October 1940). In *Autobiography*, 261, 361, he expresses his contempt for the American Institute of Architects and the Federal Housing Association.

81. Rand, *The Fountainhead*, final screenplay, 20 June 1948, pp. 130–31, Fountainhead Material, WBA, CTL-USC.

82. Preliminary script, n.d., Fountainhead Material, WBA, CTL-USC.

83. Ayn Rand to Henry Blanke, c. October 1945, box 33, file B, ARA. This note may not have been sent, since there is no typed copy in the archives.

84. Ibid.

85. Ibid.

86. Ibid.

87. Frank Lloyd Wright to Ayn Rand, 23 April 1944, quoted in Berliner, *Letters of Ayn Rand*, 112. Gerald Loeb to Ayn Rand, 4 October 1944, box 33, file LO, ARA. Wright's comments were reported by Loeb.

88. Frank Lloyd Wright to Henry Blanke, n.d., Frank Lloyd Wright Correspondence, copied from the Frank Lloyd Wright Foundation, ARA.

89. Frank Lloyd Wright to Gerald Loeb, 25 June 1948, Frank Lloyd Wright Correspondence, copied from the Frank Lloyd Wright Foundation, ARA.

90. Frank Lloyd Wright, quoted in "Frank Lloyd Wright Pans Stars' Homes," *Citizen*, 24 January 1950, clipping, Fountainhead Material, WBA, CTL-USC.

91. Production notes, box 1, file 7, Fountainhead Material, WBA, CTL-USC. On 3 March 1948, there was a request for Wright's *Autobiography* from the Los Angeles Public Library. His letters, two lectures, and *In the Nature of Materials* were also obtained on 7 April 1948. On 22 April 1948, *An Autobiography* was purchased by Henry Blanke. Vidor reported that he and Carrere inspected all of Wright's buildings in southern California. See Higham and Greenberg, *Celluloid Muse*, 240.

92. Neumann, *Film Architecture*, 126. For a further discussion of Wright's influence on the set designs, see Saint, *Image of the Architect*.

93. Karal Ann Marling, "A Note on New Deal Iconography: Futurology and the Historical Myth," *Prospects* 4 (1979): 421–40; Steven Gelber, "Working to Prosperity: California's New Deal Murals," *California History* 58 (Summer 1979): 98–127.

94. Rand in Gilbert, "Skyscrapers 'Like Finger of God' Inspired Ayn Rand to Write."

95. See my "Cannons Cannot Silence the Muses': The American-Soviet Art Alliance

and Propaganda during World War II," unpublished paper delivered at the American Studies Association Annual Conference, Boston, November 1993.

96. Ayn Rand to Mrs. Blodget, 28 August 1943, quoted in Berliner, *Letters of Ayn Rand,* 92.

97. Ayn Rand, "A Speech to Architects," c. 1943, in *The Objectivist Forum,* December 1985, 11, courtesy ARA.

98. Mumford, "Intolerable City," 283. For a comprehensive discussion of Mumford's more than decade-long attack on and the general disaffection with the skyscraper, see my *Skyscraper in American Art,* 93–97, 119–21.

99. Edmund Wilson, "Progress and Poverty," *New Republic* 68 (20 May 1931): 14.

100. Rand, *The Fountainhead,* 446.

101. David E. Nye writes in *American Technological Sublime,* 72: "In a physical world that is increasingly desacralized, the sublime represents a way to reinvest the landscape and the works of men with transcendent significance." The infusion of the skyscraper with spiritual significance was particularly pronounced in the 1920s, when Rand arrived in the United States. See "Aspects of Skyscraper Enthusiasm: Rationality and Transcendence," in my *Skyscraper in American Art,* 72–77. Prior to that, until about 1913, most observers worried that the skyscraper's great height threatened the spiritual values embodied in lofty ecclesiastical architecture.

102. Bossom, *Building to the Skies,* 65.

103. Rand, *The Fountainhead,* final script, 20 June 1948, p. 52, Fountainhead Material, WBA, CTL-USC.

104. Roland Marchand, in *Advertising the American Dream,* 240–42, discusses how the businessman's gaze dominated the new man-made landscape. He claims that the Olympian perspectives from their offices represented a visualization of their power and fantasies of dominion.

105. Vidler, "Framing Infinity," 51–63.

106. For additional information on the Singer Building, which was demolished in 1968, see my *Skyscraper in American Art*; Arnold Lehmann, "The New York Skyscraper: A History of Its Development, 1870–1939" (PhD diss., Yale University, 1974); and Landau and Condit, *Rise of the New York Skyscraper.*

107. Rand, *The Fountainhead,* 180, 283.

108. Harriman, *Journals of Ayn Rand,* 231.

109. For Aristotelian notions of biology, see Jennifer Bloomer, "The Matter of the Cutting Edge," in *Desiring Practices: Architecture, Gender, and the Interdisciplinary,* ed. Katerina Ruedi, Duncan McCorquodale, and Sarah Wigglesworth (London: Black Dog, 1996), 10–31.

110. Branden, *Passion of Ayn Rand,* 135.

111. Neal reported in *As I Am,* 97, that this scene was intended to imply sex without being censored by the Hays Office. At the time, she and Cooper were in the nascent stages of a love affair, which supposedly began after the film. Stephen Jackson, a Production Code administrator, wrote to Jack Warner on 24 June 1948, advising him to eliminate the word "frigid" from the screenplay and to dress Francon more fully: "The utmost care will be required to eliminate overemphasis on her lusting for the man." Production Code Material, Warner Bros. file, MHLC.

112. In Rand's notes on Bossom's *Building to the Skies,* she wrote, "He praises women's interest in the architecture of the home. (That's the reason for the monstrosities we have!) Some architects will not work for a woman client, regardless of the fee. (Good for them.)" 4 June 1937, in Harriman, *Journals of Ayn Rand,* 129.

113. For a full discussion of the feminine/masculine architectural antimony, see Beverly Gordon, "Woman's Domestic Body: The Conceptual Conflation of Women and Interiors in the Industrial Age," *Winterthur Portfolio* 31 (1996): 281–301.

114. Rand's formulation of Francon's character is discussed in Branden, *Passion of Ayn Rand,* 134.

115. Veblen, *Theory of the Leisure Class,* 179. See my "Lewis Mumford's Gendered and Classed Modernism," for a discussion of Veblen's influence on architectural modernist discourse.

116. Richard Dyer, "Postscript: Queers and Women in *Film Noir,*" in *Women in Film Noir,* ed. E. Anne Kaplan, new ed. (London: British Film Intitute, 1978; repr., 1998), 123–29; Lugoski, "Queering the (New) Deal," 4.

117. Berry, *Screen Styles,* 142–48.

118. Rand, *The Fountainhead,* 283. The actual rape scene appears in the novel on 217.

119. For a discussion of this theory, a popular idea beginning with Freud's *Feminine Psychology* (1931) and continuing into the 1940s and beyond, see Susan Brownmiller, *Against Our Will: Men, Women, and Rape* (New York: Bantam, 1975). For a discussion of the conflation of the skyscraper with rape, see Dolores Hayden, "Skyscraper Seduction: Skyscraper Rape," *Heresies* 1 (May 1977): 108–15. Hayden comments, "Roark 'takes' both the town and the world of cultured society Francon represents; in fact, early in the story, he rapes her and she is rapturous." Hayden also discusses the skyscraper as an image of Manifest Destiny.

120. Rand, *The Fountainhead,* 700 (the afterword). Robert Connell employed the term "marginalized masculinity" in *Masculinities.* Marginalized masculinities include homosexuals and men of color, who often occupy the same cultural position as the feminine. Toohey adheres to all the stereotypes associated with the depiction of gay characters enumerated by Richard Dyer in "Homosexuality and *Film Noir,*" in *The Matter of Images: Essays on Representation* (London: Routledge, 1993), 52–69.

121. Durgnat and Simon, *King Vidor,* 261.

122. Harriman, *Journals of Ayn Rand,* 165; Branden, *Passion of Ayn Rand,* 144.

123. Rand, *The Fountainhead,* 572.

124. Ayn Rand to Sylvia Austen, 29 July 1946, quoted in Berliner, *Letters of Ayn Rand,* 295.

125. Rand's notes on Arthur Woltersdorf, ed., *Living Architecture* (Chicago: A. Kroch, 1930), 27 February 1937, quoted in Harriman, *Journals of Ayn Rand,* 123.

126. For a thorough treatment of American public-housing policy during the Roosevelt administration and beyond, see Gail Radford, *Modern Housing for America: Policy Struggles in the New Deal Era* (Chicago: University of Chicago Press, 1996). Ickes's statement appears on p. 94. See also Harry C. Bredemeyer, *The Federal Public Housing Movement: A Case Study in Social Change* (New York: Ayer, 1980); "Public Housing," 345–55; C. W. Short and R. Stanley Brown, *Public Buildings: A Survey of Architecture of Projects*

Constructed by Federal and Other Governmental Bodies between the Years 1933 and 1939 (Washington, D.C.: Public Works Administration, 1939); Catherine Bauer, *A Citizen's Guide to Public Housing* (Poughkeepsie, N.Y.: Vassar College, 1940); Richard Pommer, "The Architecture of Urban Housing during the Early 1930s," *Journal of the Society of Architectural Historians* 37 (1978): 235–64.

127. For a discussion of this campaign, see Bredemeyer, *Federal Public Housing Movement,* 127–48. He provides a list of all the organizations that supported the National Real Estate Board, including the American Institute of Architects, the United States Chamber of Commerce, and various banks.

128. Rand, *The Fountainhead,* 693.

129. Hine, *Men at Work.*

130. Several sources have assisted me in my discussion of gender construction in *The Big Clock* due to their exploration of gender in film noir in general, although I favor the relational model advocated by Connell in *Masculinities.* These include Kaplan, *Women in Film Noir*; Jon Tuska, *Dark Cinema: American Film Noir in Cultural Perspective* (Westport, Conn.: Greenwood, 1984); Frank Krutnik, *In a Lonely Street: Film Noir, Genre, Masculinity* (London: Routledge, 1991); Robert J. Corber, *In the Name of National Security: Hitchcock, Homophobia and the Political Construction of Gender in Cold War America* (Durham, N.C.: Duke University Press, 1993); Dyer, "Homosexuality and *Film Noir,*" in *The Matter of Images,* 52–72; R. Barton Palmer, *Hollywood's Dark Cinema: American Film Noir* (New York: Twayne, 1994). See note 3 above for additional scholarship on the film.

131. R. Barton Palmer is one of the few scholars to analyze the film's narrative structure in political terms, arguing that the adaptation has more in common with a thriller, a "socially conservative genre form," than with film noir due to the Strouds' reestablishment of patriarchal law. Palmer also explores the relationship between the novel and the film's political intentions, although I hold different conclusions concerning the results of this exchange between author and screenwriter. Palmer has not examined the various scripts by Jonathan Latimer. See Palmer, "*Film Noir* and the Genre Continuum," 141–53.

132. The skyscraper's association with the media, especially newspapers, has been explored by Solomonson, *Chicago Tribune Tower Competition.*

133. Fearing, *The Big Clock,* 18.

134. Ibid., 15.

135. C. Wright Mills, *White Collar* (New York: Oxford University Press, 1953), 193–97.

136. Edward Dimendberg claims that the "nonsynchronous character of *film noir* is best apprehended as a tension between a residual American culture and urbanism of the 1920s and 1930s and its liquidation by the technological and social innovations accompanying World War II." See *Film Noir and the Spaces of Modernity,* 3.

137. Fearing, *The Big Clock,* 5.

138. Ibid., 10.

139. Henry-Russell Hitchcock and Philip Johnson, *The International Style* (New York: W. W. Norton, 1932; repr., 1966). The original title was *The International Style: Architecture since 1922.*

140. Barnard, *The Great Depression and the Culture of Abundance,* 41.

141. Several scholars have pointed to the use of pulp as a source for forbidden or transgressive material, including Barnard above. See also Paula Rabinowitz, *Black & White and Noir: America's Pulp Modernism* (New York: Columbia University Press, 2002).

142. Walter Benjamin, "The Author as Producer" (1934), reproduced in *Understanding Brecht,* trans. Anna Bostock, intro. by Stanley Mitchell (London: NLB, 1973), 85–103.

143. For biographical information on Fearing, see Harry R. Warfel, "Kenneth Flexner Fearing," in *American Novelists of Today* (New York: American Book, 1951), 146; "Kenneth Fearing, Author, Was 59," *New York Times,* 27 June 1961; Santora, "Poetry and Prose of Kenneth Flexner Fearing"; Ryley, *Kenneth Fearing: Complete Poems;* Barnard, *The Great Depression and the Culture of Abundance;* "Kenneth (Flexner) Fearing, 1902–1961," http://galenet.galenetgroup.com, 1–8.

144. "Portrait of a Cog" appeared in Ryley, *Kenneth Fearing: Complete Poems,* 197–98.

145. Ibid., 109–10. For a particularly good analysis of "Dirge," see Barnard, *The Great Depression and the Culture of Abundance,* 111–16. Barnard links the poem to the Marxist critique of capitalism's mechanizing regime as analyzed by both the Frankfurt school and the *New Masses* group, with which Fearing was affiliated. Barnard also likens Fearing's style to the frozen frames of both cinema and comic strips.

146. Fearing, *The Big Clock,* 27.

147. Fearing, quoted in Ryley, *Kenneth Fearing: Complete Poems,* xix.

148. This viewpoint is held by Santora, who interviewed various family members. In a letter from his first wife, Rachel Landon, to Patricia Santora, 30 December 1980, the former wrote that he was "a humanist who could also be a detached observer with sympathetic leanings toward the oppressed and exploited." See "Poetry and Prose of Kenneth Fearing," 12. But, as Ryley observed in *Kenneth Fearing: Complete Poems,* xvii, "nobody had to consult Marx to be appalled by the inequities of American capitalism in the Great Depression." Fearing himself later told the FBI that he had been a fellow traveler since 1933.

149. Fearing, quoted in Ryley, *Kenneth Fearing: Complete Poems,* xx.

150. Kenneth Fearing, *The Hospital* (New York: Random House, 1939).

151. Kenneth Fearing, *Clark Gifford's Body* (New York: Random House, 1942).

152. Fearing, "Reading, Writing, and the Rackets," xx.

153. Fearing, *The Big Clock,* 19; W. A. Swanberg, *Luce and His Empire* (New York: Charles Scribner's Sons, 1972), 153. Time-Life Inc. relocated to these new quarters in 1938.

154. Fearing, *The Big Clock,* 21.

155. Ibid., 19.

156. Fearing, "Reading, Writing, and the Rackets," x.

157. Swanberg, *Luce and His Empire,* 214.

158. James L. Baughman, *Henry Luce and the Rise of the American News Media* (Boston: Twayne, 1987), 103. See also Robert E. Herzstein, *Henry Luce: A Political Portrait of the Man Who Created the American Century* (New York: Macmillan, 1994).

159. Paul Arthur, "Shadows on the Mirror: *Film Noir* and Cold War America,

1945–1957" (PhD diss., New York University, 1985); Brian Neve, *Film and Politics in America: A Social Tradition* (London: Routledge, 1992). See also Richard Maltby, *"Film Noir*: The Politics of the Maladjusted Text," *Journal of American Studies* 18 (April 1984): 49–71. Maltby cautions against a zeitgeist approach to cinema, chastising film historians who would locate a one-to-one correspondence between historical events and the cinematic text. The most cultural history can do, he argues, is to establish a chain of plausibility for the relationship between a cultural production and a particular set of circumstances. He prefers to establish a chain of metaphor and coincidence between the "social problem crime film" and the announcement of the media blacklist in 1947. In a brief discussion of *The Big Clock* and other crime films of the period, Maltby argues that "the central protagonist of these movies is not marked as a figure of difference by conventional signs of heroism—the possession of exceptional abilities or dynamic moral certainty"—but wants to simply "re-establish a normality which has been disrupted at the start of the movie" (p. 67). While I agree with Maltby's assessment of the character's effort to reestablish normality, it is clear that Stroud possesses exceptional qualities that provide for the defeat of Janoth and the implied redemption of the corporation and skyscraper space.

160. According to James Naremore, *More Than Night: Film Noir in Its Contexts* (Berkeley and Los Angeles: University of California Press, 1998), 104, "the first decade of *film noir* was largely the product of a socially committed fraction or artistic movement in Hollywood, composed of 'Browderite' communists . . . and Wallace Democrats." He goes on to argue "that many of the best thrillers of the 1940s and early 1950s were expressions of the Popular Front and radical elements of the New Deal." While Latimer's political views are unknown, this characterization certainly applies to Fearing, who had no idea when he wrote the novel that it would be adapted to the screen.

161. Larry Ceplair and Steven Englund, *The Inquisition in Hollywood: Politics in the Film Community, 1930–1960* (New York: Anchor, 1980), 109. See also Nancy Lynn Schwartz, *The Hollywood Writers' Wars* (New York: Alfred A. Knopf, 1982).

162. Ceplair and Englund, *Inquisition in Hollywood,* 161.

163. Fearing in Ryley, *Kenneth Fearing: Complete Poems,* 238–39.

164. Fearing, "Reading, Writing, and the Rackets," xiv.

165. Ibid.

166. According to Ryley, *Kenneth Fearing: Complete Poems,* xxii, the painter Alice Neel was the model for Louise Patterson.

167. Fearing, "Reading, Writing, and the Rackets," xix.

168. Fearing, *The Big Clock,* 27.

169. Ibid., 3.

170. Ibid., 65.

171. Latimer, preliminary script, 4 November 1946, p. 46, PSC, MHLC.

172. Fearing, *The Big Clock,* 175.

173. For further information on Latimer, see Pauline Gale, "There's Money in Mystery," *The Writer* 54 (December 1941): 370–72; James R. McCahery, "Jonathan W. Latimer: An Interview," *Megavore* 11 (1980): 16–22; Bill Brubaker, *Stewards of the House: The Detective Fiction of Jonathan Latimer* (Bowling Green, Wis.: Bowling Green State University Popular Press, 1993).

174. McCahery, "Jonathan W. Latimer: An Interview," 19.

175. Palmer, *"Film Noir* and the Genre Continuum," 141–53.

176. Lehmann, "New York Skyscraper," 260–69. The Daily News Building also included "changing maps concerning the weather, the almanac, the time, and news bulletins."

177. Michel Foucault, *Discipline and Punish: The Birth of the Prison* (1975), trans. Alan Sheridan (New York: Vintage, 1979). See especially 195–228.

178. *The Big Clock,* directed by John Farrow (Paramount Studios, 1948; DVD, Universal Noir Collection, 2004).

179. Herzstein, *Henry Luce,* 270.

180. Alan Balfour, *Rockefeller Center: Architecture as Theater* (New York: McGraw-Hill, 1978). See also Koolhaas, *Delirious New York,* 178–207; Carol Herselle Krinsky, *Rockefeller Center* (New York: Oxford University Press, 1978); Stern, Gilmartin, and Mellins, *New York 1930,* 617–71.

181. "Movies—Just Fair *(The Big Clock),*" *New Republic* 118 (3 May 1948): 30; In C. V. Terry, "High-Powered Whodunit in Reverse," *New York Times,* 22 September 1946, the author referred to the Janoth Building in Fearing's novel as "high above the teeming Radio City pavements."

182. Carol Herselle Krinsky, "Rockefeller Center Sculpture," *Sculpture Review* 58 (Spring 1999): 30.

183. Latimer, preliminary script, 4 November 1946, p. 8, PSC, MHLC.

184. Swanberg, *Luce and His Empire,* 146.

185. Latimer, preliminary script, 4 November 1946, p. 4, PSC, MHLC. In this script, the painting is identified as a depiction of two angry faces.

186. David Riesman, *The Lonely Crowd: A Study of the Changing American Character* (New Haven: Yale University Press, 1950), xv.

187. William H. Whyte Jr., *The Organization Man* (New York: Simon & Schuster, 1956), 3. See also Vance Packard, *The Status Seekers* (New York: David Mackay, 1960).

188. Riesman, *Lonely Crowd,* 128. This translation from the Latin is Riesman's.

189. Whyte, *Organization Man,* 404.

190. Latimer, preliminary script, 4 November 1946, p. 78, PSC, MHLC.

191. Fearing, *The Big Clock,* 54.

192. According to Sylvia Harvey, in "Woman's Place: The Absent Family in *Film Noir,*" in Kaplan, *Women in Film Noir,* 35–46, in most film noirs, the institution of the family is absent or frustrated. In *The Big Clock,* the temporarily destabilized family is restored and presented as the normal fulfillment of desire.

193. The son appears in one of the last scripts, dated 17 February 1947, p. 9, PSC, MHLC. In prior scripts (4 November 1946 and 17 December 1946), Latimer renders the Strouds as childless, perhaps to underline Janoth's undermining of their heterosexual bond.

194. Fearing, "Reading, Writing, and the Rackets," xix.

195. Janey Place, "Women in *Film Noir,*" in Kaplan, *Women in Film Noir,* 47–68. Place differentiates between the "spider woman" and the "nurturing woman." Place also argues that the profligate expression of their sexuality, which is mingled with danger, may represent the character's quest for autonomy.

196. Fearing, *The Big Clock,* 71, 47.

197. Simon Callow, *Charles Laughton: A Difficult Actor* (New York: Gröve, 1988), 27–28. Callow explores in detail the furtive nature of Laughton's liaisons. He indulges in a bit of psychologizing, conjecturing that Laughton's ugliness might have prompted his need for beautiful men. Laughton's wife Elsa Lanchester feels that the furtiveness of his encounters represented both his guilt and need to sin. According to Christopher Isherwood, even when Laughton was fully reconciled to his homosexuality late in his life, he spoke of his relationships with tactful evasion. Appreciation is extended to my colleague Diane Borden for encouraging me to explore Laughton's biography as a way to reinforce my thesis.

198. Fearing, *The Big Clock,* 56.

199. Latimer, preliminary script, 4 November 1946, p. 7, PSC, MHLC. According to Naremore, *More Than Night,* 98–99, "classical *noir* was obsessed with sexual perversity. The villains in these pictures tend to be homosexual aesthetes . . . who threaten the values of democracy and somewhat proletarian masculinity." Ayn Rand imbued Ellsworth Toohey with these characteristics prior to the advent of noir by consulting modernist architectural discourse, itself informed by medical and psychiatric discourse.

200. Dyer, "Postscript: Queers and Women in *Film Noir,*" 123.

201. Fearing, *The Big Clock,* 85.

202. Dyer, "Homosexuality and *Film Noir,*" 67.

203. Latimer, preliminary script, 4 November 1946, 49–50, PSC, MHLC.

204. See my "Ayn Rand and King Vidor's Film *The Fountainhead,*" especially 317–19.

205. Fearing, *The Big Clock,* 85, 64, 81.

206. Corber, *In the Name of National Security,* 9–11. See also Robert J. Corber, *Homosexuality in Cold War America: Resistance and the Crisis of Masculinity* (Durham, N.C.: Duke University Press, 1997).

207. David K. Johnson, *The Lavender Scare: The Cold War Persecution of Gays and Lesbians in the Federal Government* (Chicago: University of Chicago Press, 2004), 1.

208. For a discussion of sexual conformity in the suburbs, see Elaine Tyler May, *Homeward Bound: American Families in the Cold War Era* (New York: Basic Books, 1998), especially 82–84.

209. Krutnik, *In a Lonely Street,* 125. In this description, Krutnik is referring to the film *The Maltese Falcon,* directed by John Huston (Warner Bros., 1941; DVD, Warner Home Video, 2005).

210. Joseph Breen to Luigi Luraschi, 8 February 1946, p. 1, *The Big Clock,* Production Code Files, MHLC. For a discussion of film noir, the Production Code, and the black list, see Naremore, *More Than Night,* 97–107.

211. Graham Thompson, *Male Sexuality under Surveillance: The Office in American Literature* (Iowa City: University of Iowa Press, 2003), 98. Thompson's discussion of elevator space concerns its depiction in Sloan Wilson's 1955 novel, *The Man in the Gray Flannel Suit.*

212. In a letter from Harry Caplan to Russell Holman (Paramount Pictures in New York), 12 March 1947, Caplan advises Holman that he is sending a contingent of pho-

tographers "to photograph a panoramic sky-line shot of New York just before dark and again directly after the lights are turned on in the building." In another letter from Dick Maibaum (Richard Maibaum was the producer of the film) to Gordon Jennings, 6 April 1947, Maibaum is still contemplating this visit. Both letters: Paramount Production Material, file 2, MHLC. In another letter, 17 April 1947, the former is deciding whether to play "the film in retrospect." In that event, Maibaum suggests starting the film "with a pan shot of the New York skyline at 10:45 a.m. and then move in and down toward the lobby entrance of the Janoth Building." They decided to retain the retrospective perspective of Stroud and employ a pan of the skyline at night. Paramount Production Material, file 1, MHLC.

213. For a discussion of the use of eighteenth-century notions of the picturesque, as articulated by Uvedale Price and William Gilpin, and promoted by the late nineteenth-century architectural critic Mariana Griswold Van Rensselaer, see my *Skyscraper in American Art,* 28–39. Van Rensselaer and Henry James supported the use of the picturesque in skyscraper imagery as a method for obfuscating its supposedly harsh commercial properties. Artists Childe Hassam and Joseph Pennell most commonly employed the picturesque in their depiction of skyscrapers.

214. Latimer, preliminary script, 17 February 1947, p. 1, PSC, MHLC.

215. The shot is also meant to underscore that the film opens at night during the time when there is a building-wide search for Stroud, who is entrapped within the clock. It may also signify that Janoth Enterprise employees are forced to work at all times of the day and night.

216. In a work authorization form, dated 5 March 1947, it was reported that $5,000 was budgeted, and $5,845 was the estimated cost for a miniature of the exterior of the Janoth Building. Paramount Production Material, file 2, MHLC.

217. Frank Lloyd Wright, *When Democracy Builds,* new ed., rev. and enl. (Chicago: University of Chicago Press, 1945), 30. The book was originally titled *The Disappearing City* (New York: William Farquhar Payson, 1932).

218. Hans Dreier, quoted in Anson Bailey Cutts, "Homes of Tomorrow in Movies of Today," *California Arts & Architecture* 54 (November 1938): 16; quoted in Juan Antonio Ramirez, *Architecture for the Screen: A Critical Study of Set Design in Hollywood's Golden Age,* trans. John F. Moffit (Jefferson, N.C.: McFarland, 2004), 195.

219. For information on Hans Dreier, see Hans Dreier, "Designing the Sets," in *We Make the Movies,* ed. Nancy Naumberg (New York: W. W. Norton, 1937), 80–89; Beverly Heisner, *Hollywood Art Direction in the Days of the Great Studios* (Jefferson, N.C.: McFarland, 1990); Affron and Affron, *Sets in Motion*; Ramirez, *Architecture for the Screen.* It is ironic that Boris Leven, one of Dreier's colleagues at Paramount, characterized him as somewhat of an authoritarian, who ran the operation like a military hierarchy. See Heisner, *Hollywood Art Direction,* 167. According to Ramirez, *Architecture for the Screen,* 38, Dreier was one of the most directly involved set designers. He was trained as an architect in Munich. In 1919, he began work at Universum Film AG in Berlin. He arrived in the United States in 1923, and from 1928 he served as the supervising art director at Paramount. He admired the Bauhaus, employing its spirit of teamwork and artistic training.

220. Hitchcock and Johnson, *International Style,* 13. According to "Big City Hustle-Bustle," *The Big Clock,* press book, 1948, p. 5, NYPLPA, Roland Anderson combined the actual shots of New York with set designs to create a convincing effect.

221. André Bazin, "William Wyler, or the Jansenist of Directing," *Review du Cinéma* 1 (1948): 149–73. Bert Cardullo, ed., *Bazin at Work: Major Essays and Reviews from the Forties and Fifties,* trans. Alain Piette and Bert Cardullo (New York: Routledge, 1997), 1–18. My appreciation is extended to Mark Shiel for bringing this reference to my attention.

222. *"The Big Clock,"* *New Yorker* 50 (1 May 1948), Paramount clipping file, MHLC.

223. Ockman, "Mirror Images," 191.

224. "Sensational Manhunt Behind 'Big Clock,'" *The Big Clock,* press book, p. 3, NYPLPA.

225. The use of the term "blind alleys" is borrowed from Richard Dyer who employs it to characterize the film noir narrative structure. He claims that the gay characters frequently constitute one of the "blind alleys of the narrative." See Dyer, "Homosexuality and *Film Noir,*" 67. I use it to refer to the spatial structure in *The Big Clock.*

226. According to Robert A. M. Stern, Thomas Mellins, and David Fishman, *New York 1960: Architecture and Urbanism between the Second World War and the Bicentennial* (New York: Monacelli, 1960), 46, Raymond M. Hood's McGraw Hill Building (1931) was the first International Style building in New York, but it had little impact. Virtually no corporate structures were built in the city for the next fifteen years. The International Style was first experienced by the public at the New York World's Fair. Early examples include Ely Jacques Kahn and Robert Alan Jacobs's Universal Pictures Building (1947) and Emery Roth & Sons' 505 Park Avenue (1949).

227. Frank Lloyd Wright, "Of Thee I Sing," *Shelter* (April 1932), reproduced in Bruce Brooks Pfeiffer, ed., with an intro. by Kenneth Frampton, *Frank Lloyd Wright: Collected Writings,* vol. 3: *1931–39* (New York: Rizzoli, Frank Lloyd Wright Foundation, 1992–95), 113–15. There are five volumes of the collected writings: vol. 1: *1894–1930*; vol. 2: *1930–32*; vol. 3: *1931–39*; vol. 4: *1939–49*; vol. 5: *1949–59.*

228. Frank Lloyd Wright, "For All May Raise the Flowers Now For All Have Got the Seed," *T-Square* (February 1932), reproduced in Pfeiffer, *Frank Lloyd Wright: Collected Writings,* 3:117–20. This article and "Of Thee I Sing" were written in response to the International Style exhibition at New York's Museum of Modern Art.

229. Frank Lloyd Wright, "The Art and Craft of the Machine" (1901), lecture by Wright to the Arts and Crafts Society, at Hull House, Chicago, 6 March 1901, and to the Western Society of Engineers, 20 March 1901, reproduced in *Frank Lloyd Wright: Writings and Buildings,* selected by Edgar J. Kaufmann and Ben Raeburn (New York: Meridian, 1960), 55–73.

230. Frank Lloyd Wright, "To the Fifty-Eighth," *Journal of the Royal Institute of Architects* (October 1939) as a rebuttal to criticisms spawned by a lecture he gave in London in May of 1939, reproduced in Pfeiffer, *Frank Lloyd Wright: Collected Writings,* 4:29. Other attacks on the International Style appeared in "American Architecture Today," *Weekly Bulletin of Michigan Society of Architects,* 14 July and 21 July 1931,

"Architecture of Individualism," *Trend,* March–April 1934, and *Architectural Forum* 68 (January 1938), entire issue devoted to Wright, all in Pfeiffer, *Frank Lloyd Wright: Collected Writings,* 3:50–57, 167–69, and 277–90 respectively.

231. Wright's views were echoed by architect Robert Woods Kennedy who claimed that buildings were environments in nature and that "man's spirit and intelligence are as important to his total adjustment as his body is." He argued that the "International-ist position does not allow man a soul." He also accused the style of favoring a "robot-like, impersonal concept of man." In accord with Mumford, he viewed the style to be as rigid as traditionalism. See "After the International Style—Then What?" *Architectural Forum* 99 (September 1953): 130–33, 186, 190, 194.

232. Wright, *When Democracy Builds,* 1, 7.

233. Lewis Mumford, "The Skyline—Status Quo," *New Yorker* 23 (11 October 1947): 104–10.

234. Hugh Morrison, "After the International Style—What?" *Architectural Forum* 72 (May 1940): 345–47.

235. Mumford, "The Skyline—Status Quo," 107, 109.

236. Ibid., 110.

237. The results of the symposium were published as "What Is Happening to Modern Architecture: A Symposium at the Museum of Modern Art," *Museum of Modern Art Bulletin* 15 (Spring 1948): 4–21. An excerpt from Mumford's "Skyline" column essay was reproduced, along with commentary and reactions from Alfred H. Barr Jr., Henry-Russell Hitchcock, Walter Gropius, Eero Saarinen, George Nelson, Ralph T. Walker, Christopher Tunnard, Frederick Gutheim, Marcel Breuer, Gerhard Kallmann, Talbot Hamlin, Lewis Mumford, and written correspondence from Carl Koch, Lewis Mumford, and Alfred H. Barr Jr. in response to the symposium. For discussions of the symposium, see Meredith Clausen, *Pietro Belluschi* (Cambridge, Mass.: MIT Press, 1994), 207–08, particularly concerning Mumford's call for a regional modernism, and Robert Wojtowicz, *Lewis Mumford and American Modernism: Eutopian Themes for Architecture and Urban Planning* (Cambridge: Cambridge University Press, 1996), 107–09. See Wojtowicz, 91–96, for an excellent discussion of Mumford's initial reaction to the International Style exhibition of 1932.

238. Hitchcock, in "What Is Happening to Modern Architecture," 10.

239. Barr, in ibid., 7.

240. Gropius, in ibid., 10–12.

241. Mumford, in ibid., 18–19. See also Lewis Mumford to Alfred H. Barr Jr., 20 February 1948, p. 21 in the same volume.

242. Elizabeth Gordon, "The Threat to the Next America," *House Beautiful* 95 (April 1953): 126–30, 250–51.

4. MID-CENTURY CORPORATE RENEWAL AND GENDER REALIGNMENT

1. Steven Cohan, *Masked Men: Masculinity and the Movies in the Fifties* (Bloomington: Indiana University Press, 1997), claims that many fifties films stage a crisis in a man's home life that calls his manhood into question, ultimately vindicating their breadwinner's

status. I would add that this "staged" crisis occurs in skyscraper films in the workplace as well as the domestic sphere. Male characters must seek reconciliation between these two spatial realms to fully realize their manhood.

2. "Space Planning Called New Art," *New York Times,* 9 May 1954; Jane Krieger, "Office Beautiful in Big Business," *New York Times,* 24 May 1959; John P. Callahan, "Office Designers Help Tenants Make Best Use of Costly Space," *New York Times,* 1 June 1958; "Outlook Is Good for Remodeling," *New York Times,* 27 February 1955.

3. William Attwood, "The American Male: Why Does He Work So Hard?" *Look* 22 (4 March 1958): 74; Packard, *Status Seekers,* 21.

4. See Donald Albrecht and Chrysanthe Broikos, eds., *On the Job: Design and the American Office* (Washington, D.C.: National Building Museum, 2000); Reinhold Martin, *The Organizational Complex: Architecture, Media, and Corporate Space* (Cambridge, Mass.: MIT Press, 2004). For sources on domestic space and the objects therein, see Kenneth T. Jackson, *Crabgrass Frontier: The Suburbanization of the United States* (New York: Oxford University Press, 1985); May, *Homeward Bound*; Elizabeth A. T. Smith et al., *Blueprints for Modern Living: History and Legacy of the Case Study Houses* (Cambridge, Mass.: MIT Press, 1989); Barbara Goldstein, ed., *Arts and Architecture: The Entenza Years* (Cambridge, Mass.: MIT Press, 1990); Lesley Jackson, *"Contemporary": Architecture and Interiors of the 1950s* (London: Phaidon, 1994); Stern, Mellins, and Fishman, *New York 1960*; Dolores Hayden, *Building Suburbia: Green Fields and Urban Growth* (New York: Pantheon, 2003); Sylvia Lavin, *Form Follows Libido: Architecture and Richard Neutra in a Psychoanalytic Culture* (Cambridge, Mass.: MIT Press, 2005).

5. Riesman, *Lonely Crowd*; Whyte, *Organization Man*; Mills, *White Collar.*

6. David Riesman and Eric Larrabee, "The Executive as Hero," *Fortune* 51 (January 1955): 108.

7. Cameron Hawley, *Executive Suite* (New York: Houghton Mifflin, 1952). In *Heyday: An Autobiography* (New York: Little, Brown, 1979), 196, the head of production at Metro-Goldwyn-Mayer, Dore Schary, claimed that he read *Executive Suite* first and bought the rights to it. He gave it to Houseman because he was too busy. According to Rob Davis, *"Executive Suite*: Big Business on the Big Screen," *Films of the Golden Age,* no. 34 (Fall 2003): 67, "The studio paid $5000 for an option against a $25,000 purchase price and began negotiating with Hawley to do a treatment."

8. John Houseman, *Unfinished Business: Memoirs, 1902–1988* (New York: Applause Theatre, 1989), 331. Ernest Lehman's notes on characters, early treatments of the story, partial scripts, and the final shooting script (3 June 1953) are located in the Ernest Lehman Collection (hereafter ELC), box 24, CTL-USC. Many of Lehman's notes and scripts are annotated. Director Robert Wise's annotated shooting script (3 June 1953) is located in the Robert Wise Collection (hereafter RWC), CTL-USC.

9. Arthur Knight, "Mr. Houseman's 'Executive Suite,'" *Saturday Review* 37 (1 May 1954): 33–34.

10. Houseman, *Unfinished Business,* 330.

11. Knight, "Mr. Houseman's 'Executive Suite,'" 34. Knight reported that in order "to get expert advice on the furniture business . . . Houseman consulted his friend Charles Eames, the designer. He personally scouted furniture plants for location work."

12. There is a paucity of contemporary scholarship on the film. See Peter Biskind, "I

Remember Poppa: *Executive Suite* and the Persistence of the Protestant Ethic," in *Seeing Is Believing: How Hollywood Taught Us to Stop Worrying and Love the Fifties* (New York: Henry Holt, 1983), 305–15, and Pina Ciarniello, "From Novel to Script: A Critical Analysis of the Techniques Involved in the Transliteration from Novel to Script with a Case Study of *Executive Suite*" (PhD diss., University of Southern California, 1979).

13. Eames moved to California in 1941. He designed sets for Cedric Gibbons at Metro-Goldwyn-Mayer, where he probably met Houseman. His experience in set design may have inspired the imaginative, set-like arrangement of his furniture in the Herman Miller showroom.

14. http://www.armstrong.com/corporatena/history_corporate.html. Cameron Hawley (1905–69) may have attended a conference sponsored by the Container Corporation of America in 1951 devoted to "the role of design on business today." Held in Aspen, Colorado, it included some two hundred business executives, product designers, graphic designers, and educators. One of the speakers at the conference was Don Wallance, whose name is similar to the hero of *Executive Suite,* who spoke about the responsibility of designing with the consumer in mind.

15. "A Designer's Home of His Own," *Look* 29 (September 1951): 148.

16. Hawley, *Executive Suite,* 230.

17. Ibid.

18. Ibid., 140.

19. "A Designer's Home of His Own," 152.

20. The best secondary source material on Eames includes Paul Schrader, "Poetry of Ideas: The Films of Charles Eames," *Film Quarterly* 23 (Spring 1970): 2–19; Owen Gingrich, "A Conversation with Charles Eames," *American Scholar* 46 (Summer 1977): 326–37; R. Craig Miller, "Interior Design and Furniture," in Detroit Institute of Art and Metropolitan Museum of Art, *Design in America: The Cranbrook Vision, 1925–1950* (New York: Harry N. Abrams, 1983), 91–144; John Neuhart, Marilyn Neuhart, and Ray Eames, *Eames Design: The Work of Charles and Ray Eames* (New York: Abrams, 1989); Pat Kirkham, *Charles and Ray Eames: Designers of the Twentieth Century* (Cambridge, Mass.: MIT Press, 1995); Donald Albrecht, ed., *The Work of Charles and Ray Eames: A Legacy of Invention* (New York: Abrams, 1997); Beatriz Colomina, "Enclosed Images: The Eameses' Multimedia Architecture," *Grey Room* 2 (Winter 2001): 7–29; Tamar Zinguer, "Toy," in *Cold War Hothouses: Inventing Postwar Culture from Cockpit to Playboy,* ed. Beatriz Colomina, Annmarie Brennan, and Jeannie Kim (New York: Princeton Architectural Press, 2004), 143–67.

21. Eliot Noyes, "Charles Eames," *Arts & Architecture* 63 (September 1946): 66, 72. Noyes was later hired at IBM as the head of design.

22. Hawley, *Executive Suite,* 231.

23. Buckminster Fuller's statement is as follows: "Perhaps we have been thinking that through mass production we can get something like the old line house only slightly cheaper. The word house itself seems to have almost stopped our minds from thinking of anything other than 'conventional house.' But we must point out to ourselves that it was not long after the introduction of the automobile that our whole conception of transportation changed from the pace of the horse and buggy." It appeared in "What Is a House?" *Arts & Architecture* 61 (July 1944): 39.

24. Lehman, final shooting script, 3 June 1953, p. 1, ELC, CTL-USC.

25. Lehman, treatment, 29 January 1953, p. 3, ELC, CTL-USC.

26. Lehman, treatment, 25 March 1953, cover sheet, ELC, CTL-USC. This treatment includes an undated cover sheet with comments penciled in by Lehman, probably made at the time of the donation of these materials to the Cinema and Television Library.

27. Lehman, treatment, 25 March 1953, p. 17, ELC, CTL-USC.

28. Lehman, final shooting script, 3 June 1953, p. 26, ELC, CTL-USC.

29. Quoted in Lowell E. Redelings, "The Hollywood Scene," *Hollywood Citizen-News* 18 (April 1954): 15.

30. Riesman and Larrabee, "Executive as Hero," 109.

31. Wise, final shooting script, 3 June 1953, p. 73, RWC, CTL-USC.

32. Lehman, final shooting script, 3 June 1953, p. 73, ELC, CTL-USC.

33. See illustrations for "A Rough Sketch for a Sample Lesson for a Hypothetical Course," 1953; *Travelling Boy* (film), 1950; and *House—After Five Years of Living* (film), 1955; in Neuhart, Neuhart, and Eames, *Eames Design,* 135, 177, 199.

34. For a further discussion of the erasure of Ray Eames, see Kirkham, *Charles and Ray Eames,* especially 61–96. Kirkham also discusses the multiplicity of ways that Ray contributed to the "Eames vision," as well as the dualities inherent in that vision. Indeed many of the unlikely juxtapositions were fostered by Ray Eames, not Charles. Yet the film renders the Eames aesthetic as the product of a singular male genius.

35. *Executive Suite,* directed by Robert Wise (Metro-Goldwyn-Mayer, 1954; DVD, Warner Home Video, 2007).

36. Wise, final shooting script, 3 June 1953, p. 3, RWC, CTL-USC.

37. Hawley, *Executive Suite,* 29.

38. Ibid., 27.

39. Redelings, "Hollywood Scene," 15. In the novel, the boardroom is rendered in sixteenth-century period style.

40. Lehman, final shooting script, 3 June 1953, p. 10, ELC, CTL-USC.

41. Hawley, *Executive Suite,* 52. Lehman followed Hawley's characterization. He described Alderson in the following terms: "The man behind the desk is part of that careful pattern. He is about sixty, not a white hair out of place about his lean handsome features." See Lehman, final shooting script, 3 June 1953, p. 10, RWC, CTL-USC.

42. Philip Wylie, *Generation of Vipers* (New York: Farrar & Rinehart, 1942), 188.

43. Lehman, final shooting script, 3 June 1953, with inserted changes dated 3 July 1953, p. 49, RWC, CTL-USC.

44. Lehman, final shooting script, 3 June 1953, p. 14, ELC, CTL-USC.

45. *The Asphalt Jungle,* directed by John Huston (Warner Bros., 1950; DVD, Warner Home Video, 2004), also starred Marilyn Monroe.

46. Wise, final shooting script, 3 June 1953, insert dated 20 August 1953, p. 44, RWC, CTL-USC.

47. Lehman, preliminary script, 21 February 1953, p. 16, ELC, CTL-USC.

48. Lehman, preliminary script, 21 February 1953, p. 17, ELC, CTL-USC.

49. Wise, final shooting script, 3 June 1953, p. 32, RWC, CTL-USC.

50. Lehman, final shooting script, 3 June 1953, p. 32, ELC, CTL-USC.

51. Hawley, *Executive Suite,* 330.

52. Lehman, treatment, 29 January 1953, p. 9, ELC, CTL-USC.

53. Lehman, final shooting script, 3 June 1953, p. 62A, ELC, CTL-USC.

54. "Hollywood Discovers the U.S. Business Drama," *Newsweek* 43 (3 May 1954): 90. Most of the reviews were very favorable. Both *Newsweek* and *Time* gave it a cover story, and *Redbook* named it "Picture of the Month." Riesman and Larrabee's article in *Fortune* was the first time the magazine devoted a full-length article to a film. The reviews include "Executive Suite," *Variety,* 23 February 1954, ELC, CTL-USC; "'Executive Suite' Dynamic Drama; Certain B.O. Smash," *Hollywood Reporter,* 23 February 1954, ELC, CTL-USC; Henry Hart, *"Executive Suite," Films in Review* 5 (March 1954): 138–40; Florence Somers, *"Executive Suite," Redbook* 103 (May 1954): 6; Marilla Waite Freeman, "New Films from Books *(Executive Suite),*" *Library Journal* 79 (15 April 1954): 766; "'Executive Suite' Shines with Greatest Array of Stars Since 'Grand Hotel,'" *Los Angeles Herald & Express,* 16 April 1954, ELC, CTL-USC; Philip T. Hartung, "Big and Monkey Business," *Commonweal* 60 (30 April 1954): 96–97; Robert Kass, "Film and TV," *Catholic World* 179 (May 1954): 142–43; Bosley Crowther, "Executive Suite," *New York Times,* 7 May 1954; Otis L. Guernsey Jr., "Executive Suite," *Tribune,* 7 May 1954, ELC, CTL-USC; "Executive Suite," *Time* 63 (10 May 1954): 48; John McCarten, "Executive Suite," *New Yorker* 30 (15 May 1954): 74–75; Allan Seager, "Executive Suite: The Power and the Prize," *Nation* 37 (11 December 1954): 506–8; Knight, "Mr. Houseman's 'Executive Suite,'" 33–34; Riesman and Larrabee, "Executive as Hero," 106–11.

55. Lehman, final shooting script, 3 June 1953, p. 62B, ELC, CTL-USC.

56. Lehman, final shooting script, 3 June 1953, p. 85, ELC, CTL-USC.

57. Wise, final shooting script, 3 June 1953, p. 97, RWC, CTL-USC.

58. Auren Uris, *The Efficient Executive* (New York: McGraw-Hill, 1957), 296.

59. Perrin Stryker, "Who Are the Executives?—I," in Editors of *Fortune, The Executive Life* (New York: Doubleday, 1956), 16.

60. T. J. Jackson Lears, "A Matter of Taste: Corporate Cultural Hegemony in a Mass-Consumption Society," in *Recasting America: Culture and Politics in the Age of the Cold War,* ed. Lary May (Chicago: University of Chicago Press, 1989), 38–57.

61. Mike Davis, *Prisoners of the American Dream: Politics and Economy in the History of the American Working Class* (London: Verso, 1986), 119–20. See Davis's "Boulwarism: The First Knell," 117–21, and "The Management Offensive of 1958–1963," 121–24. The term Boulwarism has become synonymous with deunionization. See also David Harvey, *The Condition of Postmodernity: An Inquiry into the Origins of Cultural Change* (London: Basil Blackwell, 1989), especially 132–40.

62. N. F. Hall, *Making of Higher Executives: The Modern Challenges* (New York: School of Commerce, Accounts, and Finance, New York University, 1958), 1.

63. Sloan Wilson, *The Man in the Gray Flannel Suit* (New York: Simon and Schuster, 1955).

64. Crawford Greenewalt, *Uncommon Men: The Individual in the Organization* (New York: New York University Press, 1959), 78, 84. See Barbara Ehrenreich, *The Hearts of Men: American Dreams and the Flight from Commitment* (New York: Anchor/Doubleday, 1983); Elizabeth Long, *The American Dream and the Popular Novel* (Boston: Routledge

& Kegan Paul, 1985), 148–65; Catherine Jurca, *White Diaspora: The Suburb and the Twentieth-Century American Novel* (New Haven: Yale University Press, 2001). Jurca finds it odd that so much dissatisfaction is registered during a period of such material plentitude.

65. Herryman Maurer, "Who Are the Executives?—II," in *The Executive Life,* 35.

66. George Kienzle, *Climbing the Executive Ladder: A Self-Training Course for People Who Want to Succeed* (New York: McGraw-Hill, 1950), 21–26.

67. Ralph Damon, quoted in *The Executive Life,* 19. Kienzle concurred. See *Climbing the Executive Ladder,* 35.

68. William H. Whyte Jr., "How Hard Do Executives Work?" in *The Executive Life,* 65; Attwood, "The American Male," 71. Attwood also treats the pressures of commuting.

69. Charles Huston, "Management's Responsibility for Executive Health," in *The Man in Management: A Personal View,* General Management Series 189 (New York: American Management Association, 1957), 33.

70. Kienzle, *Climbing the Executive Ladder,* 224.

71. Ray Josephs, *Streamlining Your Executive Workload* (Englewood Cliffs, N.J.: Prentice-Hall, 1958), 3.

72. Richard Austin Smith, "How Executives Crack Up," in *The Executive Life,* 80.

73. Uris, *Efficient Executive,* 269. In Shepherd Mead's popular parody of the self-help book, *How to Succeed in Business without Really Trying* (New York: Simon & Schuster, 1952), in a chapter entitled "How to Stop Being a Junior Executive," 82, he encourages the upstart to assume a "look of suffering." The best way to manage this is to appear to have an ulcer. "Grow one if you can, but if you cannot, a bottle of milk placed conspicuously on the desk will do nicely, if accompanied by a pained smile."

74. Smith, "How Executives Crack Up," 85.

75. Uris, *Efficient Executive,* 280.

76. Smith, "How Executives Crack Up," 79–93. In his chapter "How to Work Under Pressure," in *Efficient Executive,* 269, Uris lists several other dramatic titles, including "Executive Crack-up," "Your Next Promotion Can Kill You," and "Why Do Executives Die Young?"

77. Smith, "How Executives Crack Up," 79.

78. Ibid., 83–84. For a further discussion of "executive menopause," see Dero A. Sauders, "Executive Discontent," *Fortune* 54 (October 1956), 156.

79. Huston, "Management's Responsibility for Executive Health," 37.

80. Smith, "How Executives Crack Up," 92.

81. Edmund Jacobson, *You Must Relax: A Practical Method for Reducing the Strains of Modern Living* (New York: Whittesley House, 1934). Other editions include New York: McGraw-Hill, 1942; New York: Blue Ribbon Books, 1946; New York: Whittesley House, 1948; New York: McGraw-Hill, 1957. Kienzle devotes considerable attention to Jacobson's book in *Climbing the Executive Ladder,* 227–34, in a chapter entitled "How to Relax." See also "How Executives Relax—The Choice: Slow Down or Blow Up," *Time* 67 (23 January 1956): 84.

82. Kienzle, *Climbing the Executive Ladder,* 234.

83. Uris, *Efficient Executive,* 283.

84. Whyte, "How Hard Do Executives Work?" 70.

85. J. Robert Moskin, "The American Male—Why Women Dominate Him?" *Look* 22 (4 February 1958): 79.

86. William H. Whyte Jr., "The Wives of Management," *Fortune* 44 (October 1951): 86–88, 204–6, 208–13; Whyte, "The Corporation and the Wife," *Fortune* 44 (November 1951): 109–13, 150–54, 156, 158.

87. In spite of the appearance of female executives, in 1956 the *New York Times* reported that female board members were still "scandalously low," since women seeking professions were still shepherded into secretarial work or stenography. Berenice Fitzgibbon, "Tips for Would-be Women Bosses," *New York Times,* 23 September 1956; "Cherchez la Femme (Executive)," *New York Times,* 3 August 1958. For a discussion of women's education after World War II, see Susan M. Hartmann, *The Home Front and Beyond: American Women in the 1940s* (Boston: Twayne, 1982), 113. Several self-help books written for men included sections on how to work with female professionals. Frederick C. Dyer's *Executive Guide to Handling People* (New York: Prentice-Hall, 1958) included a chapter entitled, "Executives and Workers with a Difference!—Working with Women in Business," in which he encouraged male executives to treat women as they themselves would like to be treated. Irving Goldenthal's *How to Be a Successful Executive* (Philadelphia: Chilton, 1960) had a section called, "The Ladies Are Joining Us," which included a close-up photograph of a screaming woman's face duplicated six times, reinforcing the stereotype of the hysterical woman, which was not echoed in the text. For favorable treatments concerning women executives, see Joy Stephens, "They Liked Their Woman Boss," *Independent Woman* 32 (February 1953): 42, which points implicitly to the novelty of the situation, while trying to counter the stereotype of the difficult female boss. See also "Keys to Executive Development," *Independent Woman* 35 (March 1956): 19–20; Dona Dickey Guyer, "Brass Hats in Petticoats," *National Businesswoman* 37 (July 1958): 18.

88. Wilson, "Acknowledgments," in *The Man in the Gray Flannel Suit*; "Young Executive in a Hurry," *Life* 44 (13 January 1958): 89–90, which concerns the new female president and director of Henry Bendel, a high-end woman's clothing store. According to Stephen M. Gelber, *Hobbies: Leisure and the Culture of Work in America* (New York: Columbia University Press, 1999), 255, 282–84, the war loosened gender distinctions with regard to household repair and home maintenance, but he claims that women's participation in the "do-it-yourself" movement of the fifties was circumscribed.

89. Thomas Watson Sr., quoted in Whyte, "The Corporation and the Wife," 111.

90. "Sizing Up Executives' Wives," *Newsweek* 49 (13 May 1957): 93.

91. Whyte, "Wives of Management," 86.

92. Whyte, "The Corporation and the Wife," 110.

93. "Sizing Up Executives' Wives," 93.

94. Whyte, "The Corporation and the Wife," 109–10. This view was also put forth in the advice literature. See Goldenthal, *How to Be a Successful Executive,* 12. The liability of "bad wives," is discussed in Carroll Shartle, *Executive Performance and Leadership* (New York: Prentice-Hall, 1956), in a section entitled "The Role of the Spouse."

95. Kienzle, *Climbing the Executive Ladder,* 57.

96. Josephs, *Streamlining Your Executive Workload,* dedication.

97. "Sizing Up Executives' Wives," 94.

98. Ibid.; Whyte, "Wives of Management," 213.

99. Ray Lewis and Rosemary Shartle, *The Managers: A New Examination of the English, German, and American Executive* (New York: Mentor, 1958), 203.

100. Martin Revson, quoted in Whyte, "The Corporation and the Wife," 150.

101. "Sizing Up Executives' Wives," 94.

102. Ibid., 95.

103. Twentieth Century–Fox's CinemaScope *The Best of Everything,* directed by Jean Negulesco (1959; DVD, Twentieth Century–Fox Home Video, 2005). The fictional Fabian Publishing Company was located in the newly completed Seagram's Building (1958).

104. Kienzle, *Climbing the Executive Ladder,* 170.

105. Shartle, *Executive Performance and Leadership,* 31, 36.

106. Whyte, "How Hard Do Executives Work?" 75.

107. Riesman, *Lonely Crowd,* xv, xviii.

108. Whyte, "How Hard Do Executives Work?" 62.

109. Chris Argyris, *Executive Leadership: An Appraisal of a Manager in Action* (New York: Harper & Brothers, 1953).

110. Uris, *Efficient Executive,* 217–26; Kienzle, *Climbing the Executive Ladder,* 177. See also M. Joseph Dooher and Vivienne Marquis, *The Development of Executive Talent* (New York: American Management Association, 1952).

111. IBM's own showroom at 590 Madison Ave. in New York had recently been remodeled by Eliot Noyes. For further discussion of Noyes's redesign of the IBM showroom and its various computers, see John Harwood, "The White Room: Eliot Noyes and the Logic of the Information Age Interior," *Grey Room* 11 (Summer 2003): 5–31; Martin, *Organizational Complex,* 168–81; Thomas J. Watson Jr., *Father & Son: My Life at IBM and Beyond* (New York: Random House, 1990), 258–62. Martin discusses the grey-suited character of the machines and likens them to a mechanical version of the Organization Man. He also points to the manner in which the machines were subject to a practice of "architecturalization," taking on the appearance of a house by Ludwig Mies van der Rohe. In my view, the modular computers also resemble the compact and colored storage cabinets being produced by Charles Eames at that time.

112. For an excellent discussion of Fox's pioneering of CinemaScope, see John Belton, *Widescreen Cinema* (Cambridge, Mass.: Harvard University Press, 1992), 138–57. See also Barry Salt, *Film Style and Technology: History and Analysis,* 2nd ed. (London: Starword, 1992), especially 246–47.

113. See "Calculatin' Emmy," *Business Machines* 40 (5 July 1957): 11, for a discussion of the IBM machines employed in the first scene. Courtesy of the IBM Corporate Archives, Somers, New York (hereafter IBMA).

114. Sidney Skolsky, "Hollywood Is My Beat," *New York Post,* 13 December 1956, IBMA.

115. Scholars who have contributed to my general ideas on human, hence gender, mediation by the computer include Sherry Turkle, *The Second Self: Computers and the Human Spirit* (New York: Simon and Schuster, 1984); Donna Haraway, *Simians, Cyborgs and Women: The Reinvention of Nature* (New York: Routledge, 1991); Martin, *Organizational Complex,* 17–27. Martin explores the dystopian implications of Wiener's theories,

which link bodies and machines in one vast network, in which humans could ulti-mately be left out of the loop, while Haraway sees the cyborg, a fusion of machine and organism, as holding possibilities for a more liberated feminine identity occasioned by a female-computer interface. In *The Human Use of Human Beings: Cybernetics and Society* (New York: Houghton Mifflin, 1950; repr., 1954), 26–27, 31–32, Norbert Wiener claimed that "words such as life, purpose, and soul are grossly inadequate to precise scientific thinking," gaining their significance from specious calls to the unity of certain phe-nomena. In Wiener's view, "life-imitating machines" also share similarities with living organisms, prompting us to refer to them as neither biological nor mechanical. Wiener also discusses at length the "performative" characteristics of machines in concert with humans, thereby suggesting the changing character of both through feedback.

116. Edmund Berkeley, *Giant Brains or Machines That Think* (New York: John Wiley, 1949); C. John Lear, "Can a Mechanical Brain Replace You?" *Collier's* 131 (April 1953): 58–63; S. Fliegers, "Will Machines Replace the Human Brain?" *American Mercury* 70 (January 1953): 53–61; Robert Kapp, "Do Electronic Brains Really Think?" *Science Digest* 33 (March 1953): 75–79.

117. "Whiz Kid," in Exhibitor's Campaign Book for *Desk Set,* 1957, p. 3, Twentieth Century–Fox Collection (hereafter TCFC), CTL-USC.

118. Wiener, *Human Use of Human Beings,* 18.

119. Tauranac, *Empire State Building,* 290–95, 335–37.

120. Emmarac is also similar to J. Presper Eckert and John Mauchley's ENIAC (1946). Early computers were often affixed with acronymic names, heir to their mili-tary legacy. Joel Shurkin, *Engines of the Mind: A History of the Computer* (New York: W. W. Norton, 1984), 250–53; Martin Campbell-Kelly and William Aspray, *Computer: A History of the Information Machine* (New York: Basic Books, 1996), 22–24; Emerson Pugh, *Building IBM: Shaping an Industry and Its Technology* (Cambridge, Mass.: MIT Press, 1995); Paul E. Ceruzzi, *A History of Modern Computing* (Cambridge, Mass.: MIT Press, 1998); Paul Rojas, *Encyclopedia of Computers and Computer History,* vol. 2 (Chi-cago: Fitzroy, Dearborn, 2001). In 1945, John von Neumann wrote a paper including the idea of a "stored program." He suggested that instructions for the computer entered on punched computer tape, or by "plug boards," "could be stored in the computer's memory as numbers." Program sequences could be made and modified by the computer as it went along. See Glen Fleck, ed., *A Computer Perspective* (by the office of Charles and Ray Eames), intro. by I. Bernard Cohen (Cambridge, Mass.: Harvard University Press, 1973), 137. EMMARAC is a comparable computer that can be programmed with an entire library's information rather than numbers, a fictional machine that was not possible in 1957.

121. See Cheryl Malone, "Imagining Information Retrieval in the Library: *Desk Set* in Historical Context," *IEEE Annals of the History of Computing,* July–September 2002, 14–21. Malone offers useful information on the history of computing in the United States and introduces several of the important theoreticians who provided information to the public, such as Wiener. She also addresses briefly the issue of the feminine space of the library, but in contrast to my own work, she views the story as one of "woman against the machine, with woman mastering the machine as part of the happy end-ing." For other articles that deal with the film's exploration of library-related issues,

see Cheryl LaGuardia, "*Desk Set* Revisited: Reference Librarians, Reality, & Research Systems' Design," *Journal of Academic Librarianship* 21 (January 1995): 7–9; Carol Colatrella, "From *Desk Set* to *The Net*: Women and Computing Technology in Hollywood Films," *Canadian Review of American Studies* 3 (2001): 1–13. My own research on *Desk Set* commenced in 2001. See my "The Film *Desk Set* (1957): Skyscrapers, Gendered Space, and the Computer," Proceedings for *Additions* to Architectural History, XIX Conference of Society of Architectural Historians of Australia and New Zealand (SAHANZ), 2002, 16pp.

122. The name Emmy also doubled as a term associated with television award ceremonies, which further asserted IBM's superiority over its competitors. The computer was first nicknamed Emmy in Marchant's play. Twentieth Century–Fox saw fit to capitalize on it when the Emmy awards were created in 1957. See "She's No Dope," in Exhibitor's Campaign Book for *Desk Set,* 1957, p. 2, TCFC, CTL-USC.

123. Phoebe Ephron and Henry Ephron, final shooting script, 7 January 1957, p. 87, coll. 73, box F-358, Twentieth Century–Fox material, Young Library, Art and Special Collections, University of California, Los Angeles (hereafter TCFM-UCLA).

124. William Marchant, *The Desk Set: A Comedy in Three Acts* (New York: Samuel French, 1955). In Marchant's version, Bunny marries Abe Cutler, a slightly feminized mother's boy, instead of Sumner. There is also much more tension between Bunny and Sumner. He classifies her as a "freak," and an "unreconstituted old maid," while one of the research librarians calls him a "robot." See 31, 73. Twentieth Century–Fox's Phoebe and Henry Ephron, writer and producer respectively, were similar to Ruth Gordon and Garson Kanin, who usually wrote for Tracy and Hepburn. See Charles Higham, *The Life of Katharine Hepburn* (New York: W. W. Norton, 1975); Henry Ephron, *We Thought We Could Do Anything: The Life of Phoebe and Henry Ephron* (New York: Norton, 1977).

125. See scripts dated 16 August 1956, 27 August 1956, and 7 January 1957, TCFC, CTL-USC.

126. Robert Jungk, *Tomorrow Is Already Here,* trans. Marguerite Waldman, with an intro. by Herbert Agar (New York: Simon and Schuster, 1954), 177–78. See also "The Thinking Machine," *Time* 55 (23 January 1950): 54–60.

127. Ephron and Ephron, final shooting script, 7 January 1957, p. 12, TCFM-UCLA.

128. Richard L. Coe, "Stars Sparkle in 'Desk Set,'" *Washington Post and Times Herald,* 28 May 1957, public relations/subject clippings, 1955–57, IBMA. Herb Stein echoed this opinion. He reported that "IBM public relations men here from New York going over 'The Desk Set' picture at 20th with Walter Lang and producer Henry Ephron for the tie-ups and mutual promotions. The IBM machines are used throughout the movie." See "Hollywood," *New York Telegraph,* 6 April 1957, public relations collection, IBMA. See also Judith Crist, "A Pair of Screen Comedies," *New York Herald Tribune,* 12 May 1957.

129. "IBM Units in Movie," *San Jose Mercury-News,* 26 May 1957, public relations/subject clippings, IBMA. See Hal Morris, "Hollywood Film Makers Role on 38 Pictures," *Los Angeles Mirror News,* 21 January 1957, IBMA. Morris reported that "several tons of equipment has been delivered to Twentieth Century Fox from International Business Machines in Poughkeepsie, New York. What's Twentieth Century doing with the electronic brain? It is the chief prop and 'heavy' in the Cinemascope film, 'The Desk

NOTES TO CHAPTER 4 ⋏ 335

Set.'" See also "IBM Machines on Display," *Box Office* (Kansas City), 17 August 1957: "Joe Ruddick manager of the Fox Theater, Joplin, Mo., arranged with IBM to display a 1900 pound accounting machine in the lobby for 'Desk Set.'" "Movie Will Feature IBM Data Machines," *Rochester Minnesota Post-Bulletin,* 22 June 1957. "IBM in Tie-up with 'Desk Set,'" *Showmen's Trade Review,* 18 May 1957.

130. "IBM to Aid 'Desk Set,'" *Motion Picture Daily,* n.d., public relations collection, IBMA. See note 128 above for Herb Stein's report in the *New York Telegraph,* 6 April 1957.

131. "'Emmerac' *[sic]* On the 'Set': Machine Steals Show," *San Diego Union,* 26 May 1957, public relations/subject clippings, IBMA. For other film reviews, see Sam Lerner, "Tracy Hepburn, I.B.M. Star in Hilarious Film," *Chicago Daily News,* 22 May 1957; James Powers, "'Desk Set' Is a Riotous Comedy with Smart Cast," *Hollywood Reporter,* 10 May 1957. Powers recognized the Ephrons' optimistic conclusion but believed that "most of us are crowded and menaced by machines of increasing size and cerebral dimensions." Bosley Crowther, "Desk Set," *New York Times,* 15 May 1957, sec. 1; "Desk Set," *Variety,* 5 May 1957, 6; Jesse Zunser, "Desk Set," *Cue,* 18 May 1957, 10–11; "Desk Set," *New Yorker* 21 (25 May 1957); "The Most Amicable Combatants," *New Yorker,* 23 September 1972, 64–67.

132. Skolsky, "Hollywood Is My Beat"; "'Emmerac' On the 'Set,'" IBMA.

133. "Office Robots," *Fortune* 45 (January 1952): 52–57, 112–14, and 117–18.

134. Shurkin, *Engines of the Mind,* 250–53; Campbell-Kelly and Aspray, *Computer,* 22–24; Pugh, *Building IBM.*

135. Rojas, *Encyclopedia of Computers and Computer History,* 2:785–88.

136. William Rodgers, *Think: A Biography of the Watsons and IBM* (New York: Stein & Day, 1965); James Cortada, *Before the Computer: IBM, NCR, Remington Rand and the Industry They Created* (Princeton, N.J.: Princeton University Press, 1993).

137. "The 701—TV Star of 'Today,'" *Business Machines* 38 (18 March 1955): 12. The following articles also appeared in the IBM publication, *Business Machines*: "Giant 'Brains' Came to Free Men's Minds," 37 (1 January 1954): 12–13; "Producing . . . 'The Right Touch,'" 38 (5 January 1955): 7; "Kerry Drake and IBM," 37 (29 January 1954): 12–13; "'Mr. 604' Stars on TVs 'Adventure' Program," 38 (5 April 1955): 8; "Highlights in Pictures," 38 (1 July 1955): 7; "The Electronic Stars of Television," 38 (7 October 1955): 3–5; "IBM on TV," 38 (7 November 1955): 5; "Checkers Anyone?" 39 (29 March 1956): 10; "How NBC and IBM Will Cover Election Night," 39 (22 October 1956): 5; "TV Plays a Role in Stockholders Meeting," 40 (17 June 1957): 14; "On TV's 'See It Now': President Watson Views Automation," 40 (5 July 1957): 7. All articles courtesy of IBMA.

138. "'Emmerac' On the 'Set,'" IBMA. See R. V. Tozzi, "Desk Set," *Films in Review* 8 (June–July 1957): 279–80.

139. Martin, *Organizational Complex,* 171–72; Watson, *Father & Son,* 259–60.

140. Martin, *Organizational Complex,* 178.

141. William Aspray and Donald deB. Beaver, "Marketing the Monster: Advertising Computer Technology," *Annals of the History of Computing* 8 (April 1986): 127–43. This article concerns IBM's advertising strategies, with emphasis on the years from 1960 on. Thanks to IBMA for providing me with at least twenty-five ads from the 1950s, which

were concentrated in business and trade periodicals. However, computer ads also appeared in *Women's Wear Daily, Fortune, Time, Business Week, U.S. News & World Report,* and *Newsweek.*

142. *The Information Machine: Creative Man and the Data Processor* (1957), color, 10 minutes. Appreciation is extended to Paul Lasewicz at IBMA for providing me with a copy of the film. The only discussion of this film occurs in Neuhart, Neuhart, and Eames, *Eames Design,* 223. Neuhart lists the date of the film as 1957, while IBM dates it as 1958. Schrader and Colomina do not explore this film in their treatments of the Eameses' films. See note 20 above. The Eameses' other films for IBM include *Introduction to Feedback* (1960), *Mathematica: A World of Numbers . . . and Beyond* (1961), *IBM Fair Presentation #1 and #2* (1962–63), and *IBM Corporation Pavilion for the New York World's Fair* (1964–65). The Eames office also designed the exhibition *A Computer Perspective* for IBM. It was the source for the 1973 book of the same title.

143. David F. Noble, *Forces of Production: A Social History of Industrial Automation* (New York: Knopf, 1984), 49.

144. John Diebold wrote widely on the improvement of jobs and working conditions realized through automation. See "Factories without Men," *Nation* 27 (19 September 1953): 227–28; "Automation and Jobs: The Effect on the Worker," *Nation* 27 (3 October 1953): 271–72; "Labor and Automation," *Automatic Control* 2 (January 1955): 48.

145. This was one of Diebold's major claims. In "Automatic Control: Today's Industrial Revolution," *Automatic Control* 1 (July 1954): 6–15, he includes a chart in which he credits automation with creating "more output, less work, and more vacation." See also "Automation and Jobs," 272, for an extensive discussion of the leisure supposedly afforded by automation, which would result in a more meaningful life, according to Diebold.

146. Paul N. Edwards, *The Closed World: Computers and the Politics of Discourse in Cold War America* (Cambridge, Mass.: MIT Press, 1996), xiii, 21, 43, 60–61.

147. Alan M. Turing, "Computing Machinery and Intelligence," *Mind* 59 (1950), 433–60, http://www.loebner.net/Prizef/TuringArticle.html.

148. *Desk Set,* directed by Walter Lang (Twentieth Century–Fox, 1957; DVD, Twentieth Century–Fox Home Entertainment, 2004).

149. Norbert Wiener, *Cybernetics; or Control and Communications in the Animal and the Machine* (Cambridge, Mass: Technology Press, 1948); Wiener, *Human Use of Human Beings.*

150. Flo Conway and Jim Siegelman, *Dark Hero of the Information Age: In Search of Norbert Wiener the Father of Cybernetics* (New York: Basic Books, 2005), 135. See also P. R. Masani, *Norbert Wiener, 1864–1964* (Basel: Birkhauser Verlag, 1990); Freeman Dyson, "The Tragic Tale of a Genius" (Review of Conway and Siegelman's *Dark Hero of the Information Age*), *New York Review of Books* 52 (14 July 2005): 10–13. Conway and Siegelman provide an excellent synopsis of the three major cybernetics conferences prior to the publication of Wiener's first book and the protagonists who participated, outside the scope of this study. Two were funded by the Josiah Macy Jr. Foundation. The first took place in New York on 13 May 1942, and included Warren McCullough, a neurophysiologist, Lawrence Kubie, a neurologist and psychoanalyst, Arturo Rosen-

blueth, a neurophysiologist, and anthropologists Gregory Bateson and Margaret Mead, among others, attesting to the interdisciplinary character of the group. The second Macy conference took place in March of 1946 and included many of the same participants, along with learning theorist Lawrence Frank, and Gestalt psychologist Heinrich Klüver. It was entitled, "The Feedback Mechanism and Circular Causal Systems in Biology and Social Science Meeting." See Conway and Siegelman, *Dark Hero of the Information Age,* 146–53, 154–70. In December 1944, Wiener organized a two-day conference at Princeton for mathematicians, engineers, and neurophysiologists working in the computer field. This conference included the mathematician John von Neumann, who was instrumental in the fabrication of the EDVAC computer in 1945.

151. Wiener, *Human Use of Human Beings,* 16.

152. Norbert Wiener, "A Scientist Rebels," *Atlantic Monthly* 179 (January 1947): 46.

153. Norbert Wiener to Walter Reuther, 13 August 1949, Wiener Papers, MIT Archives, quoted in Noble, *Forces of Production,* 76.

154. Norbert Wiener, "Cybernetics and Society," in *Cybernetics and Society: The Second Industrial Revolution, A Symposium by Norbert Wiener* (New York: Executive Techniques, 1950), 20, 23. Although Conway and Siegelman and Masani (see note 150 above) include comprehensive lists of Wiener's publications, they omit this source, which is important for evaluating Wiener's association with management and his views on the effects of computerization on white-collar labor. Other speakers included Carl Hayer, executive assistant to the Mayor's Committee on Management Survey, City of New York; Alex W. Rathe, associate professor of Management Engineering, New York University; Al Seares, vice president and general manager, Remington Rand; and Luther Gulick, president, Institute of Public Administration, and executive director, Mayor's Committee on the Management Survey, City of New York. In the introduction by Carl Hayer, he asserted that while a representative of IBM was not on the panel, "that company very kindly arranged to conduct interested groups . . . through its New York exhibit of the latest developments in its computing machines" (8).

155. Wiener, *Human Use of Human Beings,* 16, 185. John Diebold also viewed the "current obsession with the novelty and spectacular performance of automatic controls" as diverting "attention from the problems of their application to industry. Although automatic control mechanisms are *necessary* for the achievement of fully automatic factories, they are not *sufficient* in themselves." See *Automation: The Advent of the Automatic Factory* (New York: D. Van Nostrand, 1952), 2.

156. "Women's Roles in the 1950s," in http://www.enotes.com/1950-lifestyles-social-trends-american-decades/womens-roles.

157. Roddy F. Osborn, "GE and Univac: Harnessing the High Speed Computer," *Harvard Business Review* 32 (July–August 1954): 106.

158. Ellen Lupton, *Mechanical Brides: Women and Machines from Home to Office* (New York: Princeton Architectural Press, 1993), 28–41.

159. Jungk, *Tomorrow Is Already Here,* 177–78.

160. Marchant, *The Desk Set,* unrevised version, p. 9, TCFC, CTL-USC.

161. "His Other Woman," *Films and Filming* 3 (August 1957): 24.

162. Ephron and Ephron, final shooting script, 7 January 1957, p. 112, TCFM-UCLA.

Helen Kane (1904–66) was the pixie-like singer who added the suggestive boop-boop-a-doop lyrics in 1928 to her famous song, "I Wanna Be Loved by You." It also became the trademark of Betty Boop, who was based on Kane.

163. Aspray and Beaver, "Marketing the Monster," 132. See also "Thinking Machine," 54–55. Bessie is described as having "thousands of moving parts that spin and clack entertainingly."

164. Ephron and Ephron, final shooting script, 7 January 1957, p. 107, TCFM-UCLA.

165. Diebold, *Automation,* 154. Diebold devotes considerable attention to the prevailing fear of robots in order to assure the public that the concern was unfounded.

166. In "Thinking Machine," 60, Wiener claimed that computers "suffer from typical psychiatric problems," which "sometimes spread through a machine as fears and fixations spread through a psychotic human brain. These problems can be ameliorated by rest, electric shock treatment or a lobotomy." In *Desk Set,* the computer's meltdown is blamed on Miss Warriner.

167. Two years earlier, Plato (Sal Mineo) in Nicholas Ray's *Rebel Without a Cause* (Warner Bros., 1955; DVD, Warner Home Video, 1999) wore two different-colored socks to allude to his gender confusion and sexual identity crisis and his lack of parental nurturing.

168. Tracy and Hepburn made nine movies together before the latter's death in 1967 shortly after the filming of *Guess Who's Coming to Dinner,* directed by Stanley Kramer (Columbia Pictures, 1967; DVD, Columbia TriStar Home Video, 1999).

169. Jungk, *Tomorrow Is Already Here,* 166–67, 182.

170. "Space Planning Called New Art," *New York Times,* 9 May 1954. Executive handbooks also began to tout the advantages of the well–designed office for increased efficiency and promotional purposes; see Uris, "Your Office as a Tool," in *Efficient Executive,* 96–102. The best early synopses of the comprehensive nature of space planning is Michael Saphier's *Office Planning and Design* (New York: McGraw-Hill, 1968) and Maurice Mogulescu, *Profit through Design: Rx for Effective Office Planning* (New York: American Management Association, 1970). See also Leonard Manasseh and Roger Cunliffe, *Office Buildings* (New York: Reinhold, 1962).

171. Kenneth Ripnen, *Office Building and Office Layout Planning* (New York: McGraw-Hill, 1960), 3, 120–25.

172. For an explanation of the tasks involved in methods engineering, see Edward Krick, *Methods Engineering* (New York: John Wiley & Sons, 1962), 79. In summary, the methods engineer designs the productive facility and integrates human beings into the work process.

173. Ibid., 123.

174. "Lever House Complete," *Architectural Forum* 96 (June 1952): 104. Raymond Loewy designed the interior. See Jungk, *Tomorrow Is Already Here,* 160.

175. Robert Moore Fisher, *The Boom in Office Building: An Economic Study of the Past Two Decades* (Washington, D.C.: Urban Land Institute, 1966), 3–4.

176. See James S. Russell, "Form Follows Fad: The Troubled Love Affair of Architectural Style and Management Ideal," in Albrecht and Broikos, *On the Job,* 59; Lavin, *Form Follows Libido,* 6. Lavin refers to Reyner Banham who describes a "new territory confronted by architects at mid-century who could no longer claim to be responsible

for all aspects of design because much of the interior had been taken over by industrial designers and others." The architect had become a "master selector" rather than a creator. See Reyner Banham, "Design by Choice" (1961), in Banham, *Design by Choice,* ed. Penny Sparkle (New York: Rizzoli, 1981), 97–101.

177. L. Andrew Reinhard and Henry Hofmeister, "New Trends in Office Design," *Architectural Record* 97 (March 1945): 99.

178. Wallace Harrison and Max Abramowitz, "Planning the Office Building for Automation," in *Office Buildings* (New York: F. W. Dodge, 1961), 222–26. See also Ripnen, *Office Building and Office Layout Planning,* 2, 68.

179. Eric Larrabee and Massimo Vignelli, *Knoll Design* (New York: Abrams, 1990). Both Nelson and Knoll tried to relate furniture to the architectural style of the building while taking the workers' experiences into consideration. The space planners' tasks were more all encompassing. They assumed a managerial role over all operations, of which furniture design was only one component among many.

180. Maurice Mogulescu, "Housing Modern Business," *Progressive Architecture* 40 (January 1959): 11. See also Mogulescu, "Office Design as a Business Proposition," *Interiors* 116 (January 1957): 97, 172–77. Mogulescu claimed that he was not interested in designing *pretty* offices for their own sake, but those that were the result of careful planning. He stated, "The first concern is for efficiency—efficiency in current operations, efficiency for future operations, including expansion provisions to cover the long term leases, and the accomplishment of these objectives with all possible economy."

181. "Automation and Technological Change," Hearings before the Subcommittee on Economic Stabilization of the Joint Committee on the Economic Report, Congress of the United States, Eighty-Fourth Congress, 14–18 October 1955, 1–96.

182. Herbert F. Klingman, ed., *Electronics in Business: A Descriptive Reference Guide* (New York: Controllership Foundation, 1955). This 171-page annotated bibliography was designed for business professionals who wanted to educate themselves on the benefits and effects of automation. *Harvard Business Review* and the American Management Association published extensively in this area throughout the 1950s.

183. John Diebold (1926–2005) began his research on automation at the Harvard Graduate School of Business in 1949. As part of his senior project, he led a group that was researching "Making the Automatic Factory a Reality." He interviewed computer experts John von Neumann and Norbert Wiener. The results of his 1951 thesis were the basis for his subsequent book *Automation* (1952), completed when he was twenty-six years old. However, he did not coin the term automation. It was invented by D. S. Harder of the Ford Motor Company. See Wilbur Cross, *John Diebold: Breaking the Confines of the Possible* (New York: James H. Heinman, 1965), 21–34; Carl Heyel, ed., *John Diebold on Management* (Englewood Cliffs, N.J.: Prentice Hall, 1972) for an extensive bibliography on Diebold's writings.

184. Diebold, *Automation,* 45.

185. Ralph W. Fairbanks, "Electronics in the Modern Office," *Harvard Business Review* 30 (September–October 1952): 83–98, and John Diebold's "The Office of the Future," were included in the Congressional Record, 23. See Diebold, *Automation,* 90–126, and the 1955 congressional committee's section, "Automation in Data Processing and the Office," 3, 71–96. The speakers included Robert Burgess, director, Bureau of the Census, which

had adopted a computer in the 1930s; Howard Coughlin, president, Office Employees International Union; Ralph Cordiner, president, General Electric Company, which had adopted a UNIVAC; and Allen Astin, director, National Bureau of Standards.

186. Diebold in "Automation and Technological Change," 7.

187. Fairbanks, "Electronics in the Modern Office," 83–84.

188. Harry L. Wylie, "Mechanization and Automation," in *Office Management Handbook,* 2nd ed. (New York: Ronald Press, 1958), 9.3–9.4. Diebold concurred. He asserted that "between 1920 and 1950 there was a 53 percent increase in the number of factory workers against a 150 percent increase in the number of office workers." See *Automation,* 91.

189. Mogulescu, "Housing Modern Business," 11.

190. Diebold, *Automation,* 94.

191. Fisher, *Boom in Office Building,* 28.

192. Fredric Jameson, *The Geopolitical Aesthetic: Cinema and Space in the World System* (Bloomington: Indiana University Press, 1992), 3, 9. See Jameson's chapter "Totality as Conspiracy," 9–82, especially his discussion of office space and information gathering in the Library of Congress in Alan Pakula's *All the President's Men* (1976; DVD, Warner Home Video, 2006). See also Terry Smith, *Making the Modern: Industry, Art and Design in America* (Chicago: University of Chicago Press, 1993) for a discussion of the rationalized two-dimensional grid of Fordist efficiency.

193. Fairbanks, "Electronics in the Modern Office," 83–98; J. Douglas Elliott, "Will Electronics Make People Obsolete? Electronic Office Systems and the White-Collar Worker," in *The Impact of Computers on Office Management* (New York: American Management Association, 1954), 47.

194. See Wylie, *Office Management Handbook,* 9.43; Diebold, "Linking Plant and Office," in *Automation,* 93; Harrison and Abramowitz, *Office Buildings,* 222.

195. Wiener, *Human Use of Human Beings,* 161–62; Diebold, "The Problem of Leisure," in *Automation,* 165–66. In accord with Wiener, C. Wright Mills disagreed with this majority assessment. He claimed that white-collar workers were also in danger of being displaced by the computer, in "A Look at the White Collar," in *Electronics in the Office: Problems and Prospects* (New York: American Management Association, 1952), 32–36.

196. Diebold in "Automation and Technological Change," 27. See also his section "The Debasement of the Worker," in *Automation,* 158–61.

197. Elliott, "Will Electronics Make People Obsolete?" 50.

198. Osborn, "GE and Univac," 105.

199. Malone, "Imagining Information Retrieval in the Library," 14–21.

200. Pugh, *Building IBM,* 58–59.

201. Cynthia Soulliere, "The Women of ENIAC: A Historical Study of Difficulties Faced by Women Choosing a Career in Science," http://gecdsb.on.ca/d&g/women/women.htm. See also Noble, *Forces of Production,* 51, for a brief discussion of Goldstine and Grace Hopper who designed the program for the Mark I computer and later contributed to the development of COBOL. See also Fleck, *Computer Perspective,* 135.

202. Diebold in "Automation and Technological Change," 14.

203. Robert Dubin, *The World of Work: Industrial Society and Human Relations*

(Englewood Cliffs, N.J.: Prentice-Hall, 1958), 202. The subtitle "Male vs. Female" was in a chapter entitled "Automation and the Labor Force," 199–211.

204. Fairbanks, "Electronics in the Modern Office," 98.

POSTSCRIPT

1. Slavoj Žižek, "Welcome to the Desert of the Real," *South Atlantic Quarterly* 101 (Spring 2002): 386. A similar idea was put forth at the same time by Steven Bradshaw, a BBC investigative reporter, who claimed that "For years Hollywood had been showing America at risk from terrorism, religious extremism, and weapons of mass destruction. Even those in the front line in the fight against terrorism believed it was Hollywood, not Washington that saw the warning signs most clearly." See "A Warning from Hollywood," *Panorama* (BBC's Investigative News Show), 24 March 2002, http://news.bbc.co.uk/hi/english/static/audio_video/programmes/panorama/transcripts/transcript_24_03_02.txt. After September 11, 2001, Philip Stubb, Pentagon Film Liaison, was sent to Hollywood to consult various screenwriters, directors, and producers. A so-called September 11th Group was set up to brainstorm on what terrorists might be planning next.

2. Žižek claims further that the "towers stood for the center of *virtual* capitalism of speculation disconnected from the sphere of material production" ("Welcome to the Desert of the Real," 386). One might conjecture that the valorization of working-class masculinity represented an effort by the studios to restore these productive forces for strategic purposes.

3. *The Apartment,* directed by Billy Wilder (Mirisch, 1960; VHS, MGM/UA Home Video, 1988). The screenplay is by Billy Wilder and I. A. L. Diamond. All the quotations from the film are adapted from http://www.dailyscript.com/scripts/apartment.html. References to character delineation and scenery in quotations are also taken from the script.

4. *Network,* directed by Sidney Lumet (Metro-Goldwyn-Mayer, 1976; DVD, two-disc special edition, Turner Entertainment, 2006). All quotations and descriptions of characters and scenery were taken from the revised screenplay by Paddy Chayefsky, dated 14 January 1976. It appears on http://corky.net/scripts/network.html.

5. According to the director of photography, Owen Roizman, most of the film was shot in the MGM Building in New York. There was a completely empty floor that was rented by the studio; all the rooms were constructed by the production designer. See "*Network* and How It Was Photographed" (an interview with Owen Roizman), *American Cinematographer* 58 (April 1977): 384.

6. Director Sidney Lumet states that this sequence was shot in Clinton and Russell's Apthorpe Apartments (1904), which were abandoned at the time. See "Mad as Hell—The Creation of a Movie Moment," *Network,* disc 2.

7. Production designer Philip Rosenberg claims that the purposeful use of "see-through doors" and transparent spaces was designed to show the "magnitude of the network." See "The Style," in *Network,* disc 2.

8. This scene was shot in the boardroom of the New York Public Library.

9. *Wall Street,* directed by Oliver Stone (Amercent, 1987). For a discussion of Gekko's character development and a discussion of the other Wall Street "buccaneers" of the 1980s whom Stone consulted in developing the film's context, see Raymond Arsenault, "*Wall Street* (1987): The Stockbroker's Son and the Decade of Greed," *Film and History* 28 (1998): 16–27. They include Carl Icahn, Asher Edelman, James Goldsmith, T. Boone Pickens, and Michael Milliken, among others. The film's dialogue and descriptions of characters and scenery that are in quotations are taken from Stanley Weiser and Oliver Stone's script of 23 April 1987, which can be found at http://www.imsdb.com/scripts/Wall-Street.html.

10. *Working Girl,* directed by Mike Nicols (Twentieth Century–Fox, 1988); Kevin Wade wrote the screenplay. For an excellent treatment of the film, see Elizabeth G. Traube, "Transforming Heroes: Hollywood and the Demonization of Women," *Public Culture* 3 (Spring 1991): 1–28. One may use Traube's discussion of upper-class Katharine Parker (Sigourney Weaver), a negative caricature of a feminist, to understand the character of Diana Christensen in *Network.*

11. Peter Biskind, "Stone Raids Wall Street" (interview with Oliver Stone), *Premiere* 1 (December 1987): 38.

12. In "*Wall Street* (1987)," Arsenault identifies only two paradigms of paternal authority, Lou Mannheim and Carl Fox, as does Jack Boozer Jr., "Wall Street: The Commodification of Perception," *Journal of Film and Television* 17 (1989): 90–99. Peter Biskind and Barbara Ehrenreich, "Machismo and Hollywood's Working Class," in *American Media and Mass Culture,* ed. Donald Lazare (Berkeley and Los Angeles: University of California Press, 1987), 201–15, assert that to counter the increase in corporate disempowerment, Hollywood created blue-collar camaraderie as a site of resistance or defiance. Biskind, "Stone Raids Wall Street," 38.

13. According to Arsenault, "*Wall Street* (1987)," the character of Fox was based on Stone's friend Owen Morrisey, a high-risk commodities broker, and two of Ivan Boesky's lieutenants, Martin Siegel and David Brown. Stone claims that he was a composite character, based on his friend and "David Brown, a broker convicted for insider trading who served as an advisor on the film" and "was the basis for Charlie Sheen's character in our script." See Biskind, "Stone Raids Wall Street," 34.

14. In Arsenault's "*Wall Street* (1987)," 24, the author claims that Stone fails to deliver a clear message on capitalism, class, and greed, vacillating between liberal and radical critiques; it is unclear whether he is condemning a system or merely its abuses. Traube asserts in "Transforming Heroes," 31, that Stone voided even the one-sided critique of capitalism of any critical social content.

15. *The Towering Inferno,* directed by John Guillermin and Irwin Allen (Twentieth Century–Fox and Warner Bros., 1974; DVD, two-disc special edition, Twentieth Century–Fox Home Entertainment, 2006). All dialogue was taken from http://www.script-o-rama.com/movie_scripts/t/towering-inferno-script-transcript-mcqueen.html and checked for accuracy. A Fawcett-Majors Production, *Steel* (1979) was directed by Steve Carver. The story by Peter Davis was adapted by Leigh Chapman. It also pits macho Mike Catton (Lee Majors) against corrupt corporate types who try to sabotage the completion of the building. The building's owner Big Lew Cassidy (George Kennedy) dies in an accident while trying to save another construction worker. At the beginning of

the film, he says, "Tall buildings still give me a hard on." Catton, who is among the best construction workers in the state, is called upon by Big Lew's daughter, Cass Cassidy (Jennifer O'Neill) to supervise the building's completion (she also needs a real man to complete her), but he is "frozen" by a previous accident, rendering him unable to climb. Evoking the earlier *Skyscraper* (1928), by the end of the film, he gets his manhood back with the help of a multiethnic team of workers, including a Native American named Cherokee (Robert Tessier), who raise the American flag.

16. The film cost fourteen million dollars to complete, although eleven million was initially budgeted. Over $1,100,000 was devoted to the unprecedented fifty-seven miniatures that comprised the set, which were almost seven stories high.

17. Richard Martin Stern, *The Tower* (New York: David McCay, 1973); Thomas N. Scortia and Frank Robinson, *The Glass Inferno* (New York: Doubleday, 1974).

18. James Glanz and Eric Lipton, *City in the Sky: The Rise and Fall of the World Trade Center* (New York: Times Books, 2003), 118–44.

19. See Leonard Ruchelman, *The World Trade Center: Politics and Policies of Skyscraper Development* (Syracuse: Syracuse University Press, 1977), 135–36. According to Ruchelman, in 1972 a fire broke out in the sub-basement, started perhaps by propane gas, causing smoke to billow into the lobby, elevator shafts, and corridors. Another fire broke out in February 1975. It began on the eleventh floor of the North Tower, spread via the telephone cables to the ninth and the sixteenth floors, and caused about $1 million in damage. In an uncanny coincidence, *The Towering Inferno* was completed on September 11, 1974. Stern's novel also includes a disgruntled terrorist with a bomb who sets the blaze in motion, a plot device that was written out of the cinematic adaptation.

20. Stern, *The Tower,* 1.

21. The fictional glass tower is still loftier than C. Y. Lee and Partner's preeminent Taipei 101 (2003) in Taiwan, which is 1,671 feet and 101 stories tall. It is scheduled to be superseded by Skidmore, Owings, and Merrill's Burj Dubai tower, which is slated for completion in 2009.

22. The film's lobby elevator is the actual 1955 elevator located in San Francisco's Hyatt Regency Hotel at 5 Embarcadero Center. See Tony Reeves, *The Worldwide Guide to Movie Locations* (London: Titan, 2001), 403.

23. "The Story," in *The Towering Inferno,* press book, 1974, facsimile accompanying the DVD two-disc special edition.

24. The effects of the Vietnam War on masculinity are seen in Stern's book, in lines uttered by an injured police officer on the scene: "Do you think . . . that there'll be a Purple Heart in it, Frank? I've always longed to be a wounded hero." Stern, *The Tower,* 221.

25. Bradshaw, "Warning from Hollywood," *Panorama.*

26. *Die Hard,* directed by John McTiernan (Twentieth Century–Fox, 1988; DVD, Twentieth Century Fox Home Entertainment, 2007). It was based on Roderick Thorp's novel *Nothing Lasts Forever* (New York: W. W. Norton, 1979). All dialogue and descriptions of characters and scenes were taken from the screenplay by Jeb Stuart, with revisions by Steven de Souza, second revised draft, 2 October 1987 (fourth revision 30 November 1987), http://diehardnews.tripod.com/diehardnews/id3.html.

27. The Nakatomi Building in the film is actually Johnson, Fain, and Pereira's Fox

Plaza (1987) which is 492 feet and thirty-four stories high. It serves as the headquarters of Twentieth Century–Fox.

28. The same thing happens in Stern's *The Tower*; a disgruntled electrician gains entrance to the computerized control room with a bomb, killing the guard, pointing to the building's technological and human vulnerabilities.

29. The United States Bank Tower is 1,018 feet tall and includes seventy-three above-ground stories. It also has the world's highest helicopter landing pad. The tower has a large glass crown, which is illuminated at night. It is lit up in red, white, and blue on the Fourth of July.

30. *Independence Day,* directed by Roland Emmerich (Twentieth Century–Fox, 1996; DVD, Twentieth Century–Fox Home Entertainment, 2008).

31. *World Trade Center,* directed by Oliver Stone (Paramount, 2006). For thorough information on the film, including commentary from Stone, the photographer, the actors, and the real-life protagonists, see http://movies.about.com/od/worldtradecenter/World_Trade_Center_2006.htm.

32. Philip French, *"World Trade Center,"* *The Observer,* 1 October 2006, http://guardian.co.uk/theobserver/2006/Oct/01/features.review27.

33. "About the Rescue," http://www.celebritywonder.com/movie/2006_World_Trade_Center_about_the_rescue.html.

Index

Compiled by Denise E. Carlson

Merrill Schleier is professor of art, architectural history, and film studies at the University of the Pacific in Stockton, California. She is author of *The Skyscraper in American Art*.